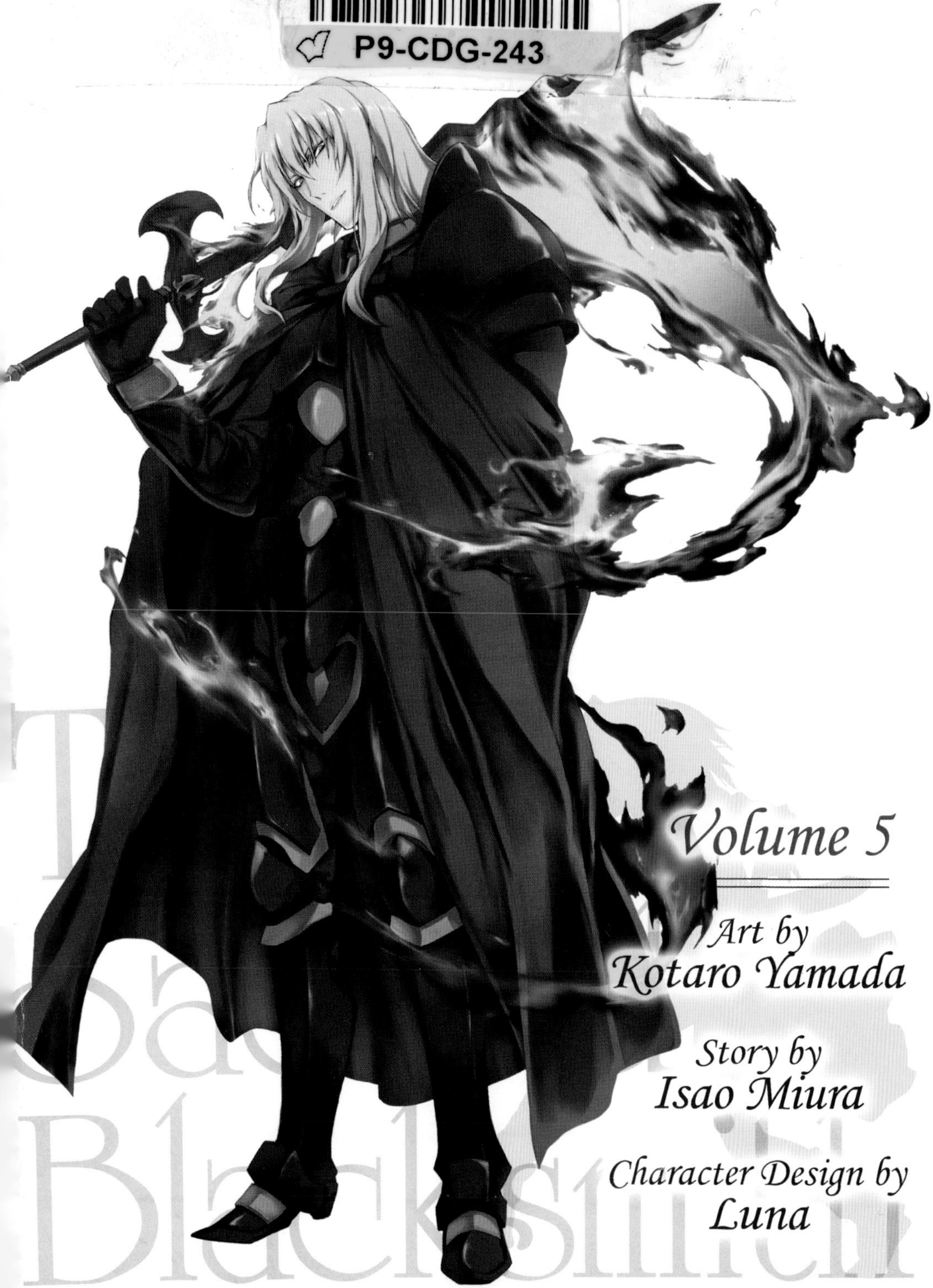

The Sacred Blacksmith

Volume 5

Art by
Kotaro Yamada

Story by
Isao Miura

Character Design by
Luna

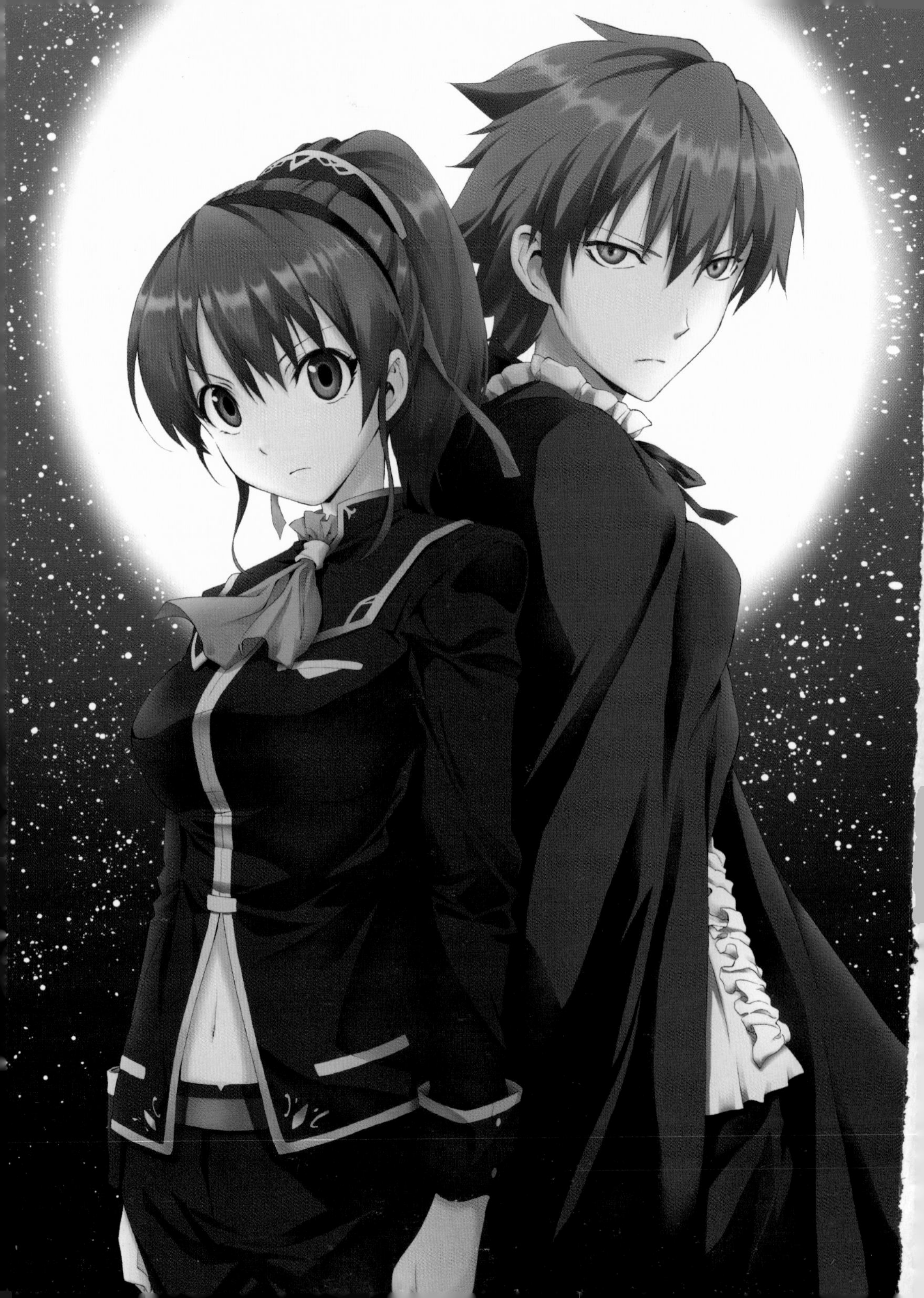

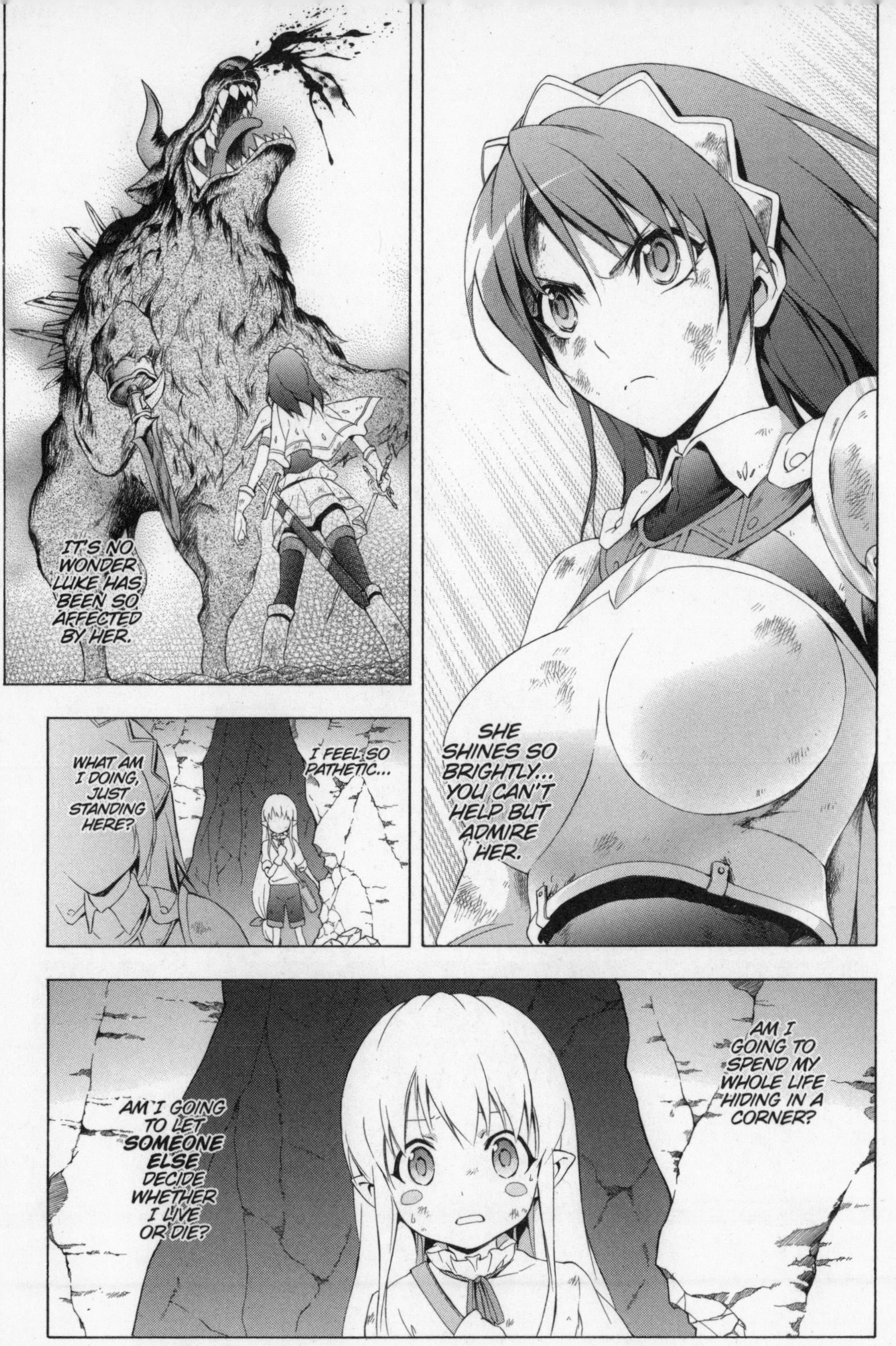
SHE SHINES SO BRIGHTLY... YOU CAN'T HELP BUT ADMIRE HER.
IT'S NO WONDER LUKE HAS BEEN SO AFFECTED BY HER.
I FEEL SO PATHETIC...
WHAT AM I DOING, JUST STANDING HERE?
AM I GOING TO SPEND MY WHOLE LIFE HIDING IN A CORNER?
AM I GOING TO LET SOMEONE ELSE DECIDE WHETHER I LIVE OR DIE?

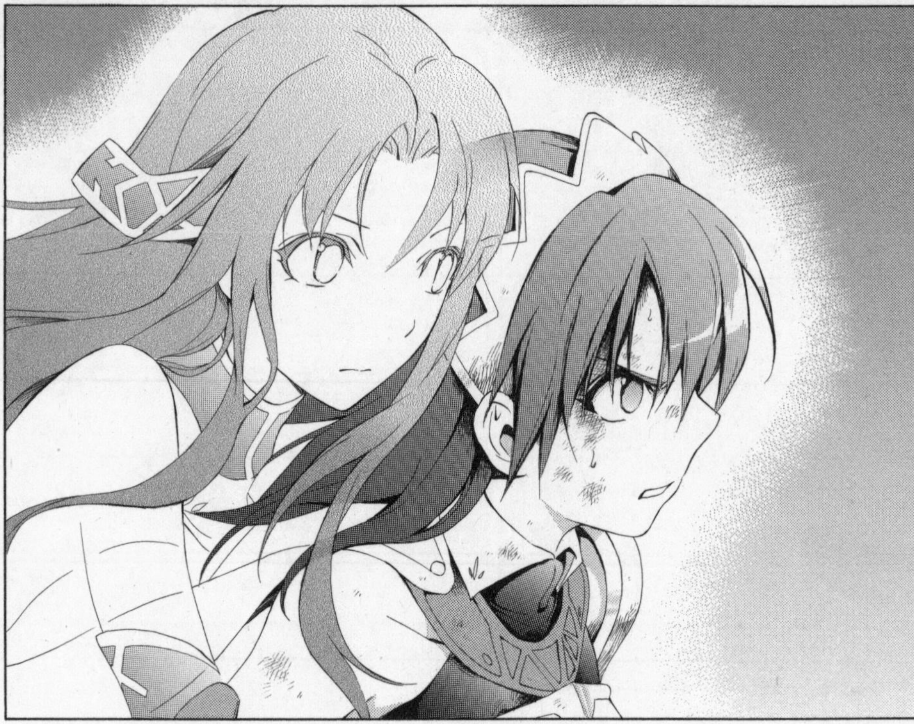

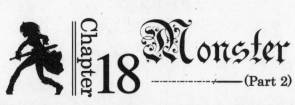

Chapter 18 Monster

(Part 2)

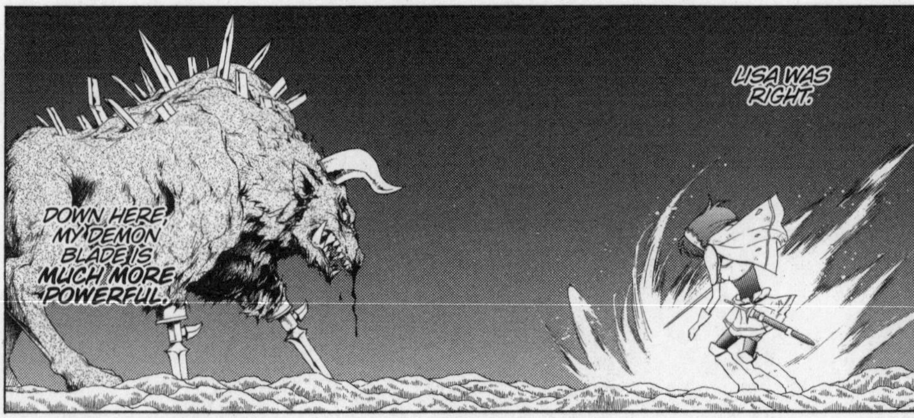
LISA WAS RIGHT.
DOWN HERE, MY DEMON BLADE IS MUCH MORE POWERFUL.

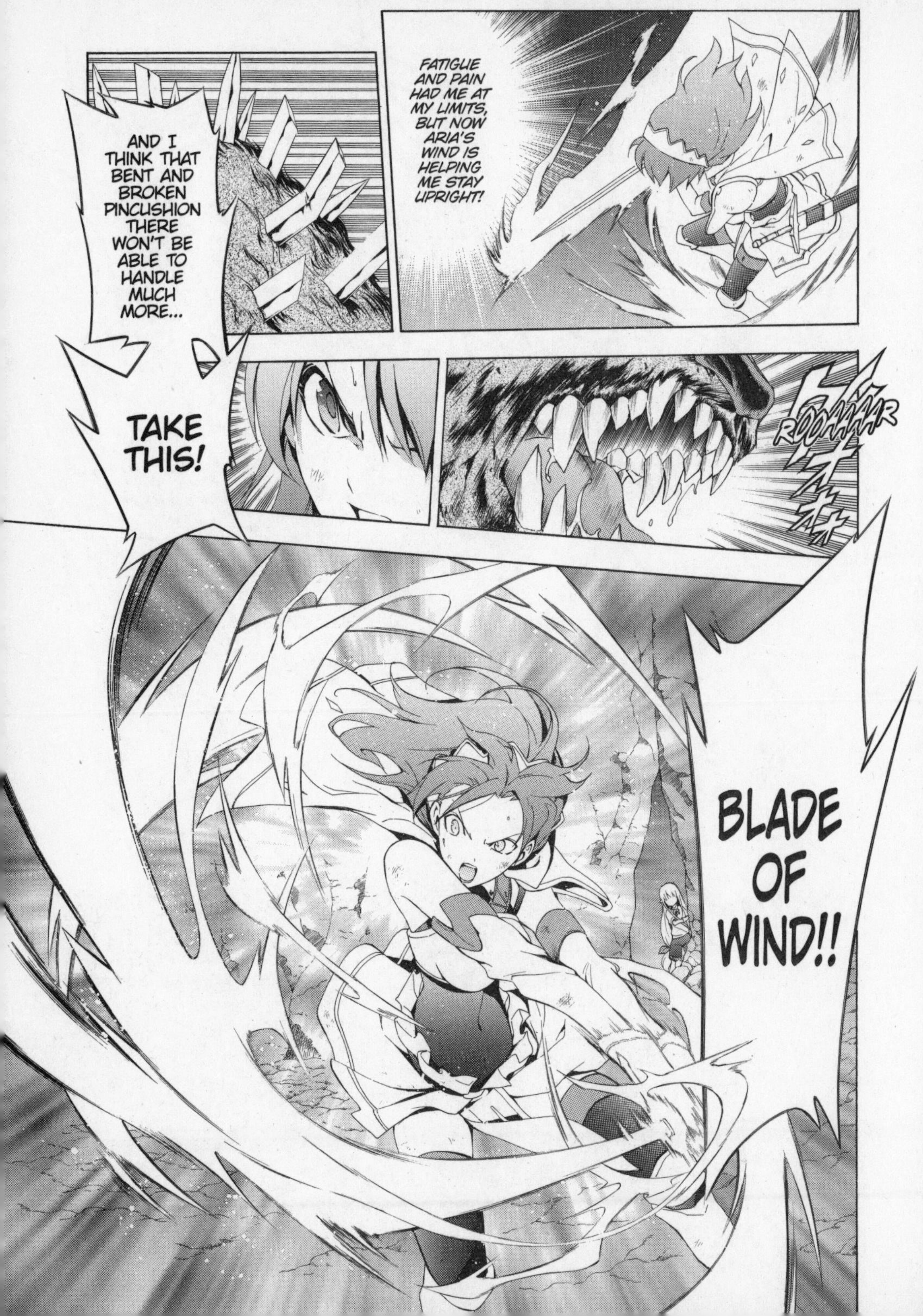
FATIGUE AND PAIN HAD ME AT MY LIMITS, BUT NOW ARIA'S WIND IS HELPING ME STAY UPRIGHT!
AND I THINK THAT BENT AND BROKEN PINCUSHION THERE WON'T BE ABLE TO HANDLE MUCH MORE...
ROOAAAAR
TAKE THIS!
BLADE OF WIND!!

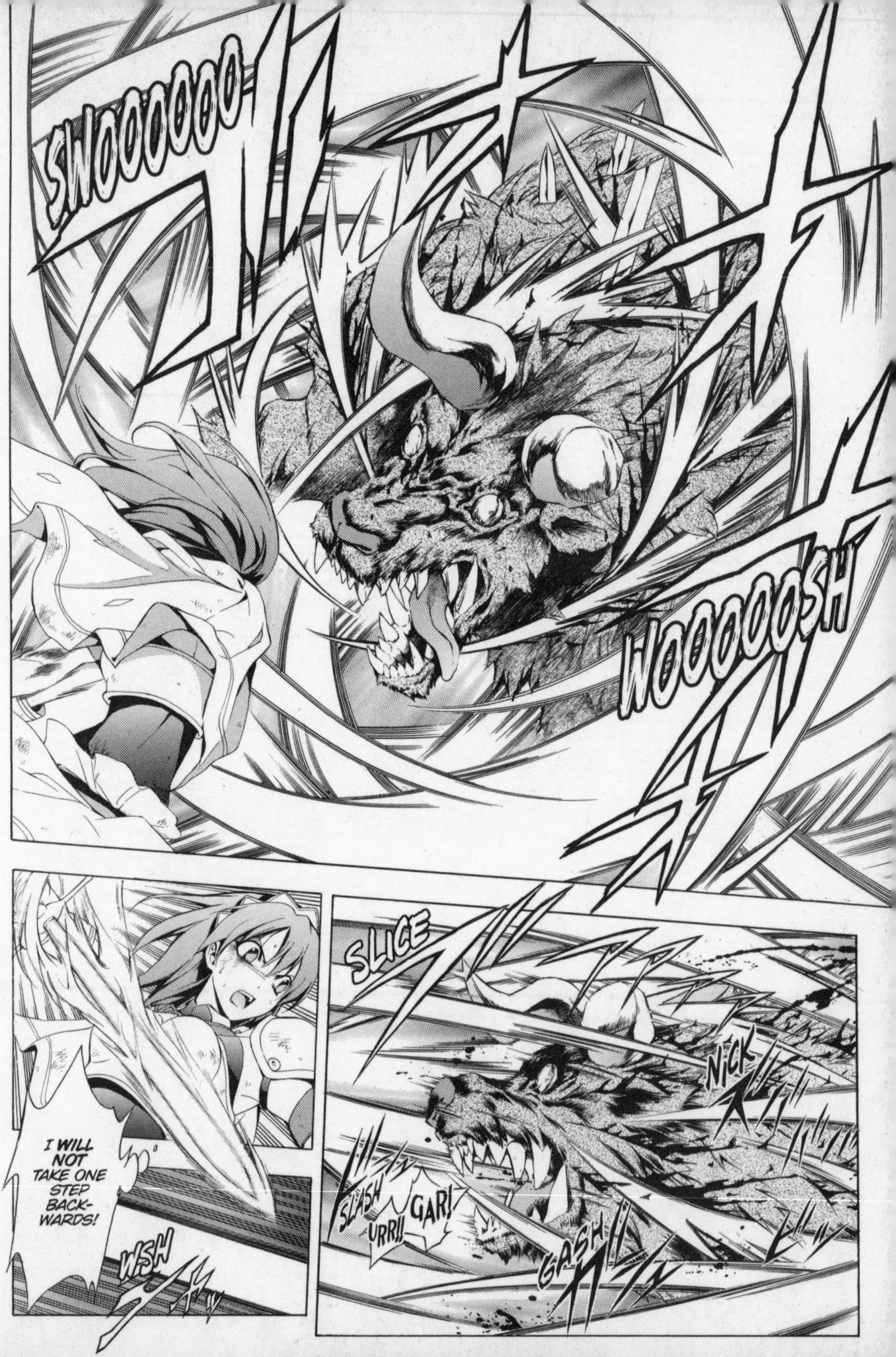
SWOOOOOO
WOOOOOSH
SLICE
NICK
GAR!
SLASH
URR!!
GASH
I WILL NOT TAKE ONE STEP BACK-WARDS!
WSH

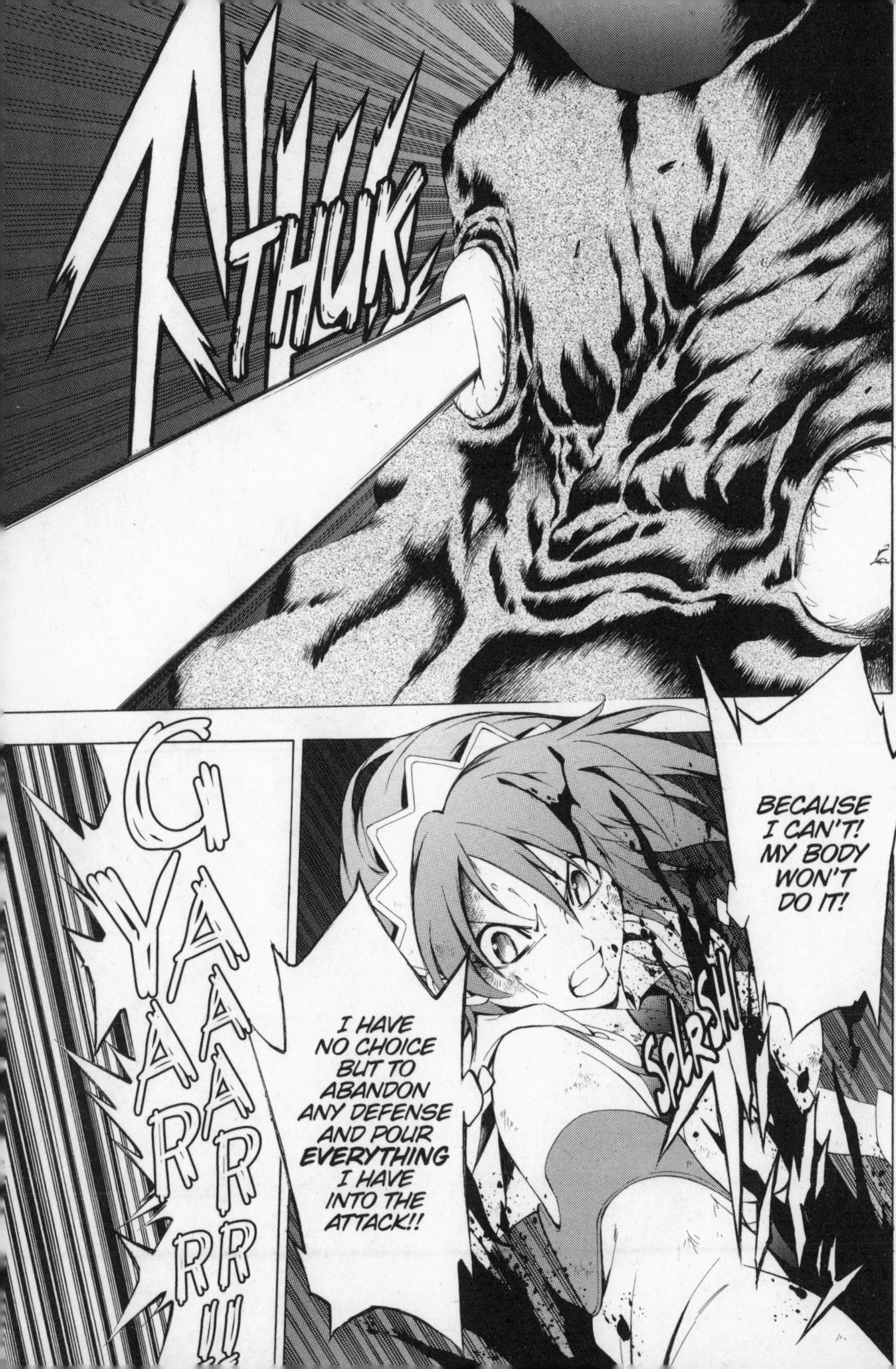
THUK
BECAUSE I CAN'T! MY BODY WON'T DO IT!
I HAVE NO CHOICE BUT TO ABANDON ANY DEFENSE AND POUR EVERYTHING I HAVE INTO THE ATTACK!!
SPLRSH
GYAAAARRRR!!

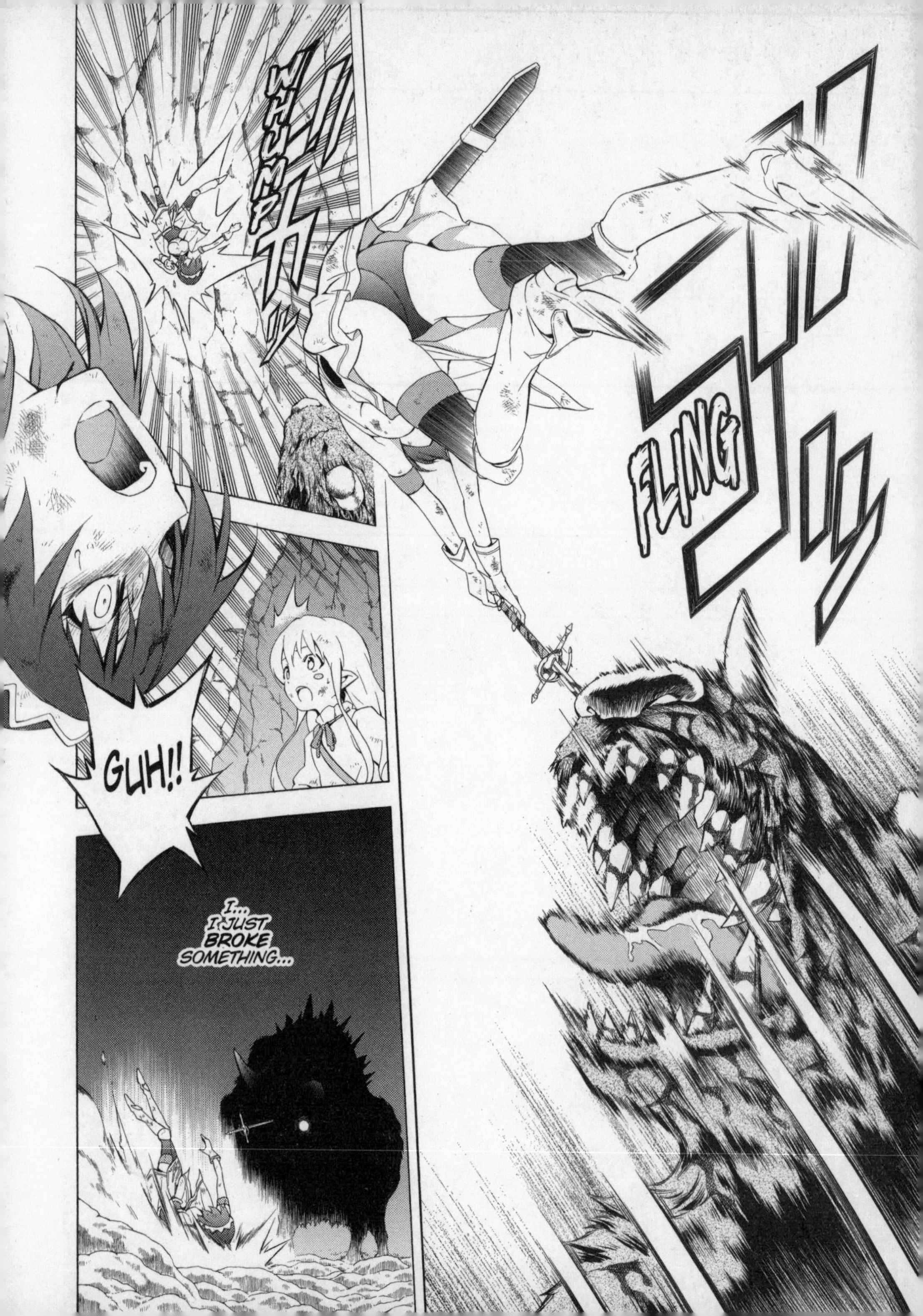
FLING
WHUMP
GUH!!
I... I JUST BROKE SOMETHING...

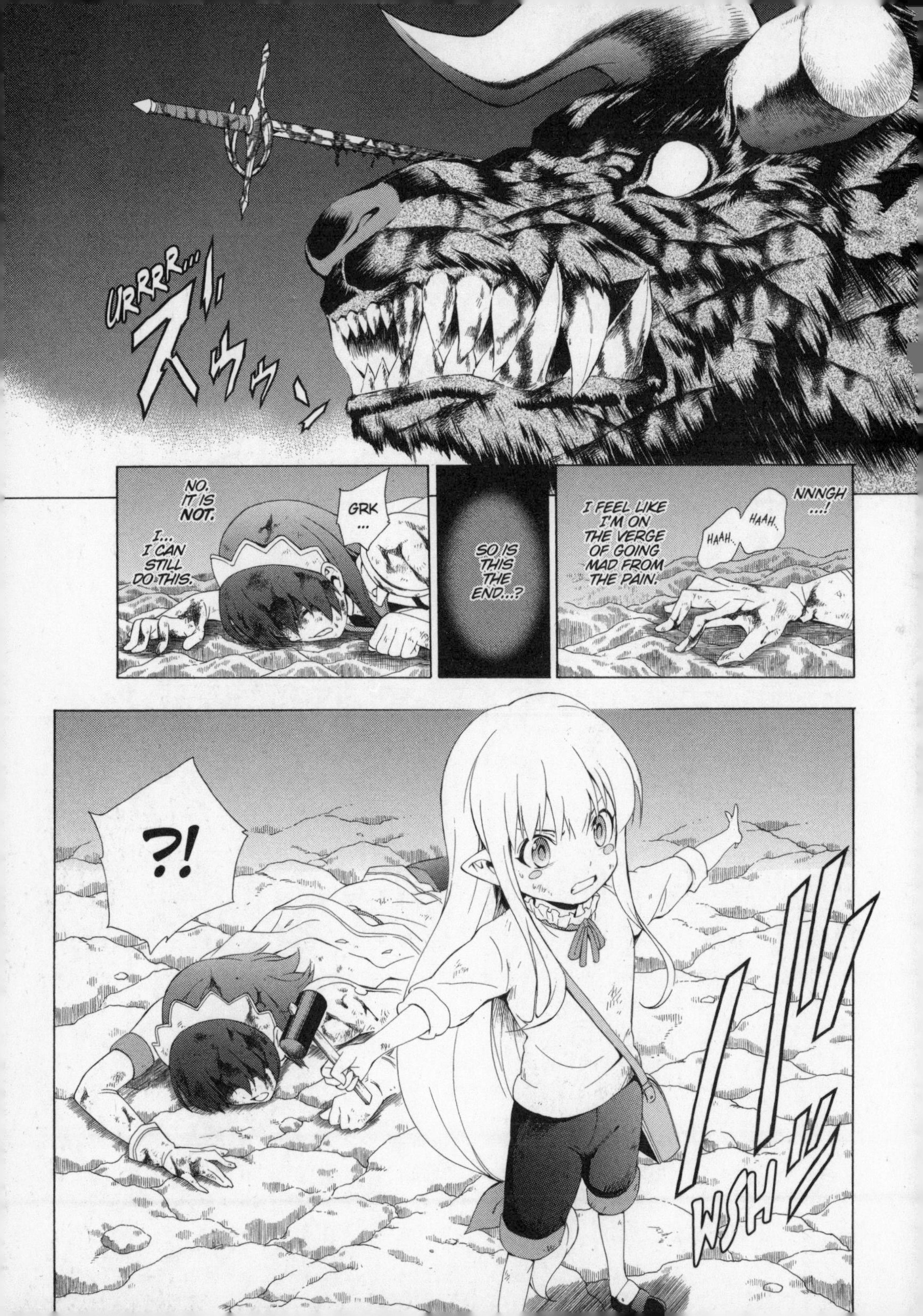
URRRR...
NNNGH...!
HAAH...
HAAH...
I FEEL LIKE I'M ON THE VERGE OF GOING MAD FROM THE PAIN.
SO IS THIS THE END...?
GRK...
NO. IT IS NOT.
I... I CAN STILL DO THIS.
WSH
?!

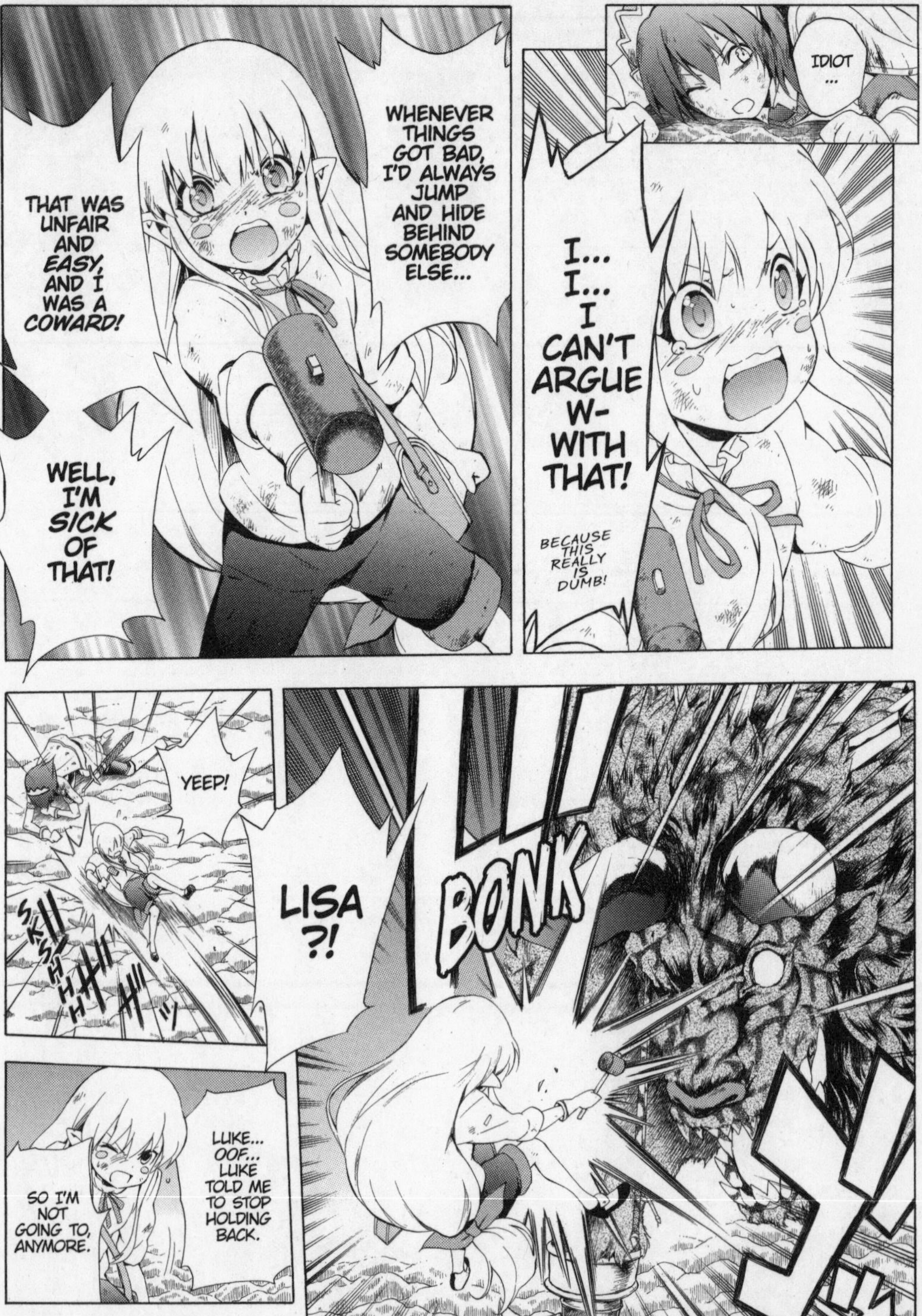
IDIOT
...
I... I... I CAN'T ARGUE W-WITH THAT!
BECAUSE THIS REALLY IS DUMB!
WHENEVER THINGS GOT BAD, I'D ALWAYS JUMP AND HIDE BEHIND SOMEBODY ELSE...
THAT WAS UNFAIR AND *EASY*, AND I WAS A *COWARD*!
WELL, I'M *SICK* OF THAT!
BONK
LISA ?!
YEEP!
SKSHHH
LUKE... OOF... LUKE TOLD ME TO STOP HOLDING BACK.
SO I'M NOT GOING TO, ANYMORE.

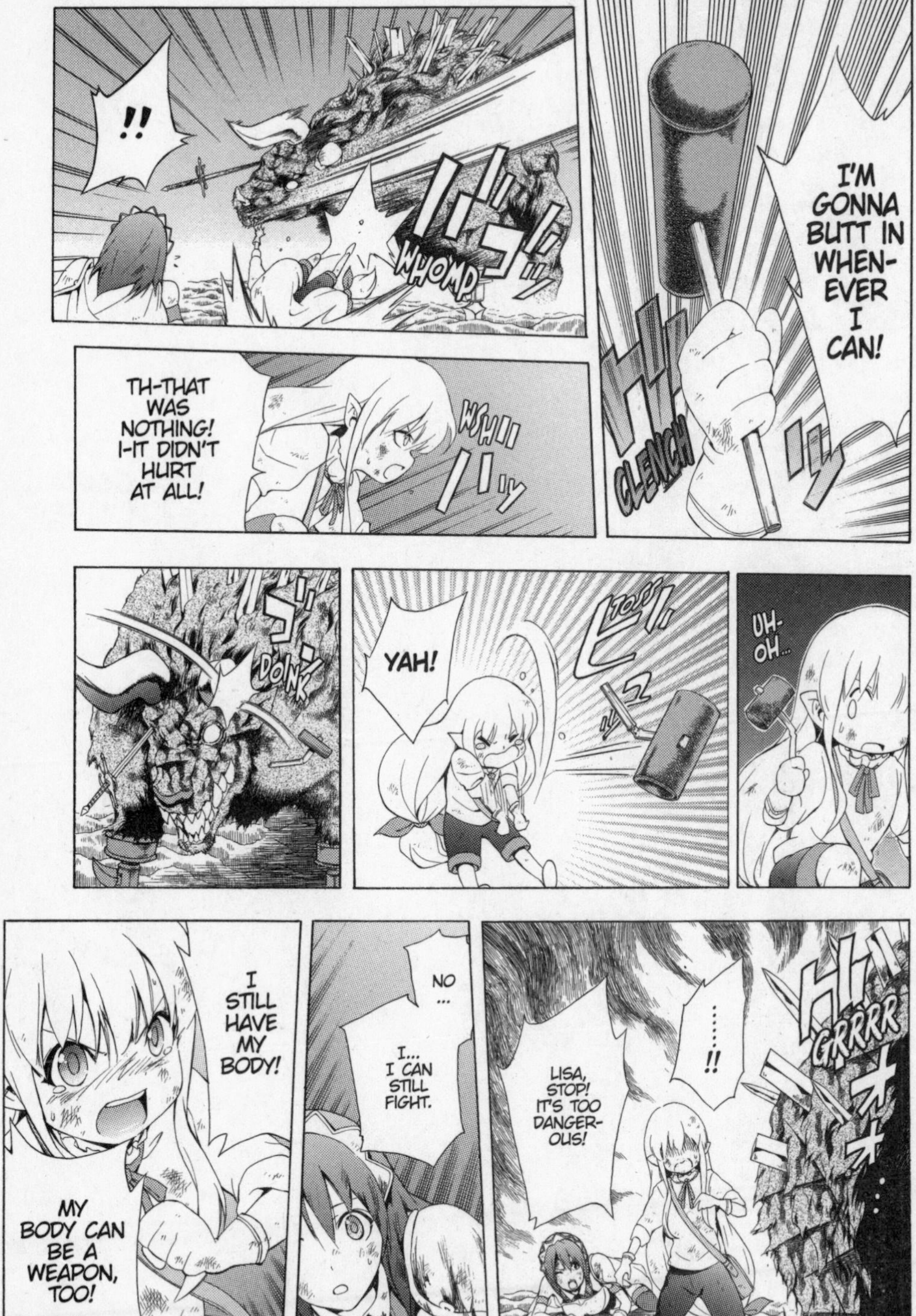
I'M GONNA BUTT IN WHEN-EVER I CAN!
CLENCH
!!
WHOMP
TH-THAT WAS NOTHING! I-IT DIDN'T HURT AT ALL!
WSHH
UH-OH...
YAH!
TOSS
DOINK
......!!
GRRRR
LISA, STOP! IT'S TOO DANGER-OUS!
NO ...
I... I CAN STILL FIGHT.
I STILL HAVE MY BODY!
MY BODY CAN BE A WEAPON, TOO!

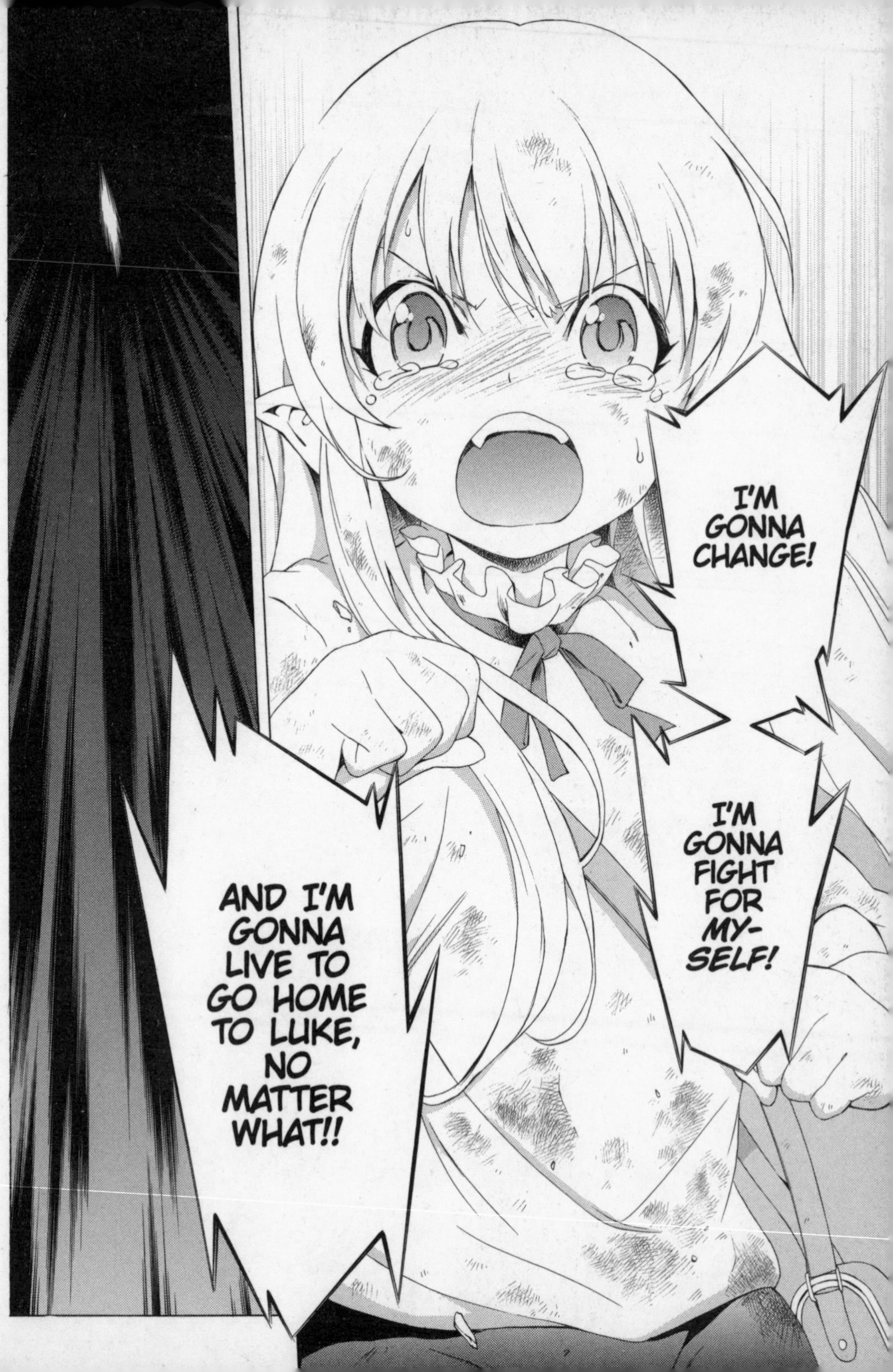
I'M GONNA CHANGE!
I'M GONNA FIGHT FOR MY-SELF!
AND I'M GONNA LIVE TO GO HOME TO LUKE, NO MATTER WHAT!!

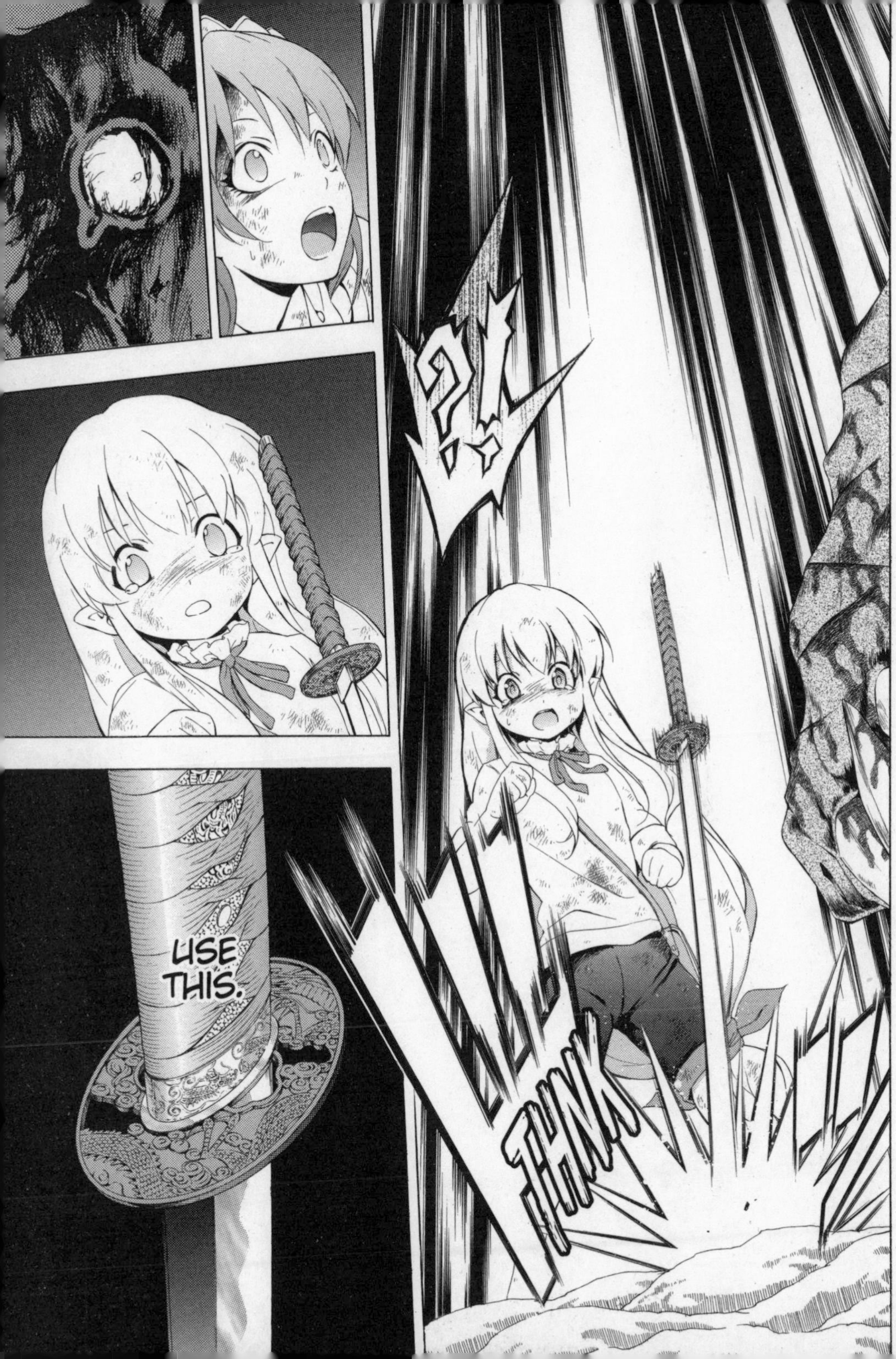
?!
USE THIS.
THUNK

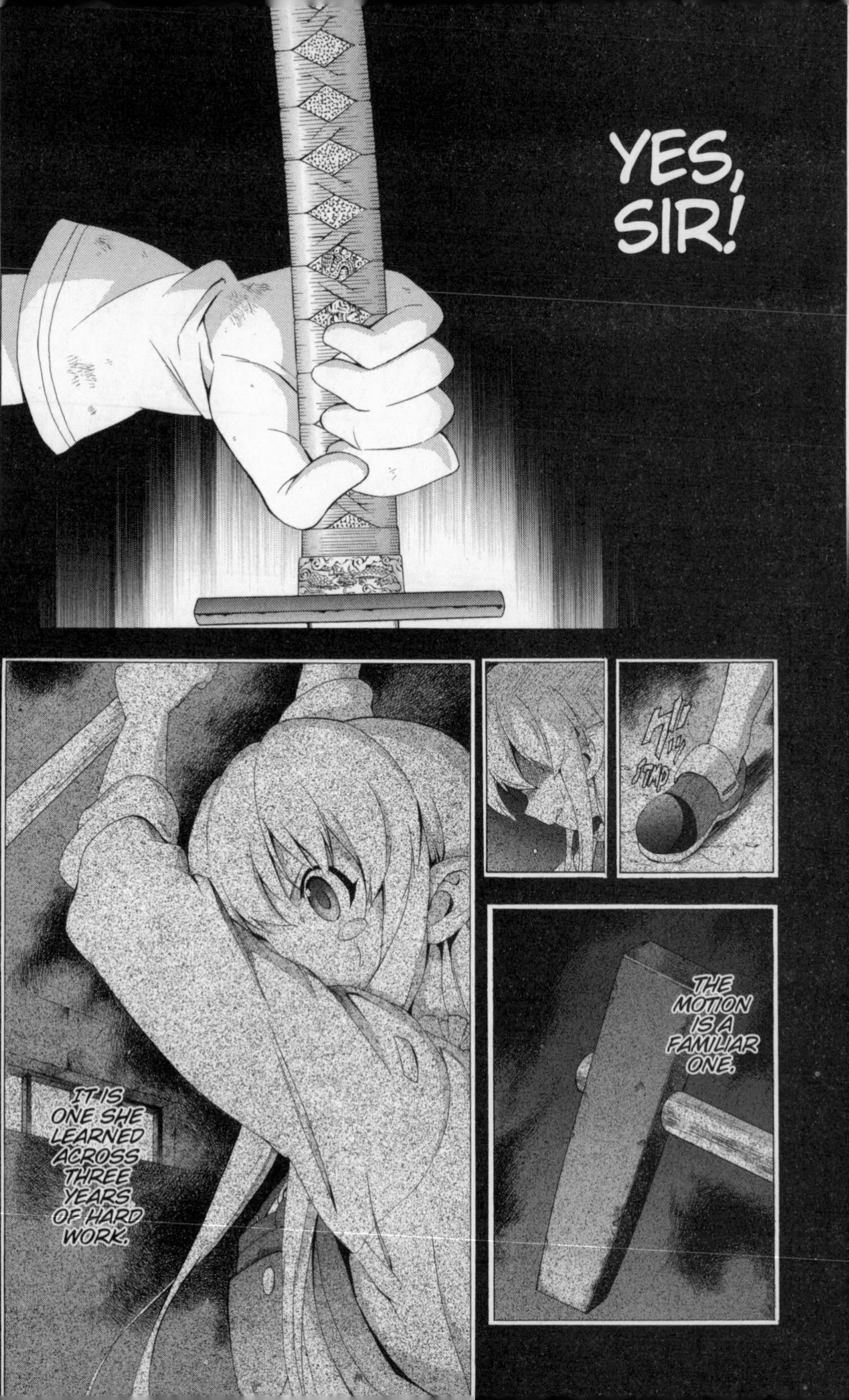
YES, SIR!
STMP
THE MOTION IS A FAMILIAR ONE.
IT IS ONE SHE LEARNED ACROSS THREE YEARS OF HARD WORK.

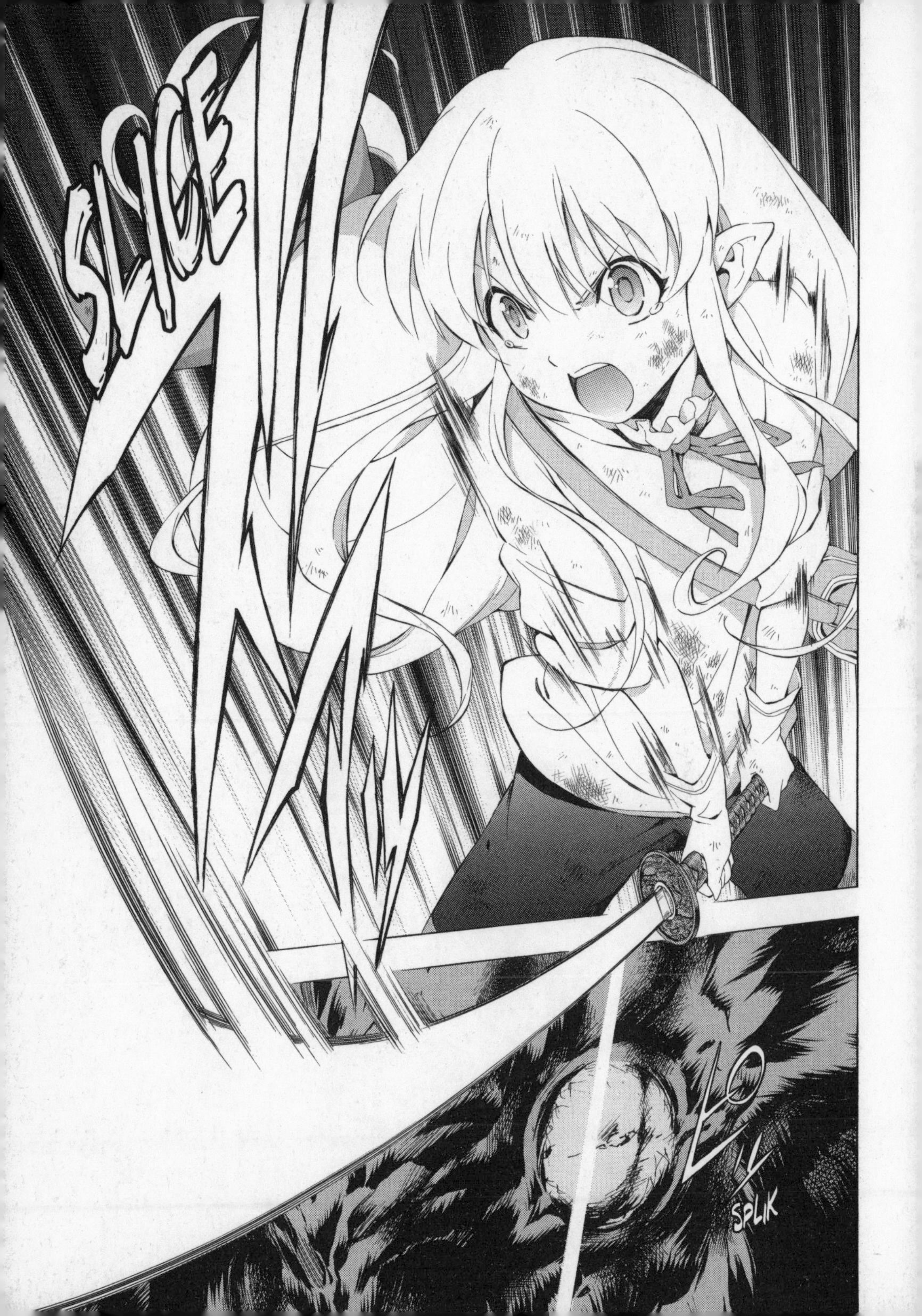
SLICE
SPLIK

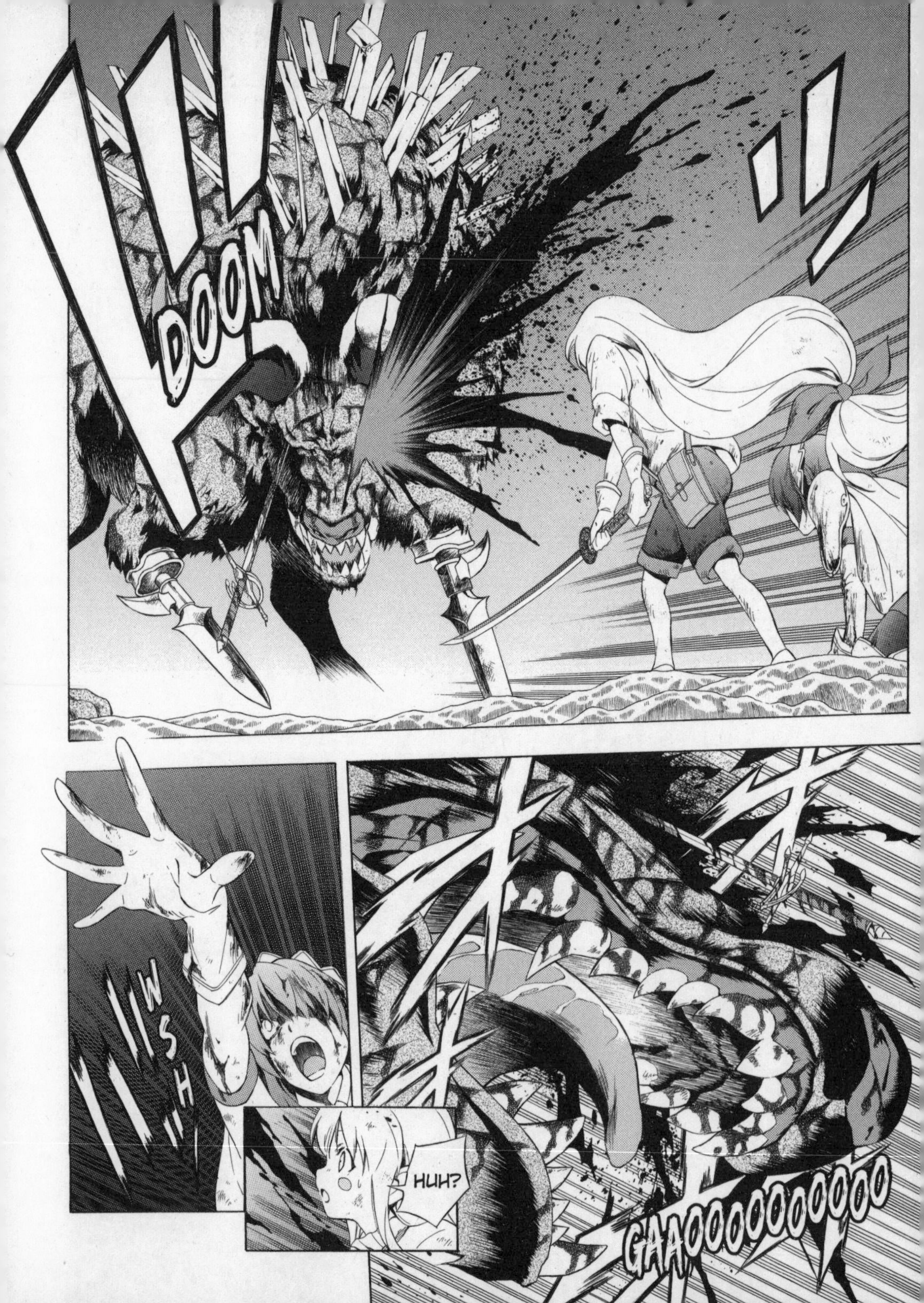
DOOM
GAAOOOOOOOOOO
WSH
HUH?

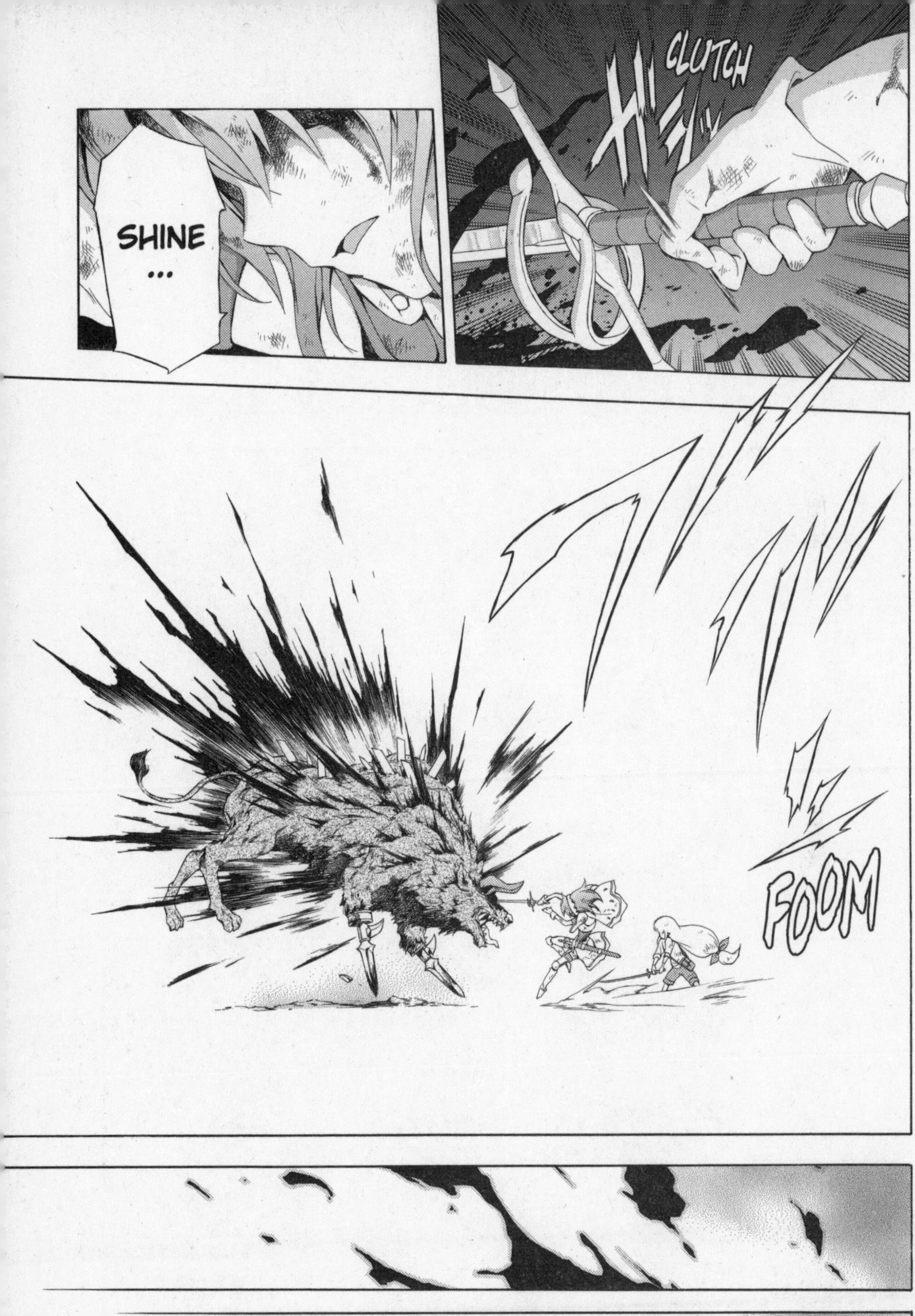
CLUTCH
SHINE ...
FOOM

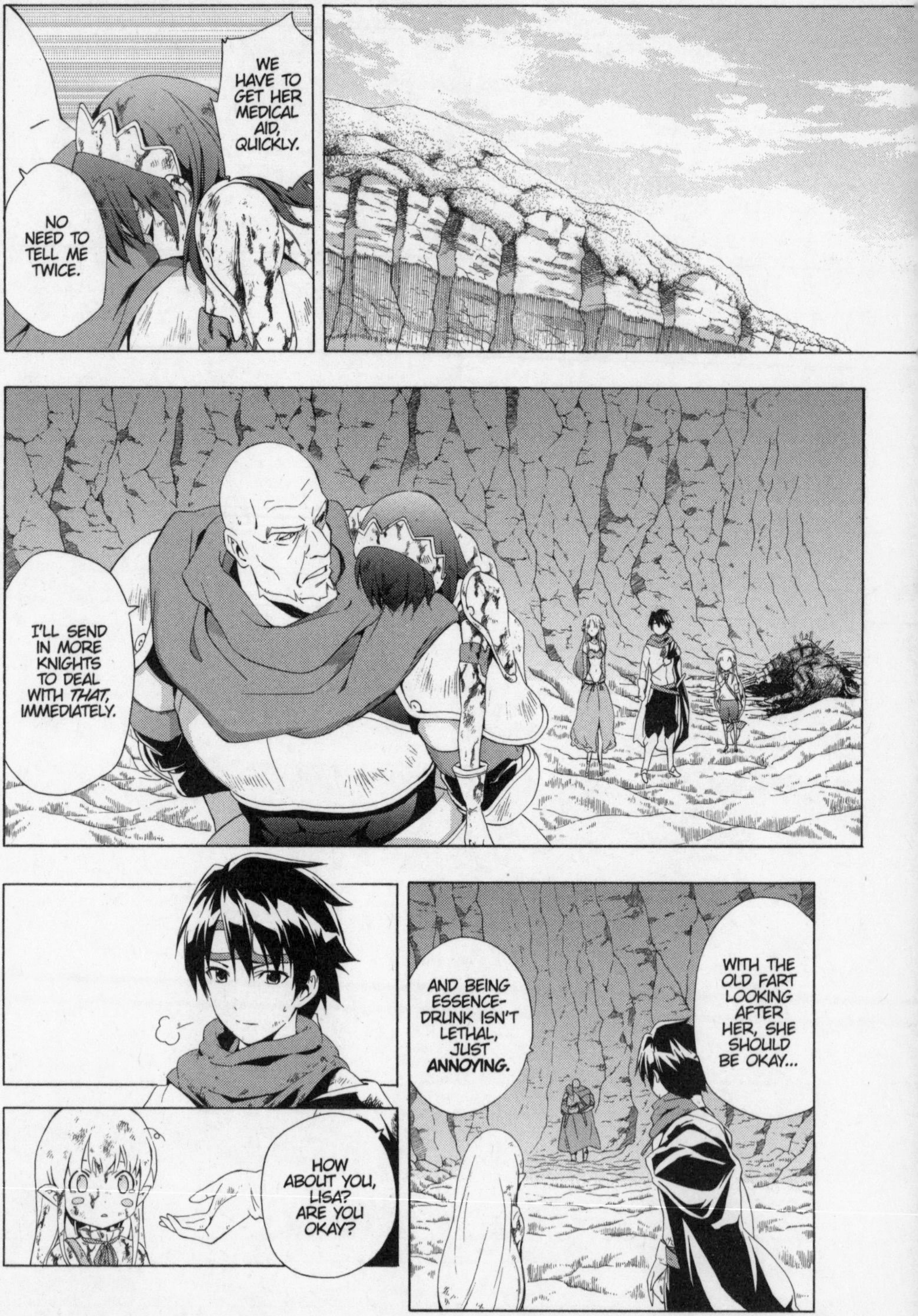
WE HAVE TO GET HER MEDICAL AID, QUICKLY.
NO NEED TO TELL ME TWICE.
I'LL SEND IN MORE KNIGHTS TO DEAL WITH *THAT*, IMMEDIATELY.
WITH THE OLD FART LOOKING AFTER HER, SHE SHOULD BE OKAY...
AND BEING ESSENCE-DRUNK ISN'T LETHAL, JUST **ANNOYING**.
HOW ABOUT YOU, LISA? ARE YOU OKAY?

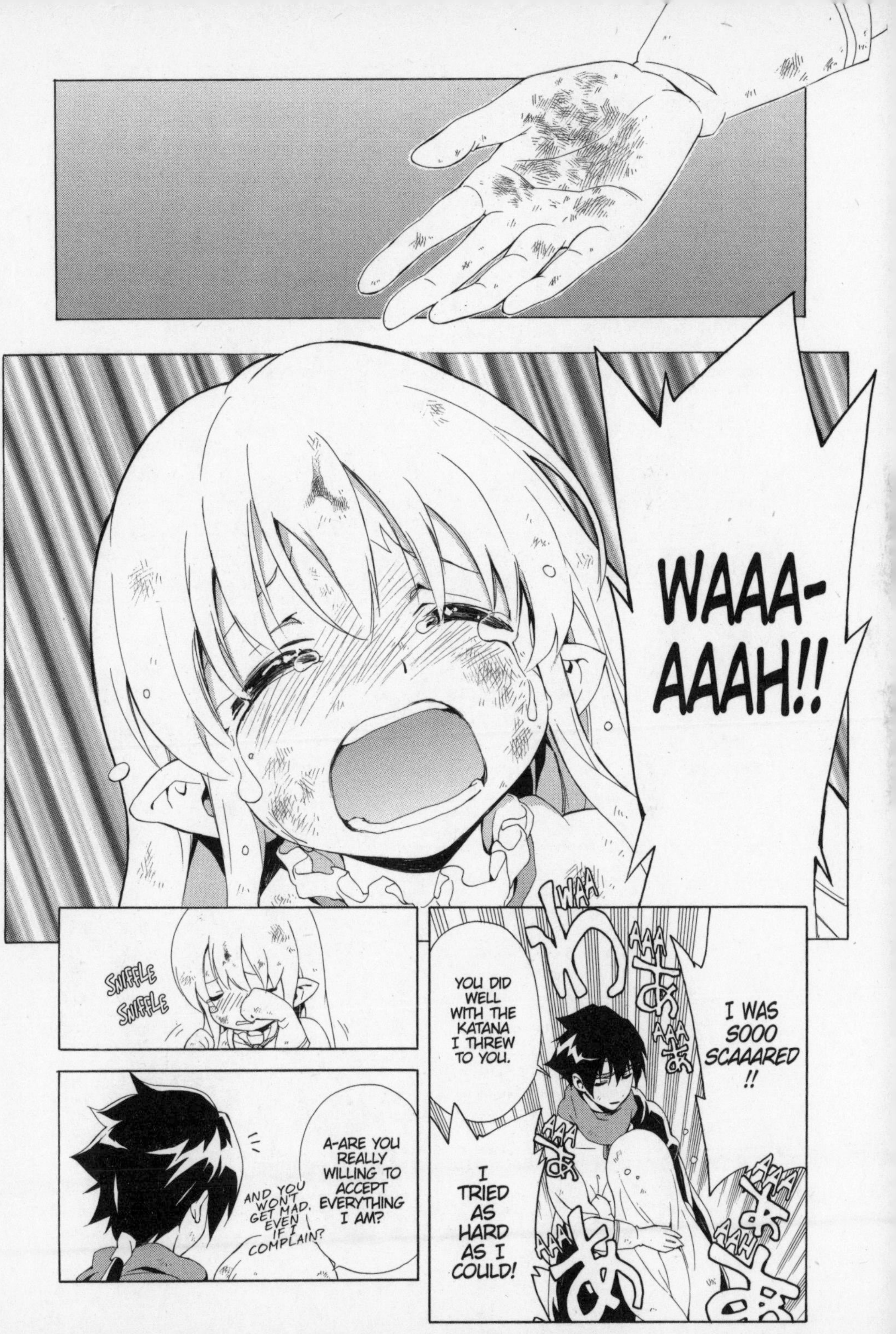
WAAAA-AAAAH!!
WAA
AAA
I WAS SOOO SCAAARED!!
YOU DID WELL WITH THE KATANA I THREW TO YOU.
I TRIED AS HARD AS I COULD!
SNIFFLE
SNIFFLE
A-ARE YOU REALLY WILLING TO ACCEPT EVERYTHING I AM?
AND YOU WON'T GET MAD, EVEN IF I COMPLAIN?

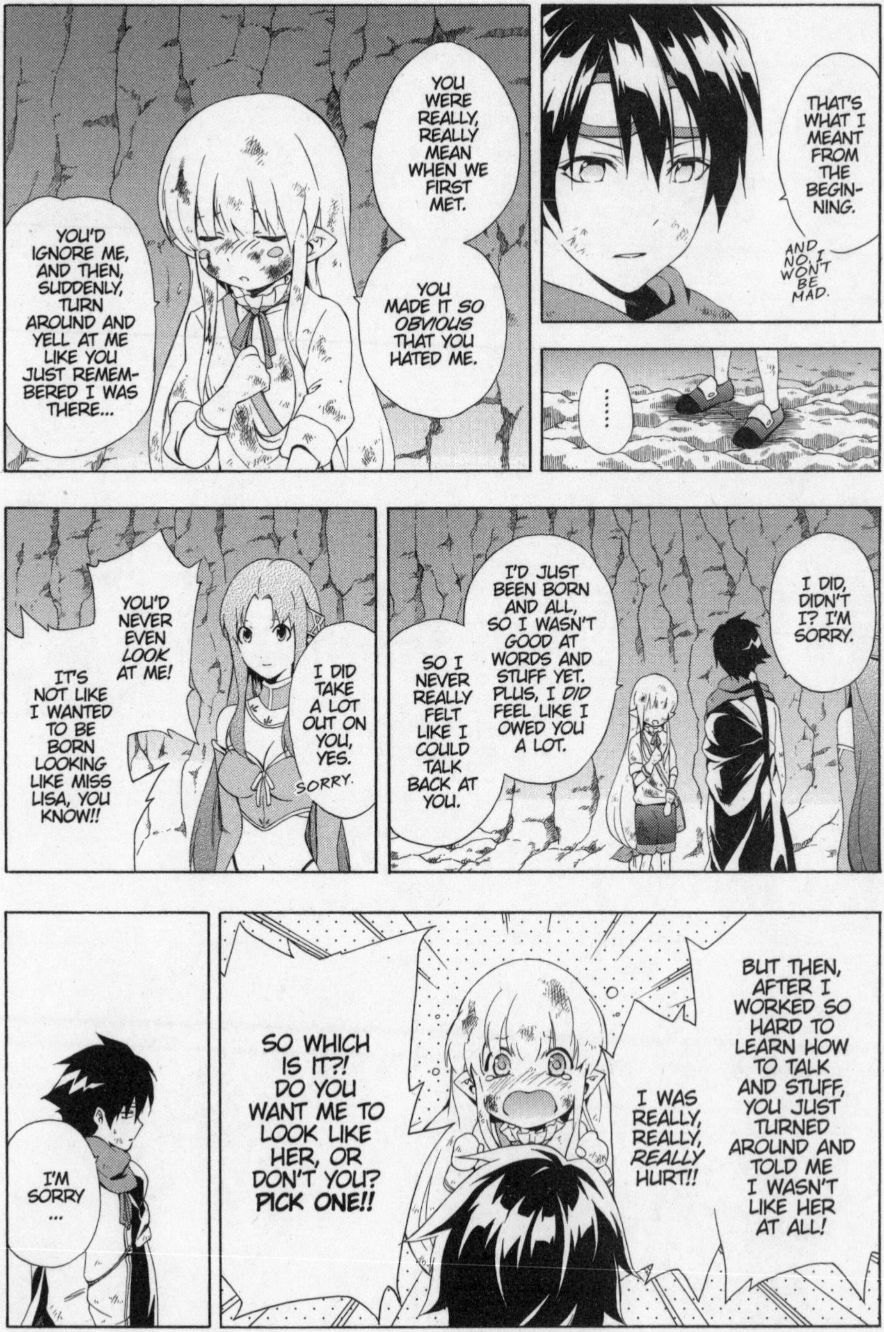
THAT'S WHAT I MEANT FROM THE BEGINNING.
AND NO, I WON'T BE MAD.
......
YOU WERE REALLY, REALLY MEAN WHEN WE FIRST MET.
YOU MADE IT *SO OBVIOUS* THAT YOU HATED ME.
YOU'D IGNORE ME, AND THEN, SUDDENLY, TURN AROUND AND YELL AT ME LIKE YOU JUST REMEMBERED I WAS THERE...
I DID, DIDN'T I? I'M SORRY.
I'D JUST BEEN BORN AND ALL, SO I WASN'T GOOD AT WORDS AND STUFF YET. PLUS, I *DID* FEEL LIKE I OWED YOU A LOT.
SO I NEVER REALLY FELT LIKE I COULD TALK BACK AT YOU.
I DID TAKE A LOT OUT ON YOU, YES.
SORRY.
YOU'D NEVER EVEN *LOOK* AT ME!
IT'S NOT LIKE I WANTED TO BE BORN LOOKING LIKE MISS LISA, YOU KNOW!!
BUT THEN, AFTER I WORKED SO HARD TO LEARN HOW TO TALK AND STUFF, YOU JUST TURNED AROUND AND TOLD ME I WASN'T LIKE HER AT ALL!
I WAS REALLY, REALLY, *REALLY* HURT!!
SO WHICH IS IT?! DO YOU WANT ME TO LOOK LIKE HER, OR DON'T YOU? PICK ONE!!
I'M SORRY ...

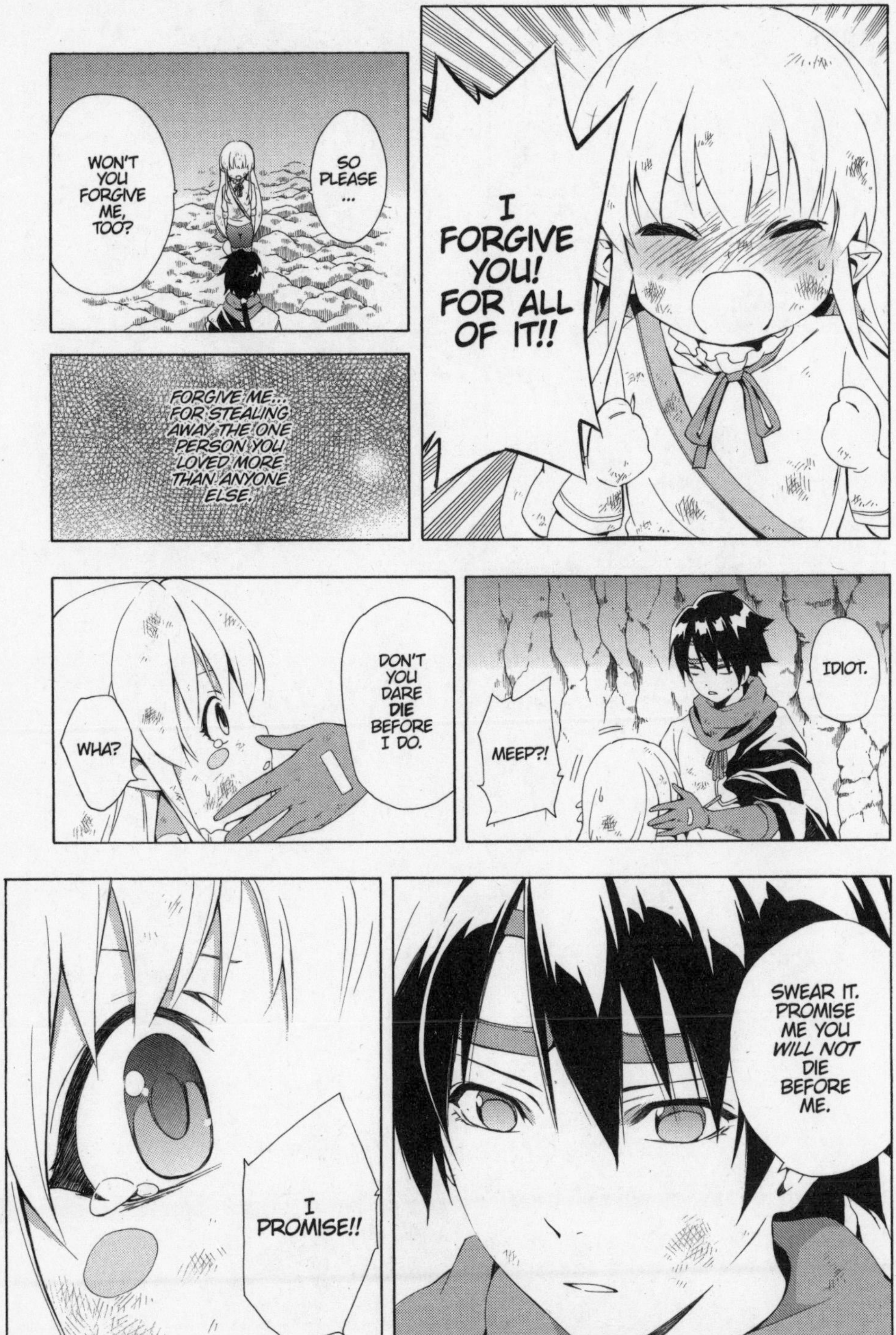
I FORGIVE YOU! FOR ALL OF IT!!
SO PLEASE ...
WON'T YOU FORGIVE ME, TOO?
FORGIVE ME... FOR STEALING AWAY THE ONE PERSON YOU LOVED MORE THAN ANYONE ELSE.
IDIOT.
MEEP?!
DON'T YOU DARE DIE BEFORE I DO.
WHA?
SWEAR IT. PROMISE ME YOU WILL NOT DIE BEFORE ME.
I PROMISE!!

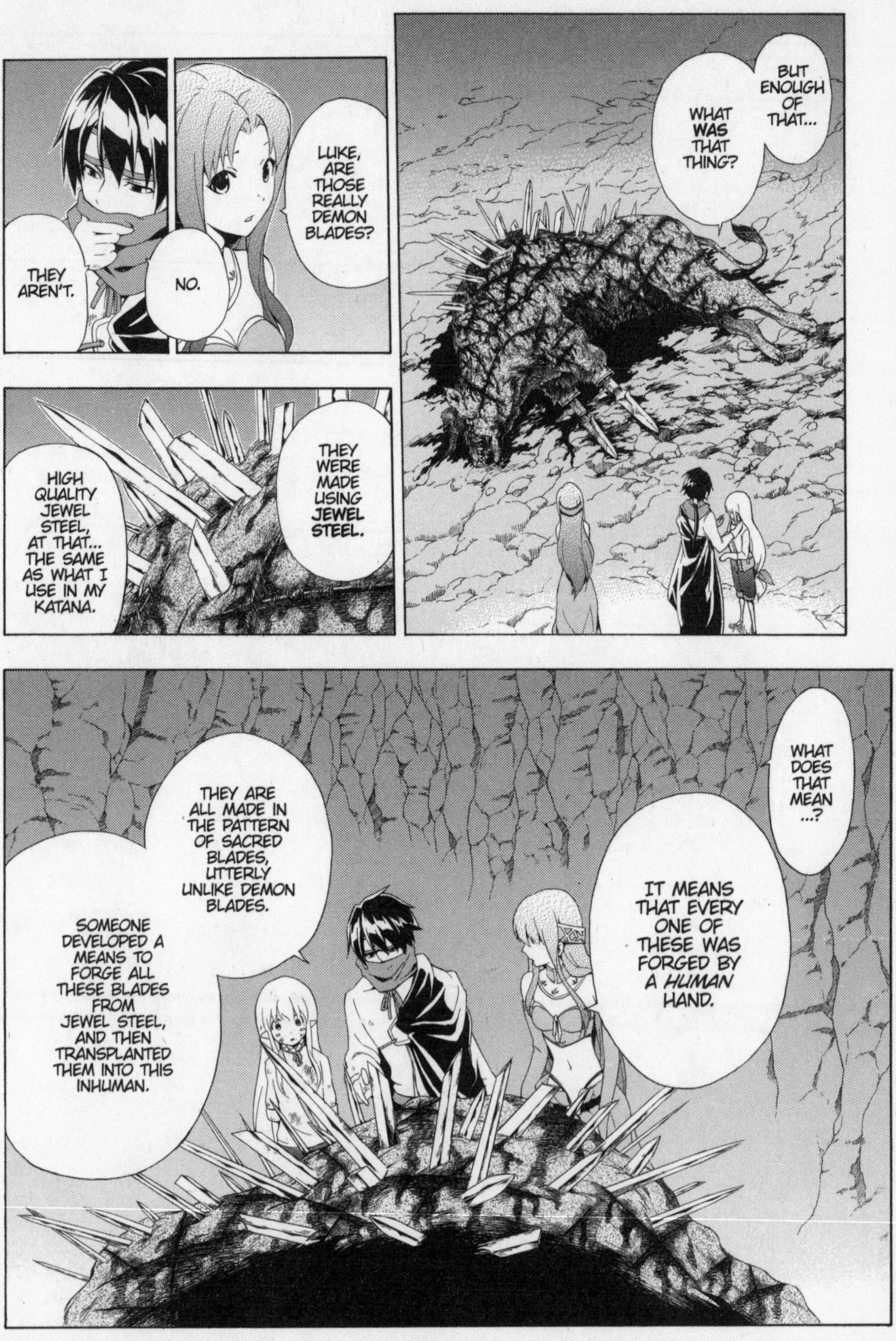
BUT ENOUGH OF THAT...
WHAT WAS THAT THING?
LUKE, ARE THOSE REALLY DEMON BLADES?
NO.
THEY AREN'T.
THEY WERE MADE USING JEWEL STEEL.
HIGH QUALITY JEWEL STEEL, AT THAT... THE SAME AS WHAT I USE IN MY KATANA.
WHAT DOES THAT MEAN ...?
IT MEANS THAT EVERY ONE OF THESE WAS FORGED BY A *HUMAN* HAND.
THEY ARE ALL MADE IN THE PATTERN OF SACRED BLADES, UTTERLY UNLIKE DEMON BLADES.
SOMEONE DEVELOPED A MEANS TO FORGE ALL THESE BLADES FROM JEWEL STEEL, AND THEN TRANSPLANTED THEM INTO THIS INHUMAN.

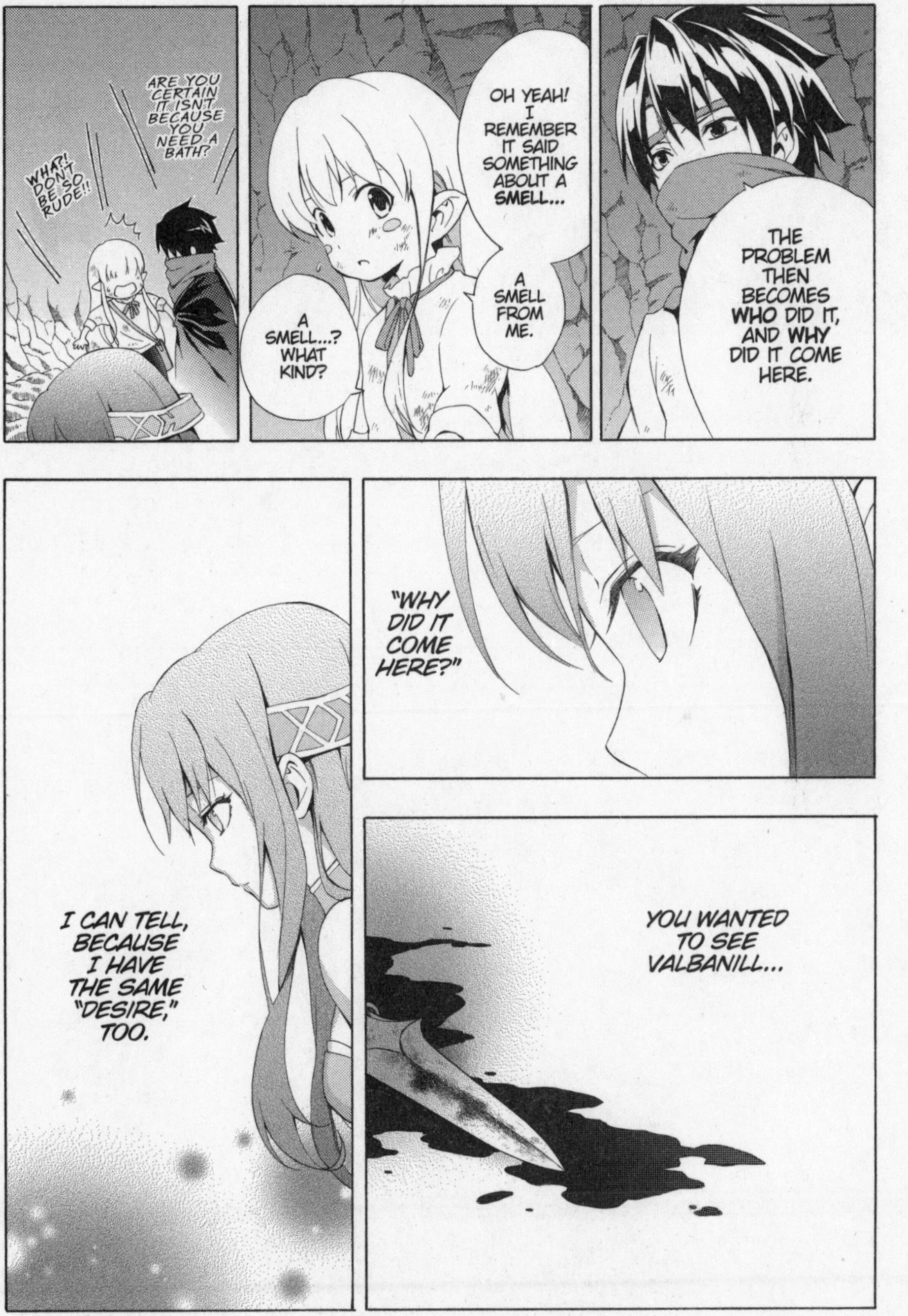
THE PROBLEM THEN BECOMES WHO DID IT, AND WHY DID IT COME HERE.
OH YEAH! I REMEMBER IT SAID SOMETHING ABOUT A SMELL...
A SMELL FROM ME.
A SMELL...? WHAT KIND?
ARE YOU CERTAIN IT ISN'T BECAUSE YOU NEED A BATH?
WHA?! DON'T BE SO RUDE!!
"WHY DID IT COME HERE?"
YOU WANTED TO SEE VALBANILL...
I CAN TELL, BECAUSE I HAVE THE SAME "DESIRE," TOO.

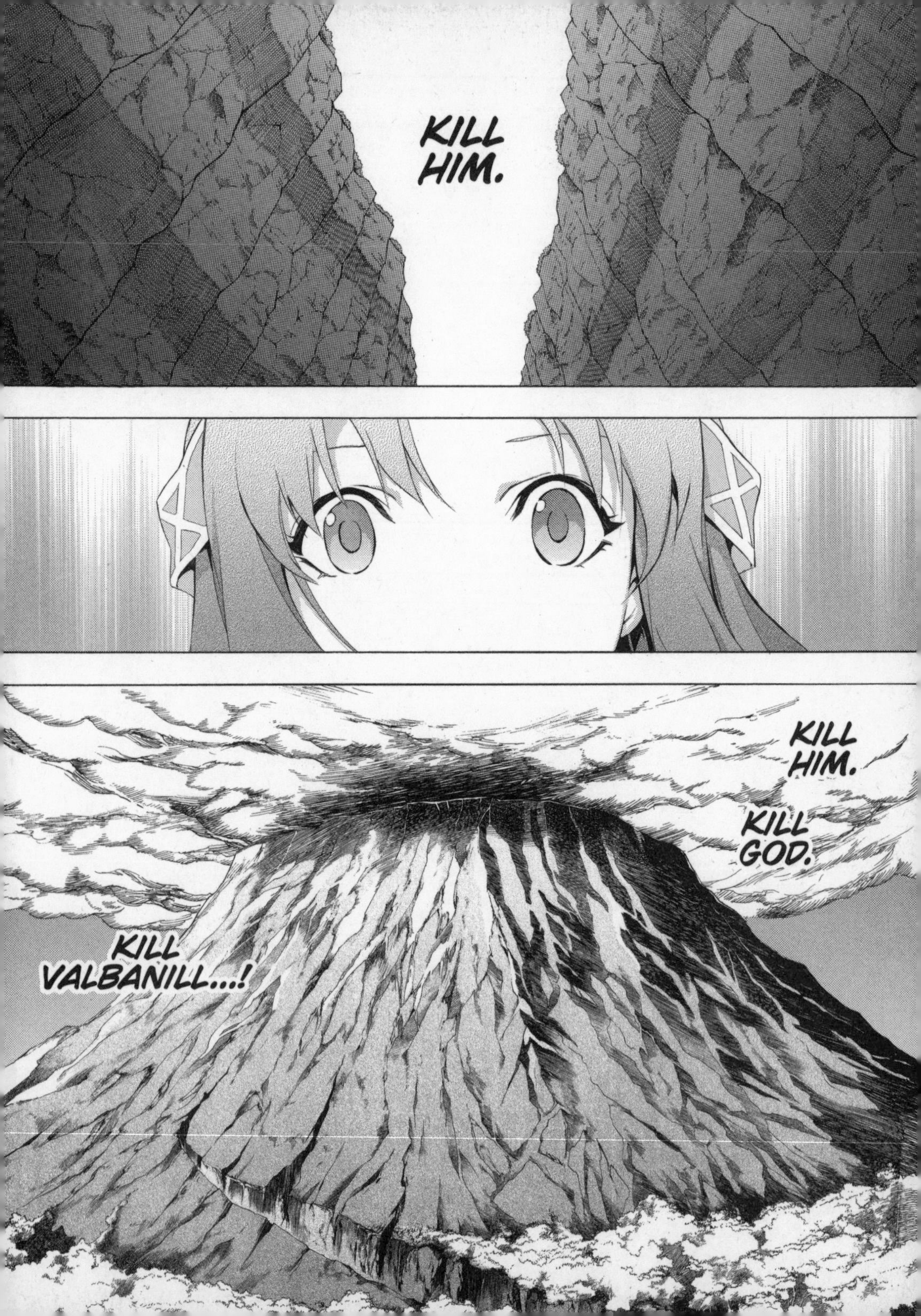
KILL HIM.
KILL HIM.
KILL GOD.
KILL VALBANILL...!

アトリエ 工房リーザ
atelier Liza BRANCH OFFICE I

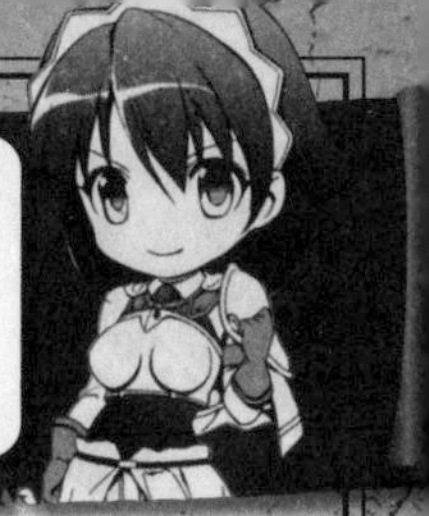
Here at the Atelier Liza Branch Office, we're going to show off everybody's passionate love for this series!

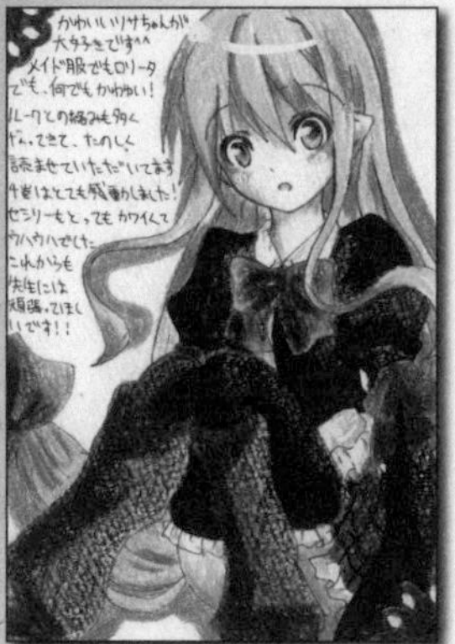

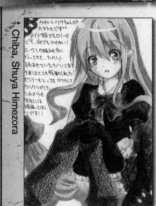

↑ Chiba, Shuya Himezora

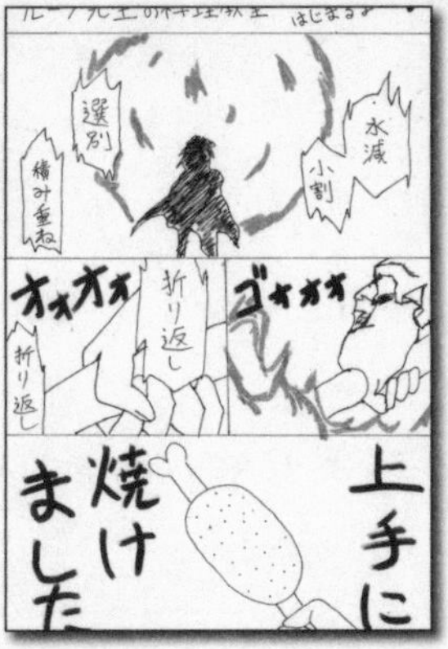
選別
積み重ね
水減
小割
オォオォ
折り返し
折り返し
ゴォオォ
上手に焼けました

↑ Aichi, Koshihikari

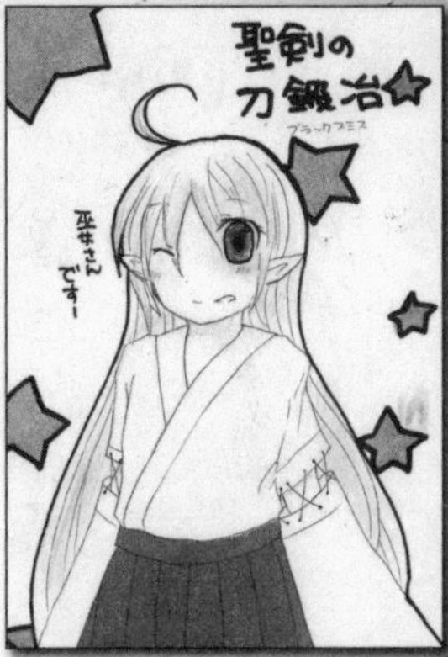
聖剣の刀鍛冶☆
ブラックスミス

↑ Yamaguchi, Kanshou Sankoku

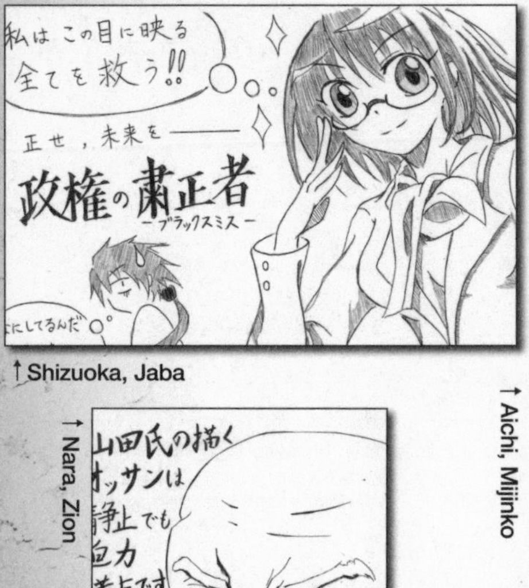
私はこの目に映る全てを救う!!
正せ，未来を——
政権の粛正者
ーブラックスミスー

↑ Shizuoka, Jaba

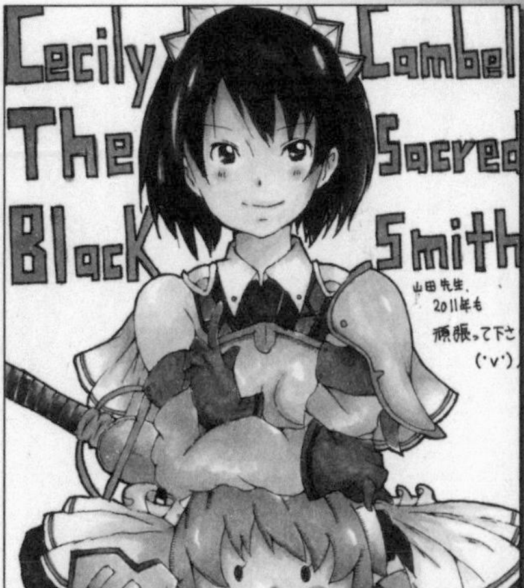
Cecily Cambel
The Sacred Black Smith
山田先生，2011年も頑張って下さ
(･v･)

↑ Aichi, Mijinko

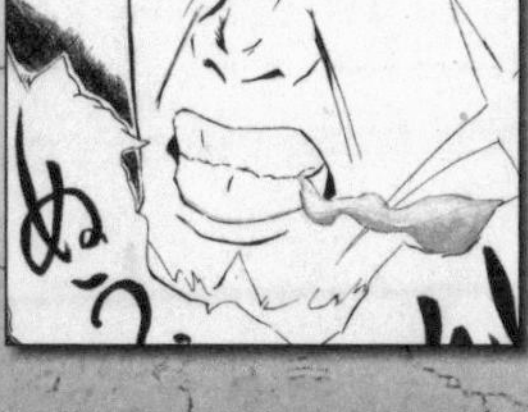
山田氏の描くオッサンは静止でも迫力満点です!!

↑ Nara, Zion

An expression of confidence is proof that one is a true knight! Come on everyone, take up the sword in your heart and stand with us!

The Sacred Blacksmith

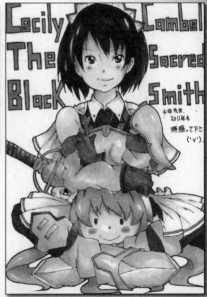

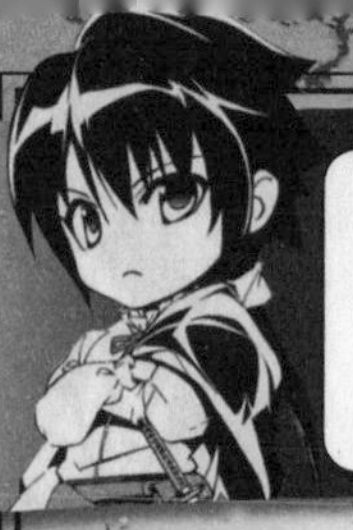

These are all well-forged pieces. Each one is more useful than Cecily, too...

アトリエ 工房リーザ atelier Liza BRANCH OFFICE II

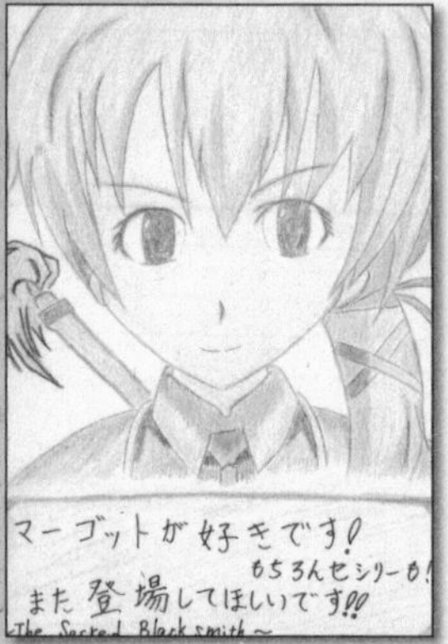
マーゴットが好きです!
もちろんセシリーも!
また登場してほしいです!!
The Sacred Blacksmith ~

↑ Saitama, Yuuji

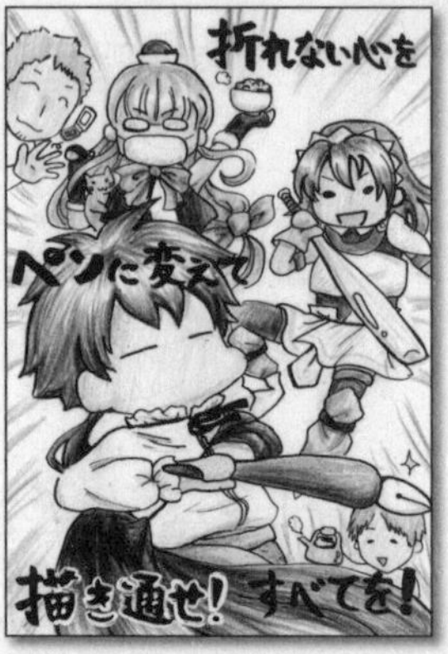
折れない心を
ペンに変えて
描き通せ! すべてを!

↑ Miyazaki, Ahri

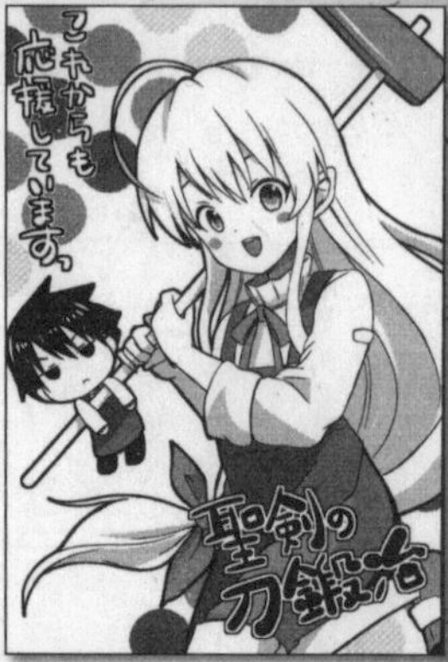
これからも応援しています。
聖剣の刀鍛冶

↑ Nagano, Kanon

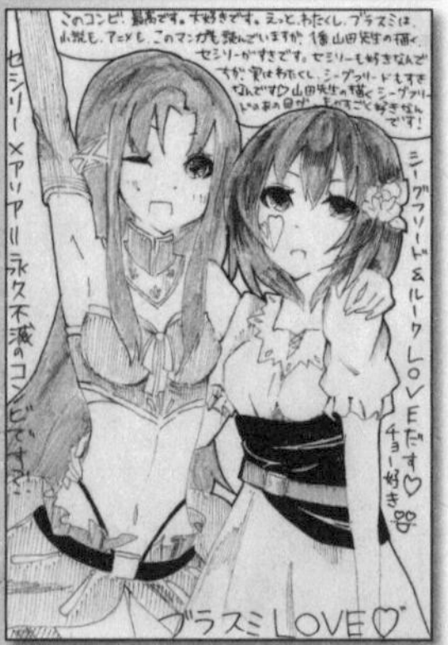
セシリー×アリア=永久不滅のコンビです
ジークフリード&ルークLOVEです ちょー好き♡
ブラスミLOVE♡

↑ Hyogo, Hibitanren

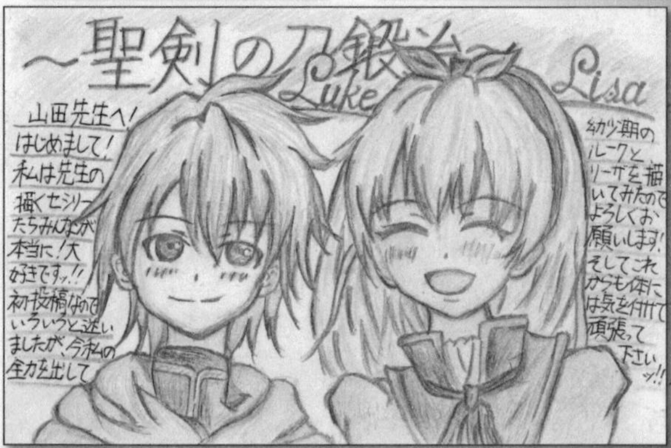
~聖剣の刀鍛冶~
Luke
Lisa
山田先生へ! はじめまして! 私は先生の描くセシリーたちみんなが本当に!大好きです!! 初投稿なのでいろいろと迷いましたが、今私の全力を出して
幼少期のルークとリーザを描いてみたのでよろしくお願いします! そしてこれからも体には気を付けて頑張って下さいッ!!

Fukushima, Kido Miri ↑

"Hibitanren," eh? I like the name. No matter what path you walk, you can only proceed through "hibitanren"--daily effort. Cecily could stand to learn that.

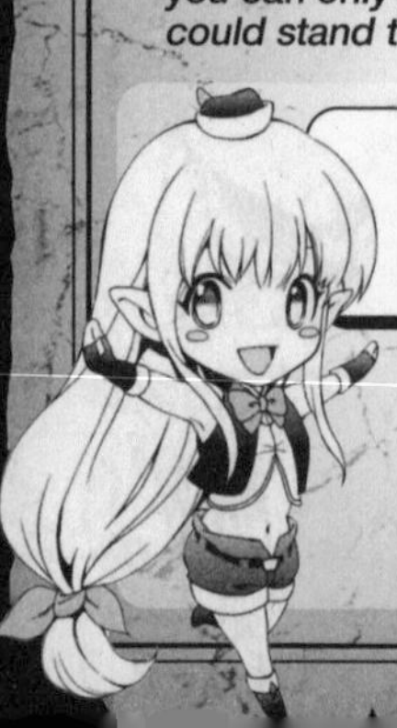

Hi, everyone! Welcome to the Atelier Liza Branch Office! Everyone whose art was displayed here will receive a personalized sketch from Yamada-sensei himself! We're still accepting submissions, so keep on sending them in*!

**Only if you live in Japan!*

The Sacred Blacksmith

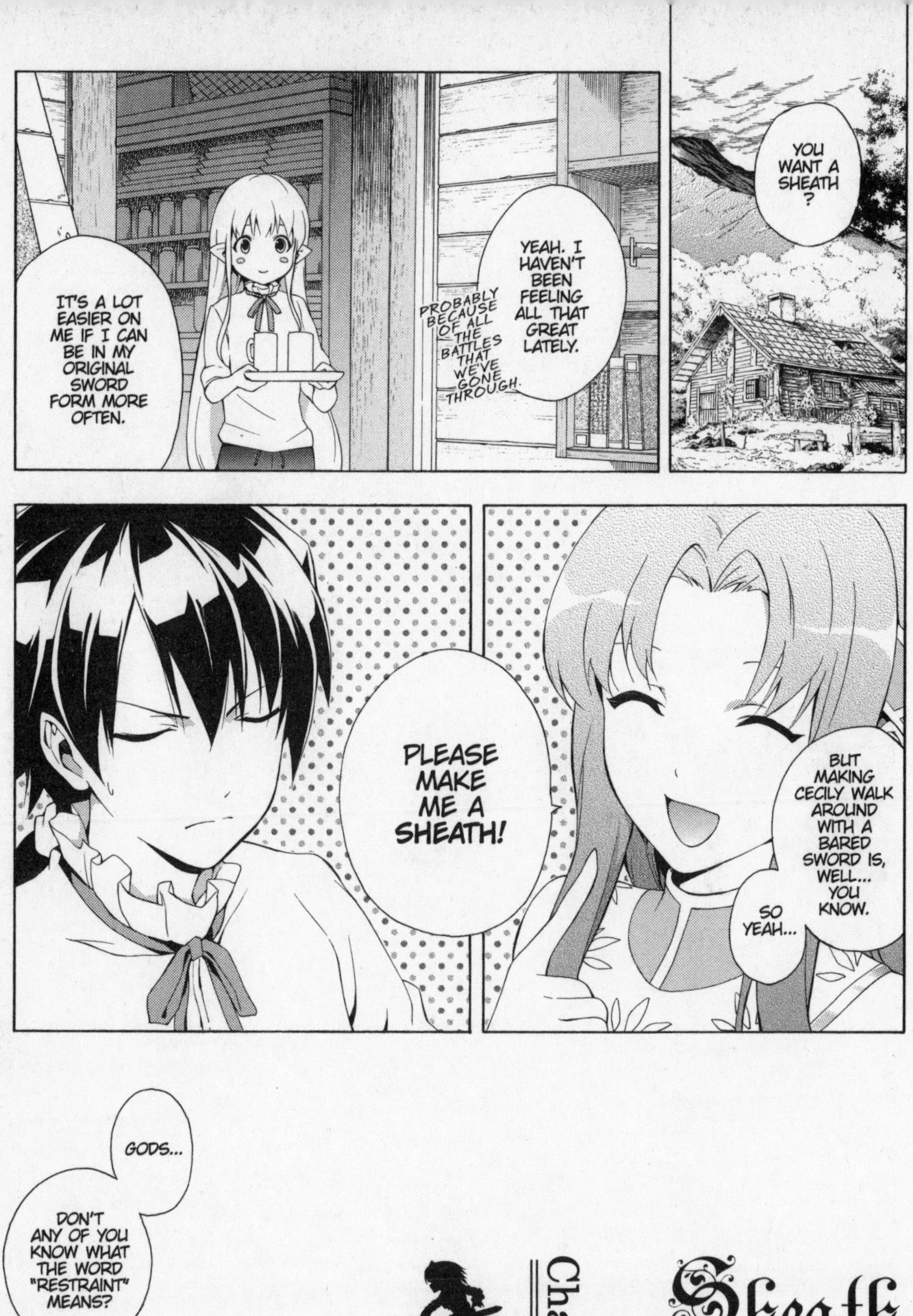
YOU WANT A SHEATH?
YEAH. I HAVEN'T BEEN FEELING ALL THAT GREAT LATELY.
PROBABLY BECAUSE OF ALL THE BATTLES THAT WE'VE GONE THROUGH.
IT'S A LOT EASIER ON ME IF I CAN BE IN MY ORIGINAL SWORD FORM MORE OFTEN.
BUT MAKING CECILY WALK AROUND WITH A BARED SWORD IS, WELL... YOU KNOW.
SO YEAH...
PLEASE MAKE ME A SHEATH!
GODS...
DON'T ANY OF YOU KNOW WHAT THE WORD "RESTRAINT" MEANS?

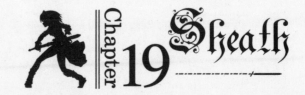

Chapter 19 Sheath

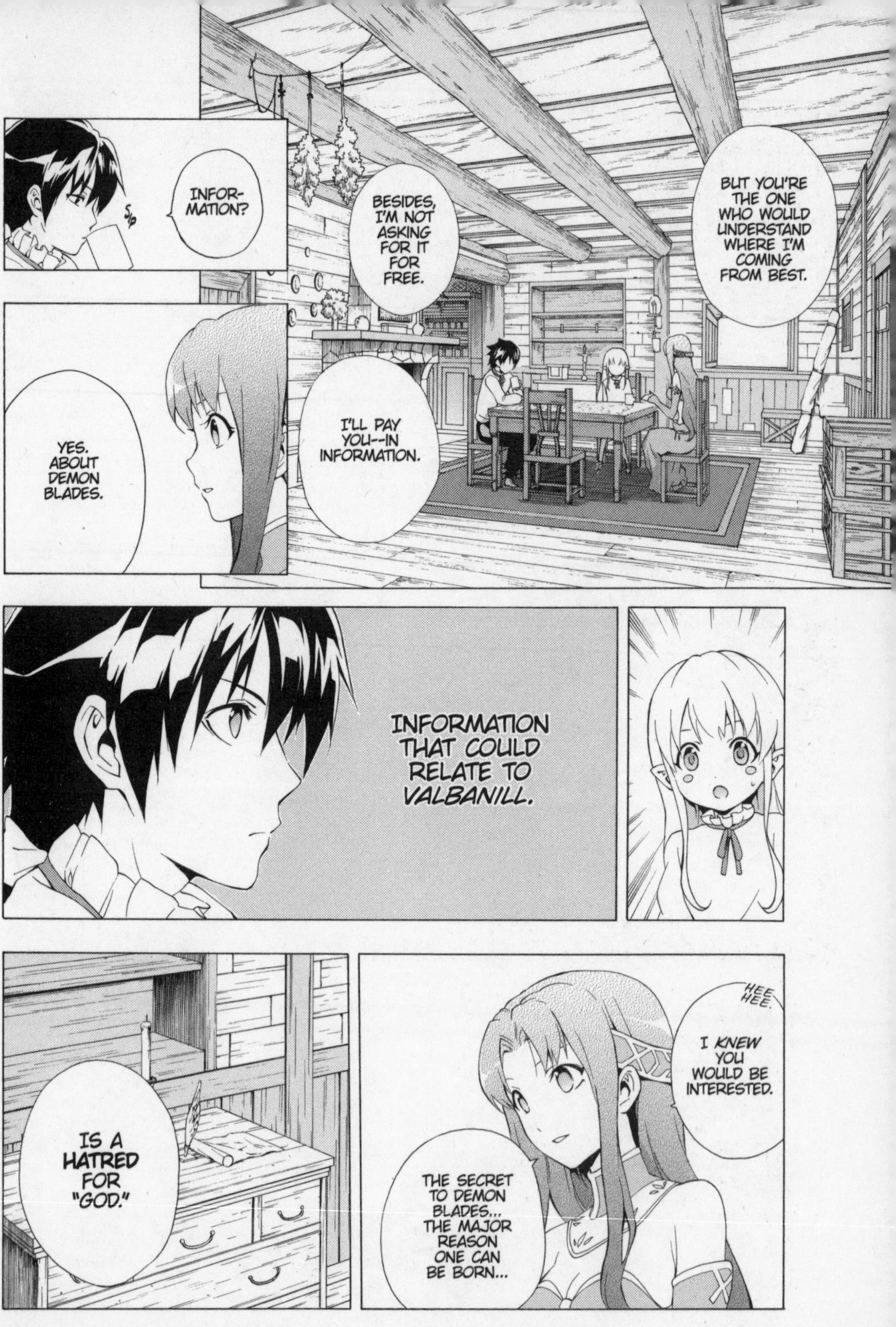
BUT YOU'RE THE ONE WHO WOULD UNDERSTAND WHERE I'M COMING FROM BEST.
BESIDES, I'M NOT ASKING FOR IT FOR FREE.
I'LL PAY YOU--IN INFORMATION.
SIP
INFORMATION?
YES. ABOUT DEMON BLADES.
INFORMATION THAT COULD RELATE TO *VALBANILL.*
HEE HEE.
I *KNEW* YOU WOULD BE INTERESTED.
THE SECRET TO DEMON BLADES... THE MAJOR REASON ONE CAN BE BORN...
IS A **HATRED** FOR "GOD."

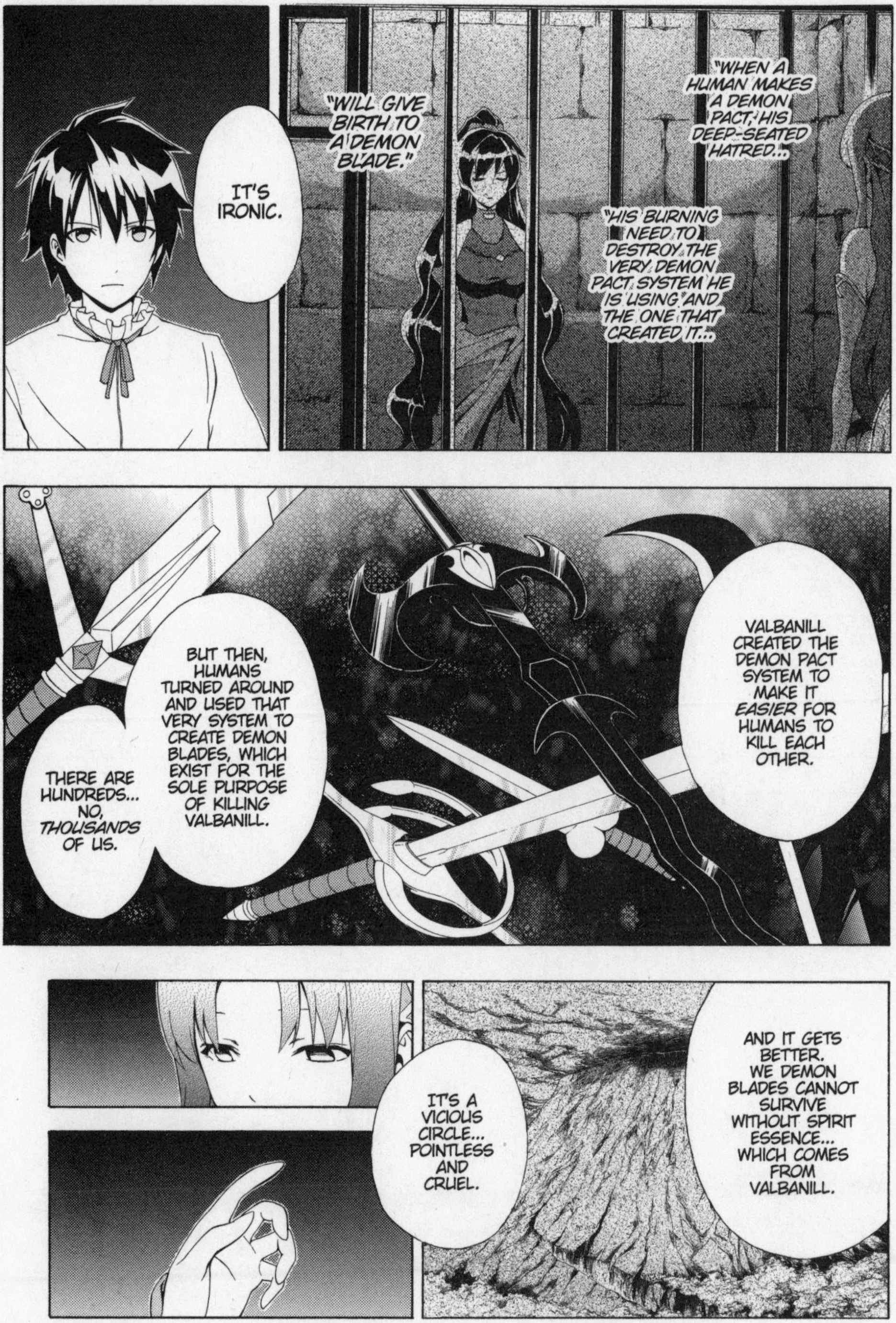
"WHEN A HUMAN MAKES A DEMON PACT, HIS DEEP-SEATED HATRED...
"HIS BURNING NEED TO DESTROY THE VERY DEMON PACT SYSTEM HE IS USING AND THE ONE THAT CREATED IT...
"WILL GIVE BIRTH TO A DEMON BLADE."
IT'S IRONIC.
VALBANILL CREATED THE DEMON PACT SYSTEM TO MAKE IT *EASIER* FOR HUMANS TO KILL EACH OTHER.
BUT THEN, HUMANS TURNED AROUND AND USED THAT VERY SYSTEM TO CREATE DEMON BLADES, WHICH EXIST FOR THE SOLE PURPOSE OF KILLING VALBANILL.
THERE ARE HUNDREDS... NO, *THOUSANDS* OF US.
AND IT GETS BETTER. WE DEMON BLADES CANNOT SURVIVE WITHOUT SPIRIT ESSENCE... WHICH COMES FROM VALBANILL.
IT'S A VICIOUS CIRCLE... POINTLESS AND CRUEL.

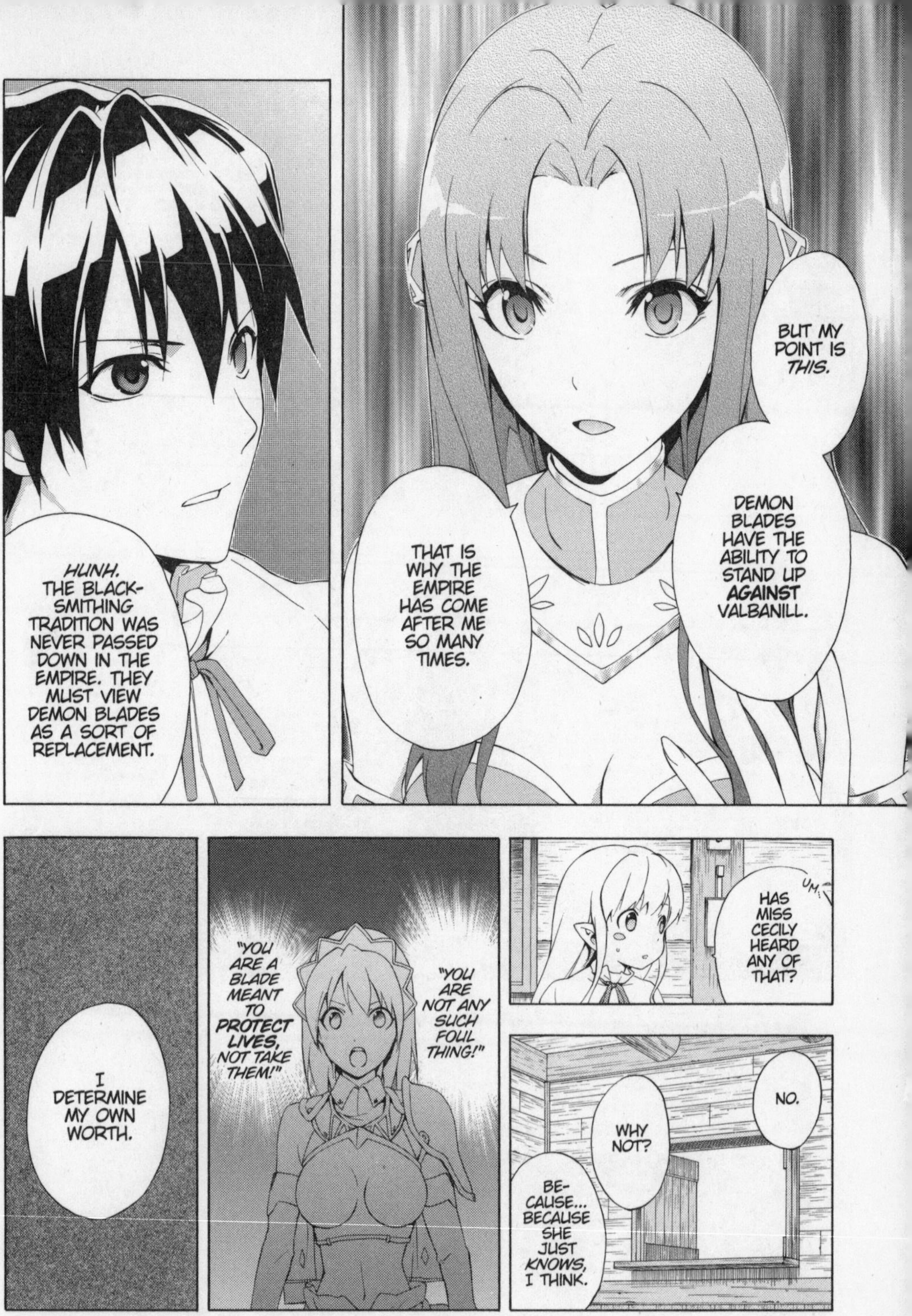
BUT MY POINT IS *THIS*.
DEMON BLADES HAVE THE ABILITY TO STAND UP **AGAINST** VALBANILL.
THAT IS WHY THE EMPIRE HAS COME AFTER ME SO MANY TIMES.
HUNH. THE BLACK-SMITHING TRADITION WAS NEVER PASSED DOWN IN THE EMPIRE. THEY MUST VIEW DEMON BLADES AS A SORT OF REPLACEMENT.
UM...
HAS MISS CECILY HEARD ANY OF THAT?
NO.
WHY NOT?
BE-CAUSE... BECAUSE SHE JUST *KNOWS*, I THINK.
"YOU ARE A BLADE MEANT TO **PROTECT LIVES,** *NOT TAKE THEM!"*
"YOU ARE NOT ANY SUCH FOUL THING!"
I DETERMINE MY OWN WORTH.

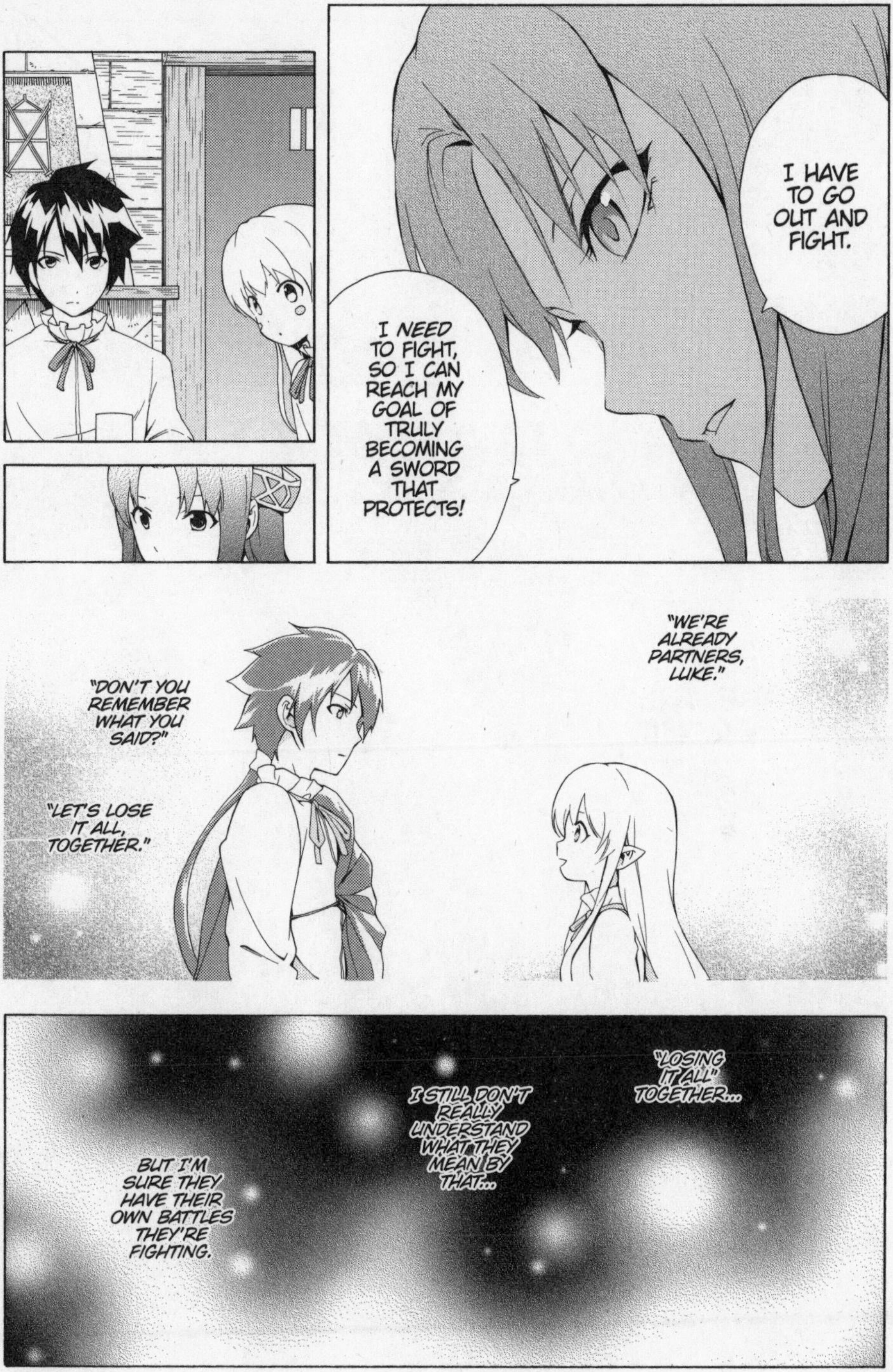
I HAVE TO GO OUT AND FIGHT.
I NEED TO FIGHT, SO I CAN REACH MY GOAL OF TRULY BECOMING A SWORD THAT PROTECTS!
"WE'RE ALREADY PARTNERS, LUKE."
"DON'T YOU REMEMBER WHAT YOU SAID?"
"LET'S LOSE IT ALL, TOGETHER."
"LOSING IT ALL" TOGETHER...
I STILL DON'T REALLY UNDERSTAND WHAT THEY MEAN BY THAT...
BUT I'M SURE THEY HAVE THEIR OWN BATTLES THEY'RE FIGHTING.

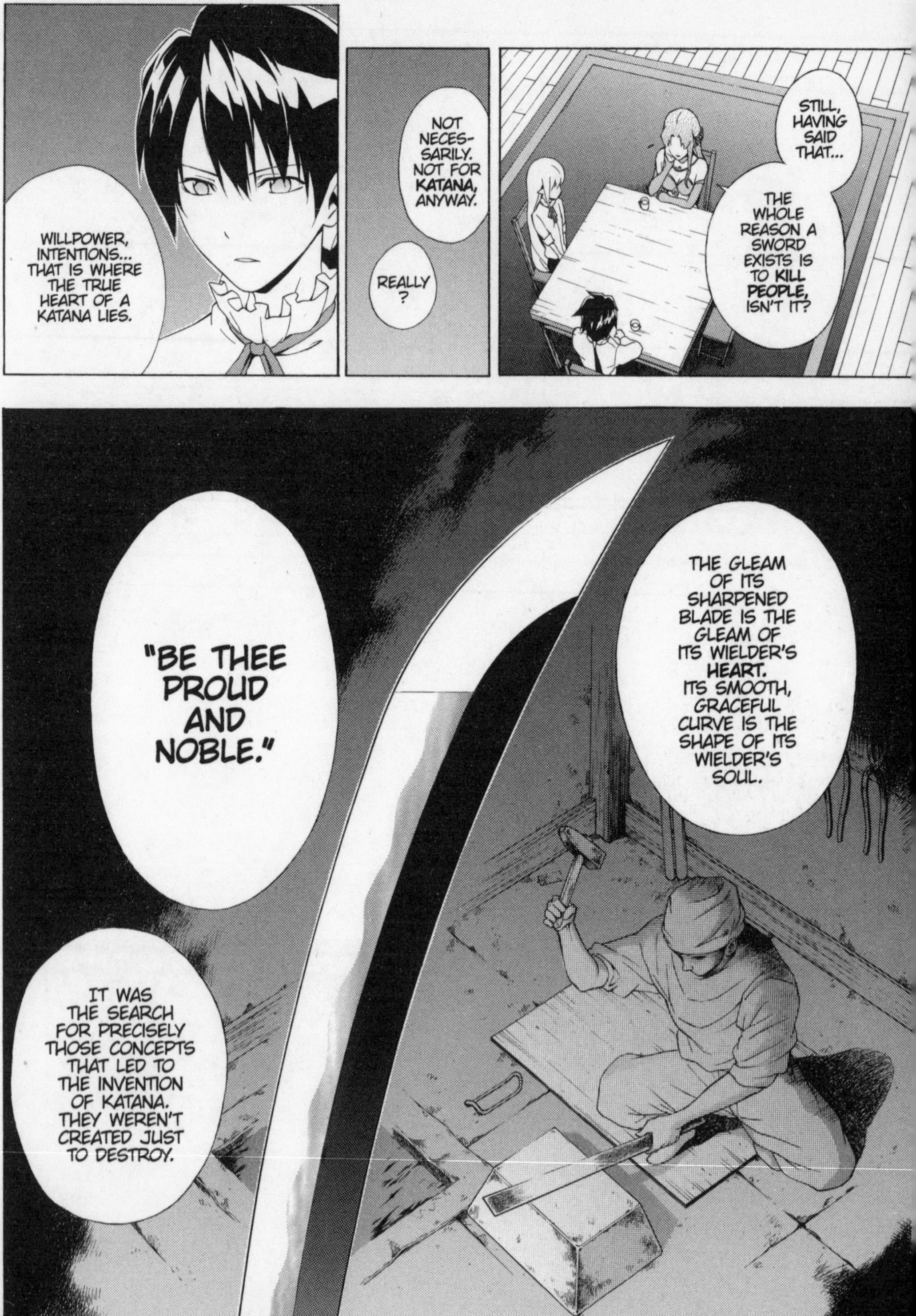
STILL, HAVING SAID THAT...
THE WHOLE REASON A SWORD EXISTS IS TO KILL PEOPLE, ISN'T IT?
NOT NECES-SARILY. NOT FOR KATANA, ANYWAY.
REALLY?
WILLPOWER, INTENTIONS... THAT IS WHERE THE TRUE HEART OF A KATANA LIES.
THE GLEAM OF ITS SHARPENED BLADE IS THE GLEAM OF ITS WIELDER'S HEART. ITS SMOOTH, GRACEFUL CURVE IS THE SHAPE OF ITS WIELDER'S SOUL.
"BE THEE PROUD AND NOBLE."
IT WAS THE SEARCH FOR PRECISELY THOSE CONCEPTS THAT LED TO THE INVENTION OF KATANA. THEY WEREN'T CREATED JUST TO DESTROY.

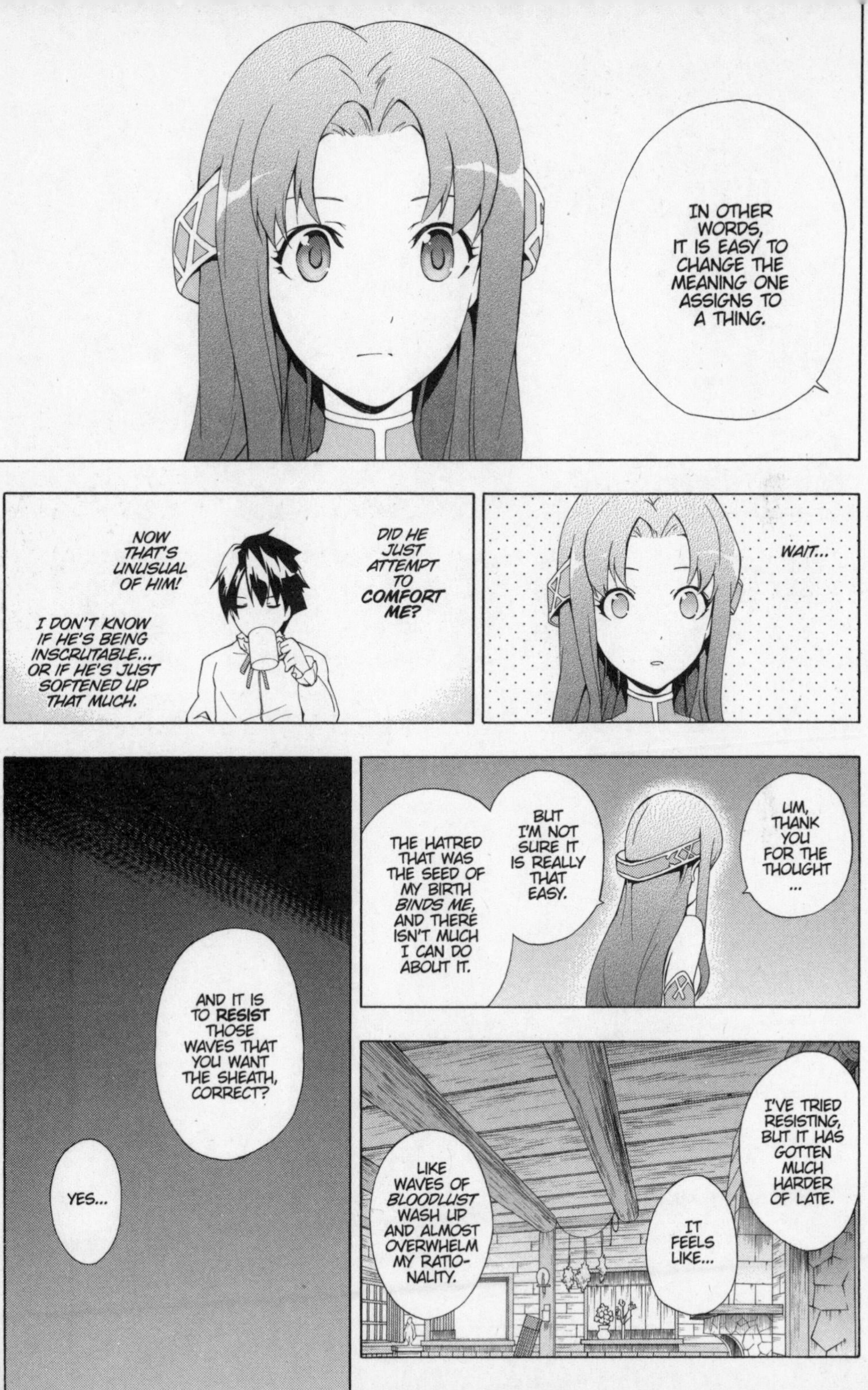
IN OTHER WORDS, IT IS EASY TO CHANGE THE MEANING ONE ASSIGNS TO A THING.
WAIT...
DID HE JUST ATTEMPT TO COMFORT ME?
NOW THAT'S UNUSUAL OF HIM!
I DON'T KNOW IF HE'S BEING INSCRUTABLE... OR IF HE'S JUST SOFTENED UP THAT MUCH.
UM, THANK YOU FOR THE THOUGHT ...
BUT I'M NOT SURE IT IS REALLY THAT EASY.
THE HATRED THAT WAS THE SEED OF MY BIRTH BINDS ME, AND THERE ISN'T MUCH I CAN DO ABOUT IT.
I'VE TRIED RESISTING, BUT IT HAS GOTTEN MUCH HARDER OF LATE.
IT FEELS LIKE...
LIKE WAVES OF BLOODLUST WASH UP AND ALMOST OVERWHELM MY RATIO-NALITY.
AND IT IS TO RESIST THOSE WAVES THAT YOU WANT THE SHEATH, CORRECT?
YES...

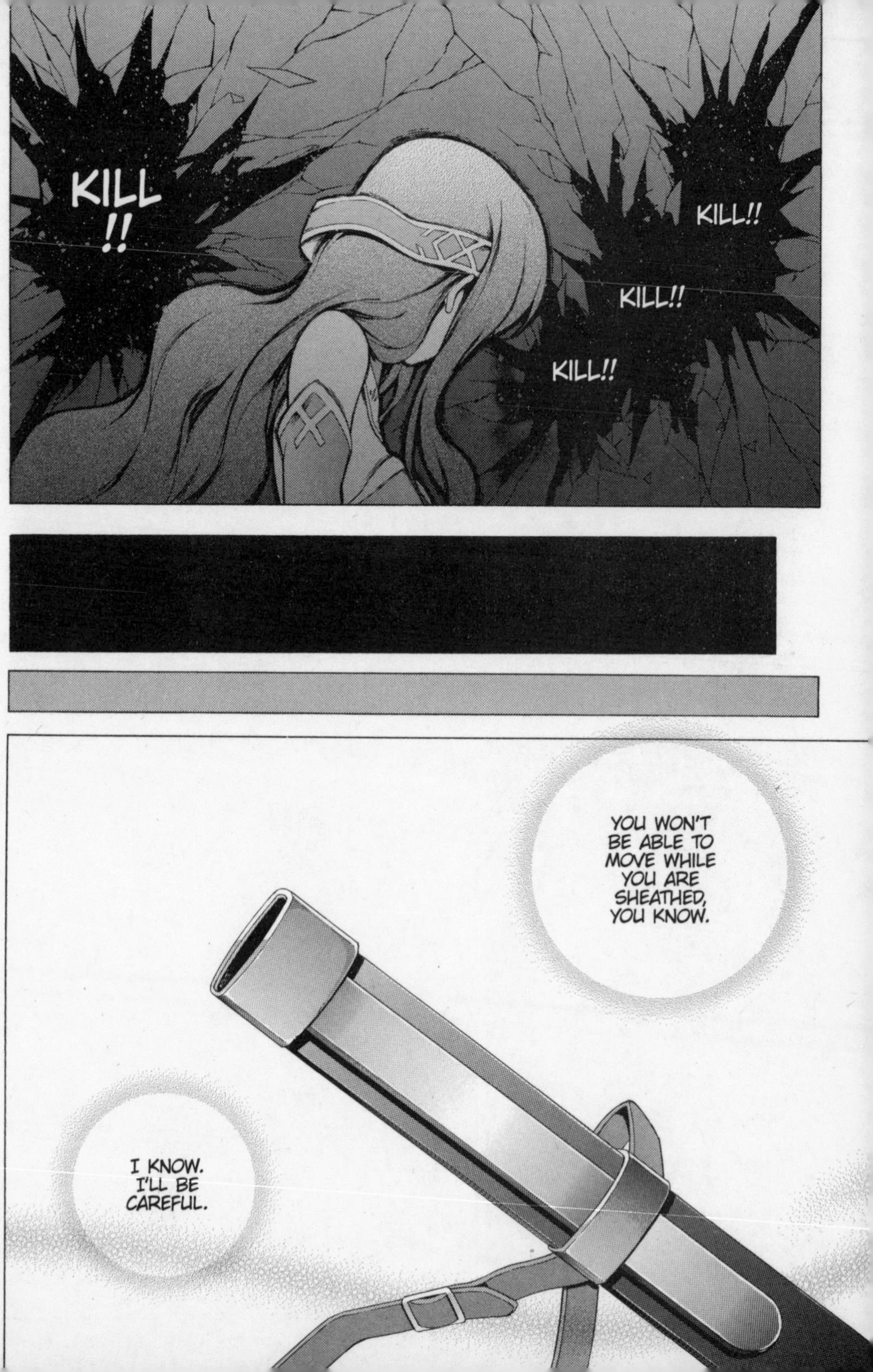
KILL!!
KILL!!
KILL!!
KILL !!
YOU WON'T BE ABLE TO MOVE WHILE YOU ARE SHEATHED, YOU KNOW.
I KNOW. I'LL BE CAREFUL.

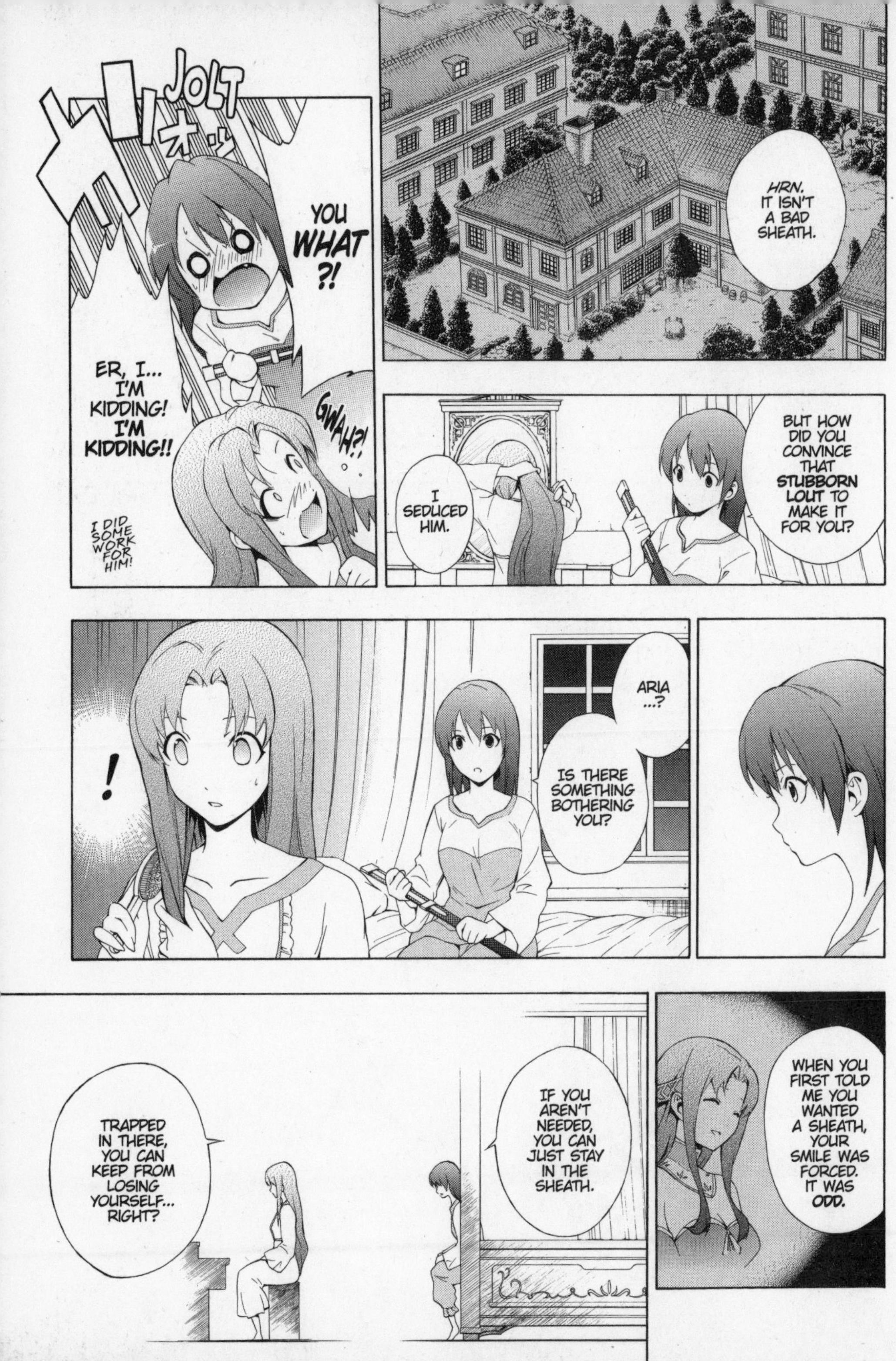
HRN. IT ISN'T A BAD SHEATH.
BUT HOW DID YOU CONVINCE THAT STUBBORN LOUT TO MAKE IT FOR YOU?
I SEDUCED HIM.
JOLT
YOU WHAT?!
ER, I... I'M KIDDING! I'M KIDDING!!
GWAH?!
I DID SOME WORK FOR HIM!
ARIA ...?
IS THERE SOMETHING BOTHERING YOU?
!
WHEN YOU FIRST TOLD ME YOU WANTED A SHEATH, YOUR SMILE WAS FORCED. IT WAS ODD.
IF YOU AREN'T NEEDED, YOU CAN JUST STAY IN THE SHEATH.
TRAPPED IN THERE, YOU CAN KEEP FROM LOSING YOURSELF... RIGHT?

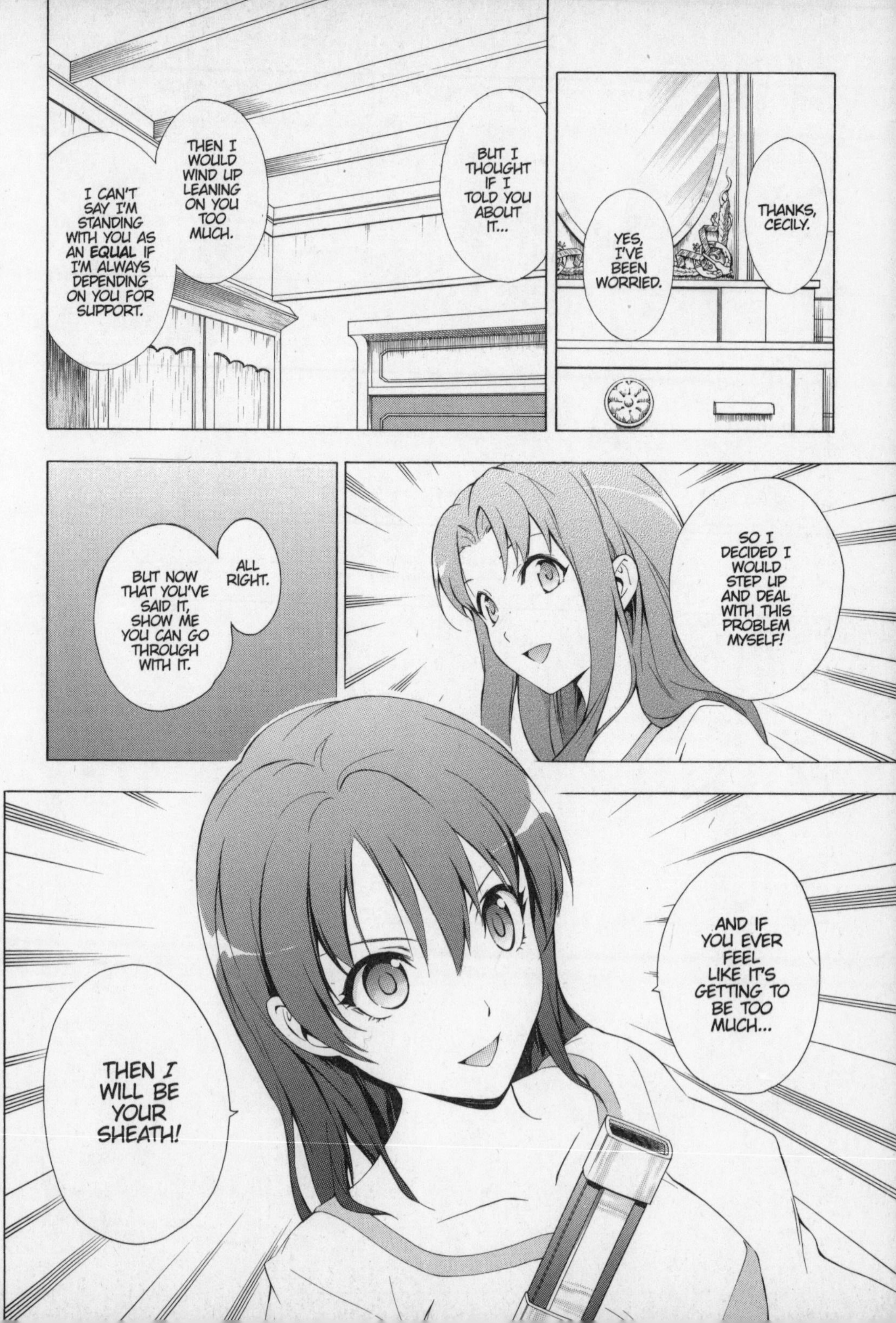
THANKS, CECILY.
YES, I'VE BEEN WORRIED.
BUT I THOUGHT IF I TOLD YOU ABOUT IT...
THEN I WOULD WIND UP LEANING ON YOU TOO MUCH.
I CAN'T SAY I'M STANDING WITH YOU AS AN **EQUAL** IF I'M ALWAYS DEPENDING ON YOU FOR SUPPORT.
SO I DECIDED I WOULD STEP UP AND DEAL WITH THIS PROBLEM MYSELF!
ALL RIGHT.
BUT NOW THAT YOU'VE SAID IT, SHOW ME YOU CAN GO THROUGH WITH IT.
AND IF YOU EVER FEEL LIKE IT'S GETTING TO BE TOO MUCH...
THEN *I* WILL BE YOUR SHEATH!

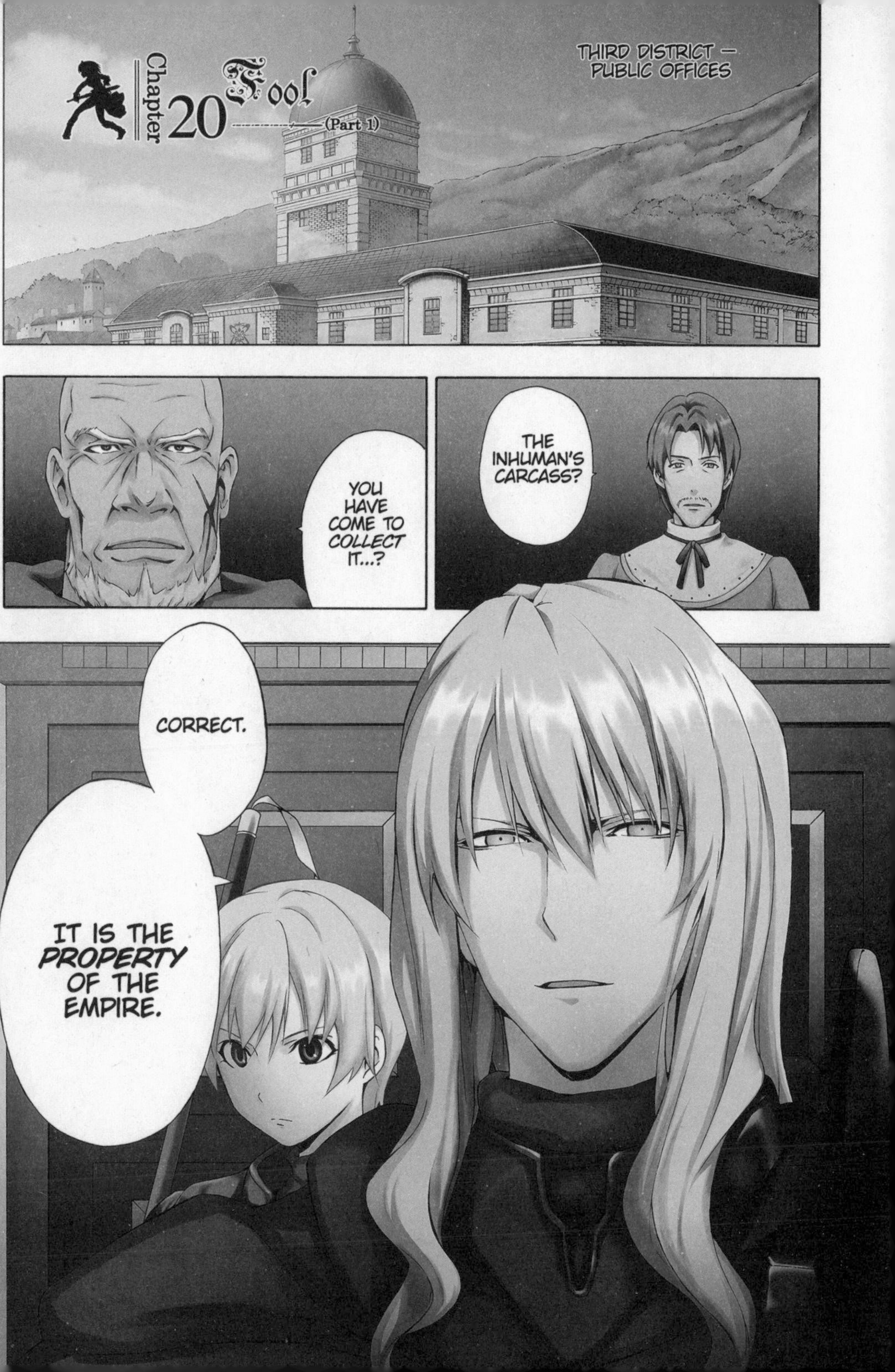
THIRD DISTRICT — PUBLIC OFFICES
Chapter 20 Fool (Part 1)
THE INHUMAN'S CARCASS?
YOU HAVE COME TO COLLECT IT...?
CORRECT.
IT IS THE *PROPERTY* OF THE EMPIRE.

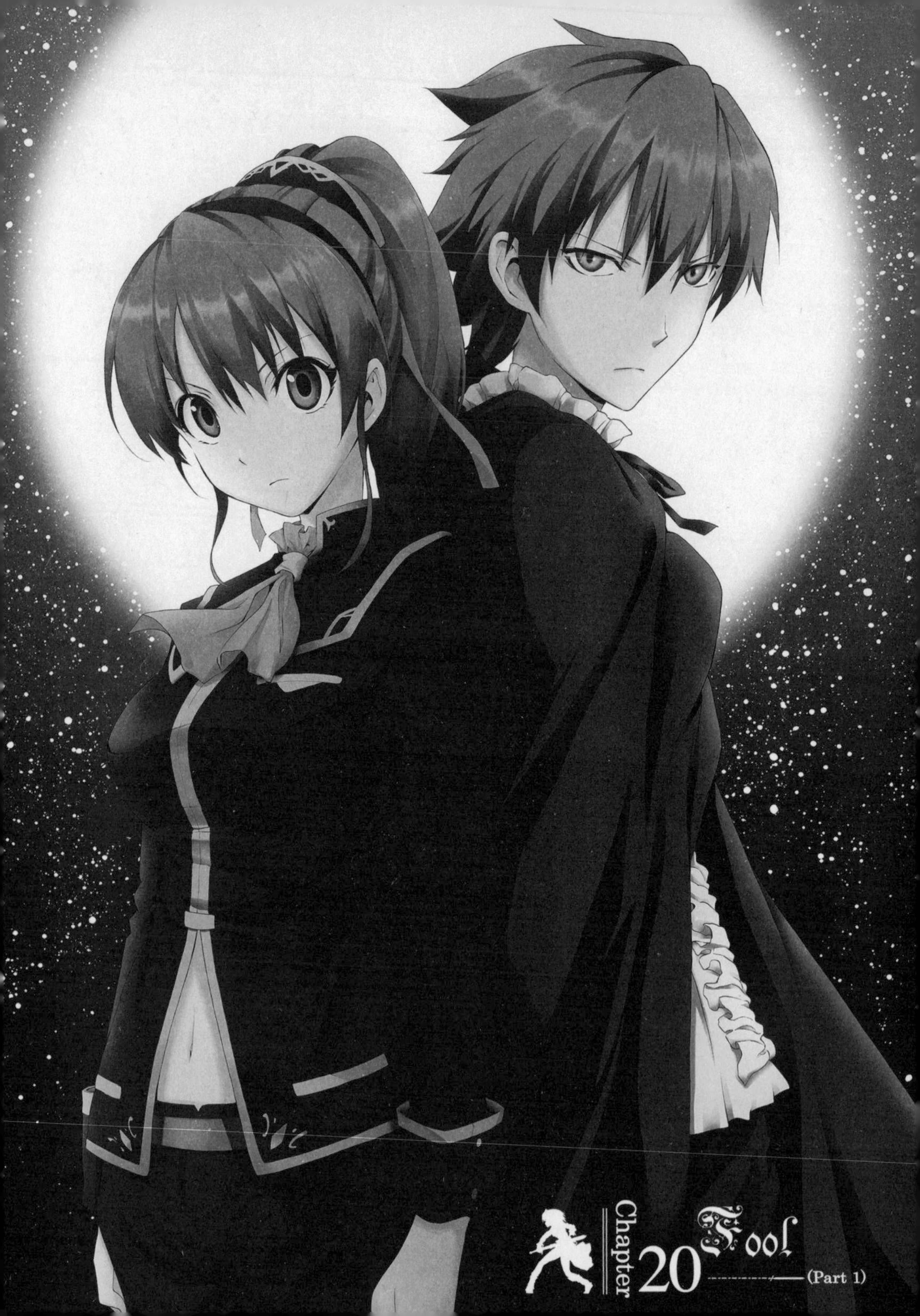

Chapter 20 Fool (Part 1)

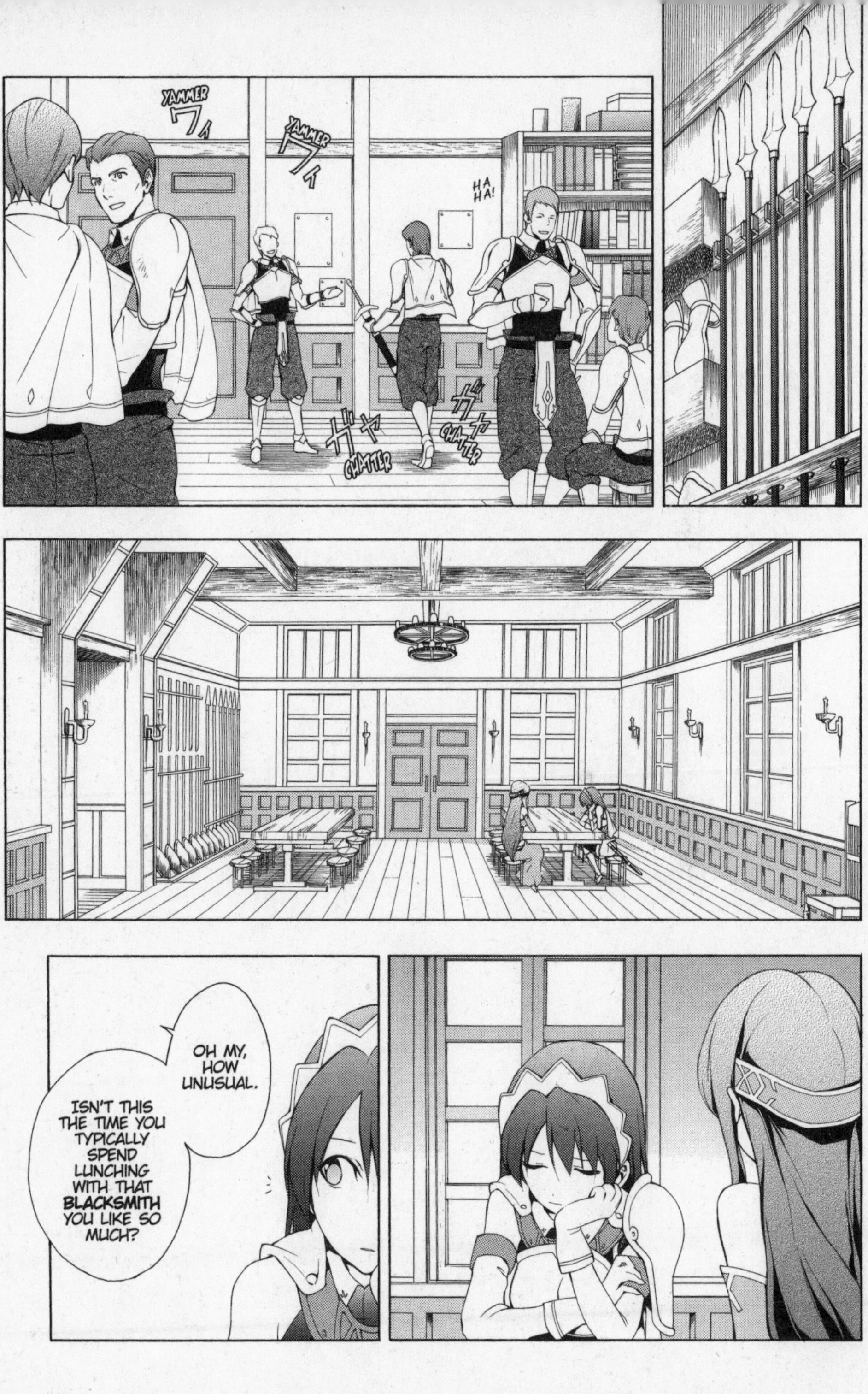

HA HA!
YAMMER
ワィ
YAMMER
ワィ
ガヤ
CHATTER
ガヤ
CHATTER
OH MY, HOW UNUSUAL.
ISN'T THIS THE TIME YOU TYPICALLY SPEND LUNCHING WITH THAT **BLACKSMITH** YOU LIKE SO MUCH?

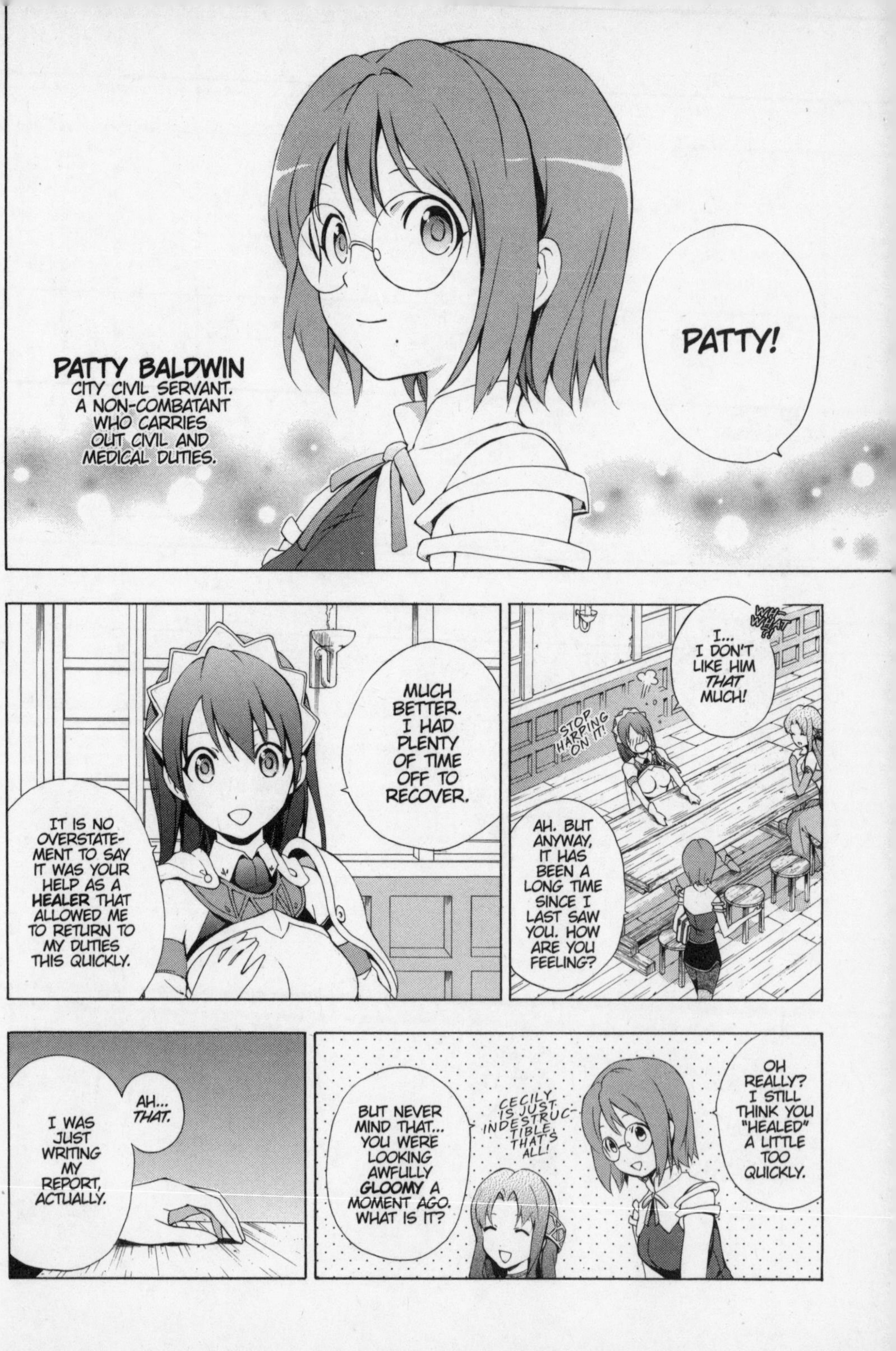
PATTY!
PATTY BALDWIN
CITY CIVIL SERVANT. A NON-COMBATANT WHO CARRIES OUT CIVIL AND MEDICAL DUTIES.
WH-WHAT!?
I... I DON'T LIKE HIM *THAT* MUCH!
STOP HARPING ON IT!
AH. BUT ANYWAY, IT HAS BEEN A LONG TIME SINCE I LAST SAW YOU. HOW ARE YOU FEELING?
MUCH BETTER. I HAD PLENTY OF TIME OFF TO RECOVER.
IT IS NO OVERSTATEMENT TO SAY IT WAS YOUR HELP AS A **HEALER** THAT ALLOWED ME TO RETURN TO MY DUTIES THIS QUICKLY.
OH REALLY? I STILL THINK YOU "HEALED" A LITTLE TOO QUICKLY.
CECILY IS JUST INDESTRUCTIBLE, THAT'S ALL!
BUT NEVER MIND THAT... YOU WERE LOOKING AWFULLY **GLOOMY** A MOMENT AGO. WHAT IS IT?
AH... *THAT.*
I WAS JUST WRITING MY REPORT, ACTUALLY.

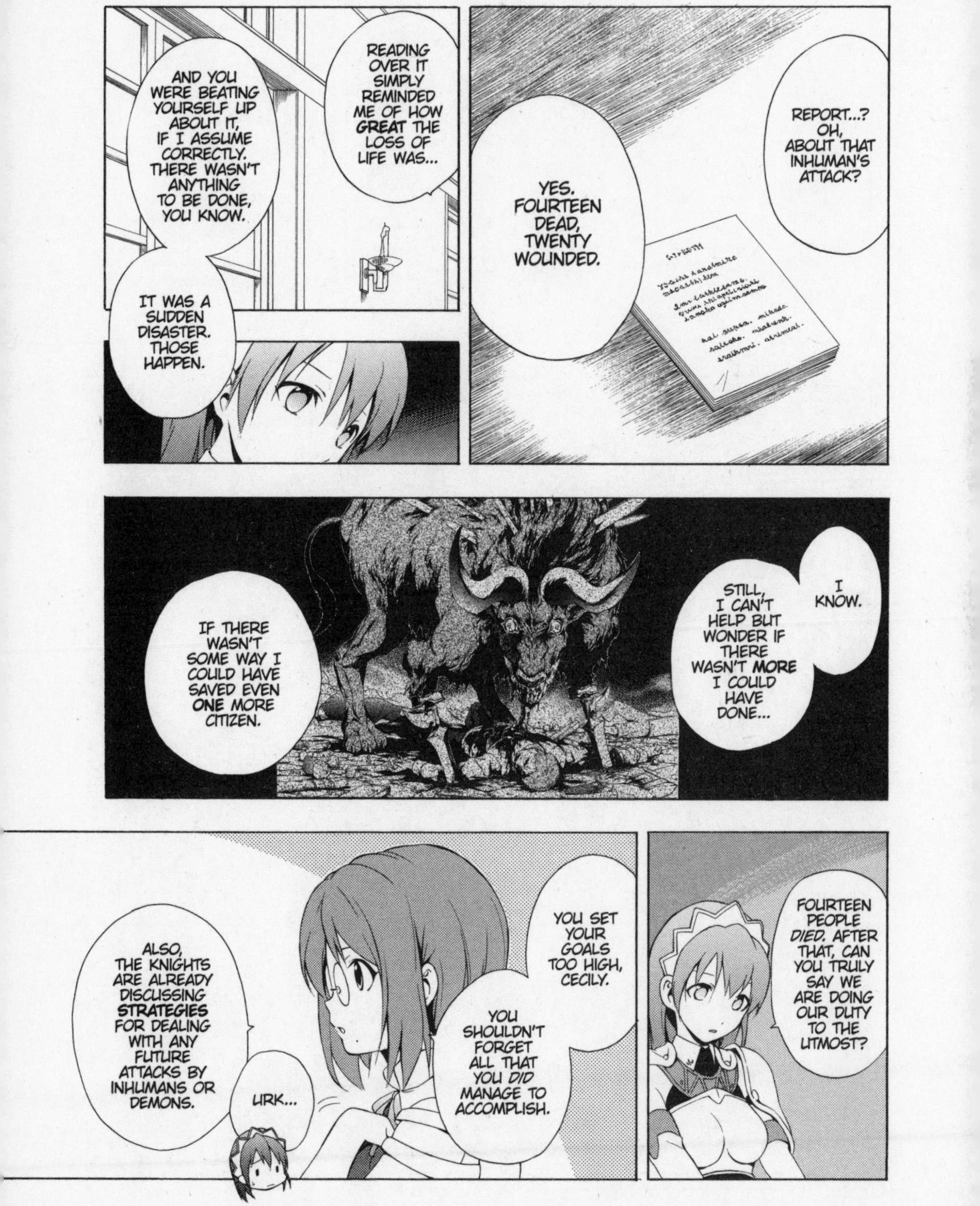
REPORT...? OH, ABOUT THAT INHUMAN'S ATTACK?
YES. FOURTEEN DEAD, TWENTY WOUNDED.
READING OVER IT SIMPLY REMINDED ME OF HOW **GREAT** THE LOSS OF LIFE WAS...
AND YOU WERE BEATING YOURSELF UP ABOUT IT, IF I ASSUME CORRECTLY. THERE WASN'T ANYTHING TO BE DONE, YOU KNOW.
IT WAS A SUDDEN DISASTER. THOSE HAPPEN.
I KNOW.
STILL, I CAN'T HELP BUT WONDER IF THERE WASN'T **MORE** I COULD HAVE DONE...
IF THERE WASN'T SOME WAY I COULD HAVE SAVED EVEN **ONE** MORE CITIZEN.
FOURTEEN PEOPLE *DIED*. AFTER THAT, CAN YOU TRULY SAY WE ARE DOING OUR DUTY TO THE UTMOST?
YOU SET YOUR GOALS TOO HIGH, CECILY.
YOU SHOULDN'T FORGET ALL THAT YOU *DID* MANAGE TO ACCOMPLISH.
ALSO, THE KNIGHTS ARE ALREADY DISCUSSING **STRATEGIES** FOR DEALING WITH ANY FUTURE ATTACKS BY INHUMANS OR DEMONS.
URK...

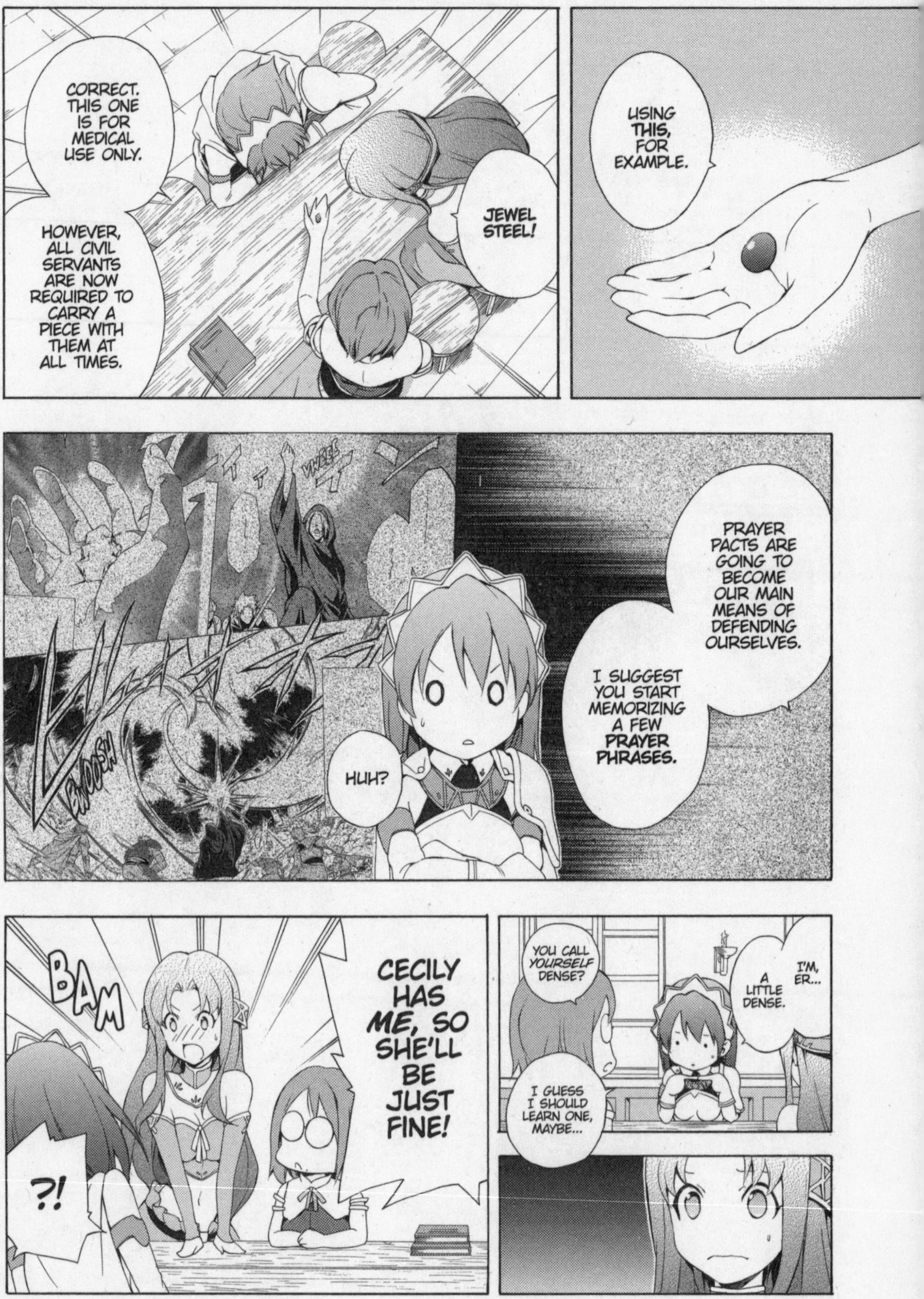
USING THIS, FOR EXAMPLE.
JEWEL STEEL!
CORRECT. THIS ONE IS FOR MEDICAL USE ONLY.
HOWEVER, ALL CIVIL SERVANTS ARE NOW REQUIRED TO CARRY A PIECE WITH THEM AT ALL TIMES.
PRAYER PACTS ARE GOING TO BECOME OUR MAIN MEANS OF DEFENDING OURSELVES.
I SUGGEST YOU START MEMORIZING A FEW PRAYER PHRASES.
HUH?
VWEEE
BWOOSH
I'M, ER... A LITTLE DENSE.
YOU CALL YOURSELF DENSE?
I GUESS I SHOULD LEARN ONE, MAYBE...
CECILY HAS ME, SO SHE'LL BE JUST FINE!
BAM
?!

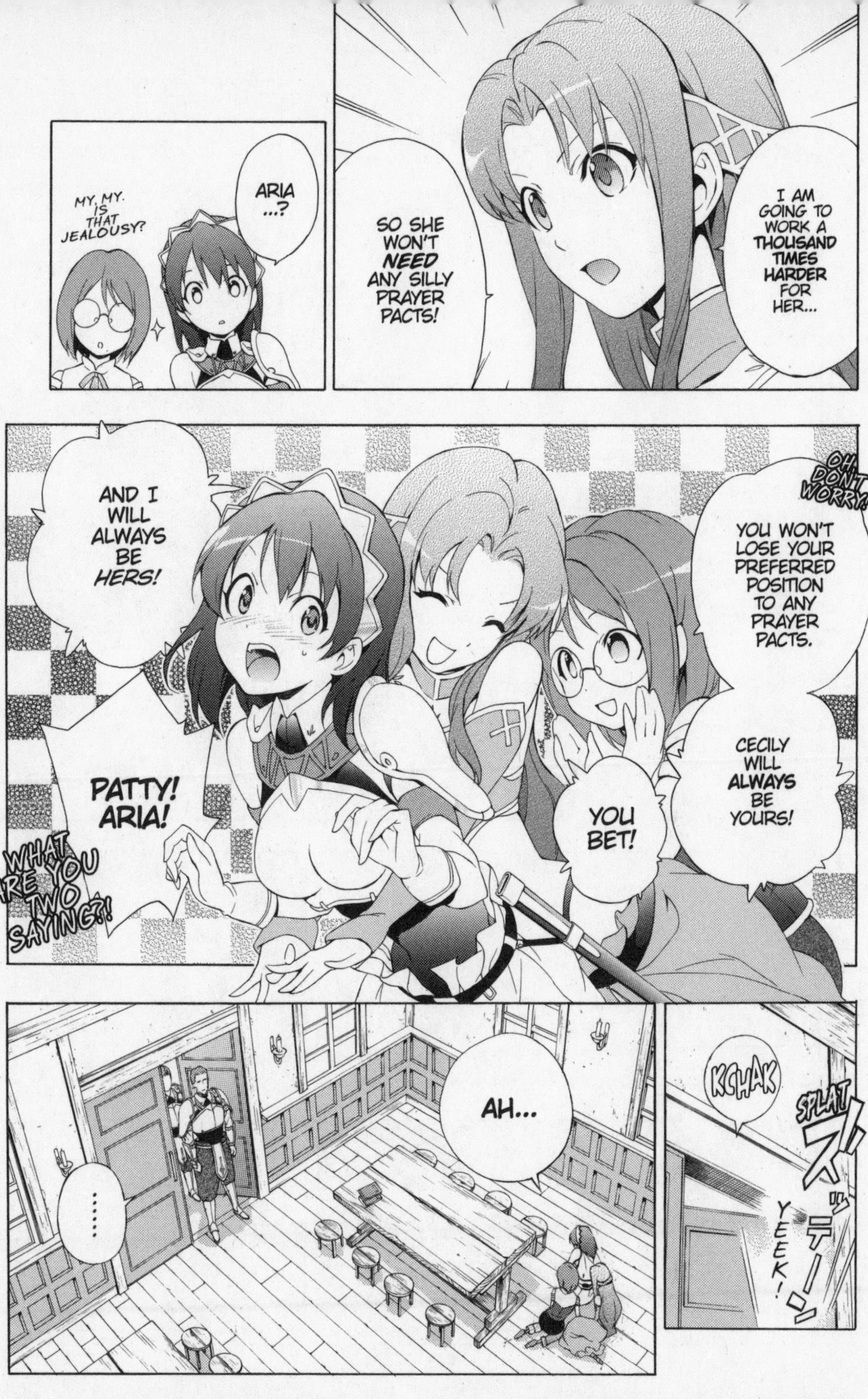
I AM GOING TO WORK A THOUSAND TIMES HARDER FOR HER...
SO SHE WON'T NEED ANY SILLY PRAYER PACTS!
ARIA ...?
MY, MY. IS THAT JEALOUSY?
OH, DON'T WORRY!
YOU WON'T LOSE YOUR PREFERRED POSITION TO ANY PRAYER PACTS.
CECILY WILL ALWAYS BE YOURS!
YOU BET!
AND I WILL ALWAYS BE HERS!
PATTY! ARIA!
WHAT ARE YOU TWO SAYING?!
KCHAK
SPLAT
YEEK!
AH...
......

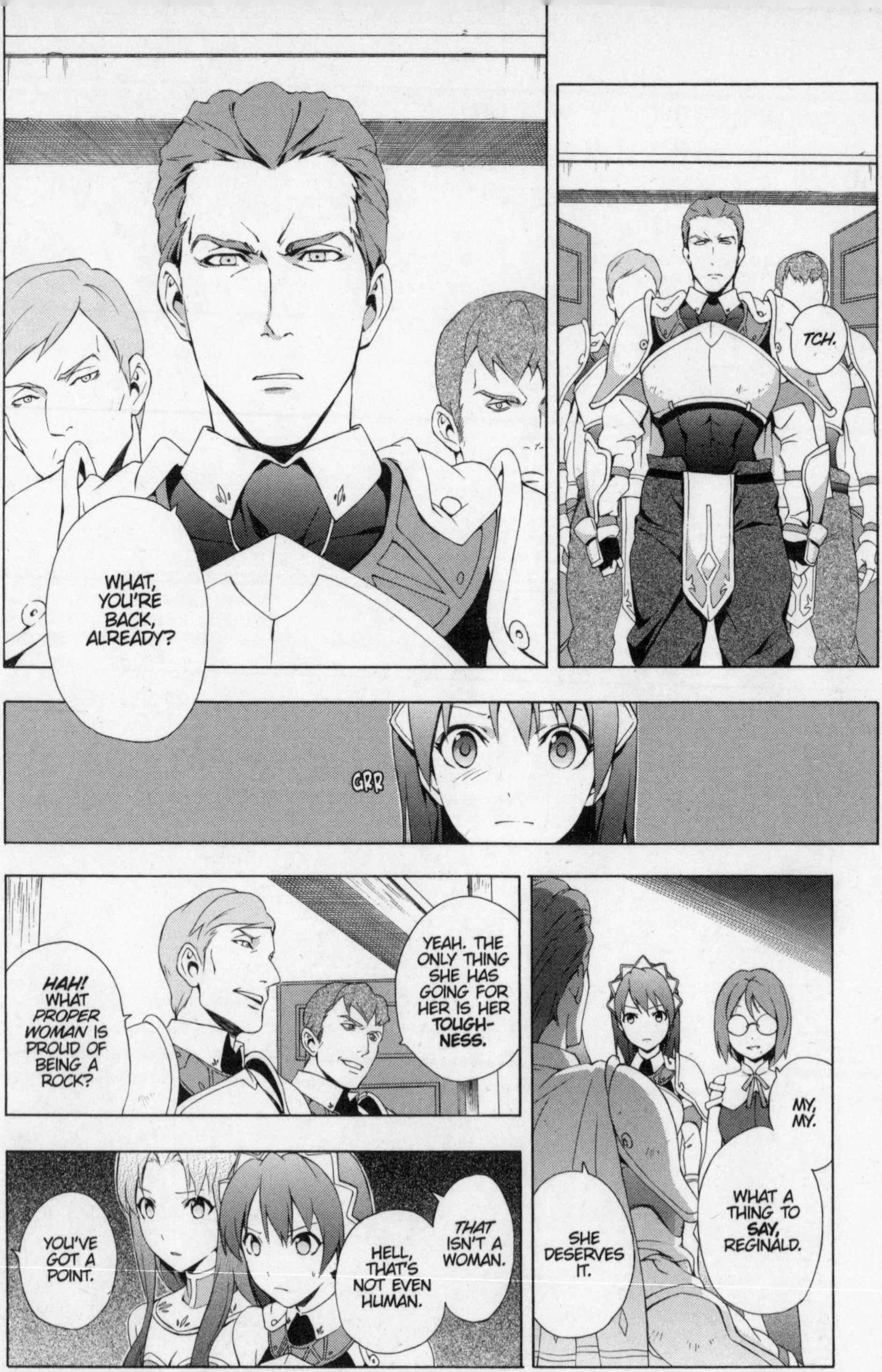
TCH.
WHAT, YOU'RE BACK, ALREADY?
GRR
MY, MY.
WHAT A THING TO SAY, REGINALD.
SHE DESERVES IT.
YEAH. THE ONLY THING SHE HAS GOING FOR HER IS HER TOUGHNESS.
HAH! WHAT PROPER WOMAN IS PROUD OF BEING A ROCK?
THAT ISN'T A WOMAN.
HELL, THAT'S NOT EVEN HUMAN.
YOU'VE GOT A POINT.

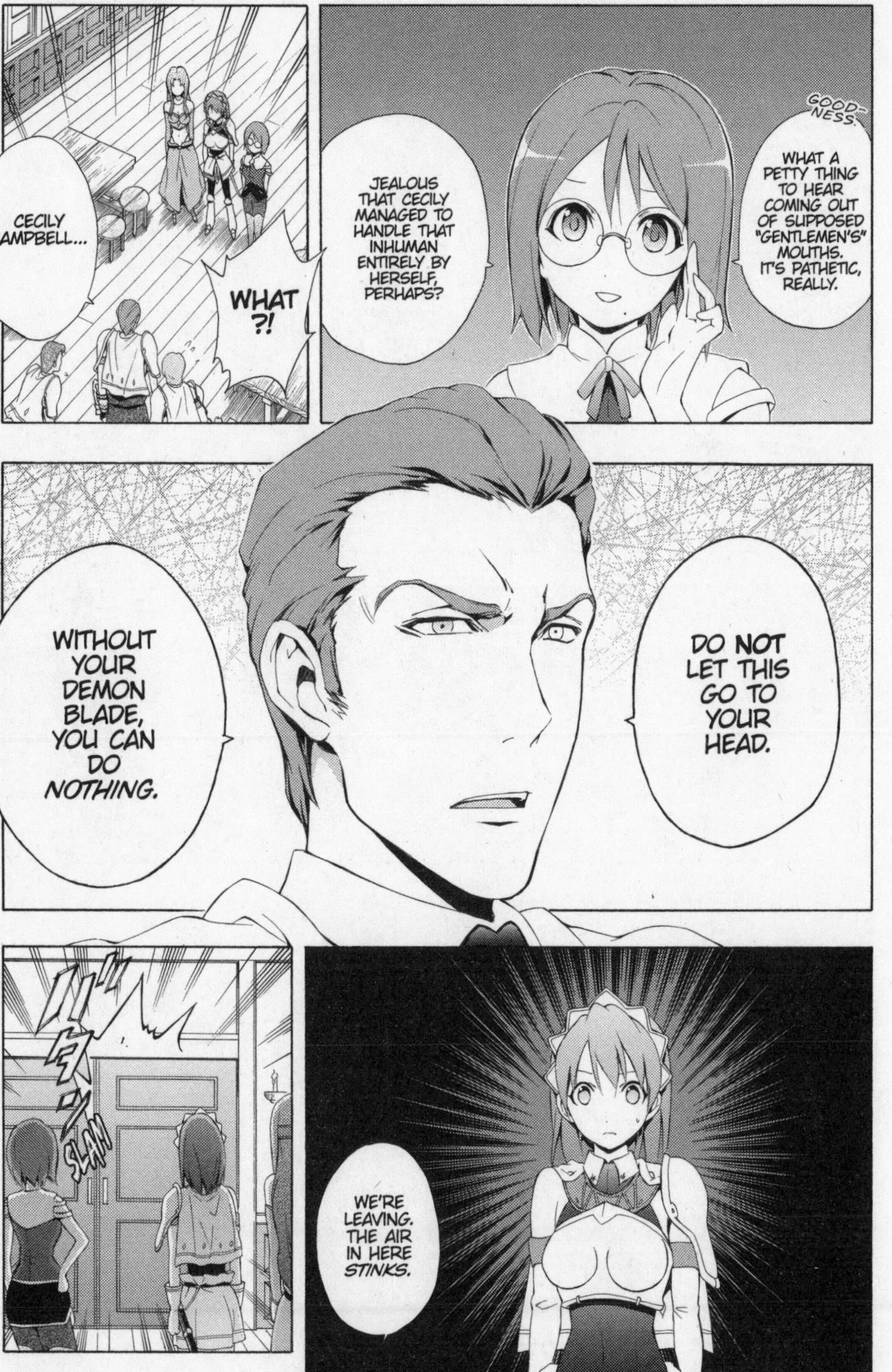
GOOD-NESS.
WHAT A PETTY THING TO HEAR COMING OUT OF SUPPOSED "GENTLEMEN'S" MOUTHS. IT'S PATHETIC, REALLY.
JEALOUS THAT CECILY MANAGED TO HANDLE THAT INHUMAN ENTIRELY BY HERSELF, PERHAPS?
WHAT ?!
CECILY CAMPBELL...
DO NOT LET THIS GO TO YOUR HEAD.
WITHOUT YOUR DEMON BLADE, YOU CAN DO NOTHING.
WE'RE LEAVING. THE AIR IN HERE STINKS.
SLAM

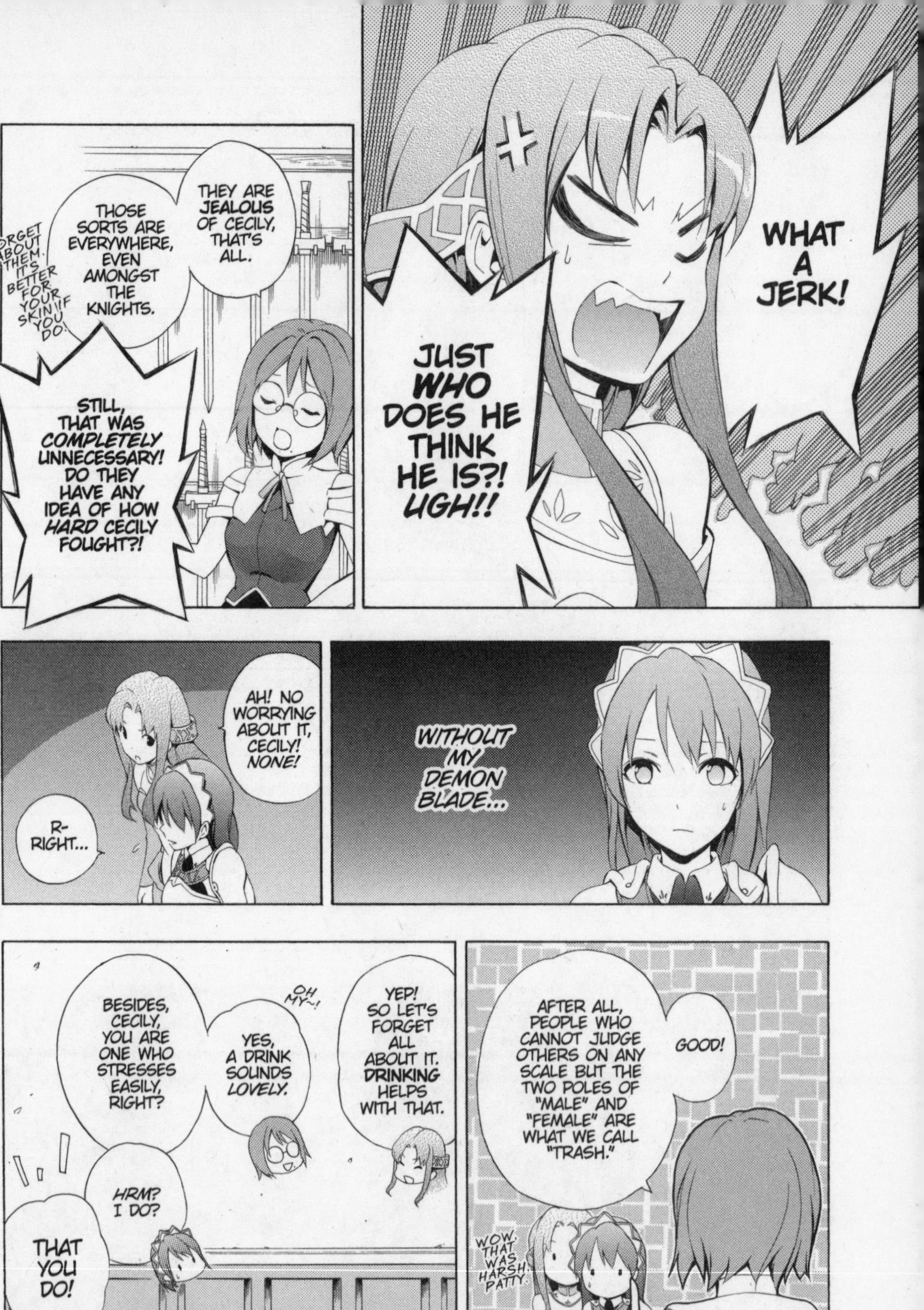
WHAT A JERK!
JUST WHO DOES HE THINK HE IS?! UGH!!
THEY ARE JEALOUS OF CECILY, THAT'S ALL.
THOSE SORTS ARE EVERYWHERE, EVEN AMONGST THE KNIGHTS.
FORGET ABOUT THEM. IT'S BETTER FOR YOUR SKIN IF YOU DO.
STILL, THAT WAS COMPLETELY UNNECESSARY! DO THEY HAVE ANY IDEA OF HOW HARD CECILY FOUGHT?!
WITHOUT MY DEMON BLADE...
AH! NO WORRYING ABOUT IT, CECILY! NONE!
R-RIGHT...
AFTER ALL, PEOPLE WHO CANNOT JUDGE OTHERS ON ANY SCALE BUT THE TWO POLES OF "MALE" AND "FEMALE" ARE WHAT WE CALL "TRASH."
GOOD!
WOW. THAT WAS HARSH, PATTY.
YEP! SO LET'S FORGET ALL ABOUT IT. DRINKING HELPS WITH THAT.
OH MY~!
YES, A DRINK SOUNDS LOVELY.
BESIDES, CECILY, YOU ARE ONE WHO STRESSES EASILY, RIGHT?
HRM? I DO?
THAT YOU DO!

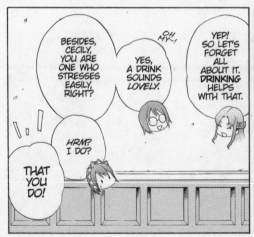

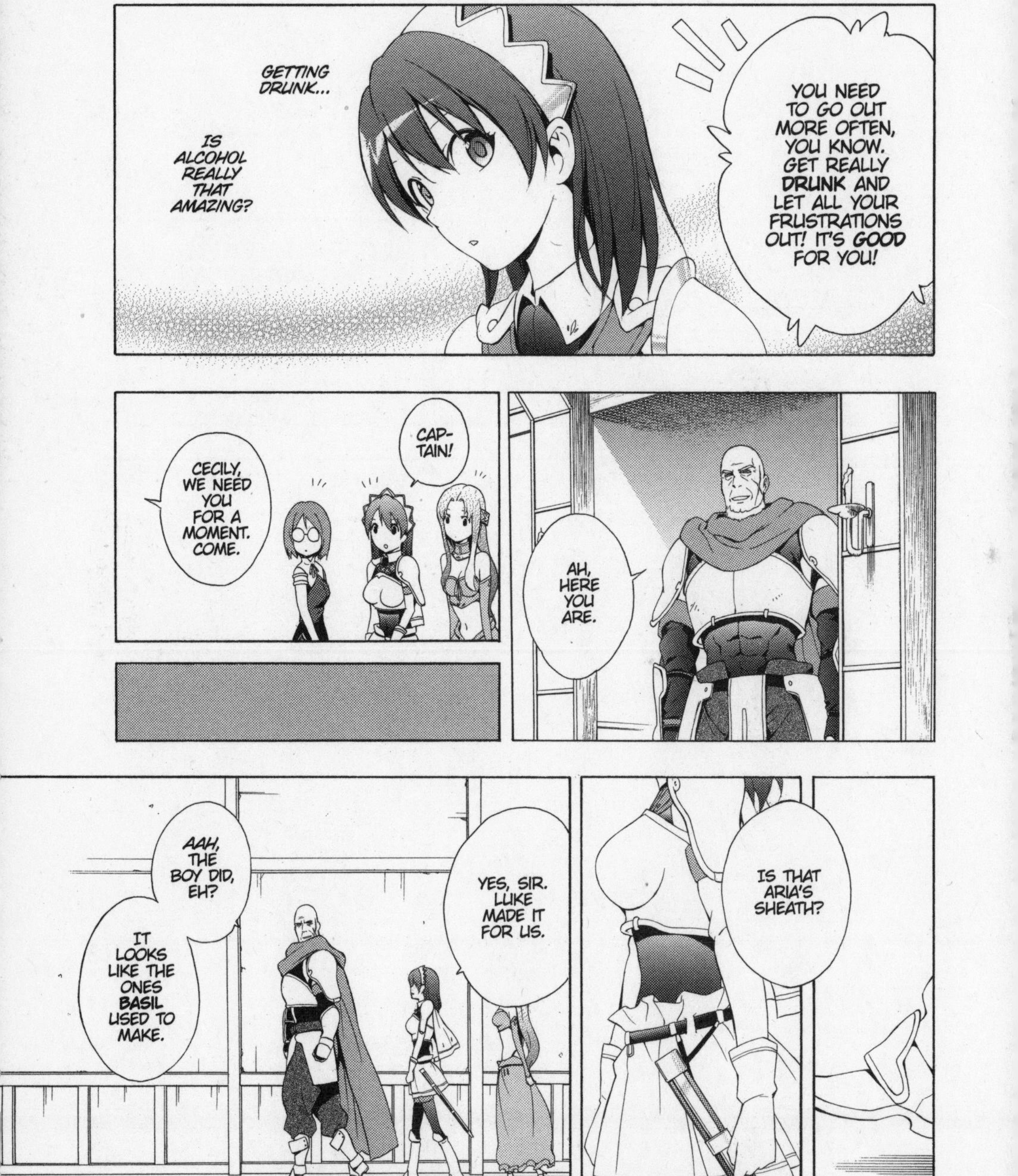
YOU NEED TO GO OUT MORE OFTEN, YOU KNOW. GET REALLY DRUNK AND LET ALL YOUR FRUSTRATIONS OUT! IT'S GOOD FOR YOU!
GETTING DRUNK...
IS ALCOHOL REALLY THAT AMAZING?
AH, HERE YOU ARE.
CAP-TAIN!
CECILY, WE NEED YOU FOR A MOMENT. COME.
IS THAT ARIA'S SHEATH?
YES, SIR. LUKE MADE IT FOR US.
AAH, THE BOY DID, EH?
IT LOOKS LIKE THE ONES BASIL USED TO MAKE.

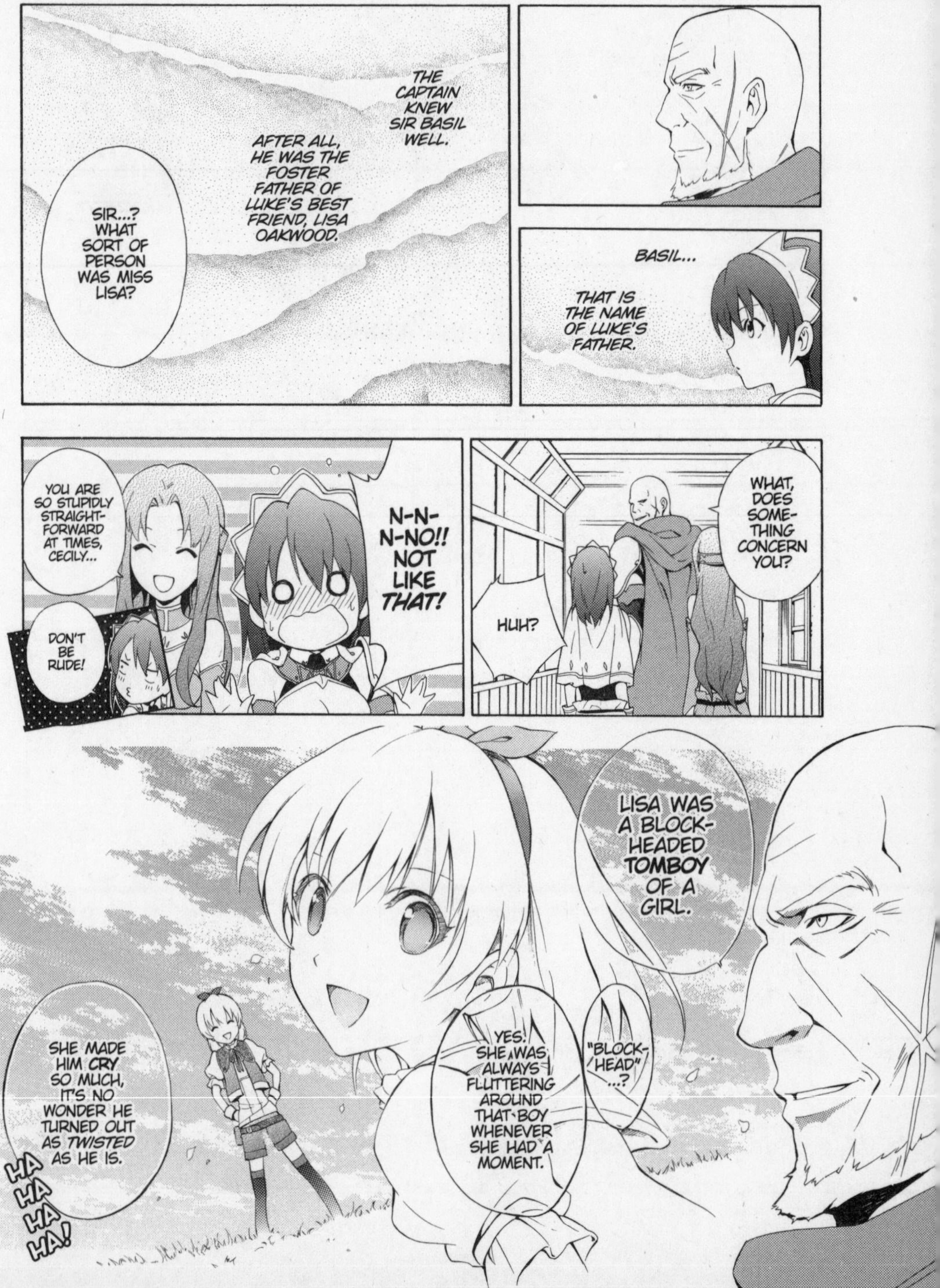
BASIL...
THAT IS THE NAME OF LUKE'S FATHER.
THE CAPTAIN KNEW SIR BASIL WELL.
AFTER ALL, HE WAS THE FOSTER FATHER OF LUKE'S BEST FRIEND, LISA OAKWOOD.
SIR...? WHAT SORT OF PERSON WAS MISS LISA?
WHAT, DOES SOME-THING CONCERN YOU?
HUH?
N-N-N-NO!! NOT LIKE *THAT*!
YOU ARE SO STUPIDLY STRAIGHT-FORWARD AT TIMES, CECILY...
DON'T BE RUDE!
LISA WAS A BLOCK-HEADED **TOMBOY** OF A GIRL.
"BLOCK-HEAD" ...?
YES. SHE WAS ALWAYS FLUTTERING AROUND THAT BOY WHENEVER SHE HAD A MOMENT.
SHE MADE HIM **CRY** SO MUCH, IT'S NO WONDER HE TURNED OUT AS *TWISTED* AS HE IS.
HA HA HA HA!

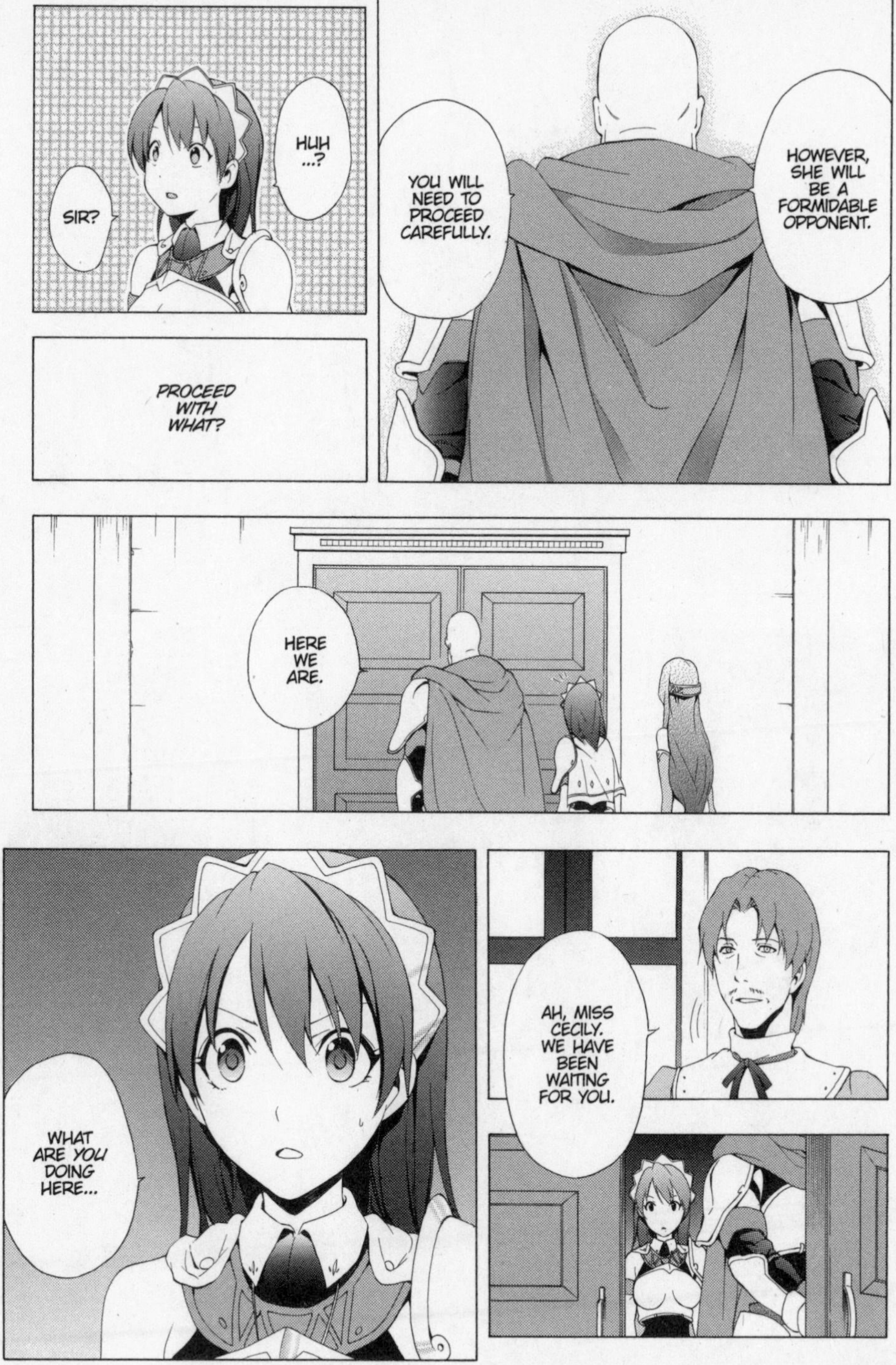
HOWEVER, SHE WILL BE A FORMIDABLE OPPONENT.
YOU WILL NEED TO PROCEED CAREFULLY.
HUH ...?
SIR?
PROCEED WITH WHAT?
HERE WE ARE.
AH, MISS CECILY. WE HAVE BEEN WAITING FOR YOU.
WHAT ARE *YOU* DOING HERE...

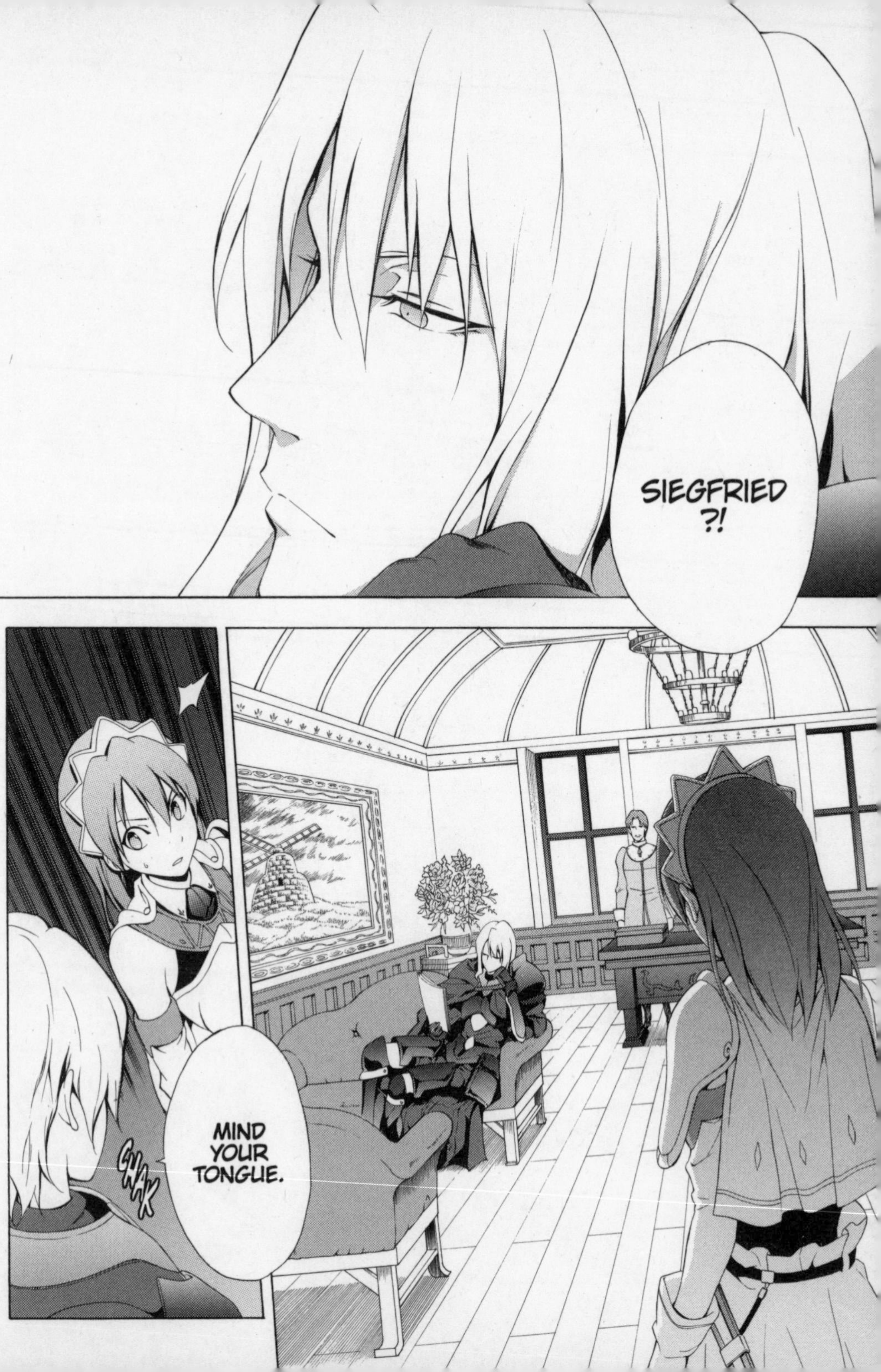
SIEGFRIED ?!
MIND YOUR TONGUE.
CHAK

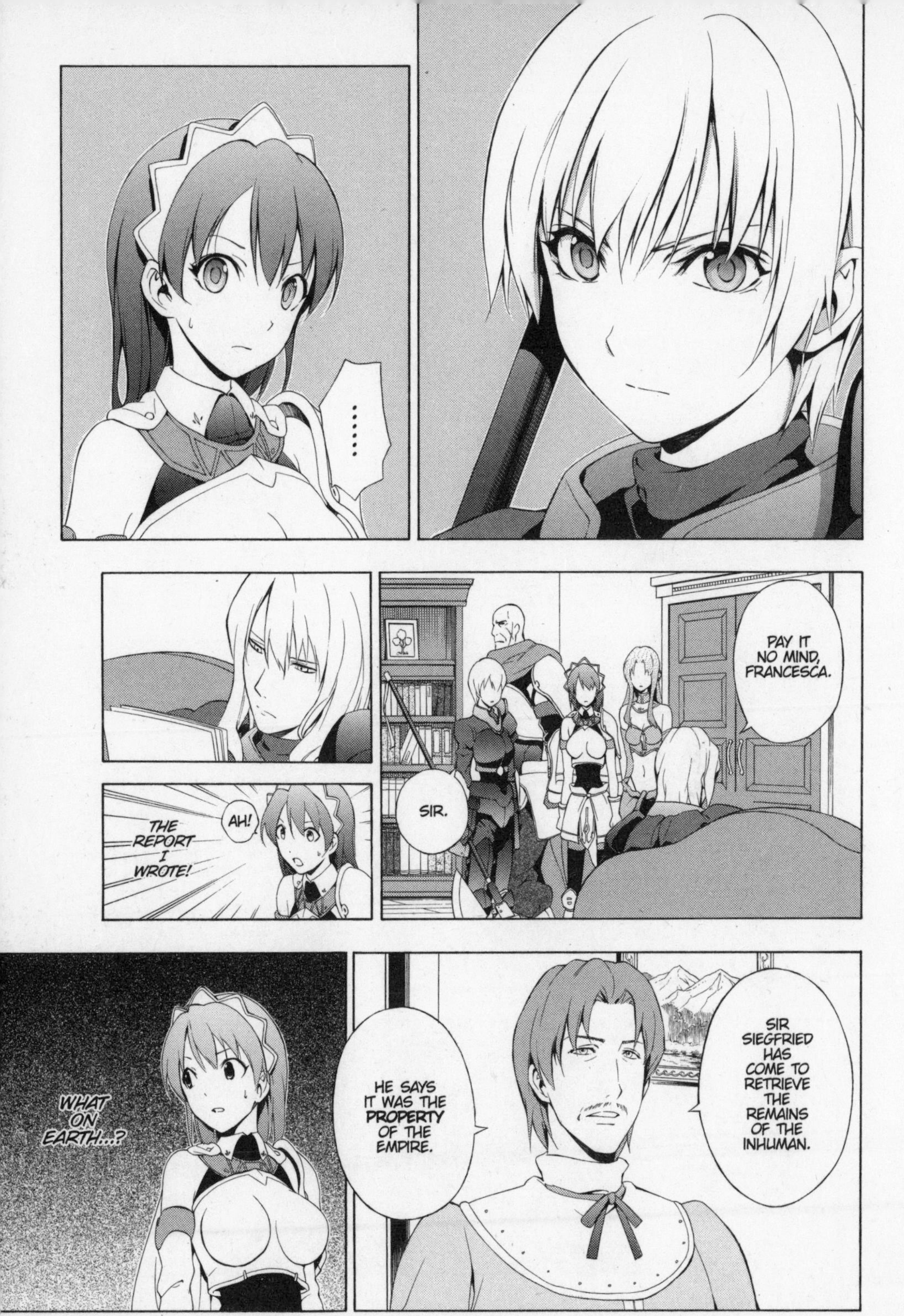
……
PAY IT NO MIND, FRANCESCA.
SIR.
AH!
THE REPORT I WROTE!
SIR SIEGFRIED HAS COME TO RETRIEVE THE REMAINS OF THE INHUMAN.
HE SAYS IT WAS THE PROPERTY OF THE EMPIRE.
WHAT ON EARTH...?

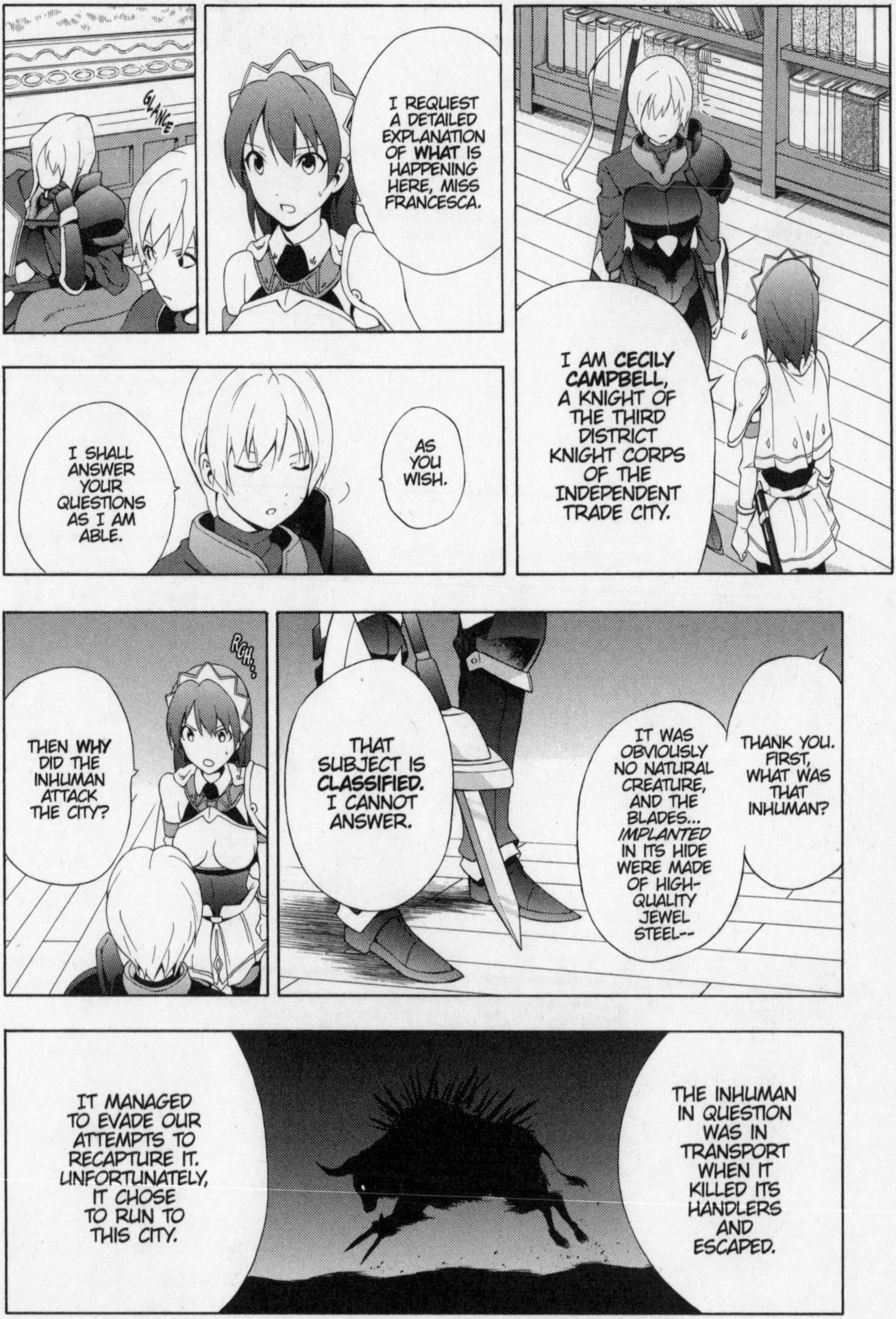
I AM CECILY CAMPBELL, A KNIGHT OF THE THIRD DISTRICT KNIGHT CORPS OF THE INDEPENDENT TRADE CITY.
I REQUEST A DETAILED EXPLANATION OF WHAT IS HAPPENING HERE, MISS FRANCESCA.
GLANCE
AS YOU WISH.
I SHALL ANSWER YOUR QUESTIONS AS I AM ABLE.
THANK YOU. FIRST, WHAT WAS THAT INHUMAN?
IT WAS OBVIOUSLY NO NATURAL CREATURE, AND THE BLADES... IMPLANTED IN ITS HIDE WERE MADE OF HIGH-QUALITY JEWEL STEEL--
THAT SUBJECT IS CLASSIFIED. I CANNOT ANSWER.
RCH
THEN WHY DID THE INHUMAN ATTACK THE CITY?
THE INHUMAN IN QUESTION WAS IN TRANSPORT WHEN IT KILLED ITS HANDLERS AND ESCAPED.
IT MANAGED TO EVADE OUR ATTEMPTS TO RECAPTURE IT. UNFORTUNATELY, IT CHOSE TO RUN TO THIS CITY.

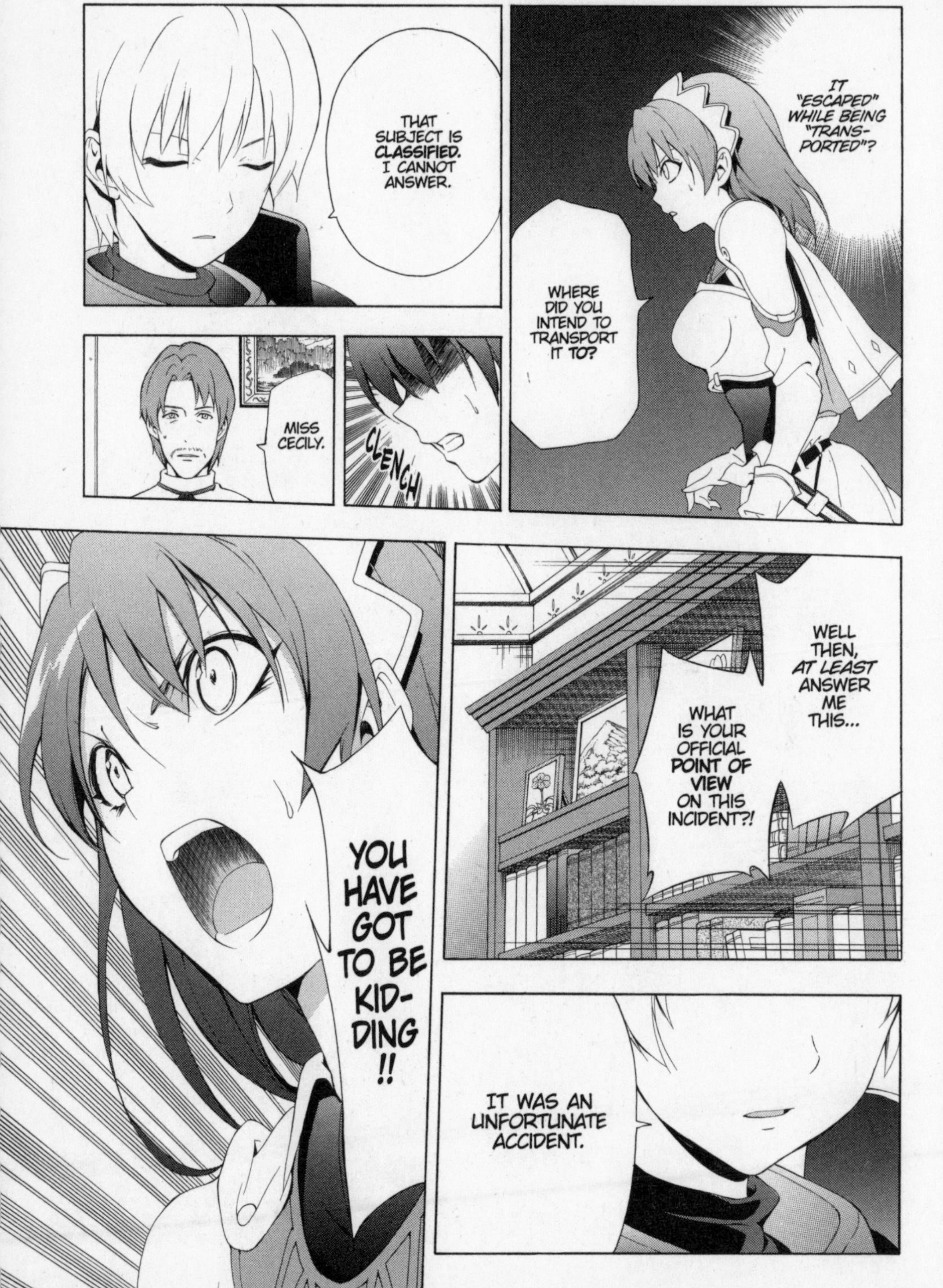
IT "ESCAPED" WHILE BEING "TRANS-PORTED"?
WHERE DID YOU INTEND TO TRANSPORT IT TO?
THAT SUBJECT IS CLASSIFIED. I CANNOT ANSWER.
CLENCH
MISS CECILY.
WELL THEN, AT LEAST ANSWER ME THIS...
WHAT IS YOUR OFFICIAL POINT OF VIEW ON THIS INCIDENT?!
IT WAS AN UNFORTUNATE ACCIDENT.
YOU HAVE GOT TO BE KID-DING!!

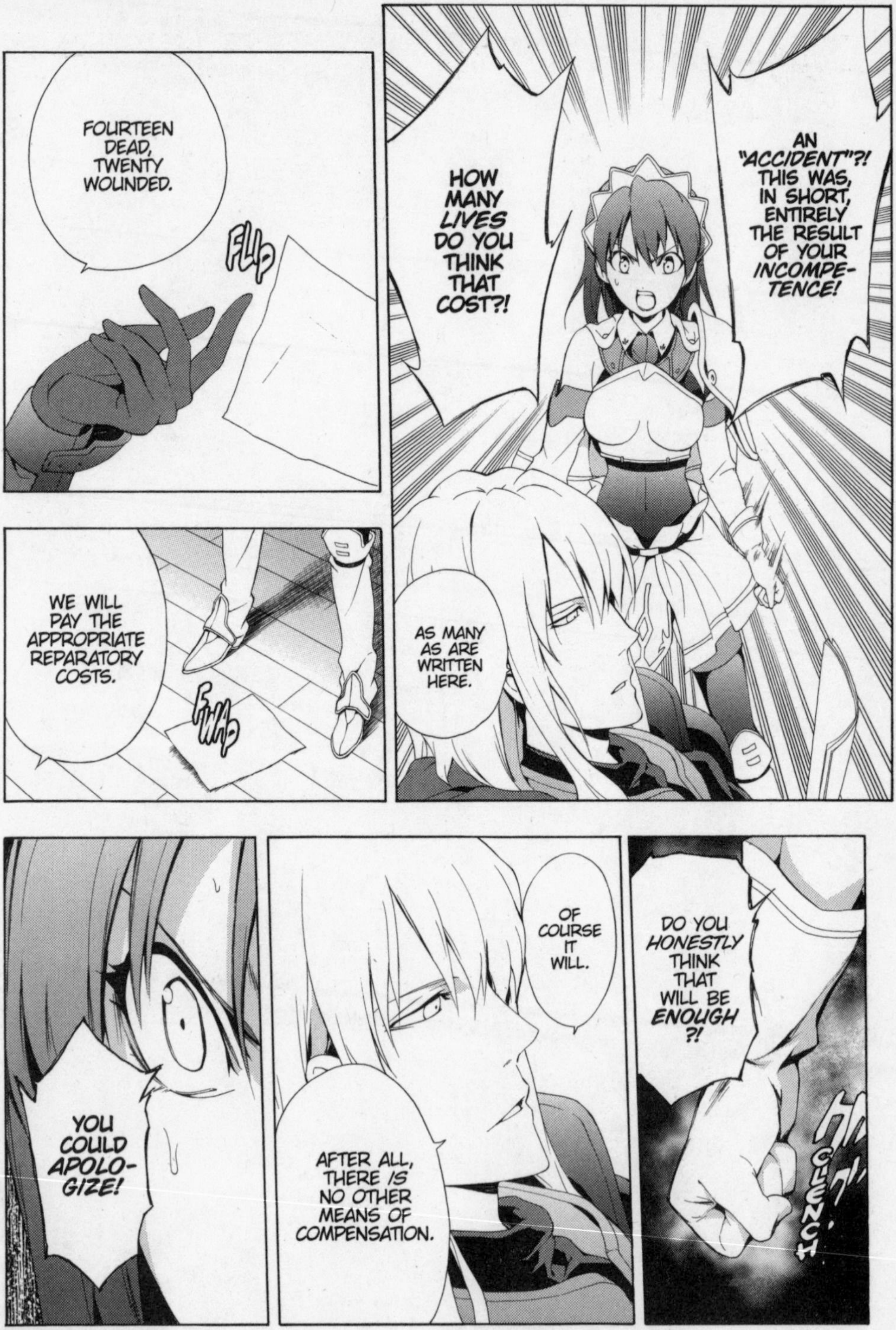
AN "ACCIDENT"?! THIS WAS, IN SHORT, ENTIRELY THE RESULT OF YOUR INCOMPETENCE!
HOW MANY LIVES DO YOU THINK THAT COST?!
AS MANY AS ARE WRITTEN HERE.
FOURTEEN DEAD, TWENTY WOUNDED.
FLIP
WE WILL PAY THE APPROPRIATE REPARATORY COSTS.
FWAP
DO YOU HONESTLY THINK THAT WILL BE ENOUGH?!
CLENCH
OF COURSE IT WILL.
AFTER ALL, THERE IS NO OTHER MEANS OF COMPENSATION.
YOU COULD APOLOGIZE!

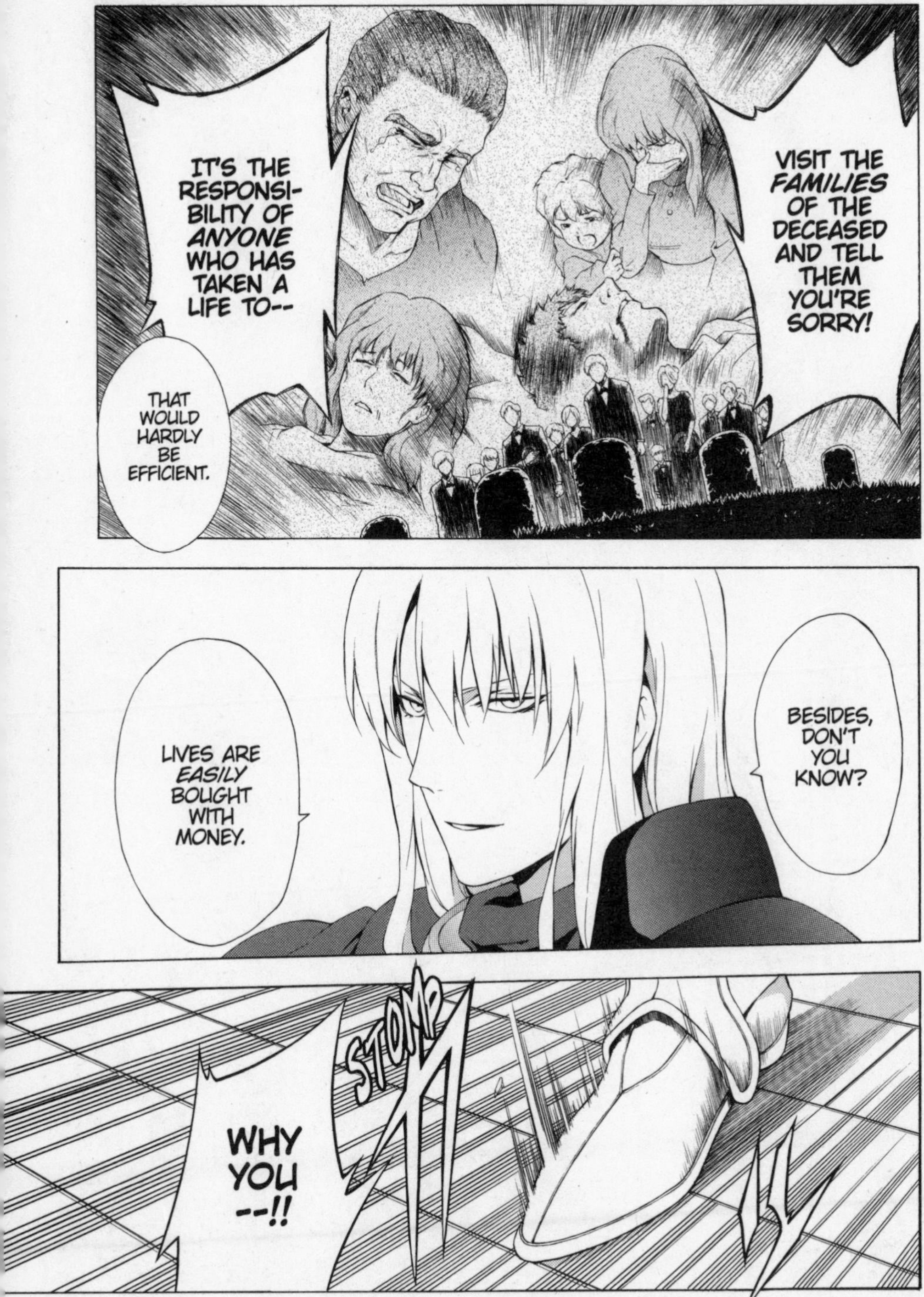
IT'S THE RESPONSIBILITY OF *ANYONE* WHO HAS TAKEN A LIFE TO--
VISIT THE *FAMILIES* OF THE DECEASED AND TELL THEM YOU'RE SORRY!
THAT WOULD HARDLY BE EFFICIENT.
BESIDES, DON'T YOU KNOW?
LIVES ARE *EASILY* BOUGHT WITH MONEY.
STOMP
WHY YOU --!!

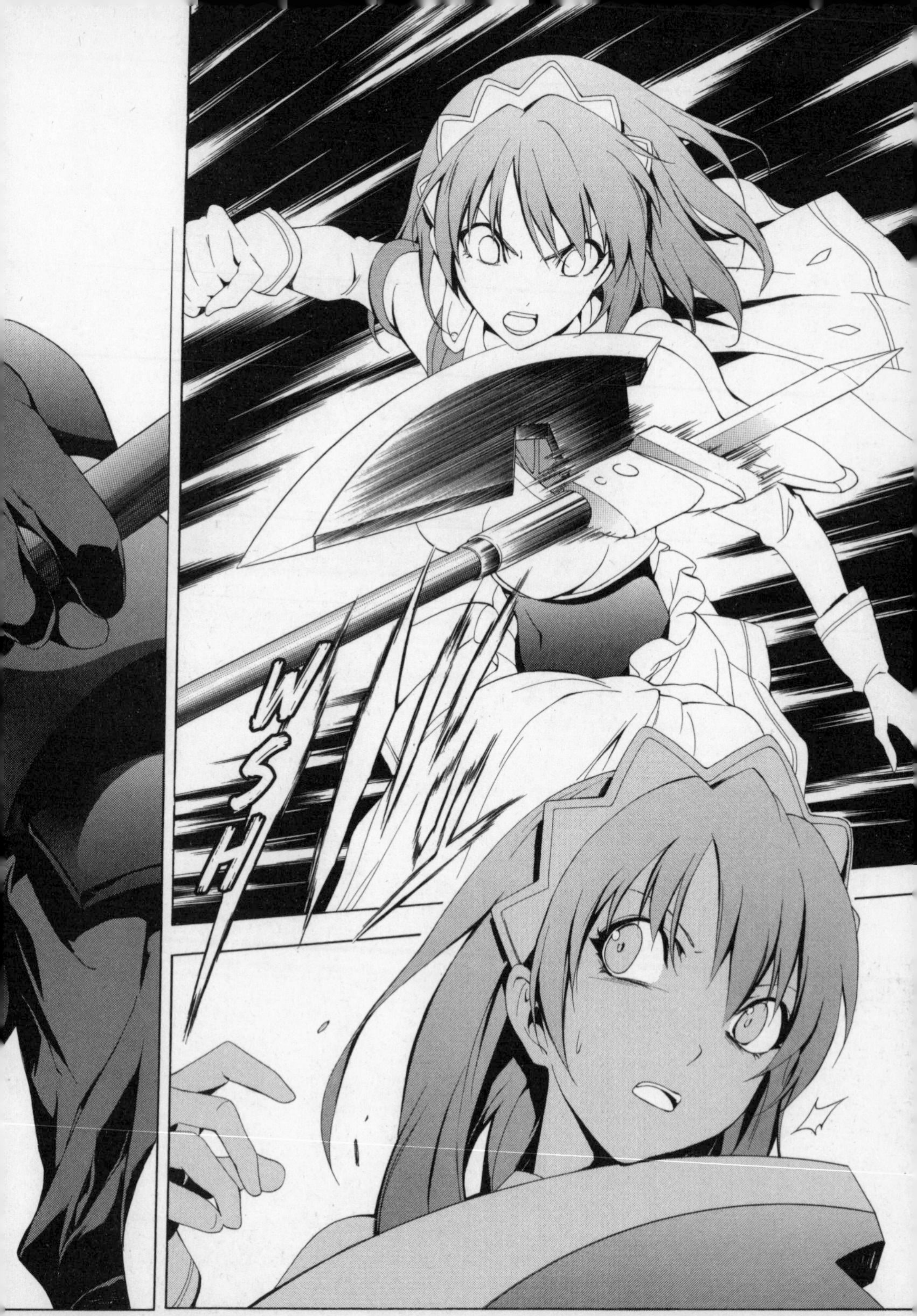
WHSH

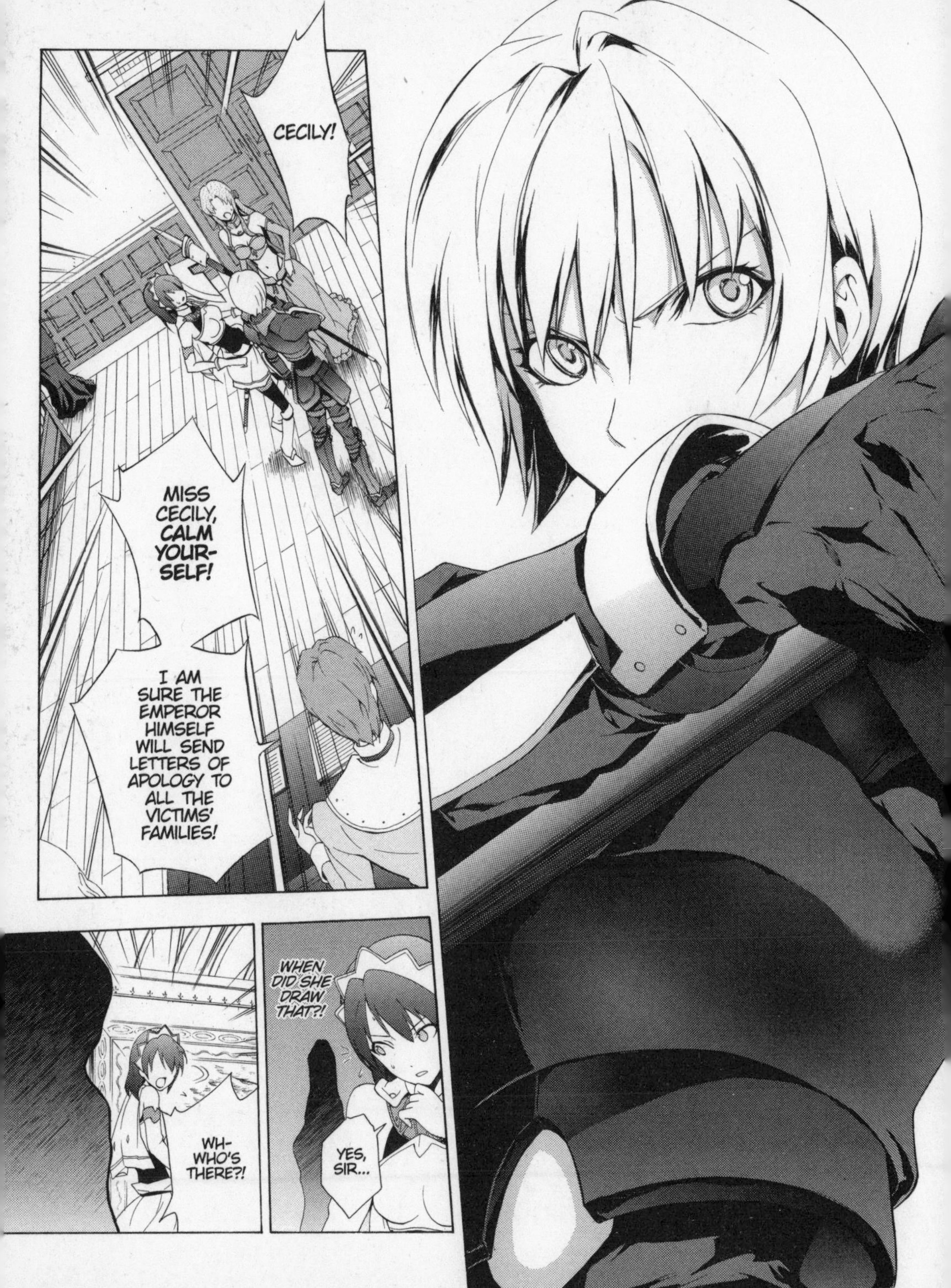
CECILY!
MISS CECILY, CALM YOURSELF!
I AM SURE THE EMPEROR HIMSELF WILL SEND LETTERS OF APOLOGY TO ALL THE VICTIMS' FAMILIES!
WHEN DID SHE DRAW THAT?!
YES, SIR...
WH-WHO'S THERE?!

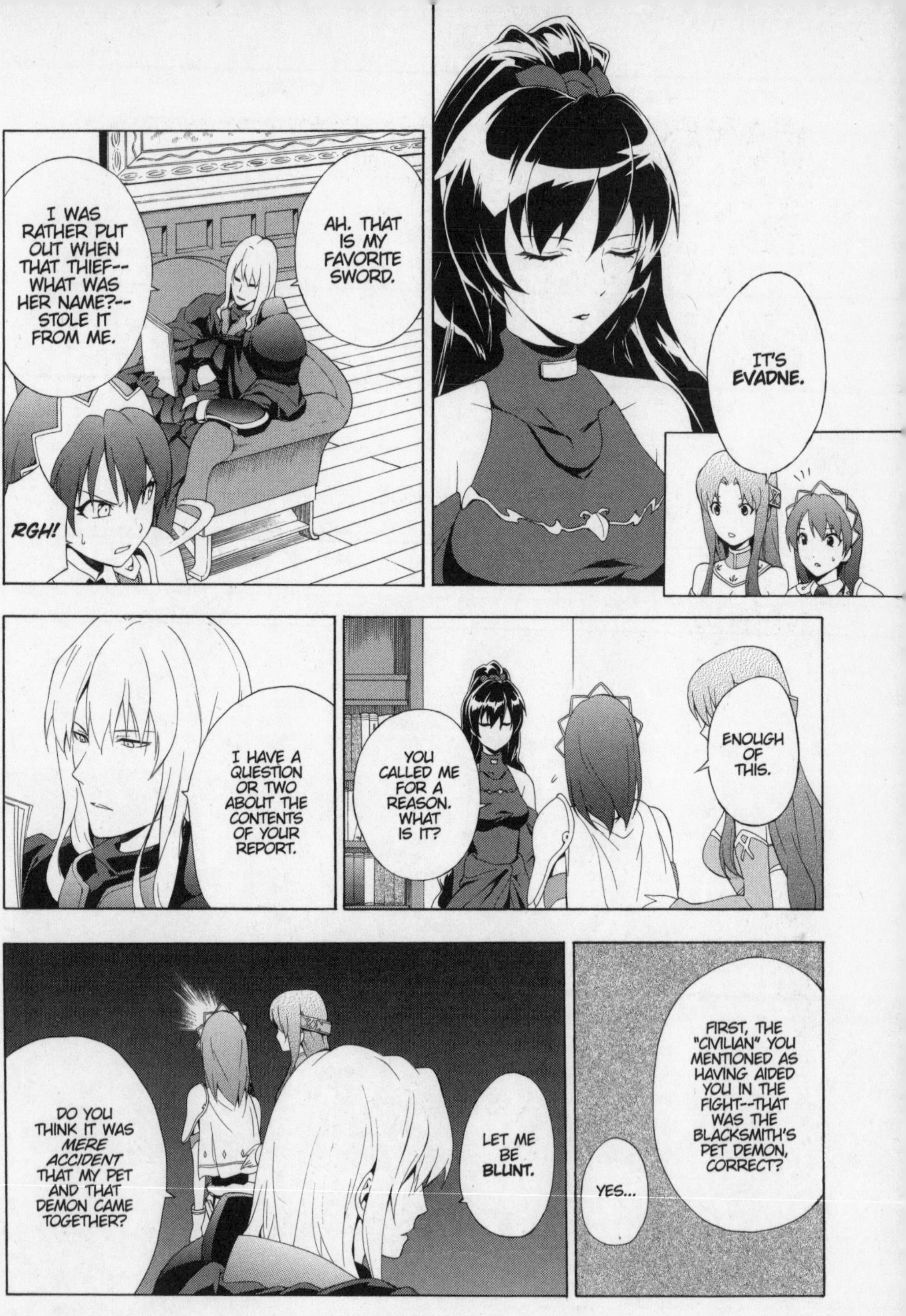
IT'S EVADNE.
AH. THAT IS MY FAVORITE SWORD.
I WAS RATHER PUT OUT WHEN THAT THIEF--WHAT WAS HER NAME?--STOLE IT FROM ME.
RGH!
ENOUGH OF THIS.
YOU CALLED ME FOR A REASON. WHAT IS IT?
I HAVE A QUESTION OR TWO ABOUT THE CONTENTS OF YOUR REPORT.
FIRST, THE "CIVILIAN" YOU MENTIONED AS HAVING AIDED YOU IN THE FIGHT--THAT WAS THE BLACKSMITH'S PET DEMON, CORRECT?
YES...
LET ME BE BLUNT.
DO YOU THINK IT WAS *MERE ACCIDENT* THAT MY PET AND THAT DEMON CAME TOGETHER?

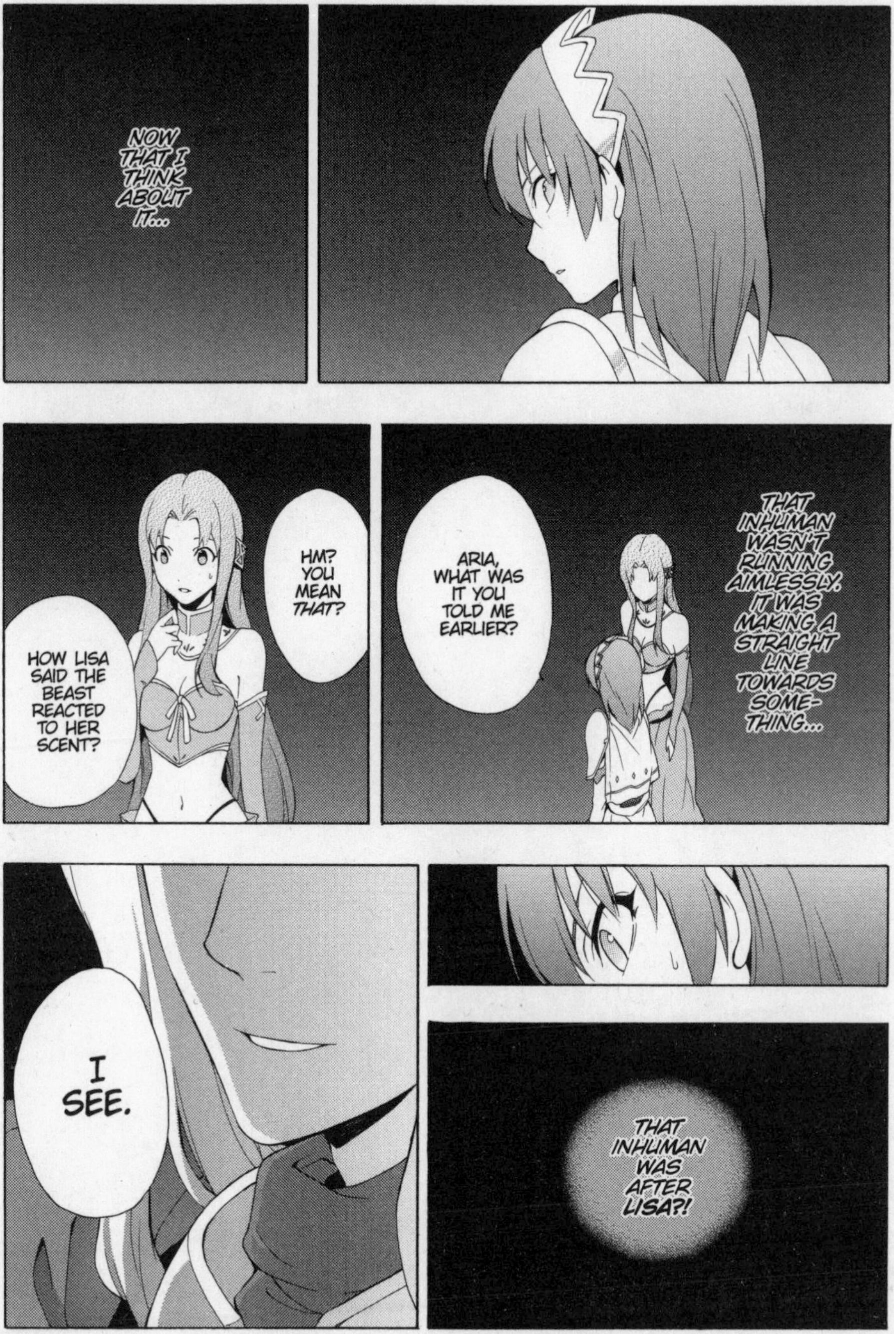
NOW THAT I THINK ABOUT IT...
THAT INHUMAN WASN'T RUNNING AIMLESSLY. IT WAS MAKING A STRAIGHT LINE TOWARDS SOME-THING...
ARIA, WHAT WAS IT YOU TOLD ME EARLIER?
HM? YOU MEAN *THAT*?
HOW LISA SAID THE BEAST REACTED TO HER SCENT?
THAT INHUMAN WAS AFTER LISA?!
I SEE.

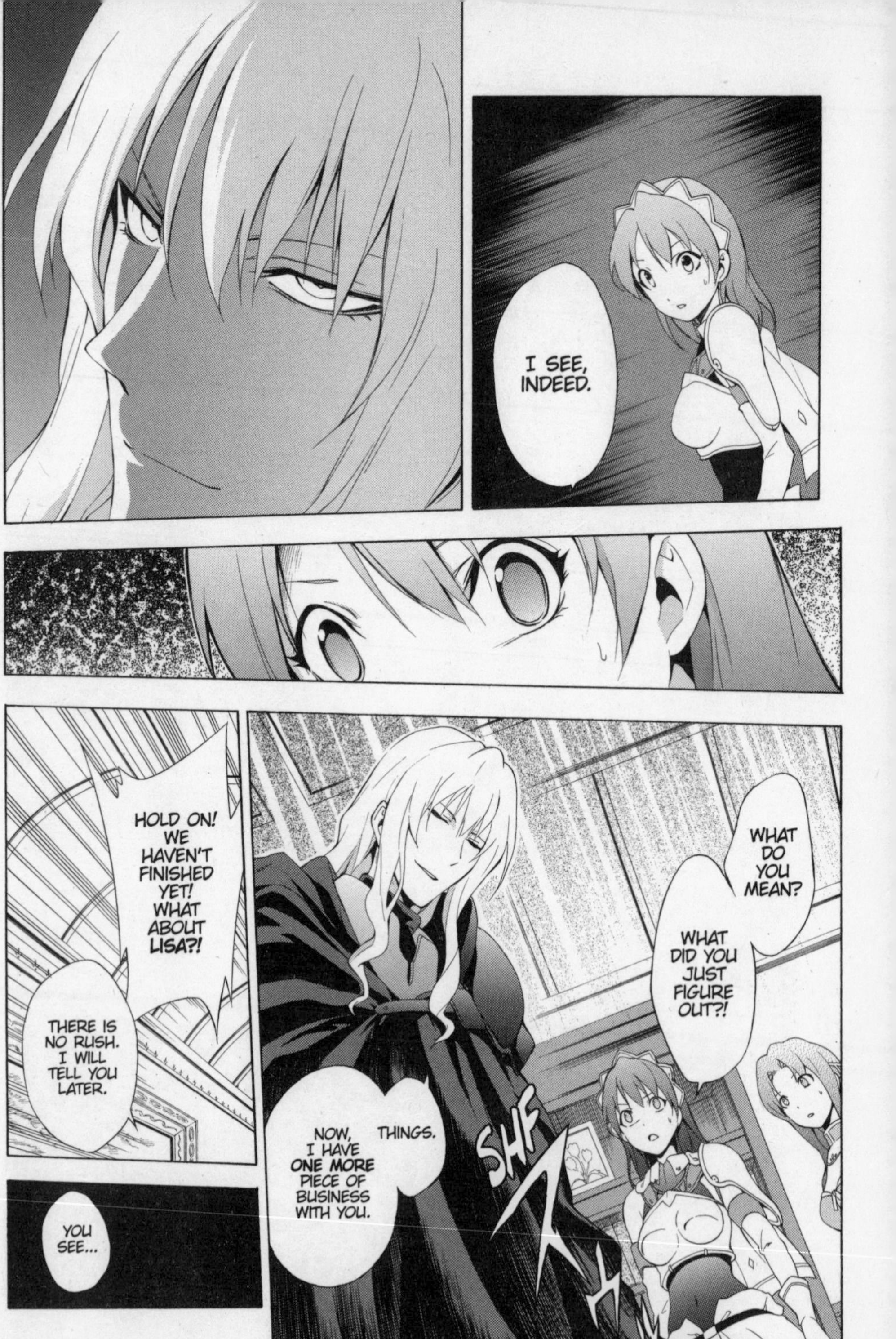
I SEE, INDEED.
WHAT DO YOU MEAN?
WHAT DID YOU JUST FIGURE OUT?!
SHF
THINGS.
NOW, I HAVE ONE MORE PIECE OF BUSINESS WITH YOU.
HOLD ON! WE HAVEN'T FINISHED YET! WHAT ABOUT LISA?!
THERE IS NO RUSH. I WILL TELL YOU LATER.
YOU SEE...

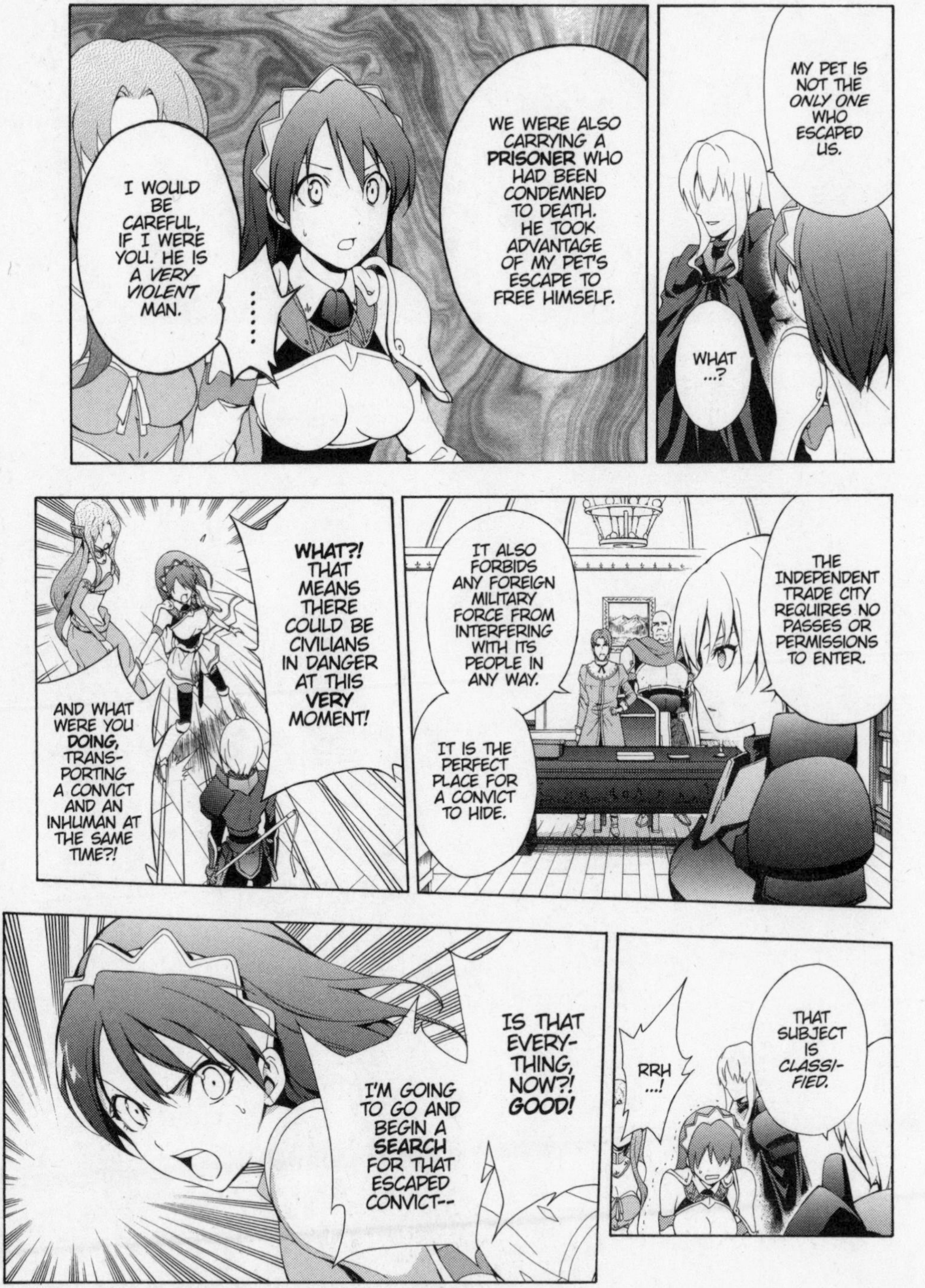
MY PET IS NOT THE ONLY ONE WHO ESCAPED US.
WHAT ...?
WE WERE ALSO CARRYING A PRISONER WHO HAD BEEN CONDEMNED TO DEATH. HE TOOK ADVANTAGE OF MY PET'S ESCAPE TO FREE HIMSELF.
......
I WOULD BE CAREFUL, IF I WERE YOU. HE IS A VERY VIOLENT MAN.
THE INDEPENDENT TRADE CITY REQUIRES NO PASSES OR PERMISSIONS TO ENTER.
IT ALSO FORBIDS ANY FOREIGN MILITARY FORCE FROM INTERFERING WITH ITS PEOPLE IN ANY WAY.
IT IS THE PERFECT PLACE FOR A CONVICT TO HIDE.
WHAT?! THAT MEANS THERE COULD BE CIVILIANS IN DANGER AT THIS VERY MOMENT!
AND WHAT WERE YOU DOING, TRANS-PORTING A CONVICT AND AN INHUMAN AT THE SAME TIME?!
THAT SUBJECT IS CLASSI-FIED.
RRH ...!
IS THAT EVERY-THING, NOW?! GOOD!
I'M GOING TO GO AND BEGIN A SEARCH FOR THAT ESCAPED CONVICT--

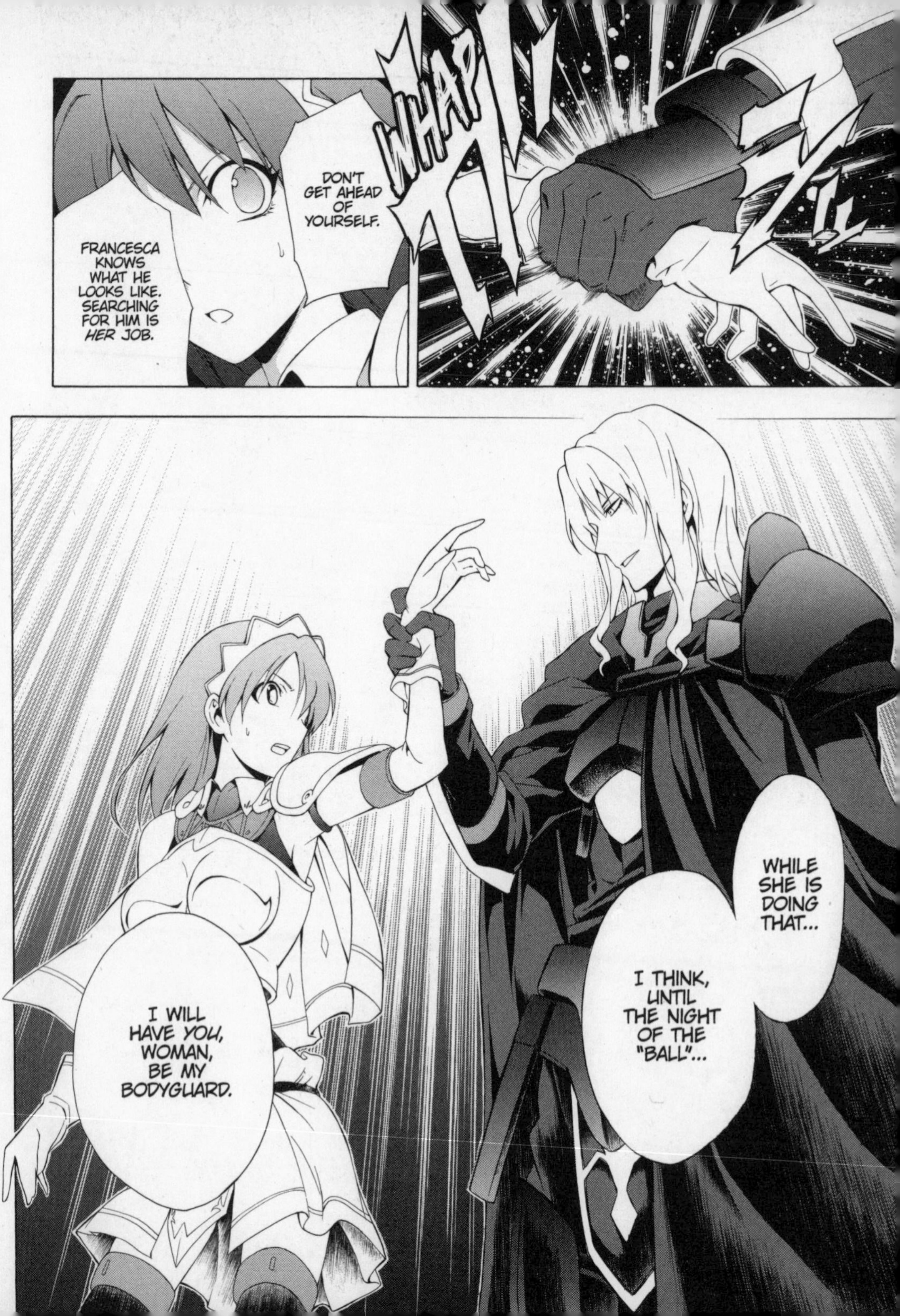
WHAP!!
DON'T GET AHEAD OF YOURSELF.
FRANCESCA KNOWS WHAT HE LOOKS LIKE. SEARCHING FOR HIM IS *HER* JOB.
WHILE SHE IS DOING THAT...
I THINK, UNTIL THE NIGHT OF THE "BALL"...
I WILL HAVE *YOU*, WOMAN, BE MY BODYGUARD.

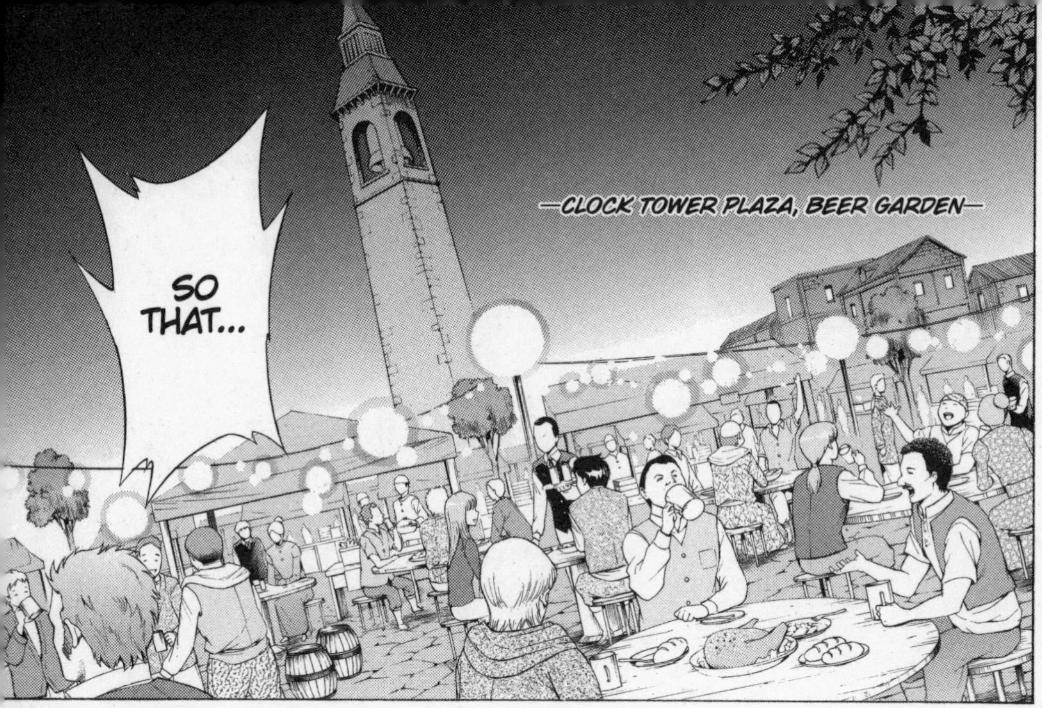
—CLOCK TOWER PLAZA, BEER GARDEN—
SO THAT...

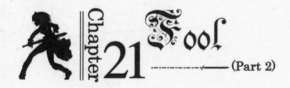

Chapter 21 Fool (Part 2)

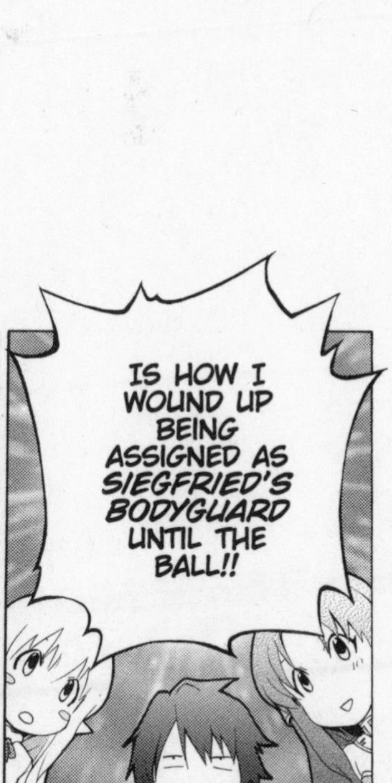
IS HOW I WOUND UP BEING ASSIGNED AS SIEGFRIED'S BODYGUARD UNTIL THE BALL!!

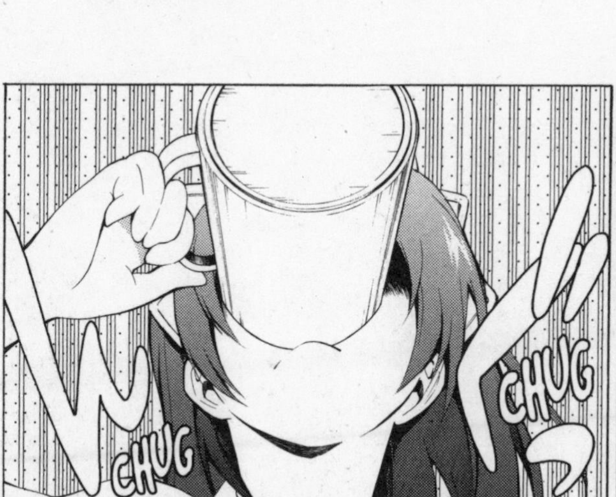
CHUG
CHUG

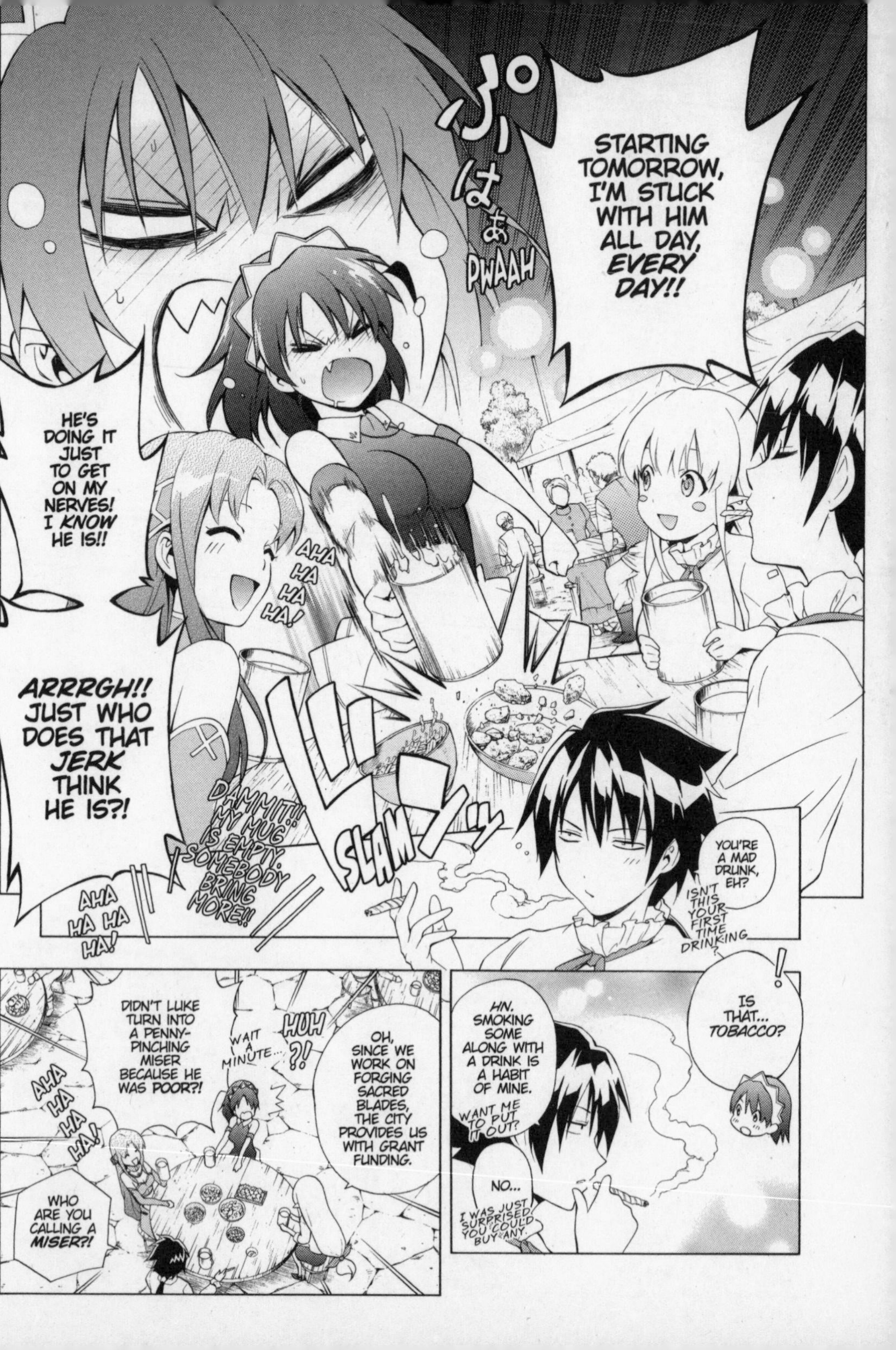

ぷはぁ
PWAAH
STARTING TOMORROW, I'M STUCK WITH HIM ALL DAY, *EVERY* DAY!!
HE'S DOING IT JUST TO GET ON MY NERVES! I *KNOW* HE IS!!
AHA HA HA HA!
ARRRGH!! JUST WHO DOES THAT *JERK* THINK HE IS?!
SLAM
DAMMIT!! MY MUG IS EMPTY. SOMEBODY BRING MORE!!
AHA HA HA HA!
YOU'RE A MAD DRUNK, EH?
ISN'T THIS YOUR FIRST TIME DRINKING?
!
IS THAT... *TOBACCO?*
HN. SMOKING SOME ALONG WITH A DRINK IS A HABIT OF MINE.
WANT ME TO PUT IT OUT?
NO...
I WAS JUST SURPRISED YOU COULD BUY ANY.
HUH?!
WAIT A MINUTE...
OH, SINCE WE WORK ON FORGING SACRED BLADES, THE CITY PROVIDES US WITH GRANT FUNDING.
DIDN'T LUKE TURN INTO A PENNY-PINCHING MISER BECAUSE HE WAS POOR?!
AHA HA HA HA!
WHO ARE YOU CALLING A *MISER?!*

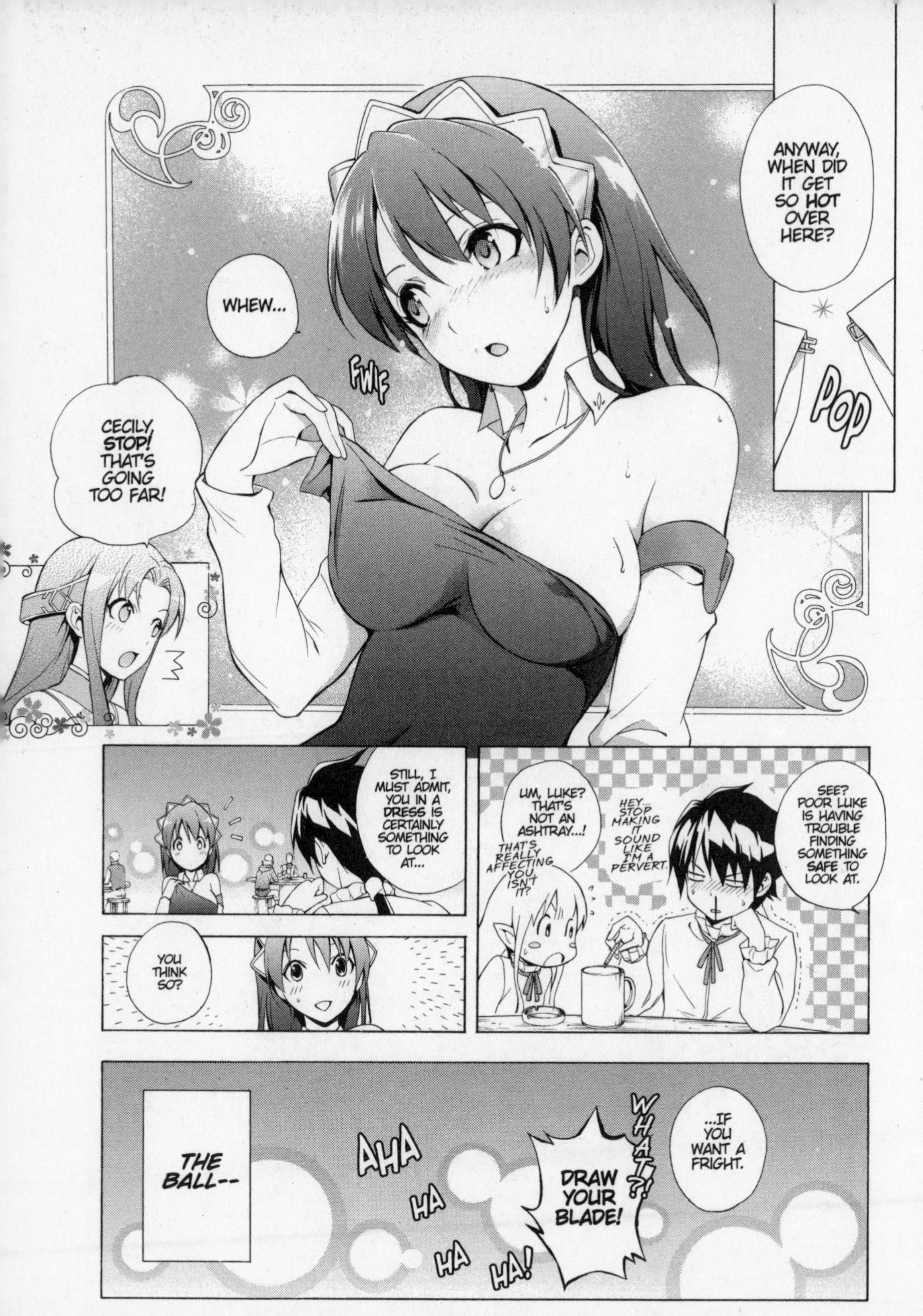

ANYWAY, WHEN DID IT GET SO HOT OVER HERE?
POP
WHEW...
FWIF
CECILY, STOP! THAT'S GOING TOO FAR!
SEE? POOR LUKE IS HAVING TROUBLE FINDING SOMETHING SAFE TO LOOK AT.
HEY... STOP MAKING IT SOUND LIKE I'M A PERVERT.
UM, LUKE? THAT'S NOT AN ASHTRAY...!
THAT'S REALLY AFFECTING YOU, ISN'T IT?
STILL, I MUST ADMIT, YOU IN A DRESS IS CERTAINLY SOMETHING TO LOOK AT...
YOU THINK SO?
...IF YOU WANT A FRIGHT.
WHAT?!
DRAW YOUR BLADE!
AHA HA HA HA!
THE BALL--

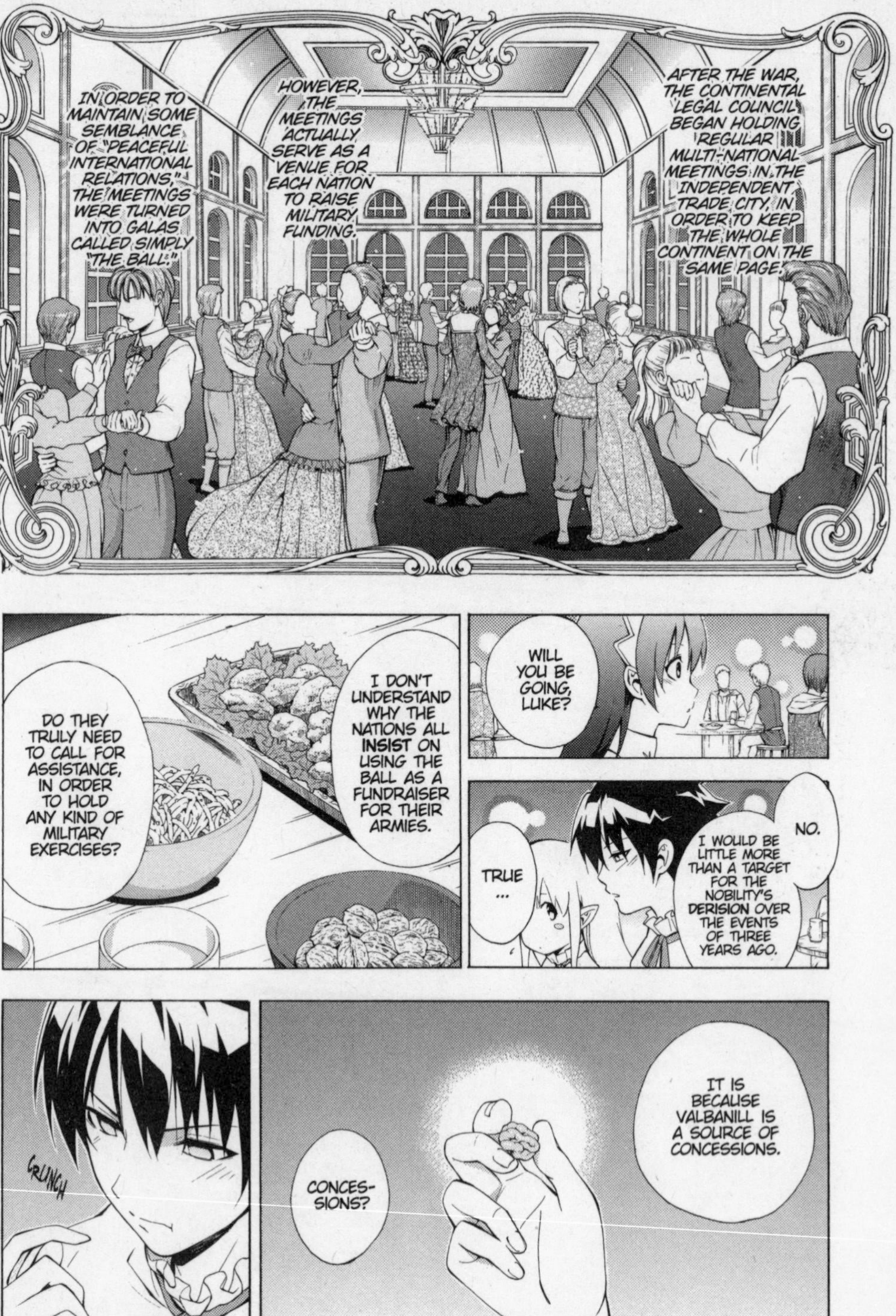
AFTER THE WAR, THE CONTINENTAL LEGAL COUNCIL BEGAN HOLDING REGULAR MULTI-NATIONAL MEETINGS IN THE INDEPENDENT TRADE CITY, IN ORDER TO KEEP THE WHOLE CONTINENT ON THE SAME PAGE.
HOWEVER, THE MEETINGS ACTUALLY SERVE AS A VENUE FOR EACH NATION TO RAISE MILITARY FUNDING.
IN ORDER TO MAINTAIN SOME SEMBLANCE OF "PEACEFUL INTERNATIONAL RELATIONS," THE MEETINGS WERE TURNED INTO GALAS CALLED SIMPLY "THE BALL."
WILL YOU BE GOING, LUKE?
NO.
I WOULD BE LITTLE MORE THAN A TARGET FOR THE NOBILITY'S DERISION OVER THE EVENTS OF THREE YEARS AGO.
TRUE ...
I DON'T UNDERSTAND WHY THE NATIONS ALL INSIST ON USING THE BALL AS A FUNDRAISER FOR THEIR ARMIES.
DO THEY TRULY NEED TO CALL FOR ASSISTANCE, IN ORDER TO HOLD ANY KIND OF MILITARY EXERCISES?
IT IS BECAUSE VALBANILL IS A SOURCE OF CONCESSIONS.
CONCES-SIONS?
CRUNCH

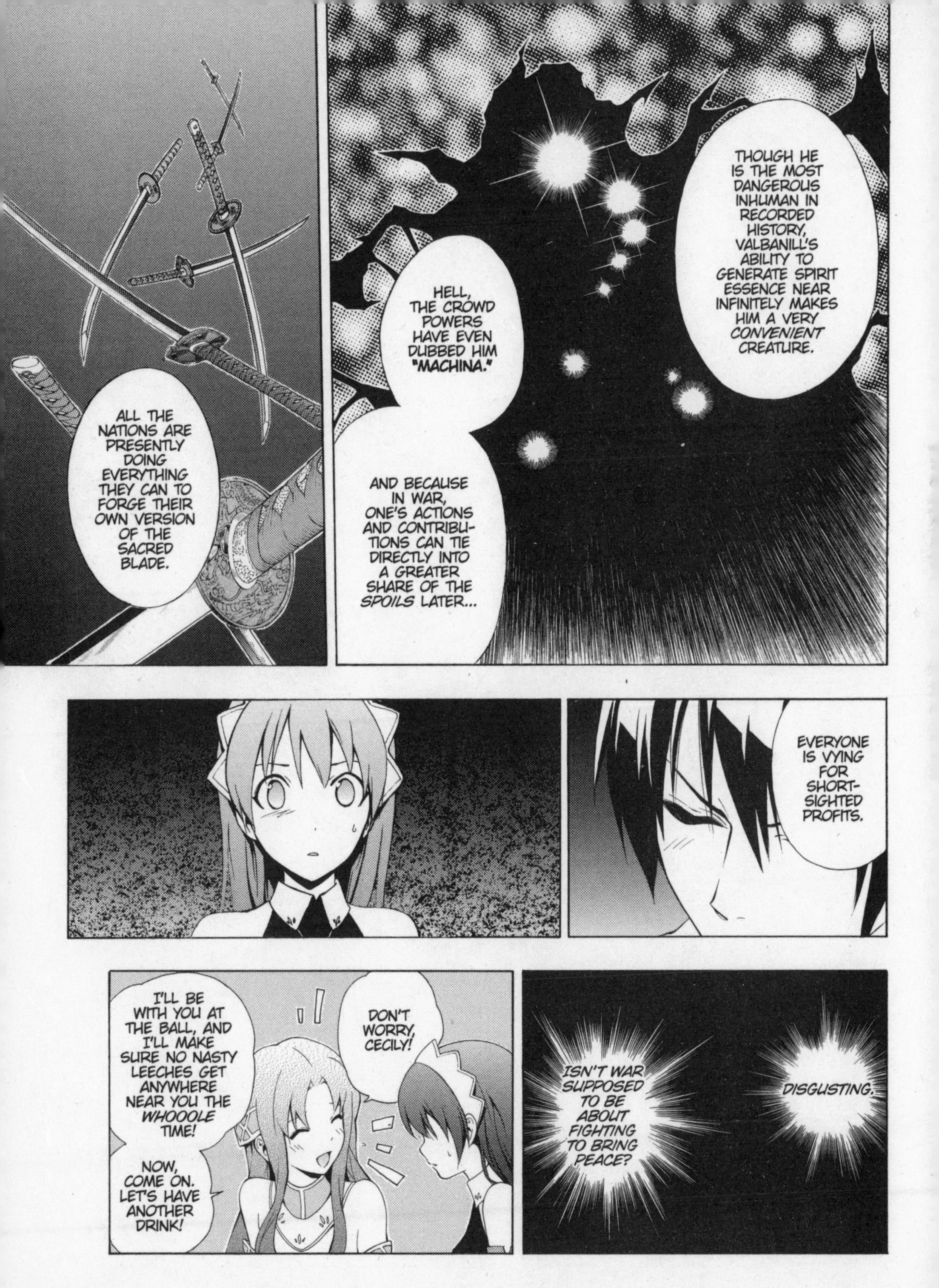
THOUGH HE IS THE MOST DANGEROUS INHUMAN IN RECORDED HISTORY, VALBANILL'S ABILITY TO GENERATE SPIRIT ESSENCE NEAR INFINITELY MAKES HIM A VERY *CONVENIENT* CREATURE.
HELL, THE CROWD POWERS HAVE EVEN DUBBED HIM **"MACHINA."**
AND BECAUSE IN WAR, ONE'S ACTIONS AND CONTRIBUTIONS CAN TIE DIRECTLY INTO A GREATER SHARE OF THE *SPOILS* LATER...
ALL THE NATIONS ARE PRESENTLY DOING EVERYTHING THEY CAN TO FORGE THEIR OWN VERSION OF THE SACRED BLADE.
EVERYONE IS VYING FOR SHORT-SIGHTED PROFITS.
DISGUSTING.
ISN'T WAR SUPPOSED TO BE ABOUT FIGHTING TO BRING PEACE?
DON'T WORRY, CECILY!
I'LL BE WITH YOU AT THE BALL, AND I'LL MAKE SURE NO NASTY LEECHES GET ANYWHERE NEAR YOU THE *WHOOOLE* TIME!
NOW, COME ON. LET'S HAVE ANOTHER DRINK!

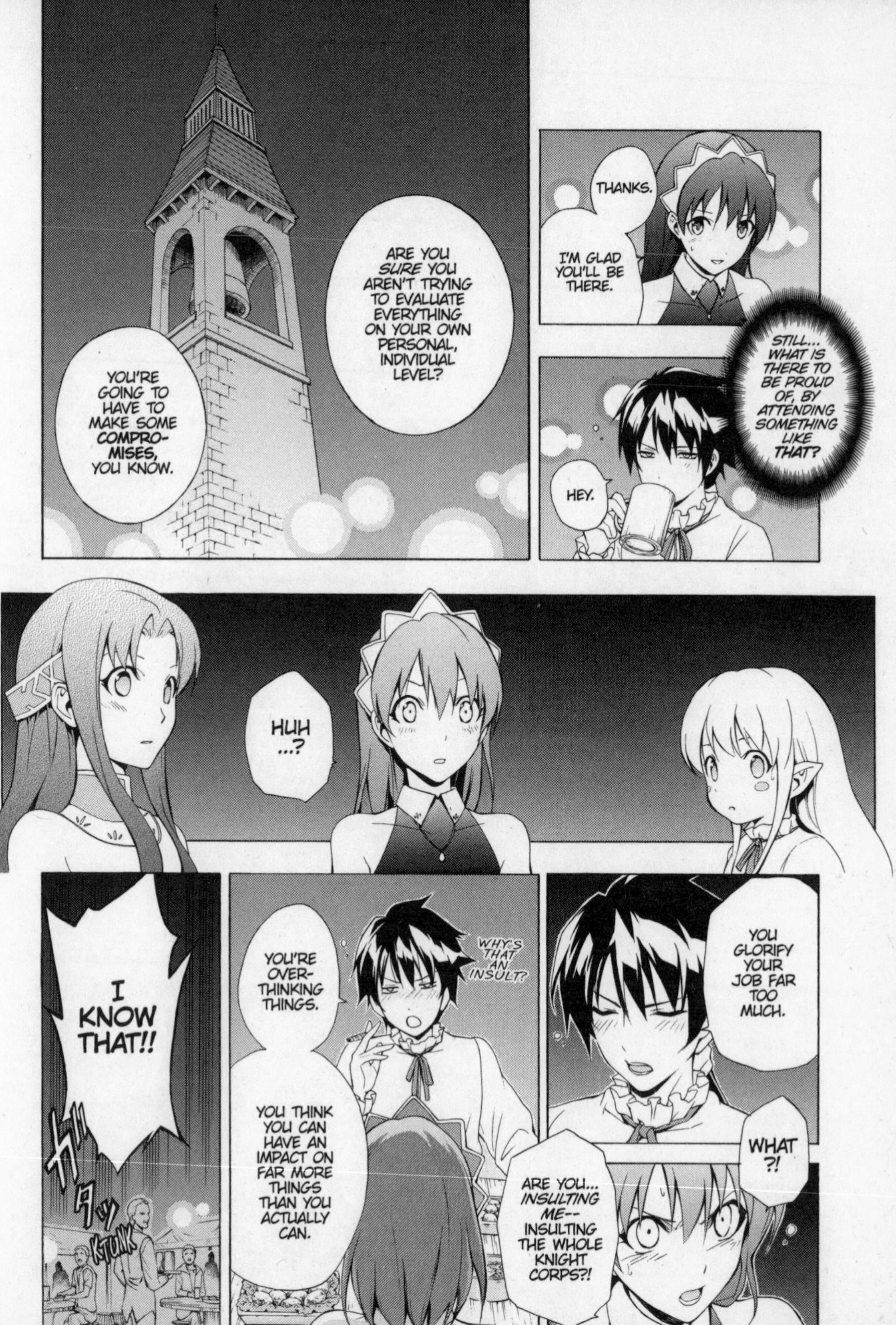
THANKS.
I'M GLAD YOU'LL BE THERE.
STILL... WHAT IS THERE TO BE PROUD OF, BY ATTENDING SOMETHING LIKE THAT?
HEY.
ARE YOU SURE YOU AREN'T TRYING TO EVALUATE EVERYTHING ON YOUR OWN PERSONAL, INDIVIDUAL LEVEL?
YOU'RE GOING TO HAVE TO MAKE SOME COMPRO-MISES, YOU KNOW.
HUH ...?
YOU GLORIFY YOUR JOB FAR TOO MUCH.
WHAT ?!
ARE YOU... INSULTING ME-- INSULTING THE WHOLE KNIGHT CORPS?!
WHY'S THAT AN INSULT?
YOU'RE OVER-THINKING THINGS.
YOU THINK YOU CAN HAVE AN IMPACT ON FAR MORE THINGS THAN YOU ACTUALLY CAN.
I KNOW THAT!!
KTONK

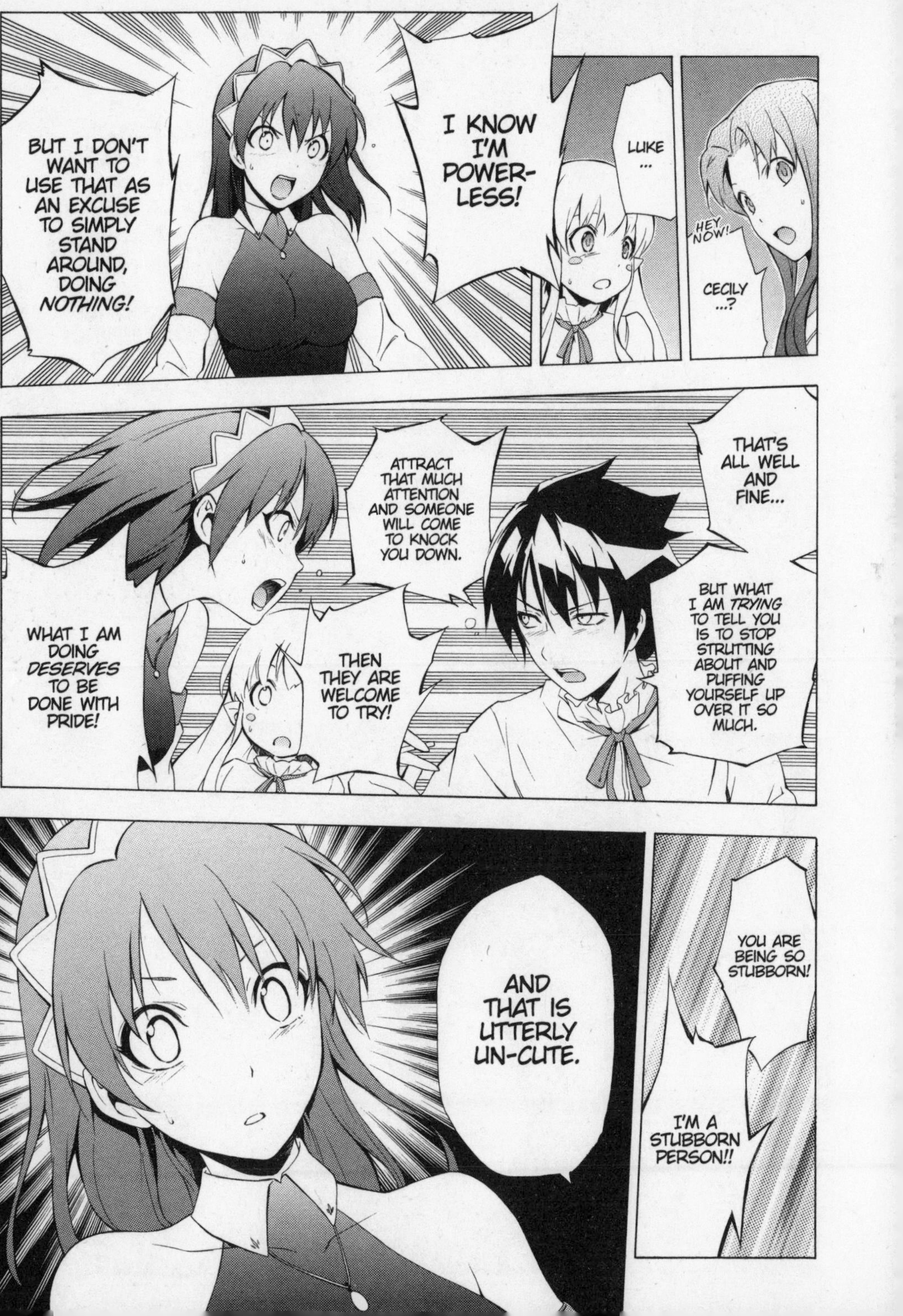
HEY NOW!
CECILY ...?
LUKE ...
I KNOW I'M POWER-LESS!
BUT I DON'T WANT TO USE THAT AS AN EXCUSE TO SIMPLY STAND AROUND, DOING *NOTHING!*
THAT'S ALL WELL AND FINE...
BUT WHAT I AM *TRYING* TO TELL YOU IS TO STOP STRUTTING ABOUT AND PUFFING YOURSELF UP OVER IT SO MUCH.
ATTRACT THAT MUCH ATTENTION AND SOMEONE WILL COME TO KNOCK YOU DOWN.
THEN THEY ARE WELCOME TO TRY!
WHAT I AM DOING *DESERVES* TO BE DONE WITH PRIDE!
YOU ARE BEING SO STUBBORN!
I'M A STUBBORN PERSON!!
AND THAT IS UTTERLY UN-CUTE.

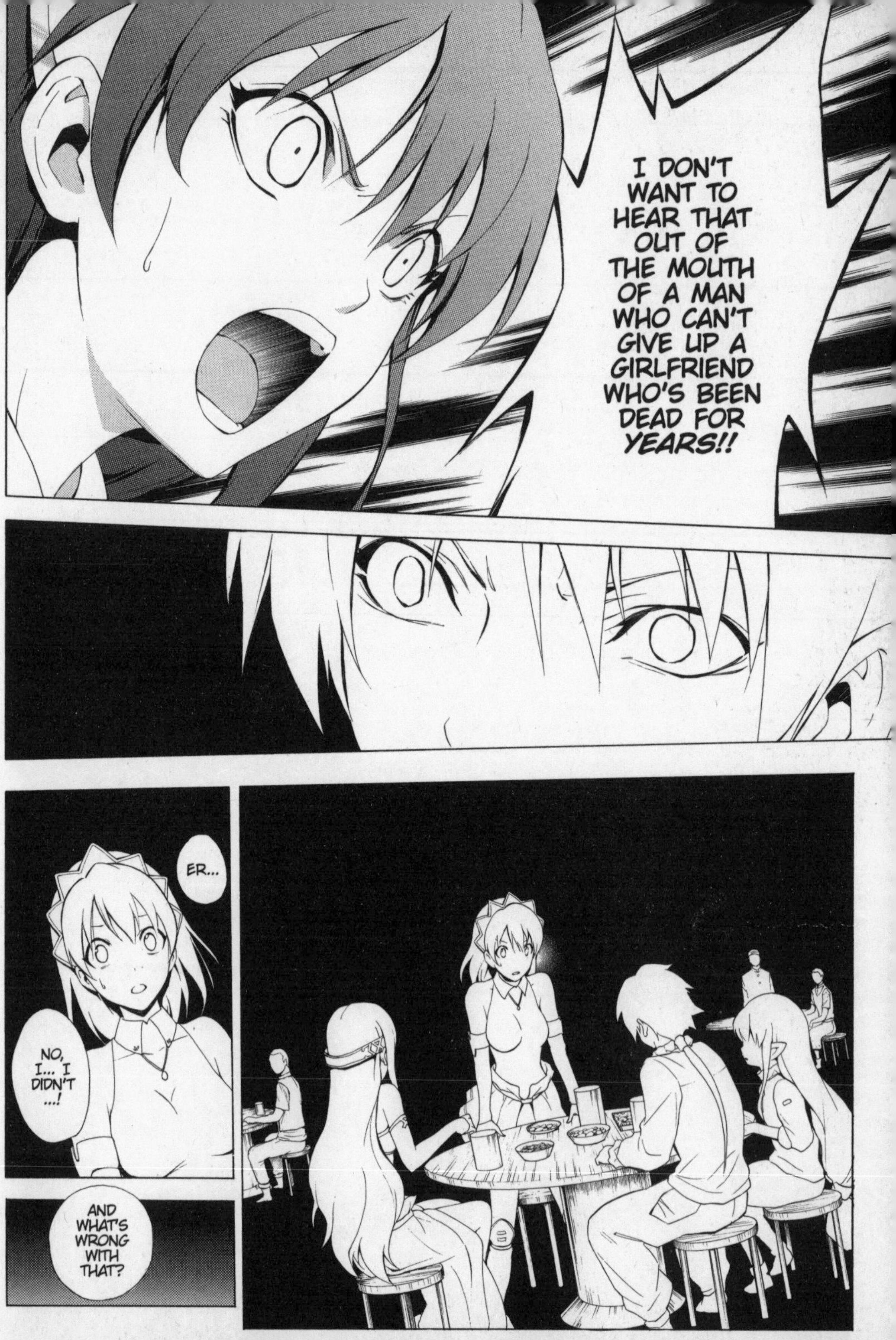
I DON'T WANT TO HEAR THAT OUT OF THE MOUTH OF A MAN WHO CAN'T GIVE UP A GIRLFRIEND WHO'S BEEN DEAD FOR YEARS!!
ER...
NO, I... I DIDN'T ...!
AND WHAT'S WRONG WITH THAT?

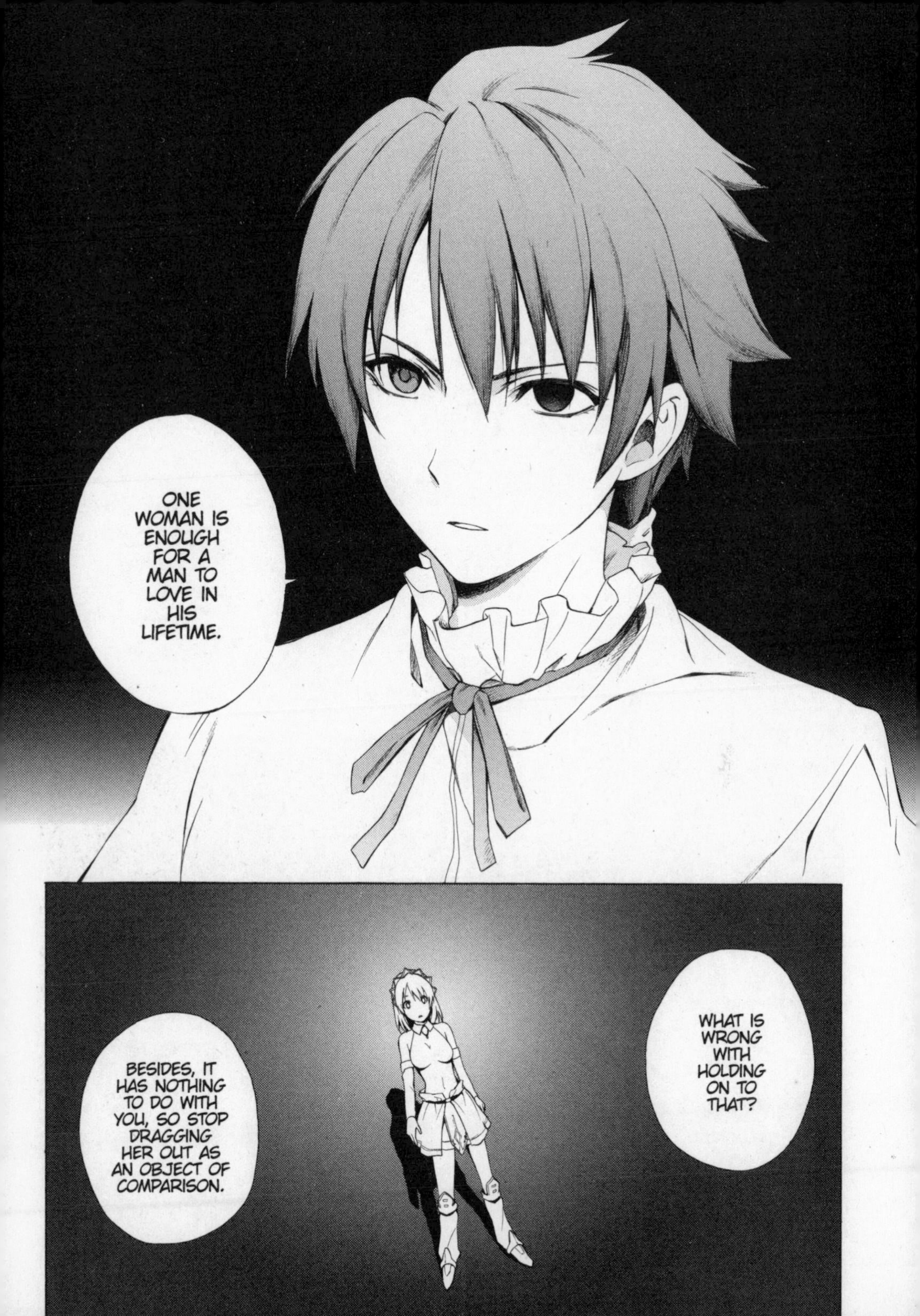
ONE WOMAN IS ENOUGH FOR A MAN TO LOVE IN HIS LIFETIME.
WHAT IS WRONG WITH HOLDING ON TO THAT?
BESIDES, IT HAS NOTHING TO DO WITH YOU, SO STOP DRAGGING HER OUT AS AN OBJECT OF COMPARISON.

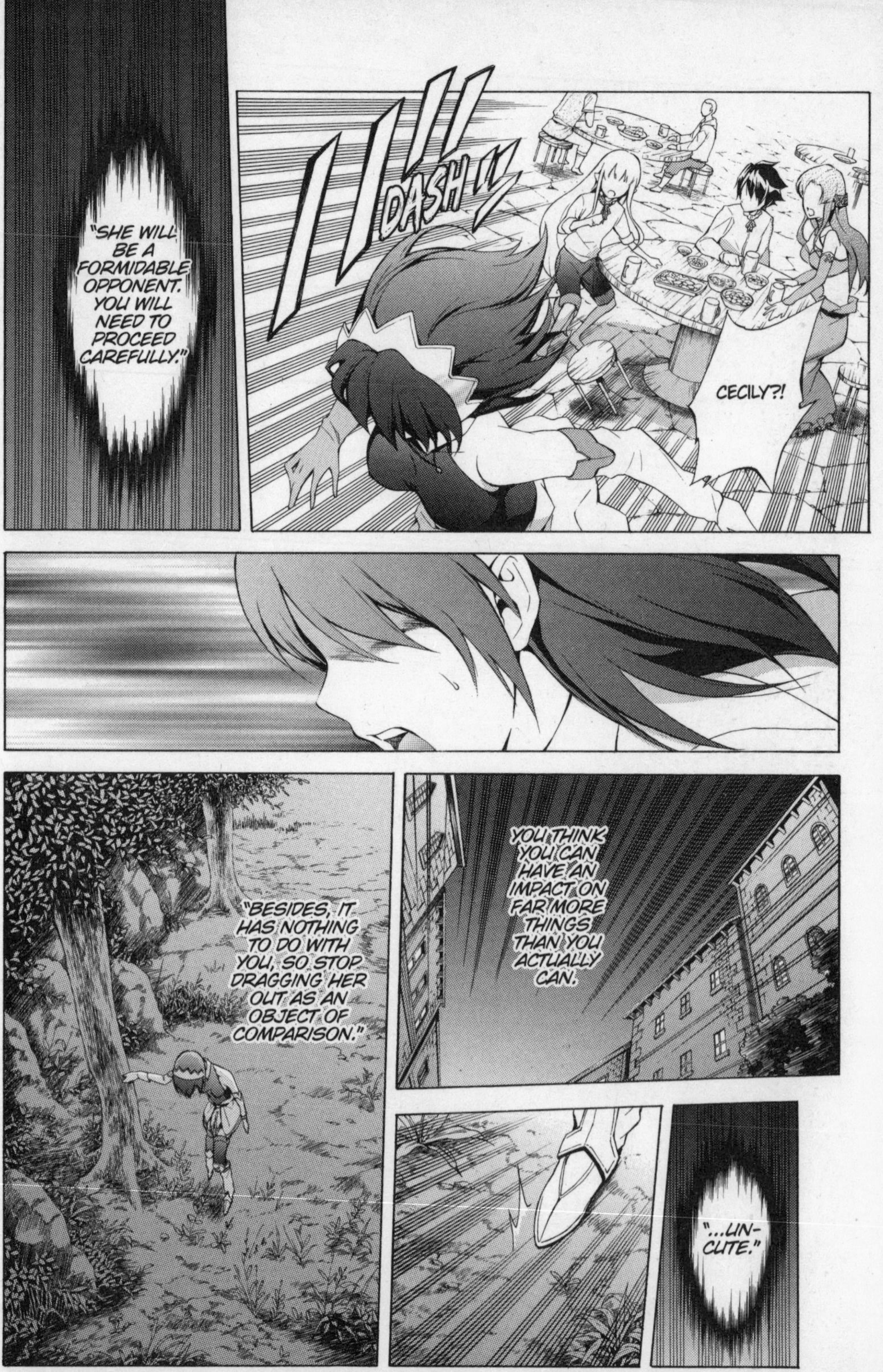
DASH
CECILY?!
"SHE WILL BE A FORMIDABLE OPPONENT. YOU WILL NEED TO PROCEED CAREFULLY."
YOU THINK YOU CAN HAVE AN IMPACT ON FAR MORE THINGS THAN YOU ACTUALLY CAN.
"...UN-CUTE."
"BESIDES, IT HAS NOTHING TO DO WITH YOU, SO STOP DRAGGING HER OUT AS AN OBJECT OF COMPARISON."

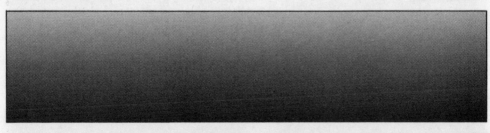

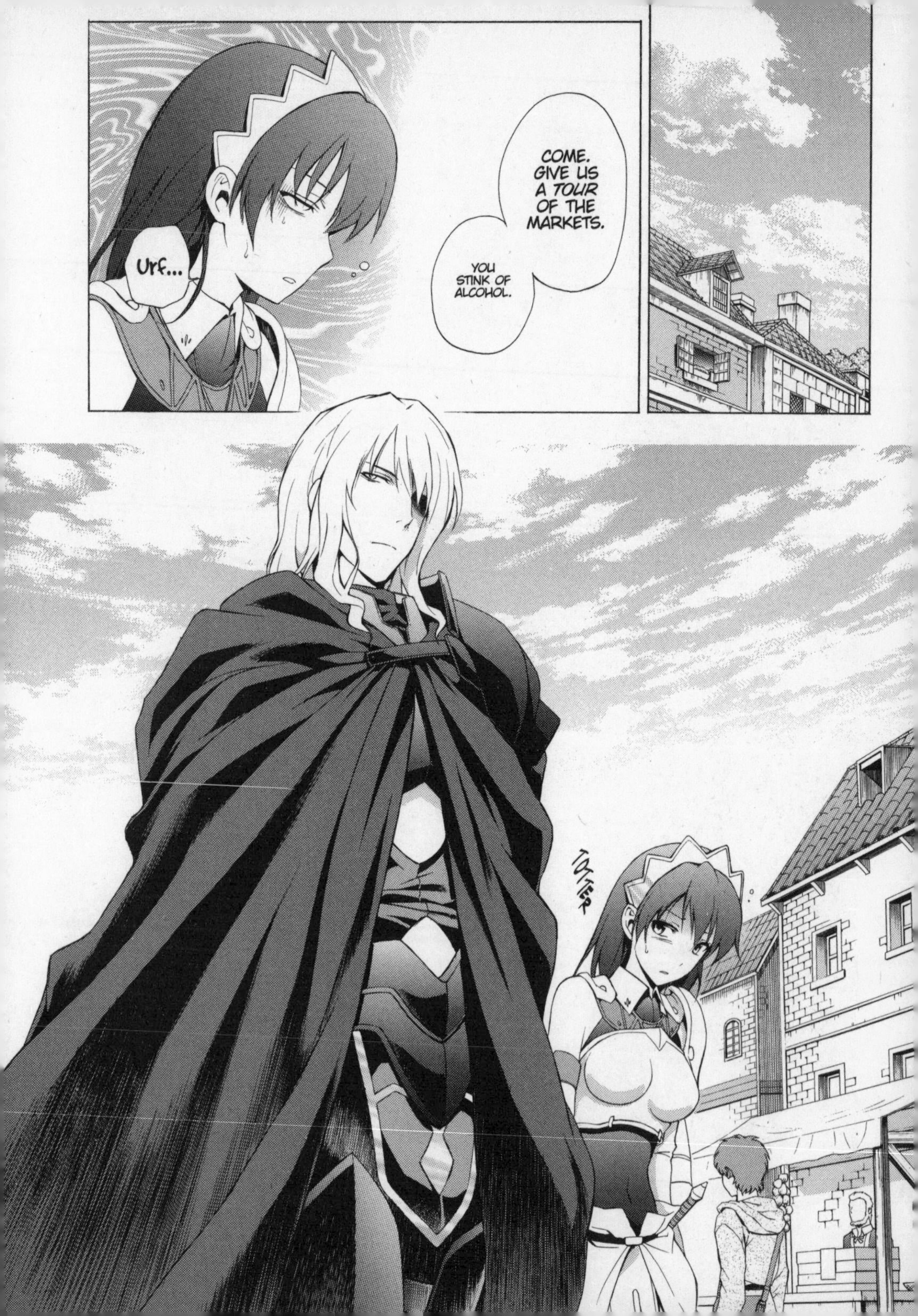
COME. GIVE US A *TOUR* OF THE MARKETS.
YOU STINK OF ALCOHOL.
Urf...
TOTTER

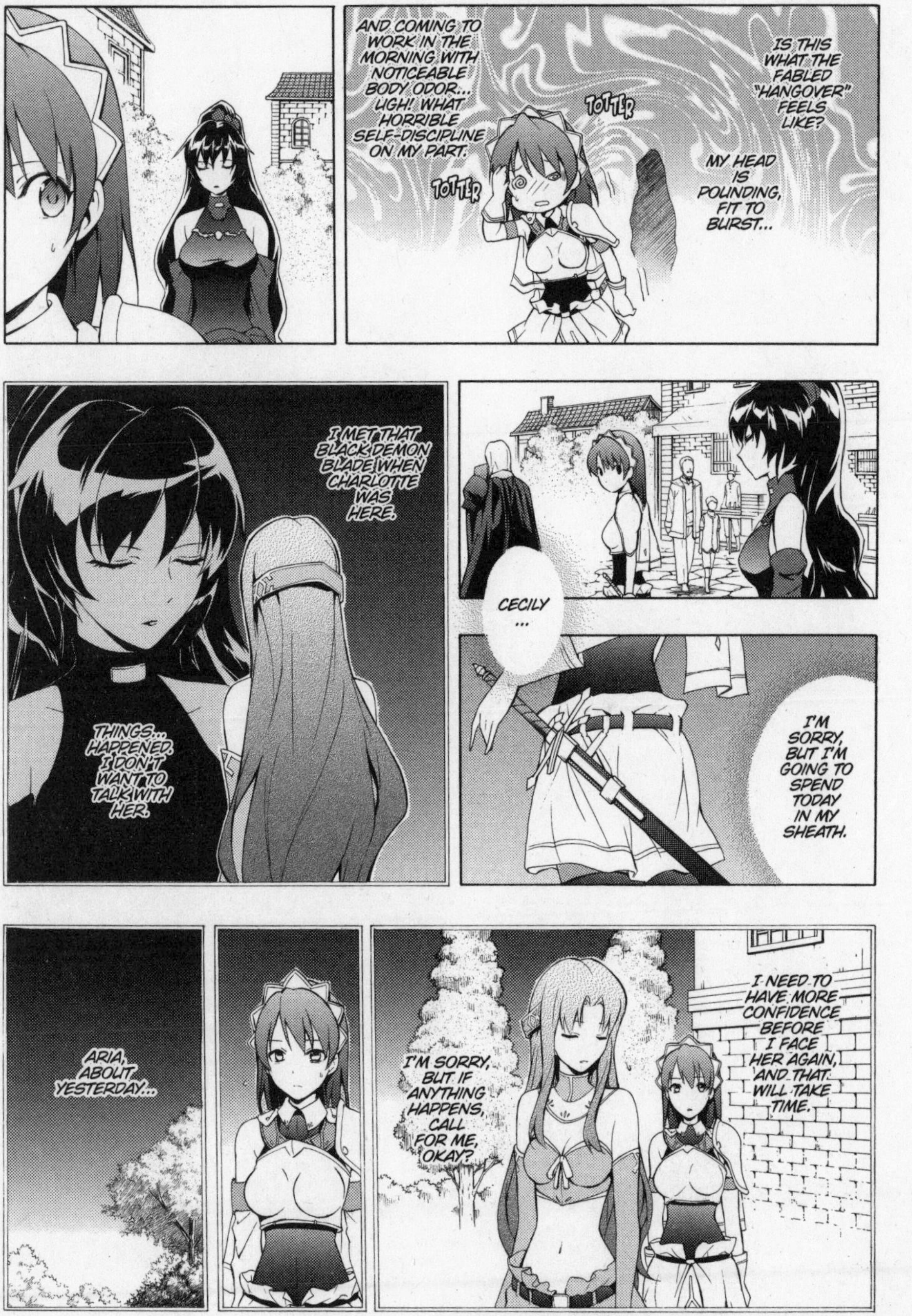
IS THIS WHAT THE FABLED "HANGOVER" FEELS LIKE?
MY HEAD IS POUNDING, FIT TO BURST...
TOTTER
AND COMING TO WORK IN THE MORNING WITH NOTICEABLE BODY ODOR... UGH! WHAT HORRIBLE SELF-DISCIPLINE ON MY PART.
TOTTER
CECILY...
I'M SORRY, BUT I'M GOING TO SPEND TODAY IN MY SHEATH.
I MET THAT BLACK DEMON BLADE WHEN CHARLOTTE WAS HERE.
THINGS... HAPPENED. I DON'T WANT TO TALK WITH HER.
I NEED TO HAVE MORE CONFIDENCE BEFORE I FACE HER AGAIN, AND THAT WILL TAKE TIME.
I'M SORRY, BUT IF ANYTHING HAPPENS, CALL FOR ME, OKAY?
ARIA, ABOUT YESTERDAY...

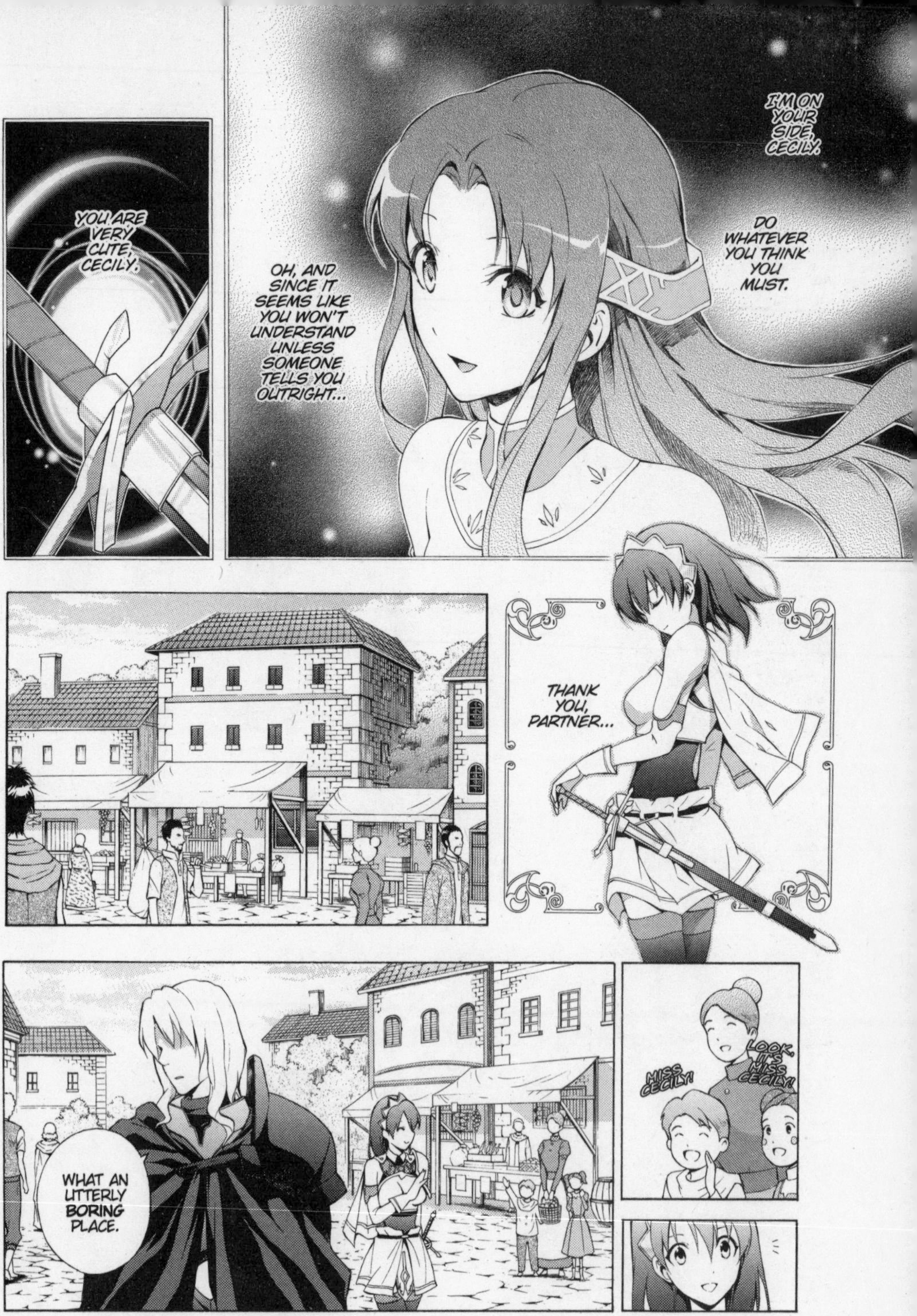
I'M ON YOUR SIDE, CECILY.
DO WHATEVER YOU THINK YOU MUST.
OH, AND SINCE IT SEEMS LIKE YOU WON'T UNDERSTAND UNLESS SOMEONE TELLS YOU OUTRIGHT...
YOU ARE VERY CUTE, CECILY.
THANK YOU, PARTNER...
LOOK, IT'S MISS CECILY!
MISS CECILY!
WHAT AN UTTERLY BORING PLACE.

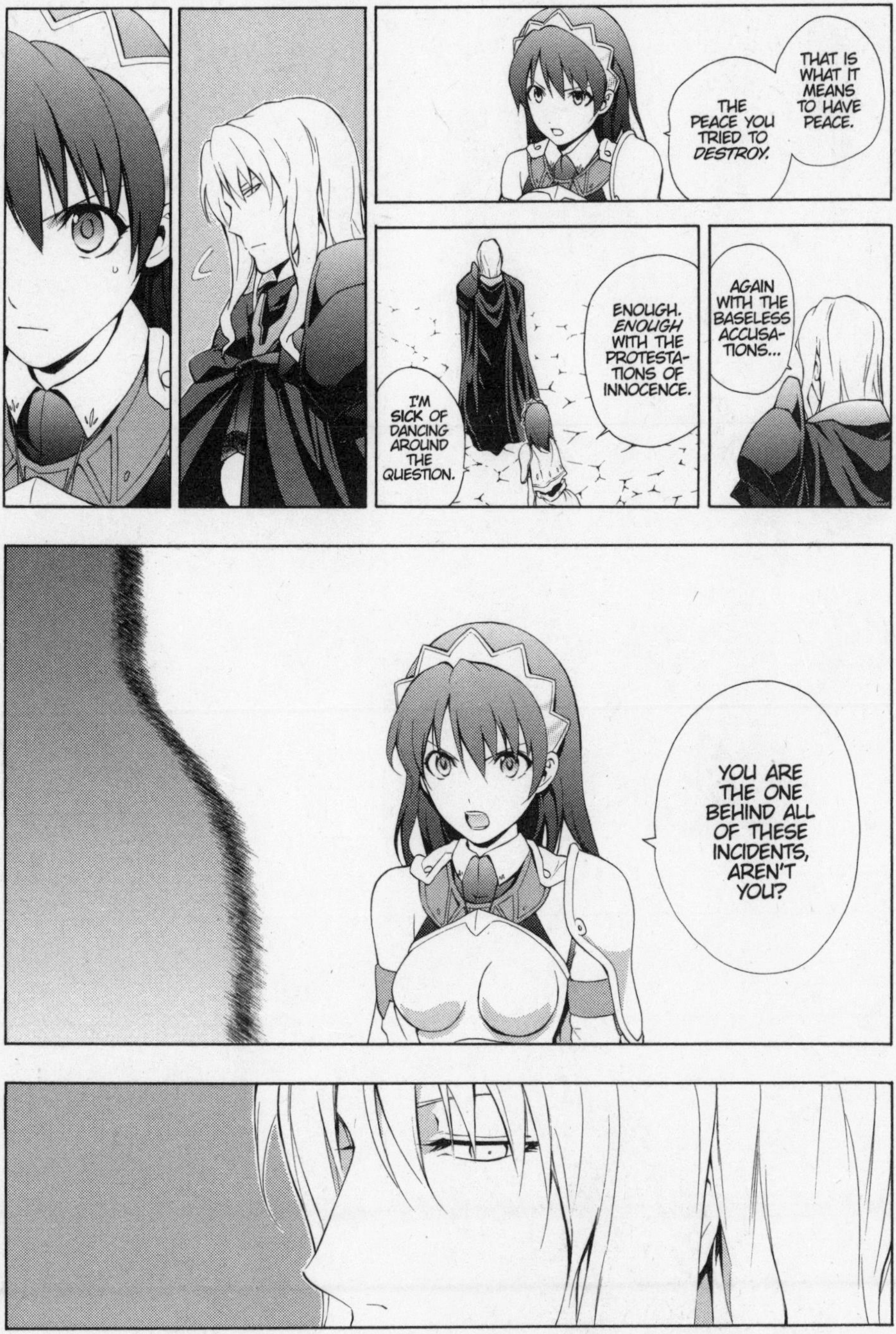
THAT IS WHAT IT MEANS TO HAVE PEACE.
THE PEACE YOU TRIED TO *DESTROY.*
AGAIN WITH THE BASELESS ACCUSA-TIONS...
ENOUGH. *ENOUGH* WITH THE PROTESTA-TIONS OF INNOCENCE.
I'M SICK OF DANCING AROUND THE QUESTION.
YOU ARE THE ONE BEHIND ALL OF THESE INCIDENTS, AREN'T YOU?

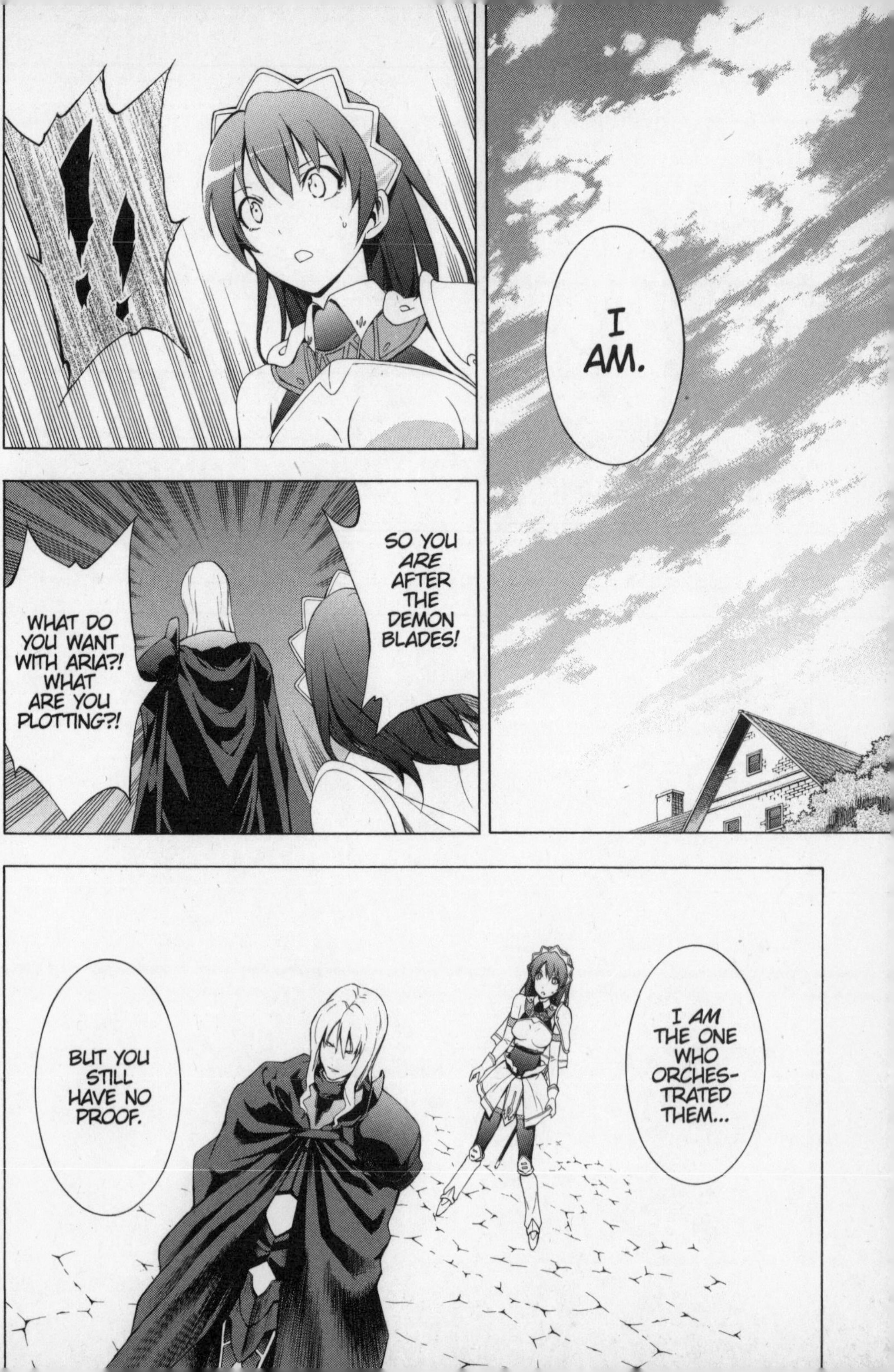

I AM.
!!
SO YOU ARE AFTER THE DEMON BLADES!
WHAT DO YOU WANT WITH ARIA?! WHAT ARE YOU PLOTTING?!
I AM THE ONE WHO ORCHES-TRATED THEM...
BUT YOU STILL HAVE NO PROOF.

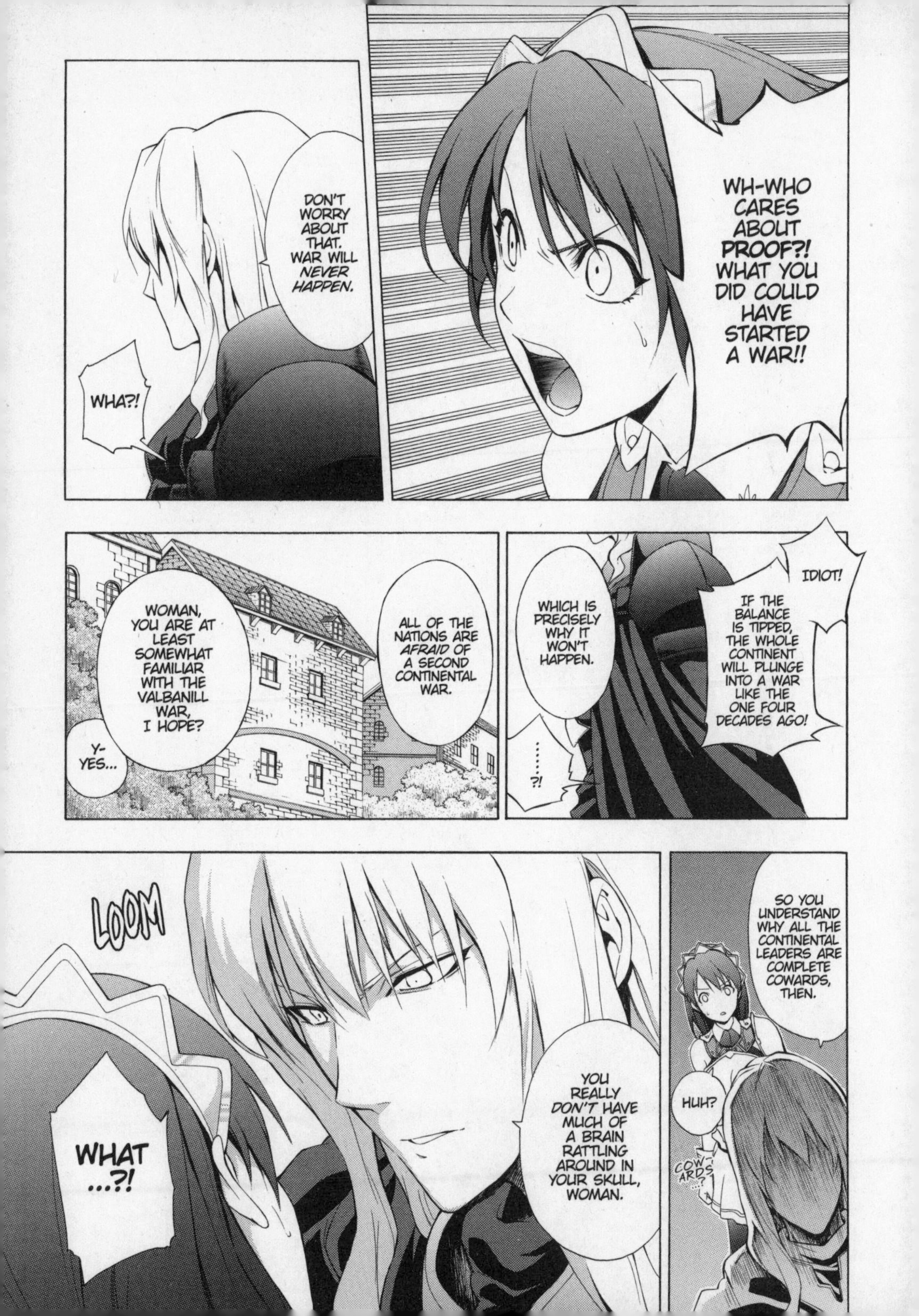
WH-WHO CARES ABOUT PROOF?! WHAT YOU DID COULD HAVE STARTED A WAR!!
DON'T WORRY ABOUT THAT. WAR WILL NEVER HAPPEN.
WHA?!
IDIOT!
IF THE BALANCE IS TIPPED, THE WHOLE CONTINENT WILL PLUNGE INTO A WAR LIKE THE ONE FOUR DECADES AGO!
WHICH IS PRECISELY WHY IT WON'T HAPPEN.
......?!
ALL OF THE NATIONS ARE AFRAID OF A SECOND CONTINENTAL WAR.
WOMAN, YOU ARE AT LEAST SOMEWHAT FAMILIAR WITH THE VALBANILL WAR, I HOPE?
Y-YES...
SO YOU UNDERSTAND WHY ALL THE CONTINENTAL LEADERS ARE COMPLETE COWARDS, THEN.
HUH?
COW-ARDS...?
LOOM
YOU REALLY DON'T HAVE MUCH OF A BRAIN RATTLING AROUND IN YOUR SKULL, WOMAN.
WHAT ...?!

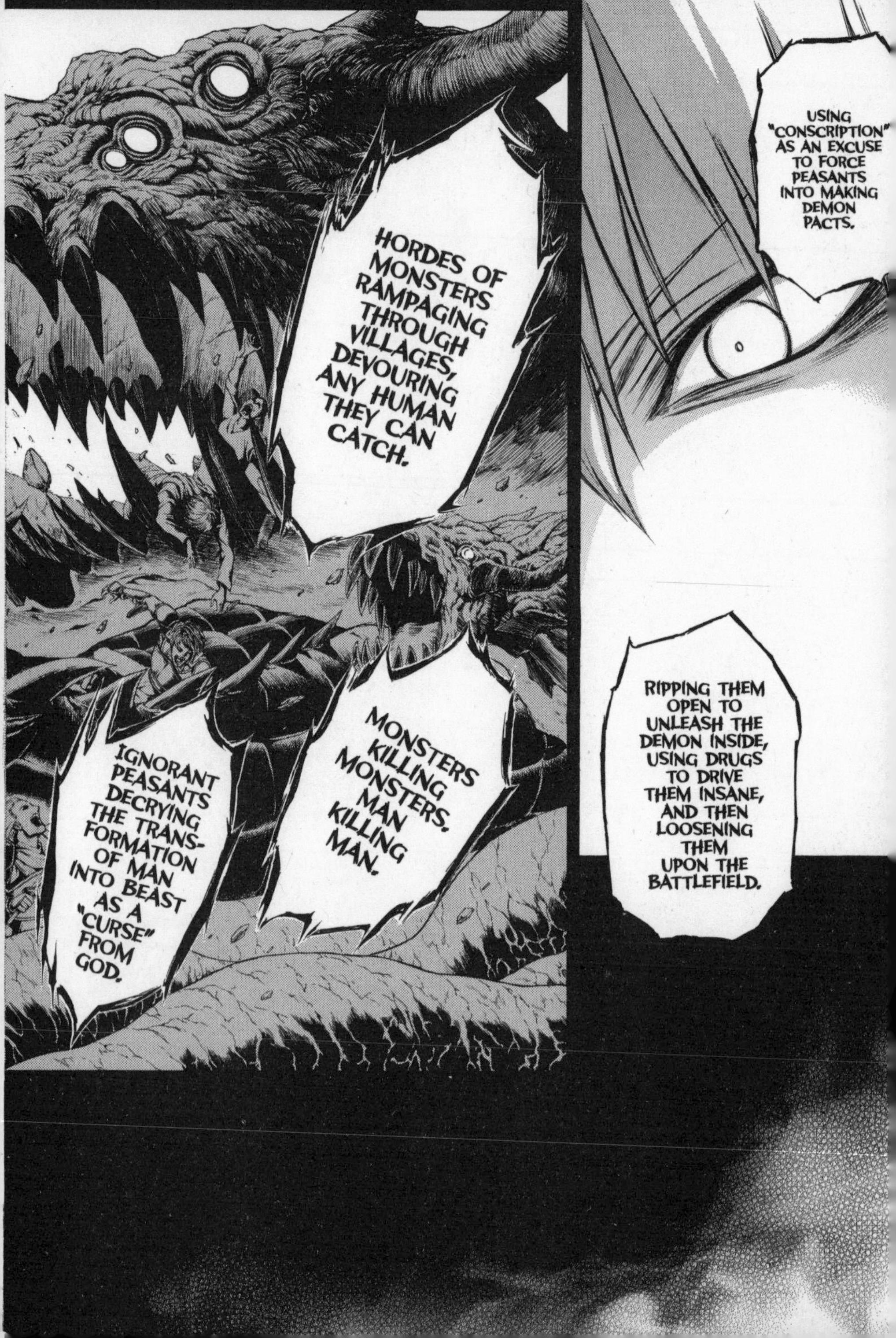
USING "CONSCRIPTION" AS AN EXCUSE TO FORCE PEASANTS INTO MAKING DEMON PACTS.
RIPPING THEM OPEN TO UNLEASH THE DEMON INSIDE, USING DRUGS TO DRIVE THEM INSANE, AND THEN LOOSENING THEM UPON THE BATTLEFIELD.
HORDES OF MONSTERS RAMPAGING THROUGH VILLAGES, DEVOURING ANY HUMAN THEY CAN CATCH.
MONSTERS KILLING MONSTERS. MAN KILLING MAN.
IGNORANT PEASANTS DECRYING THE TRANS-FORMATION OF MAN INTO BEAST AS A "CURSE" FROM GOD.

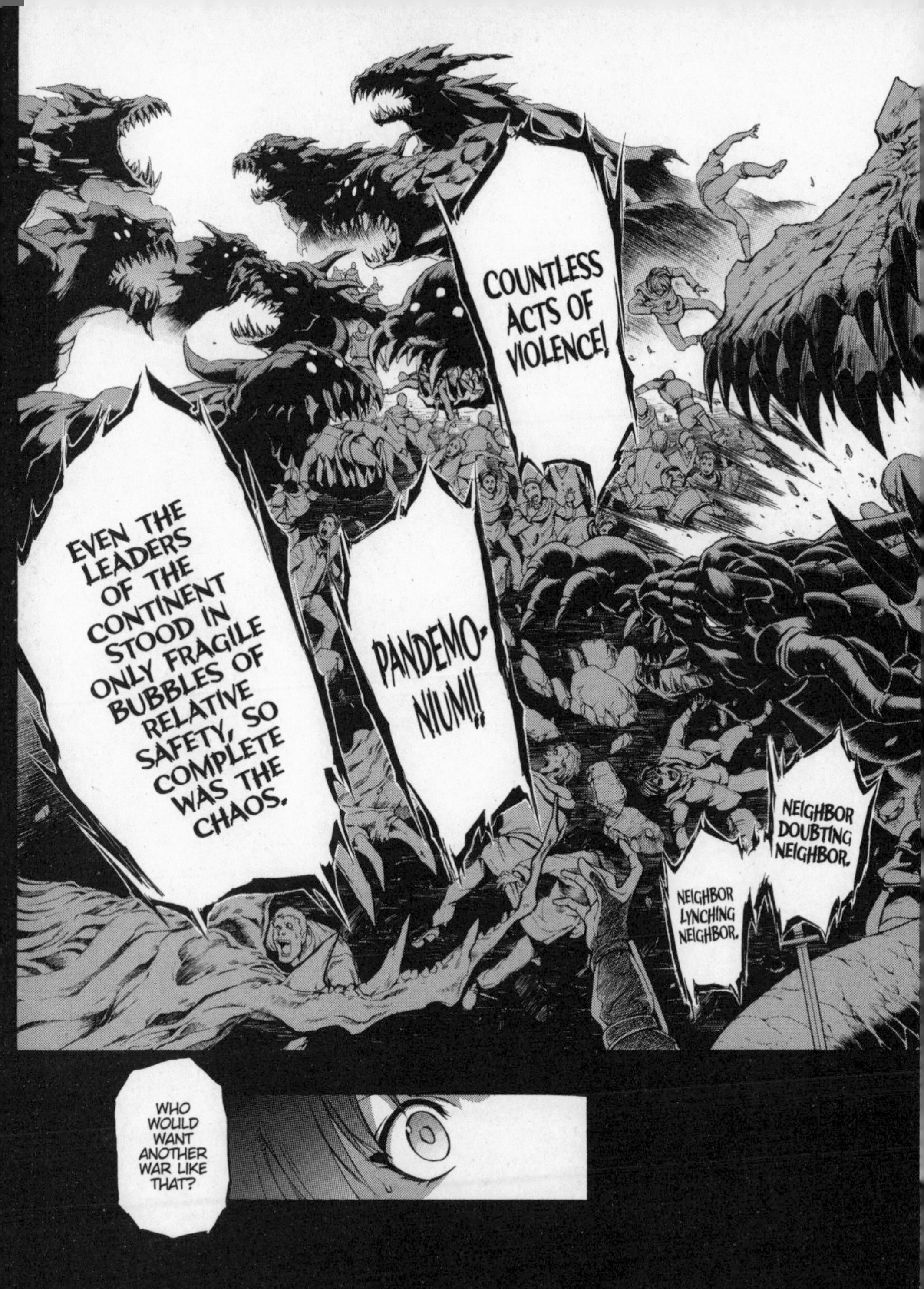
COUNTLESS ACTS OF VIOLENCE!
NEIGHBOR DOUBTING NEIGHBOR.
NEIGHBOR LYNCHING NEIGHBOR.
PANDEMO-NIUM!!
EVEN THE LEADERS OF THE CONTINENT STOOD IN ONLY FRAGILE BUBBLES OF RELATIVE SAFETY, SO COMPLETE WAS THE CHAOS.
WHO WOULD WANT ANOTHER WAR LIKE THAT?

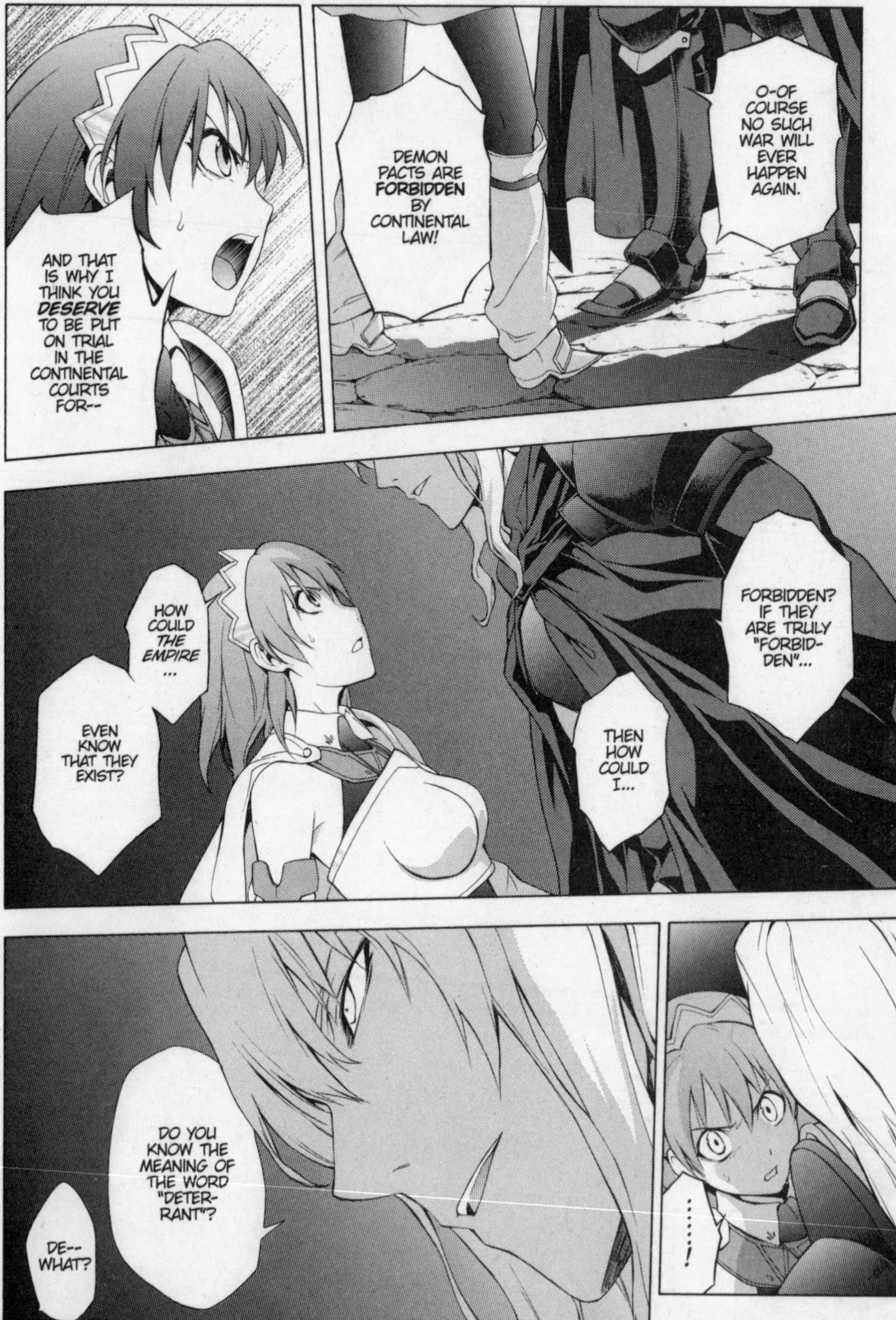
O-OF COURSE NO SUCH WAR WILL EVER HAPPEN AGAIN.
DEMON PACTS ARE **FORBIDDEN** BY CONTINENTAL LAW!
AND THAT IS WHY I THINK YOU ***DESERVE*** TO BE PUT ON TRIAL IN THE CONTINENTAL COURTS FOR--
FORBIDDEN? IF THEY ARE TRULY "FORBID-DEN"...
THEN HOW COULD I...
HOW COULD *THE EMPIRE* ...
EVEN KNOW THAT THEY EXIST?
......!
DO YOU KNOW THE MEANING OF THE WORD "DETER-RANT"?
DE-- WHAT?

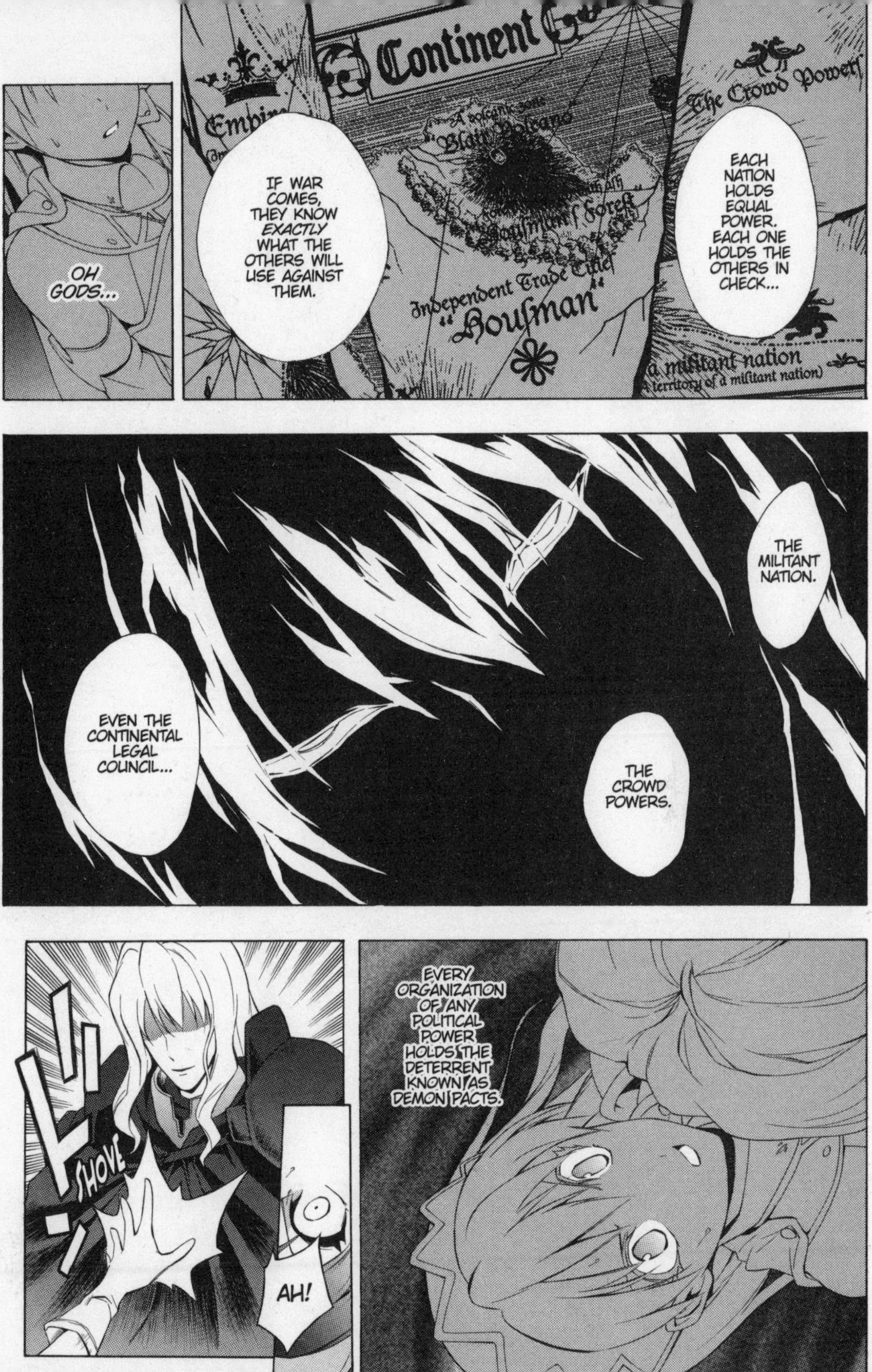
Continent
The Crowd Powers
Independent Trade City
"Housman"
a militant nation
(a territory of a militant nation)
EACH NATION HOLDS EQUAL POWER. EACH ONE HOLDS THE OTHERS IN CHECK...
IF WAR COMES, THEY KNOW *EXACTLY* WHAT THE OTHERS WILL USE AGAINST THEM.
OH GODS...
THE MILITANT NATION.
THE CROWD POWERS.
EVEN THE CONTINENTAL LEGAL COUNCIL...
EVERY ORGANIZATION OF ANY POLITICAL POWER HOLDS THE DETERRENT KNOWN AS DEMON PACTS.
SHOVE
AH!

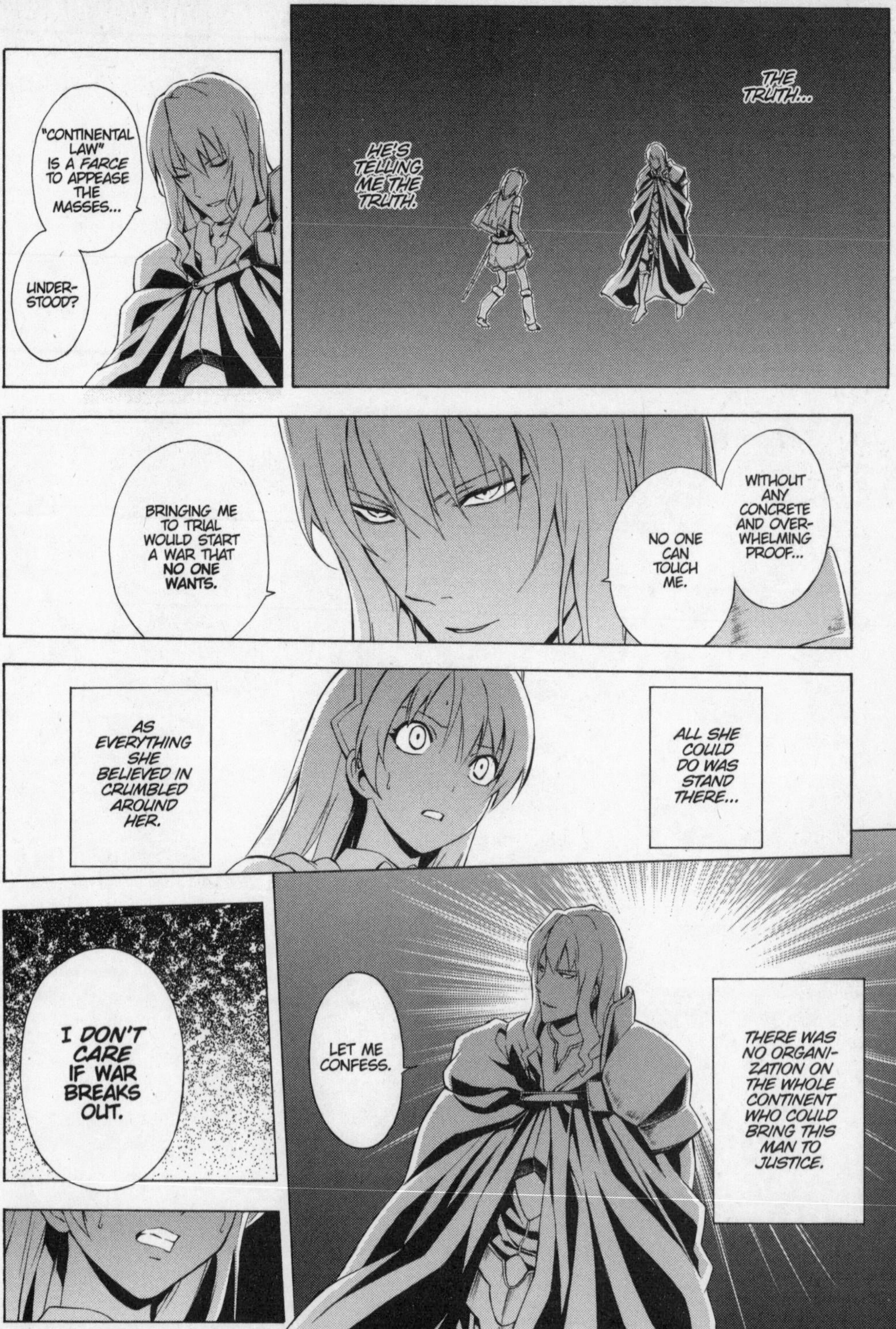
THE TRUTH...
HE'S TELLING ME THE TRUTH.
"CONTINENTAL LAW" IS A FARCE TO APPEASE THE MASSES...
UNDERSTOOD?
WITHOUT ANY CONCRETE AND OVERWHELMING PROOF...
NO ONE CAN TOUCH ME.
BRINGING ME TO TRIAL WOULD START A WAR THAT NO ONE WANTS.
ALL SHE COULD DO WAS STAND THERE...
AS EVERYTHING SHE BELIEVED IN CRUMBLED AROUND HER.
THERE WAS NO ORGANIZATION ON THE WHOLE CONTINENT WHO COULD BRING THIS MAN TO JUSTICE.
LET ME CONFESS.
I DON'T CARE IF WAR BREAKS OUT.

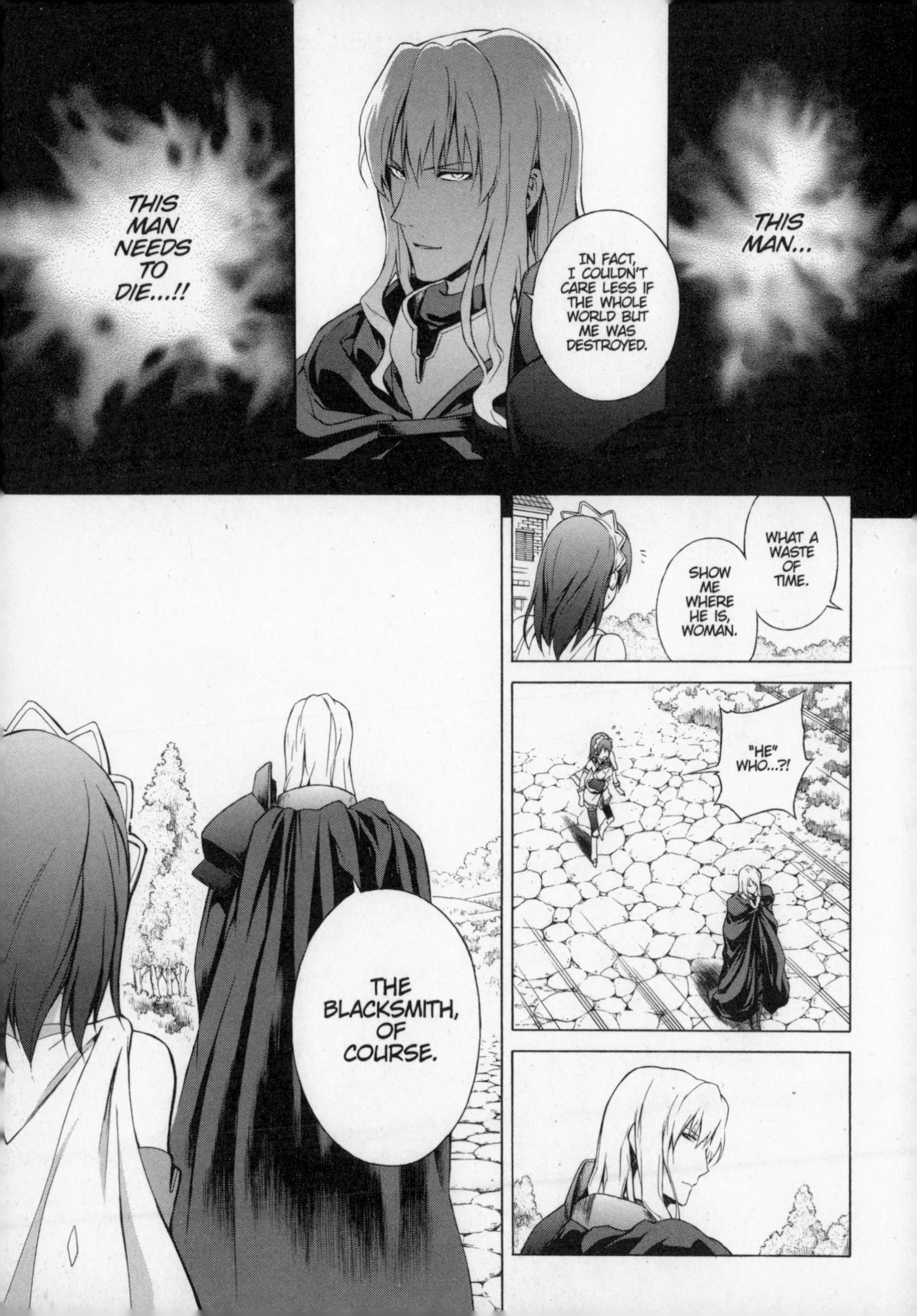
THIS MAN...
IN FACT, I COULDN'T CARE LESS IF THE WHOLE WORLD BUT ME WAS DESTROYED.
THIS MAN NEEDS TO DIE...!!
WHAT A WASTE OF TIME.
SHOW ME WHERE HE IS, WOMAN.
"HE" WHO...?!
THE BLACKSMITH, OF COURSE.

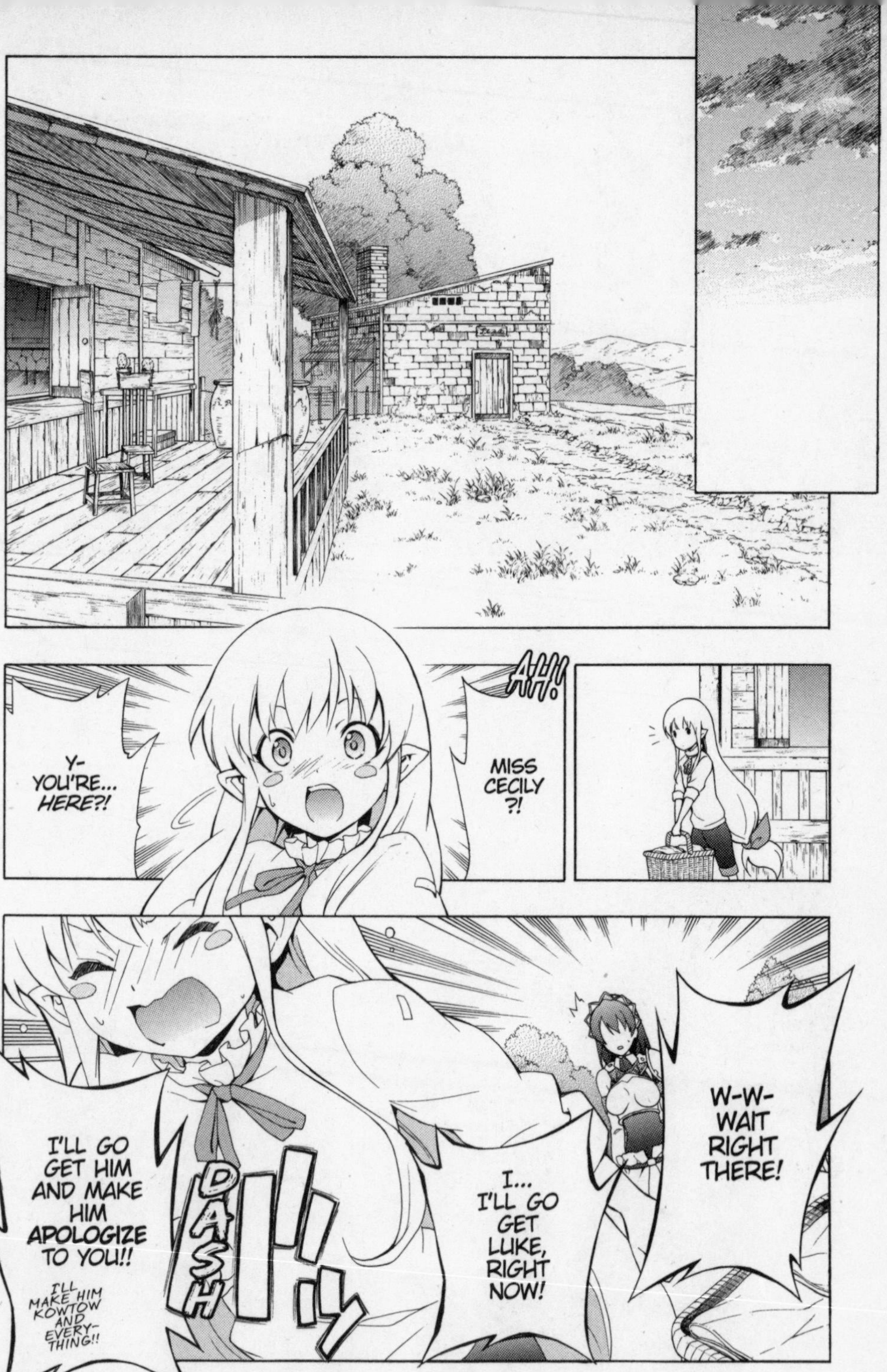
AH!!
MISS CECILY ?!
Y- YOU'RE... HERE?!
W-W-WAIT RIGHT THERE!
I... I'LL GO GET LUKE, RIGHT NOW!
DASH
I'LL GO GET HIM AND MAKE HIM APOLOGIZE TO YOU!!
I'LL MAKE HIM KOWTOW AND EVERY-THING!!

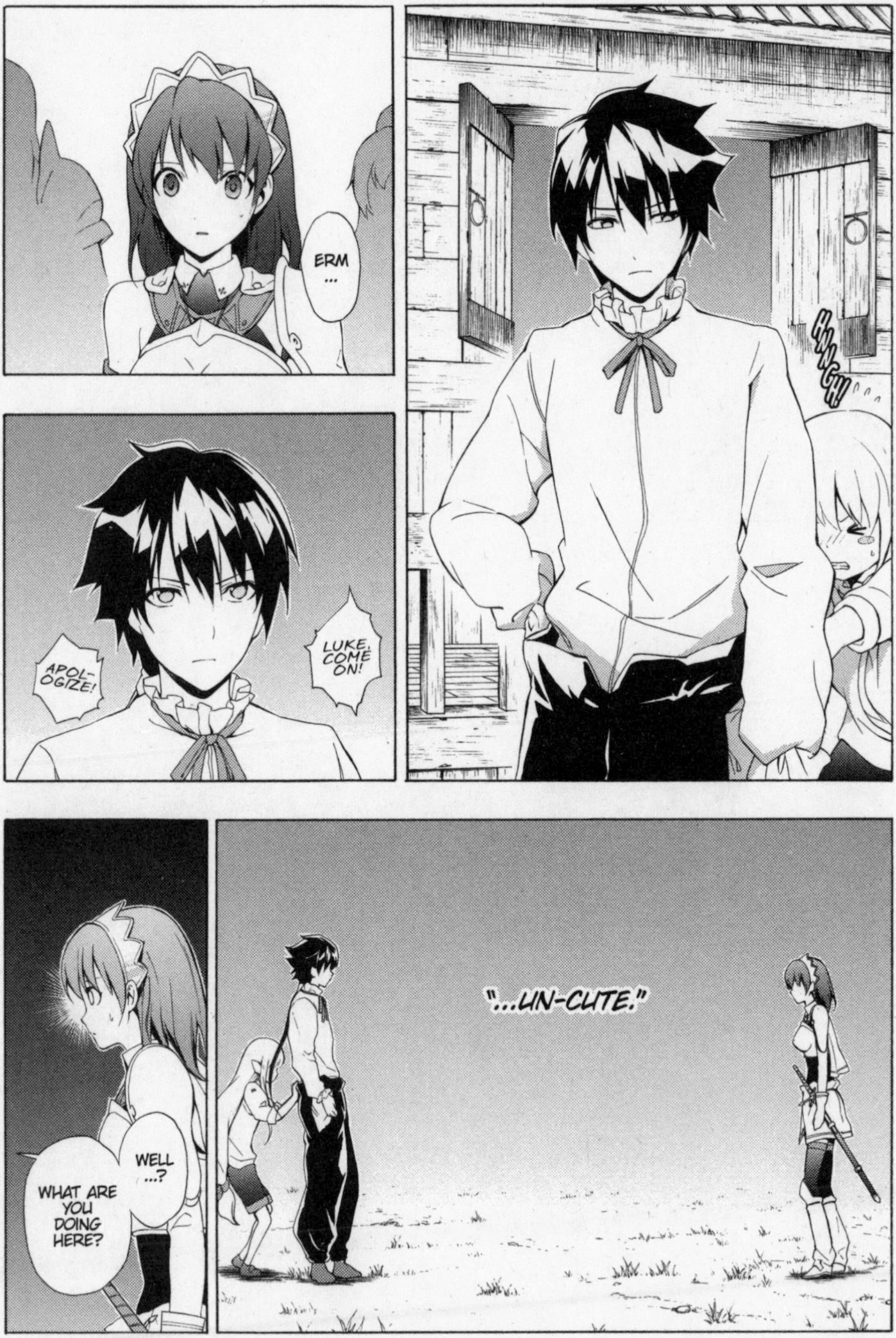
HNNGH!
ERM ...
LUKE, COME ON!
APOLOGIZE!
"...UN-CUTE."
WELL ...?
WHAT ARE YOU DOING HERE?

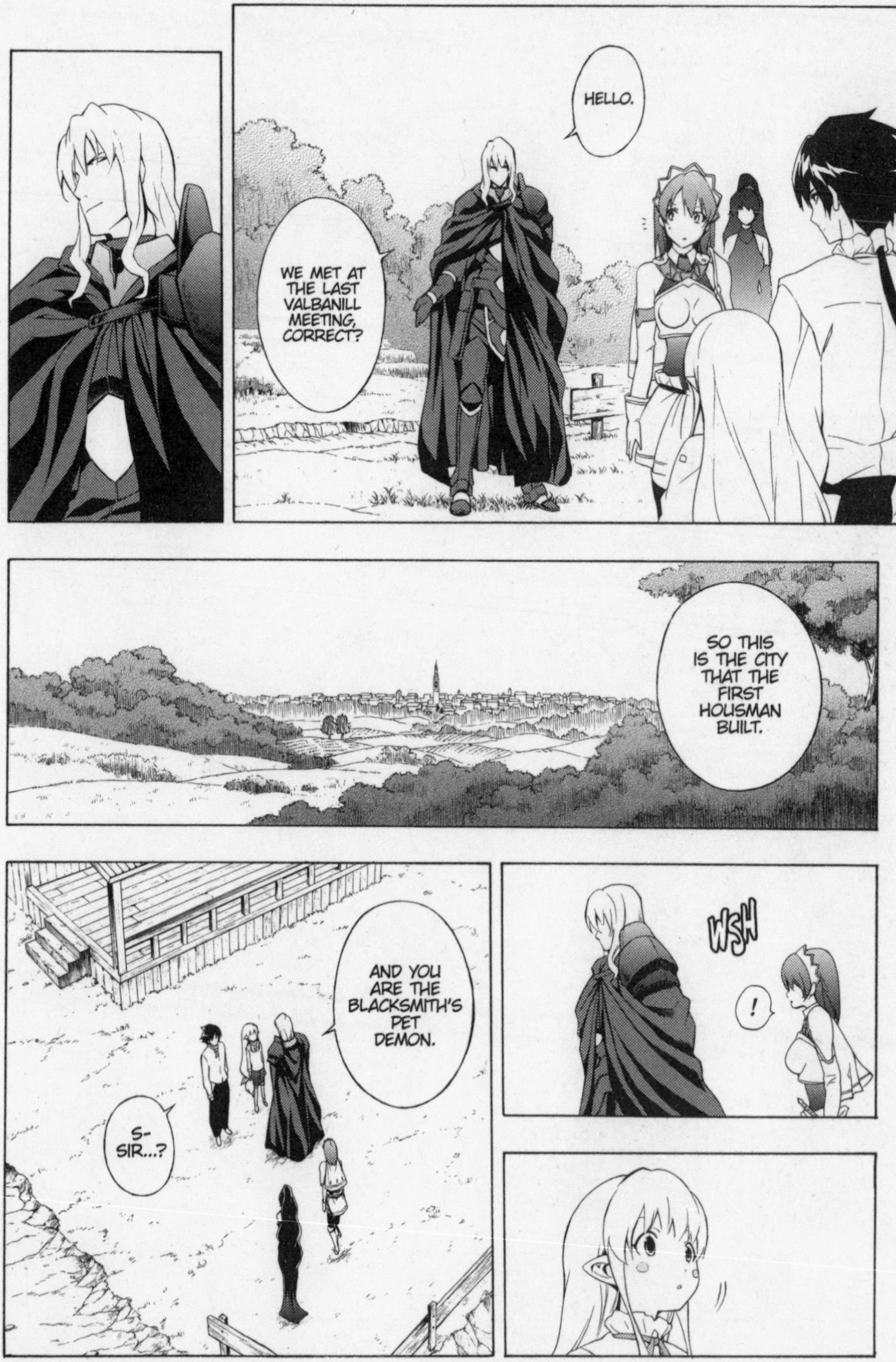
HELLO.
WE MET AT THE LAST VALBANILL MEETING, CORRECT?
SO THIS IS THE CITY THAT THE FIRST HOUSMAN BUILT.
WSH
!
AND YOU ARE THE BLACKSMITH'S PET DEMON.
S-SIR...?

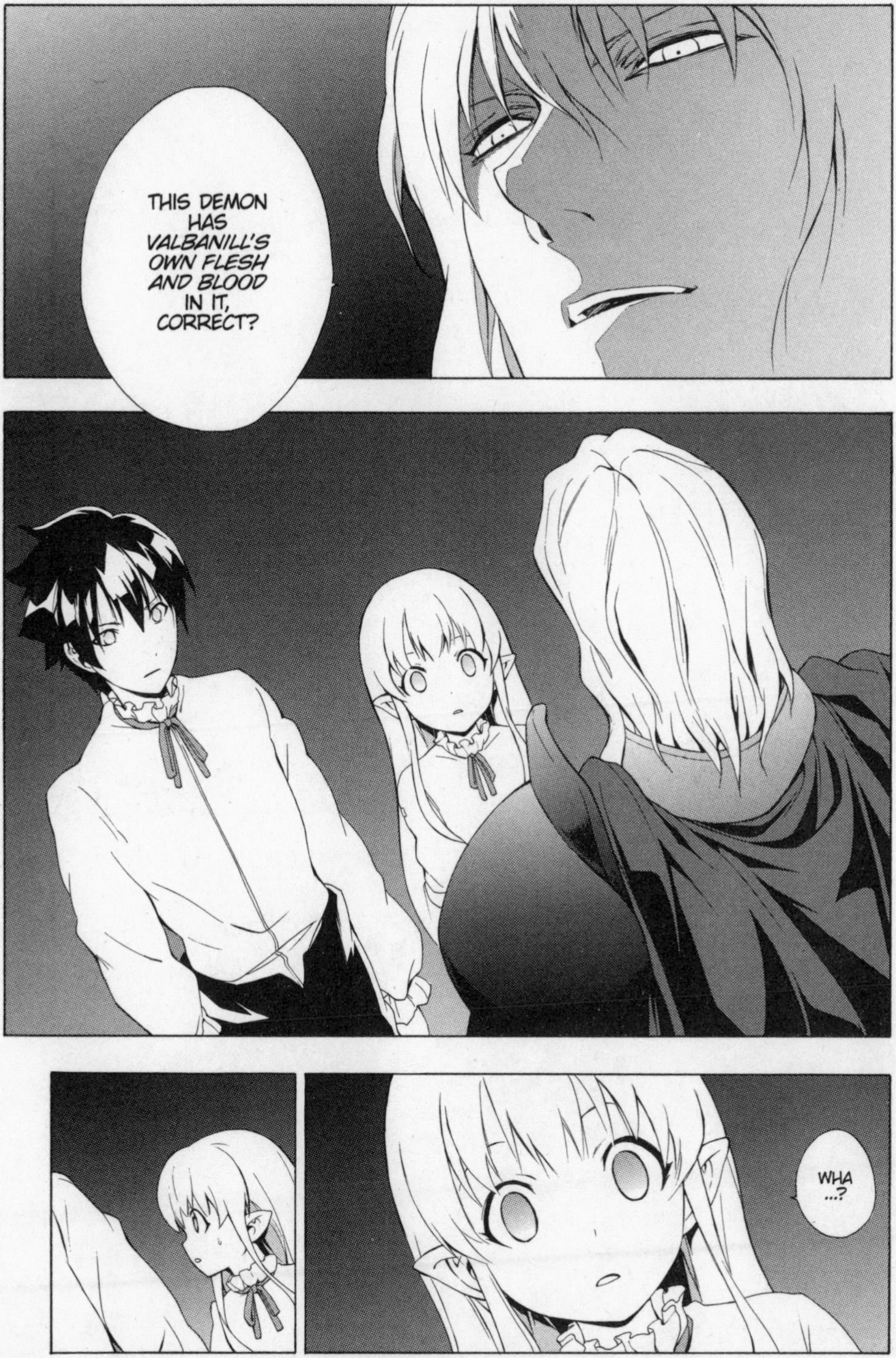
THIS DEMON HAS VALBANILL'S OWN FLESH AND BLOOD IN IT, CORRECT?
WHA ...?

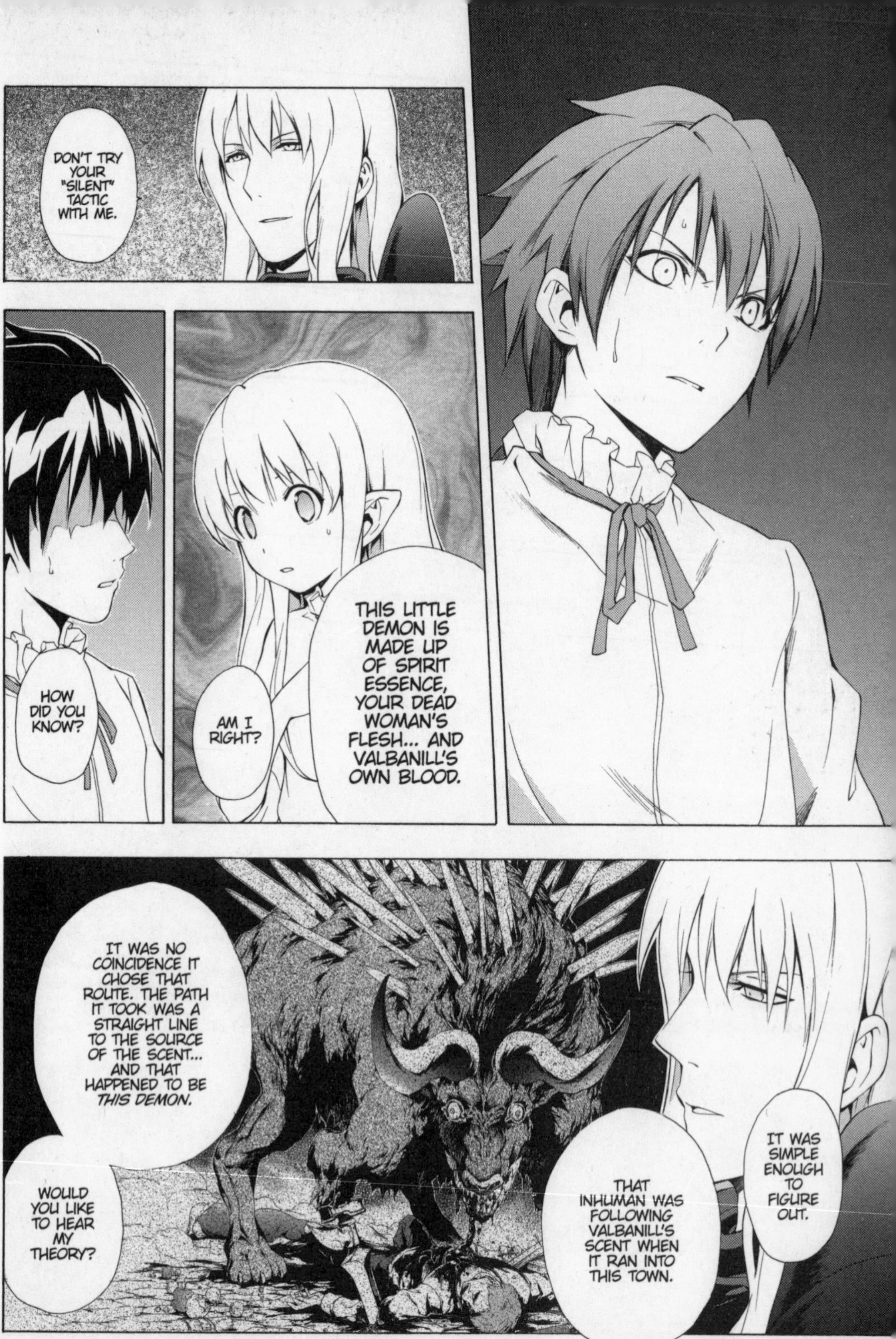
DON'T TRY YOUR "SILENT" TACTIC WITH ME.
THIS LITTLE DEMON IS MADE UP OF SPIRIT ESSENCE, YOUR DEAD WOMAN'S FLESH... AND VALBANILL'S OWN BLOOD.
AM I RIGHT?
HOW DID YOU KNOW?
IT WAS SIMPLE ENOUGH TO FIGURE OUT.
THAT INHUMAN WAS FOLLOWING VALBANILL'S SCENT WHEN IT RAN INTO THIS TOWN.
IT WAS NO COINCIDENCE IT CHOSE THAT ROUTE. THE PATH IT TOOK WAS A STRAIGHT LINE TO THE SOURCE OF THE SCENT... AND THAT HAPPENED TO BE *THIS DEMON.*
WOULD YOU LIKE TO HEAR MY THEORY?

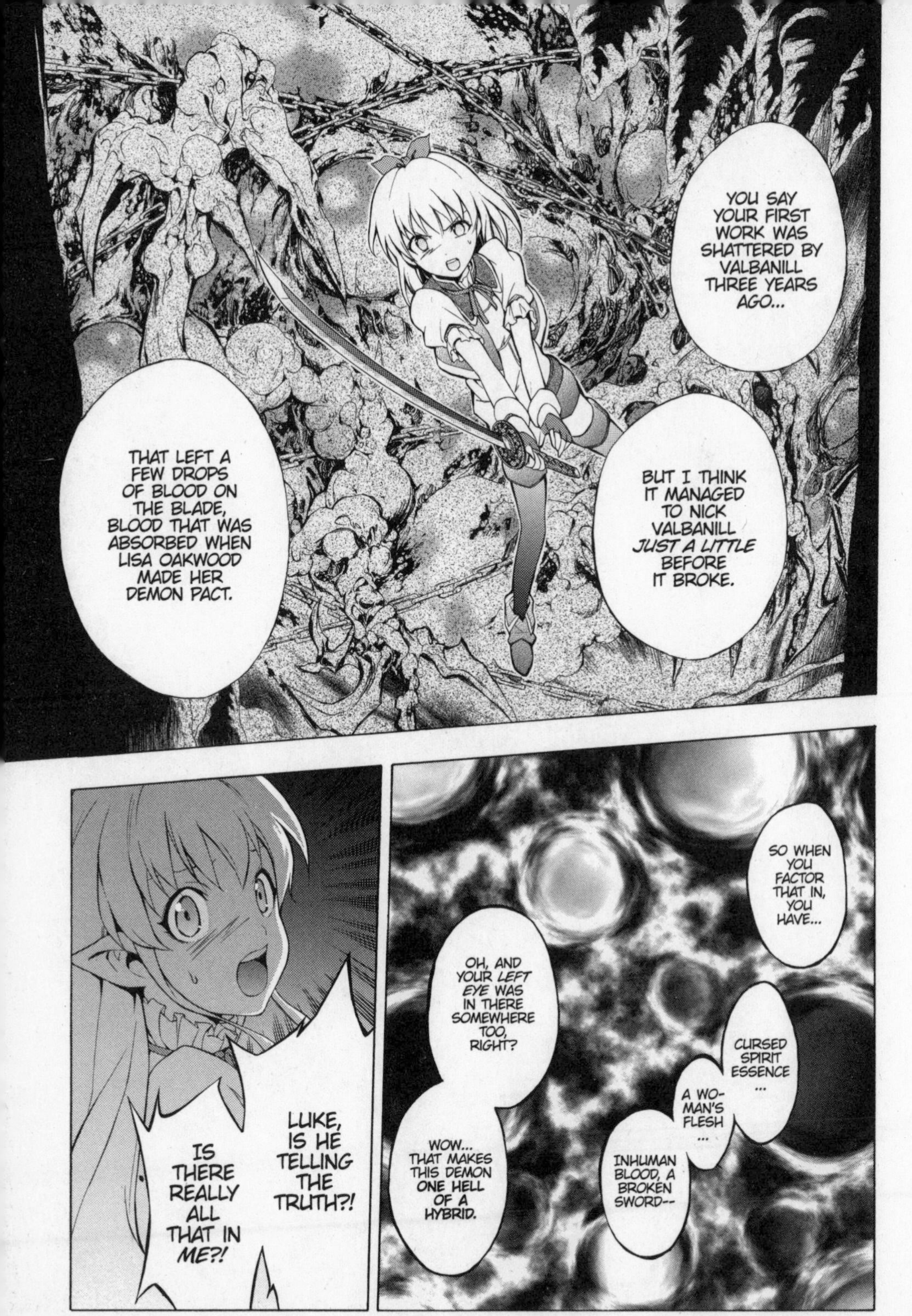
YOU SAY YOUR FIRST WORK WAS SHATTERED BY VALBANILL THREE YEARS AGO...
BUT I THINK IT MANAGED TO NICK VALBANILL *JUST A LITTLE* BEFORE IT BROKE.
THAT LEFT A FEW DROPS OF BLOOD ON THE BLADE, BLOOD THAT WAS ABSORBED WHEN LISA OAKWOOD MADE HER DEMON PACT.
SO WHEN YOU FACTOR THAT IN, YOU HAVE...
CURSED SPIRIT ESSENCE...
A WOMAN'S FLESH...
INHUMAN BLOOD, A BROKEN SWORD--
OH, AND YOUR *LEFT EYE* WAS IN THERE SOMEWHERE TOO, RIGHT?
WOW... THAT MAKES THIS DEMON ONE HELL OF A HYBRID.
LUKE, IS HE TELLING THE TRUTH?!
IS THERE REALLY ALL THAT IN *ME?!*

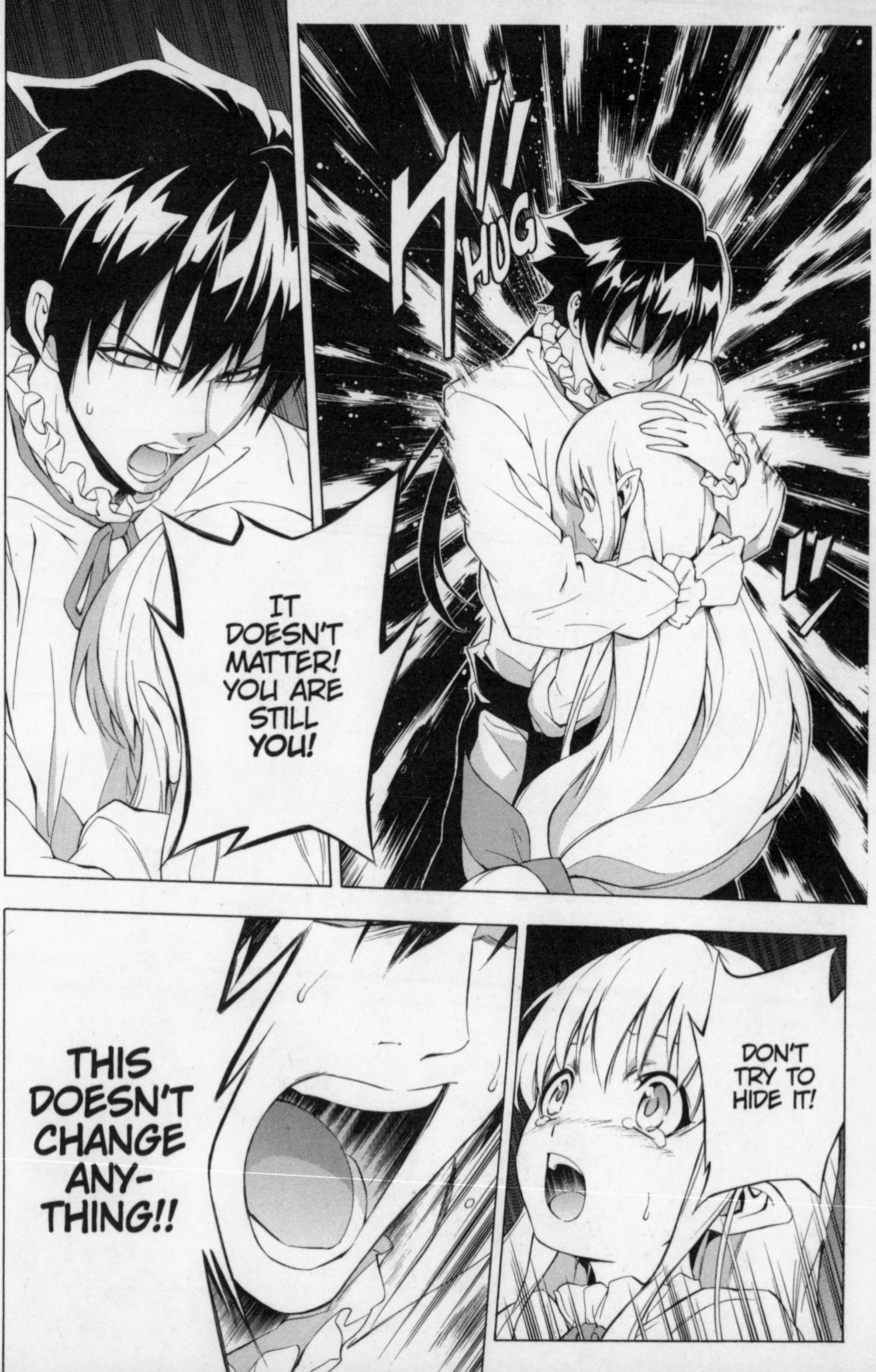
HUG
IT DOESN'T MATTER! YOU ARE STILL YOU!
DON'T TRY TO HIDE IT!
THIS DOESN'T CHANGE ANYTHING!!

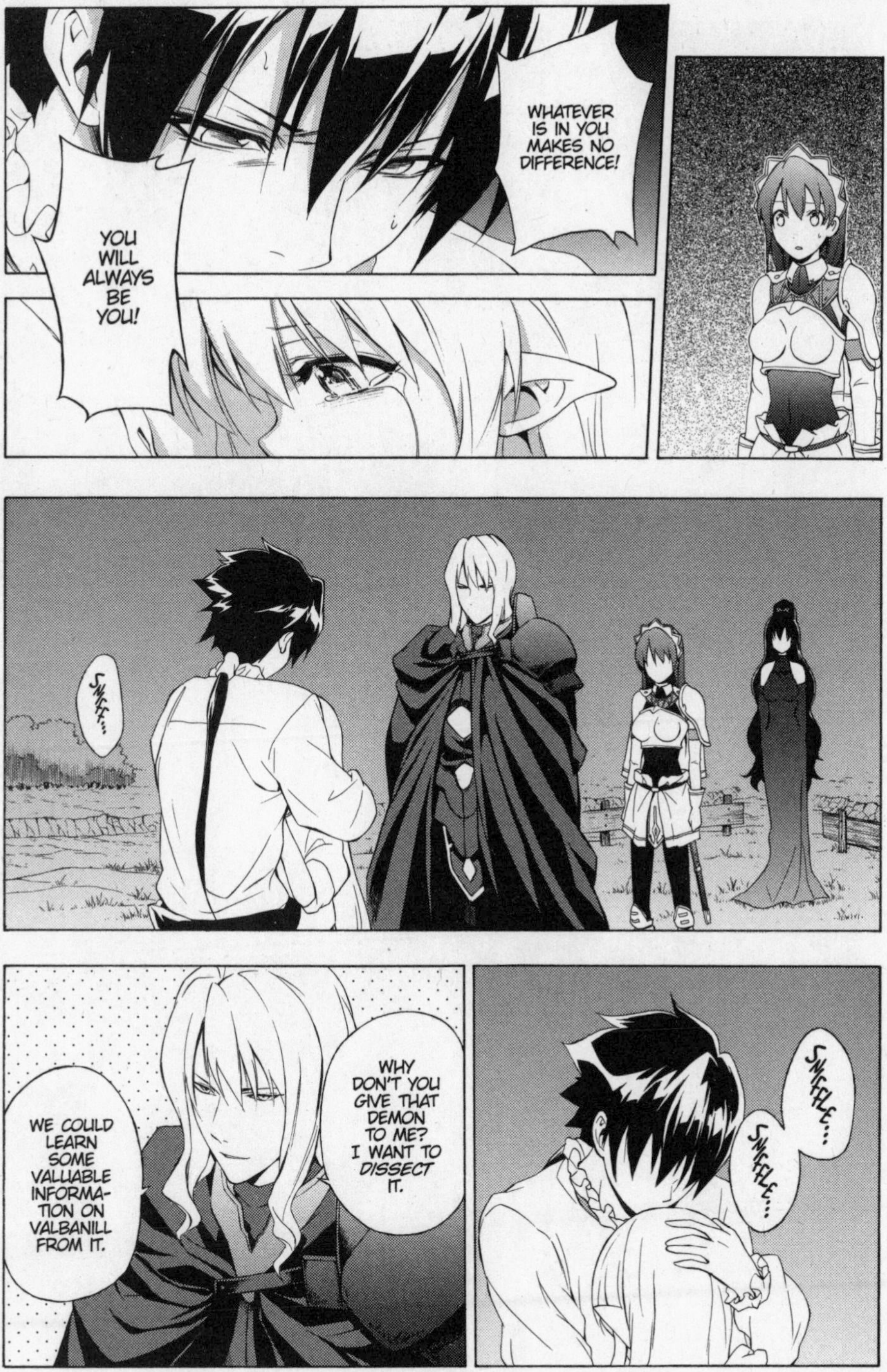
WHATEVER IS IN YOU MAKES NO DIFFERENCE!
YOU WILL ALWAYS BE YOU!
SNIFF...
SNIFFLE...
SNIFFLE...
WHY DON'T YOU GIVE THAT DEMON TO ME? I WANT TO *DISSECT* IT.
WE COULD LEARN SOME VALUABLE INFORMATION ON VALBANILL FROM IT.

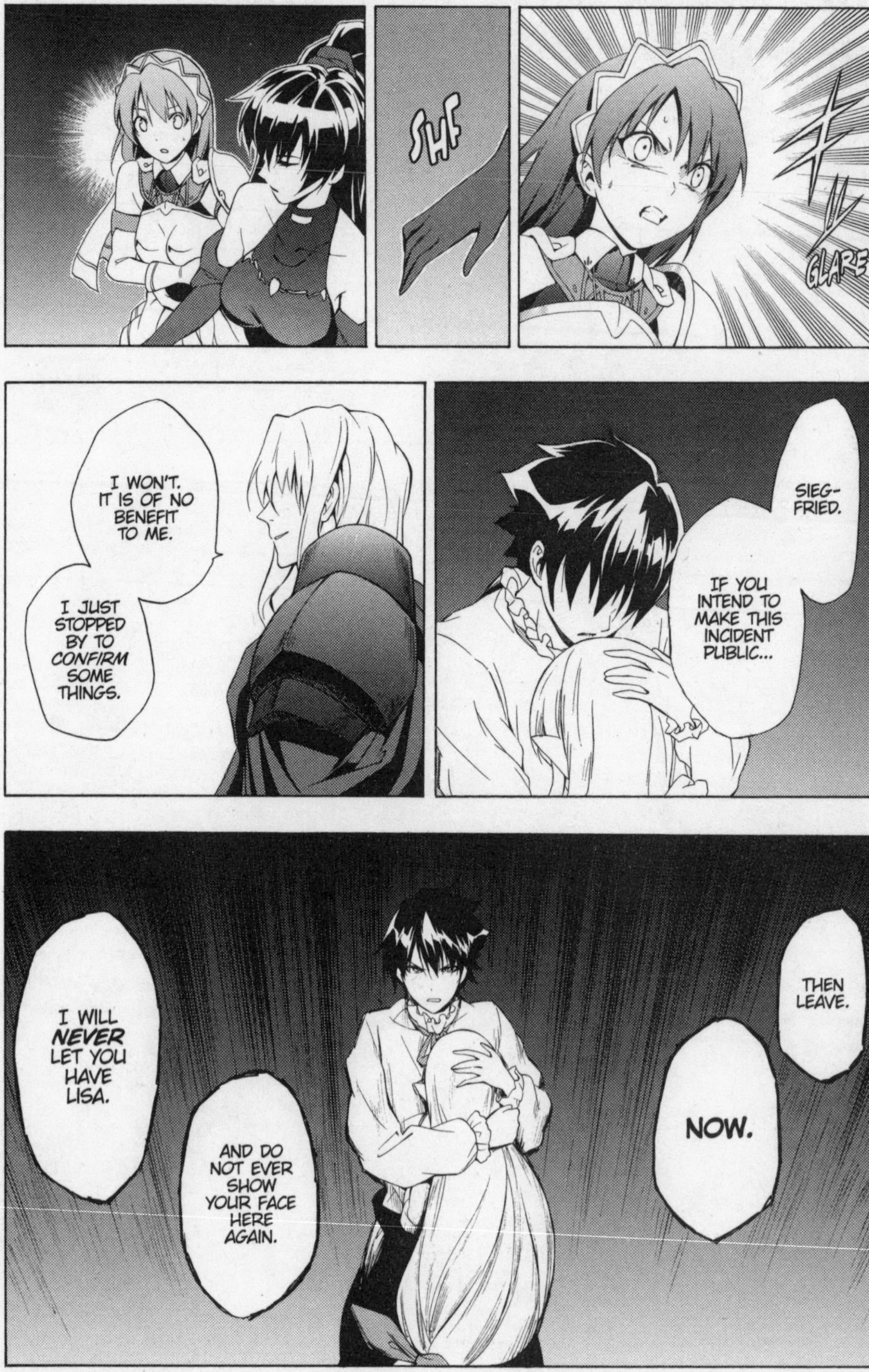
GLARE
SHF
SIEG-FRIED.
IF YOU INTEND TO MAKE THIS INCIDENT PUBLIC...
I WON'T. IT IS OF NO BENEFIT TO ME.
I JUST STOPPED BY TO *CONFIRM* SOME THINGS.
THEN LEAVE.
NOW.
I WILL **NEVER** LET YOU HAVE LISA.
AND DO NOT EVER SHOW YOUR FACE HERE AGAIN.

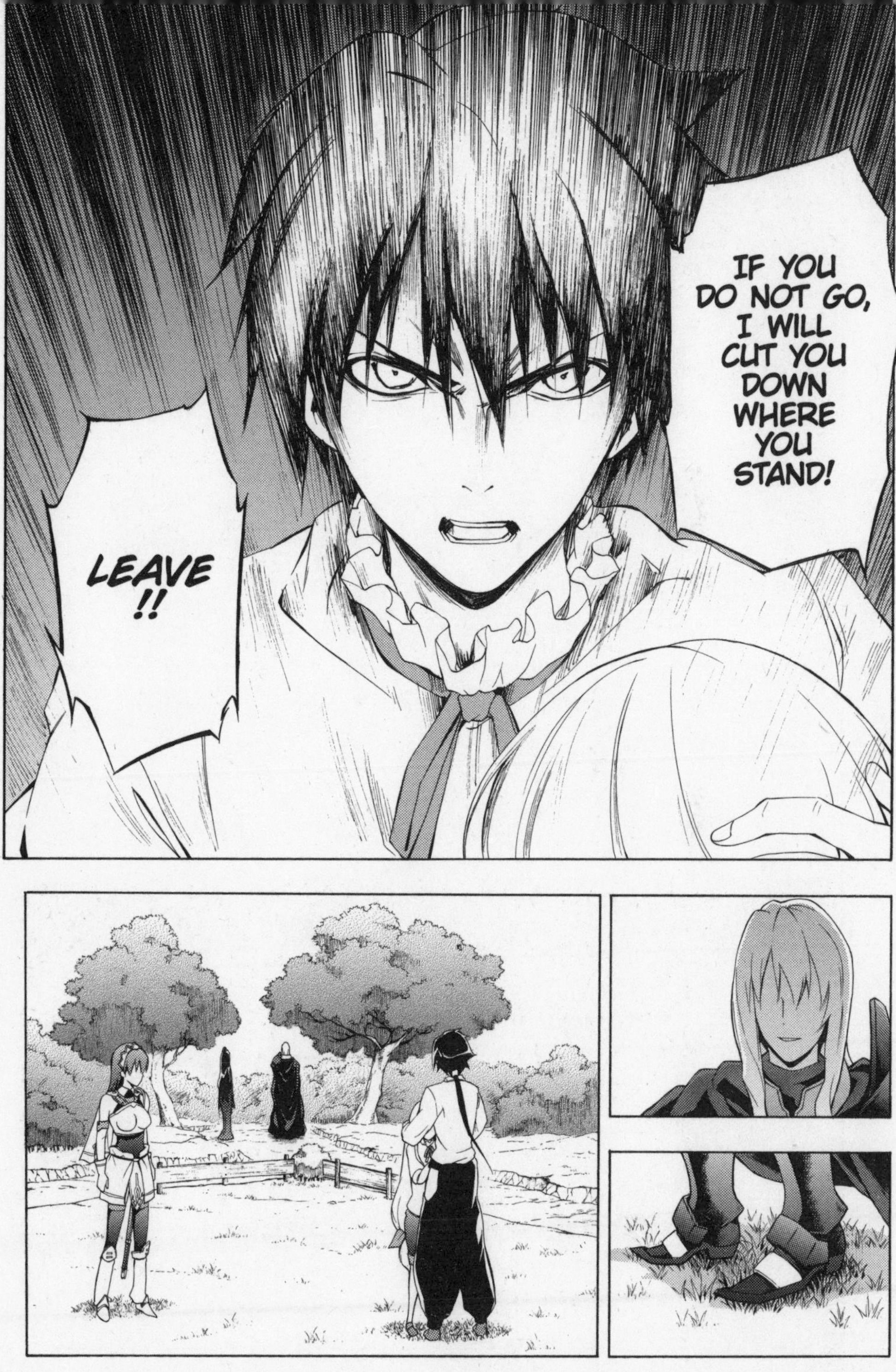
IF YOU DO NOT GO, I WILL CUT YOU DOWN WHERE YOU STAND!
LEAVE !!

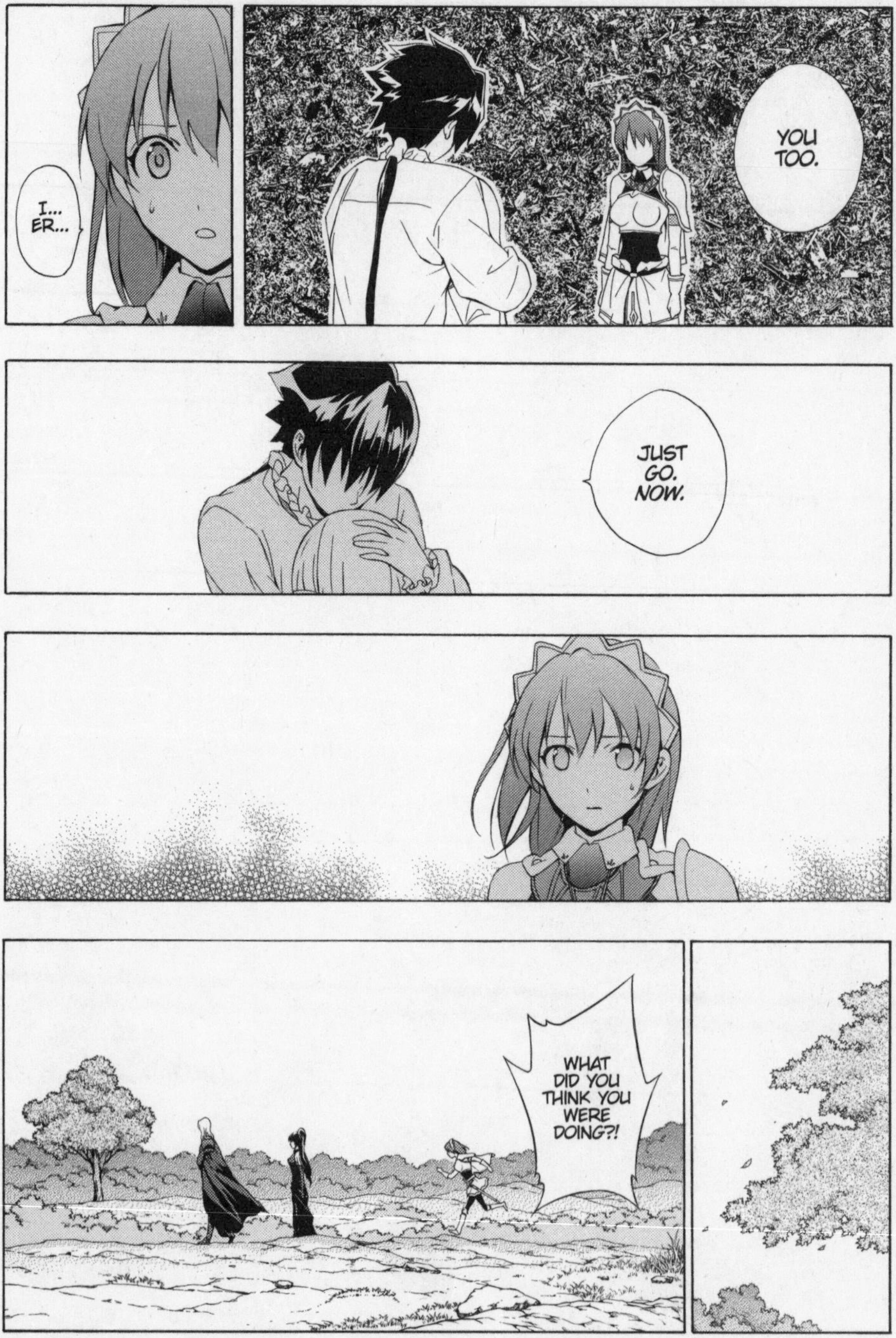
YOU TOO.
I... ER...
JUST GO. NOW.
WHAT DID YOU THINK YOU WERE DOING?!

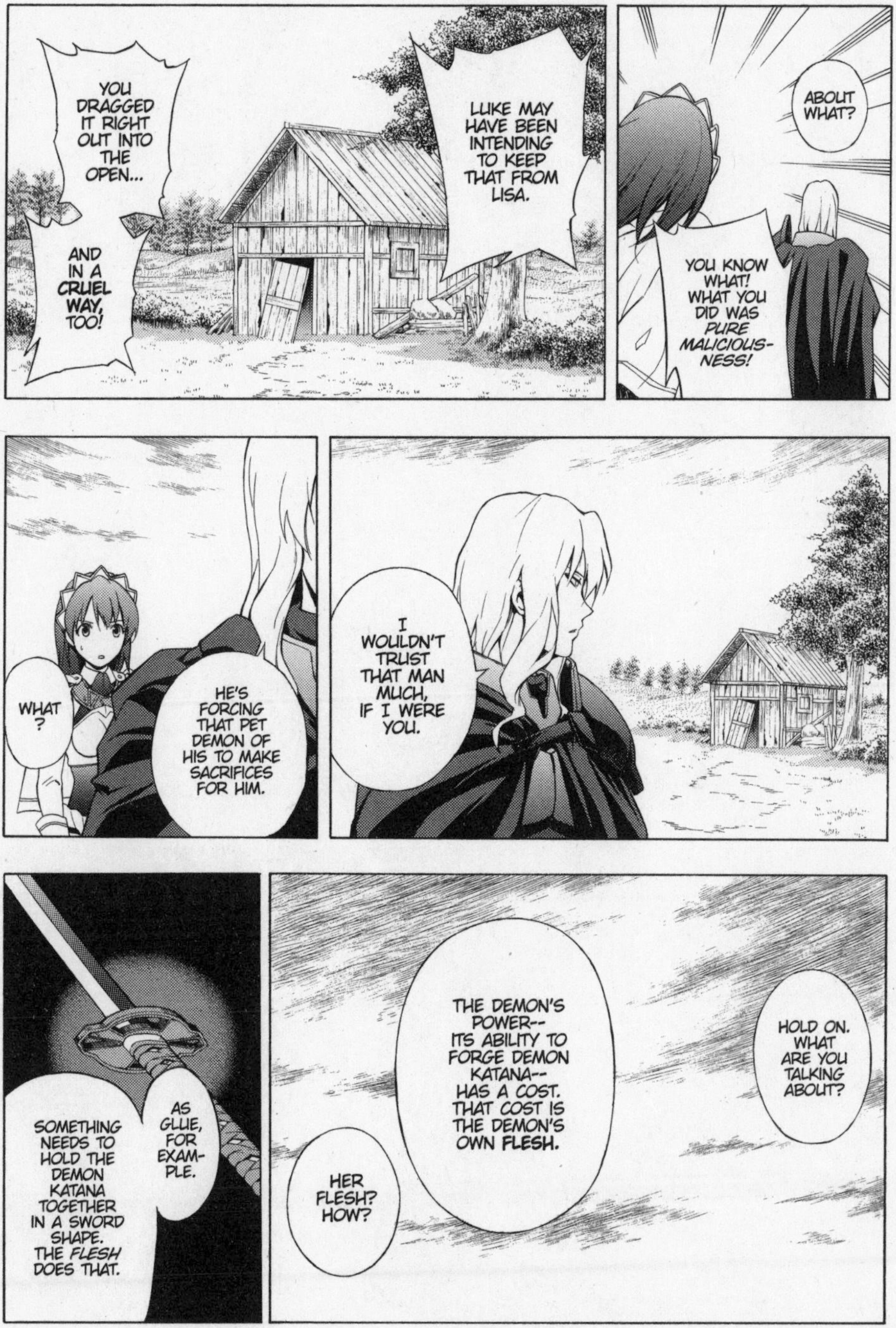
ABOUT WHAT?
YOU KNOW WHAT! WHAT YOU DID WAS PURE MALICIOUSNESS!
LUKE MAY HAVE BEEN INTENDING TO KEEP THAT FROM LISA.
YOU DRAGGED IT RIGHT OUT INTO THE OPEN...
AND IN A CRUEL WAY, TOO!
I WOULDN'T TRUST THAT MAN MUCH, IF I WERE YOU.
HE'S FORCING THAT PET DEMON OF HIS TO MAKE SACRIFICES FOR HIM.
WHAT?
HOLD ON. WHAT ARE YOU TALKING ABOUT?
THE DEMON'S POWER-- ITS ABILITY TO FORGE DEMON KATANA-- HAS A COST. THAT COST IS THE DEMON'S OWN FLESH.
HER FLESH? HOW?
AS GLUE, FOR EXAMPLE.
SOMETHING NEEDS TO HOLD THE DEMON KATANA TOGETHER IN A SWORD SHAPE. THE FLESH DOES THAT.

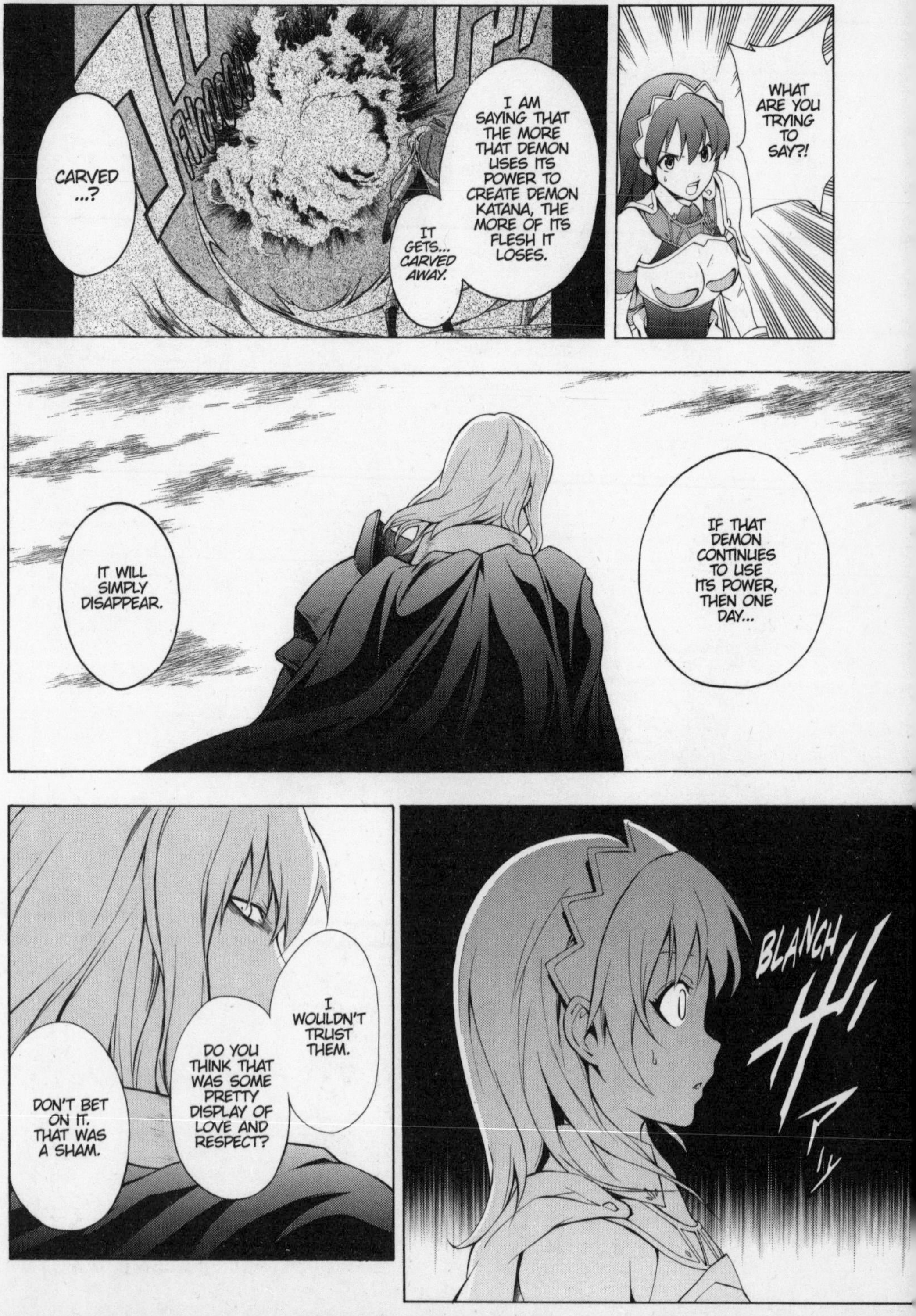
WHAT ARE YOU TRYING TO SAY?!
I AM SAYING THAT THE MORE THAT DEMON USES ITS POWER TO CREATE DEMON KATANA, THE MORE OF ITS FLESH IT LOSES.
IT GETS... CARVED AWAY.
CARVED ...?
IF THAT DEMON CONTINUES TO USE ITS POWER, THEN ONE DAY...
IT WILL SIMPLY DISAPPEAR.
BLANCH
I WOULDN'T TRUST THEM.
DO YOU THINK THAT WAS SOME PRETTY DISPLAY OF LOVE AND RESPECT?
DON'T BET ON IT. THAT WAS A SHAM.

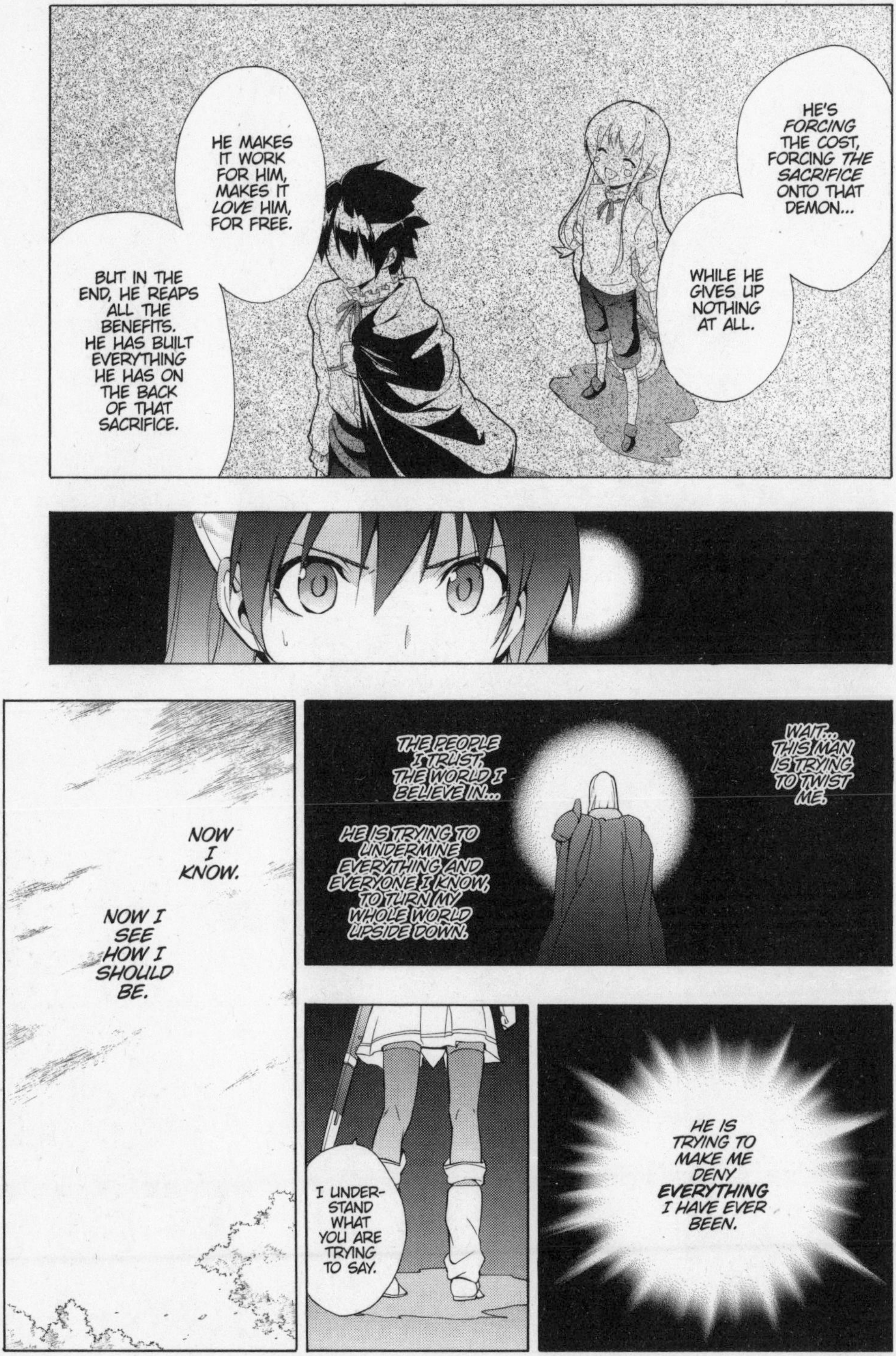
HE'S FORCING THE COST, FORCING THE SACRIFICE ONTO THAT DEMON...
WHILE HE GIVES UP NOTHING AT ALL.
HE MAKES IT WORK FOR HIM, MAKES IT LOVE HIM, FOR FREE.
BUT IN THE END, HE REAPS ALL THE BENEFITS. HE HAS BUILT EVERYTHING HE HAS ON THE BACK OF THAT SACRIFICE.
WAIT... THIS MAN IS TRYING TO TWIST ME.
THE PEOPLE I TRUST, THE WORLD I BELIEVE IN...
HE IS TRYING TO UNDERMINE EVERYTHING AND EVERYONE I KNOW, TO TURN MY WHOLE WORLD UPSIDE DOWN.
HE IS TRYING TO MAKE ME DENY EVERYTHING I HAVE EVER BEEN.
I UNDERSTAND WHAT YOU ARE TRYING TO SAY.
NOW I KNOW.
NOW I SEE HOW I SHOULD BE.

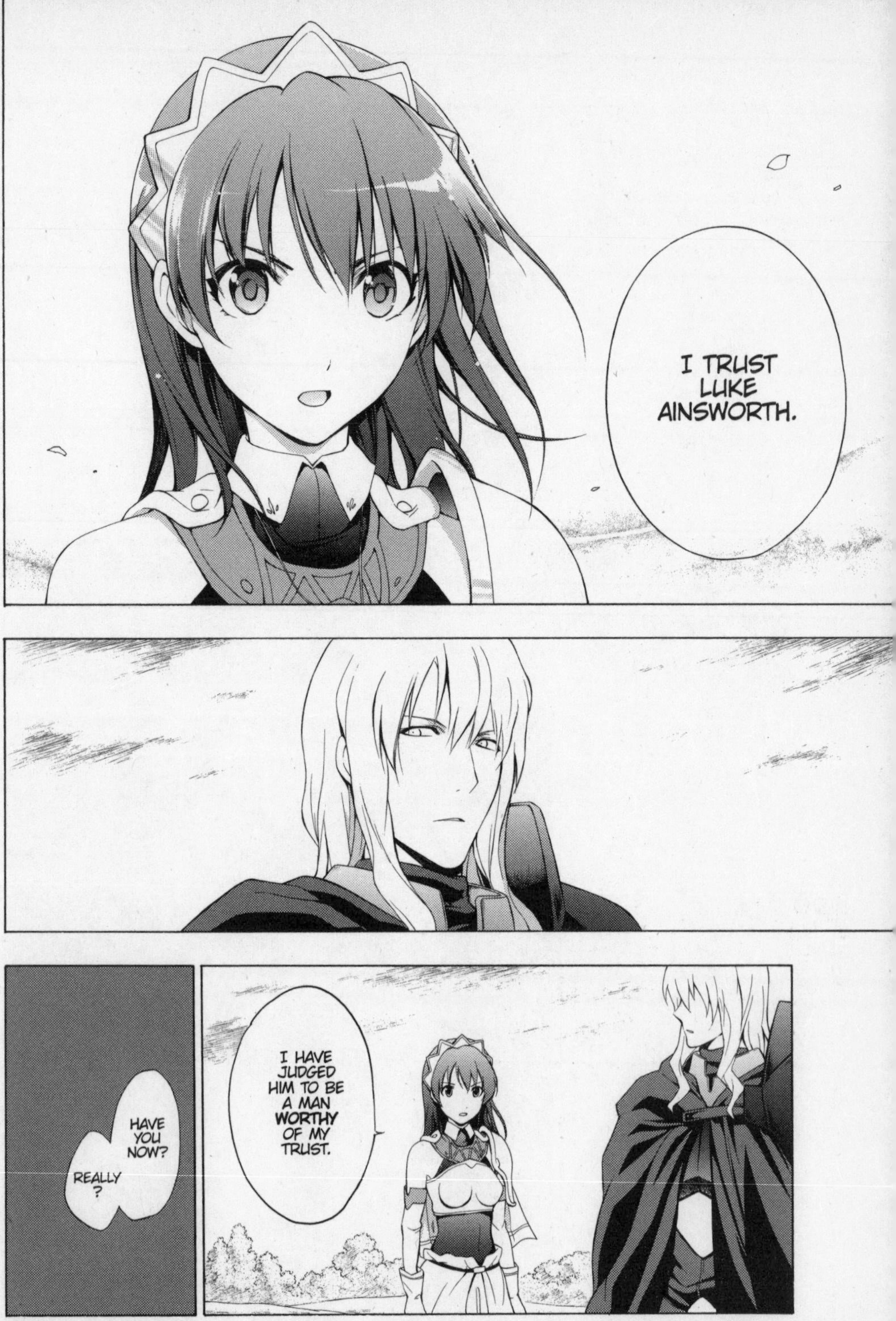
I TRUST LUKE AINSWORTH.
I HAVE JUDGED HIM TO BE A MAN WORTHY OF MY TRUST.
HAVE YOU NOW?
REALLY?

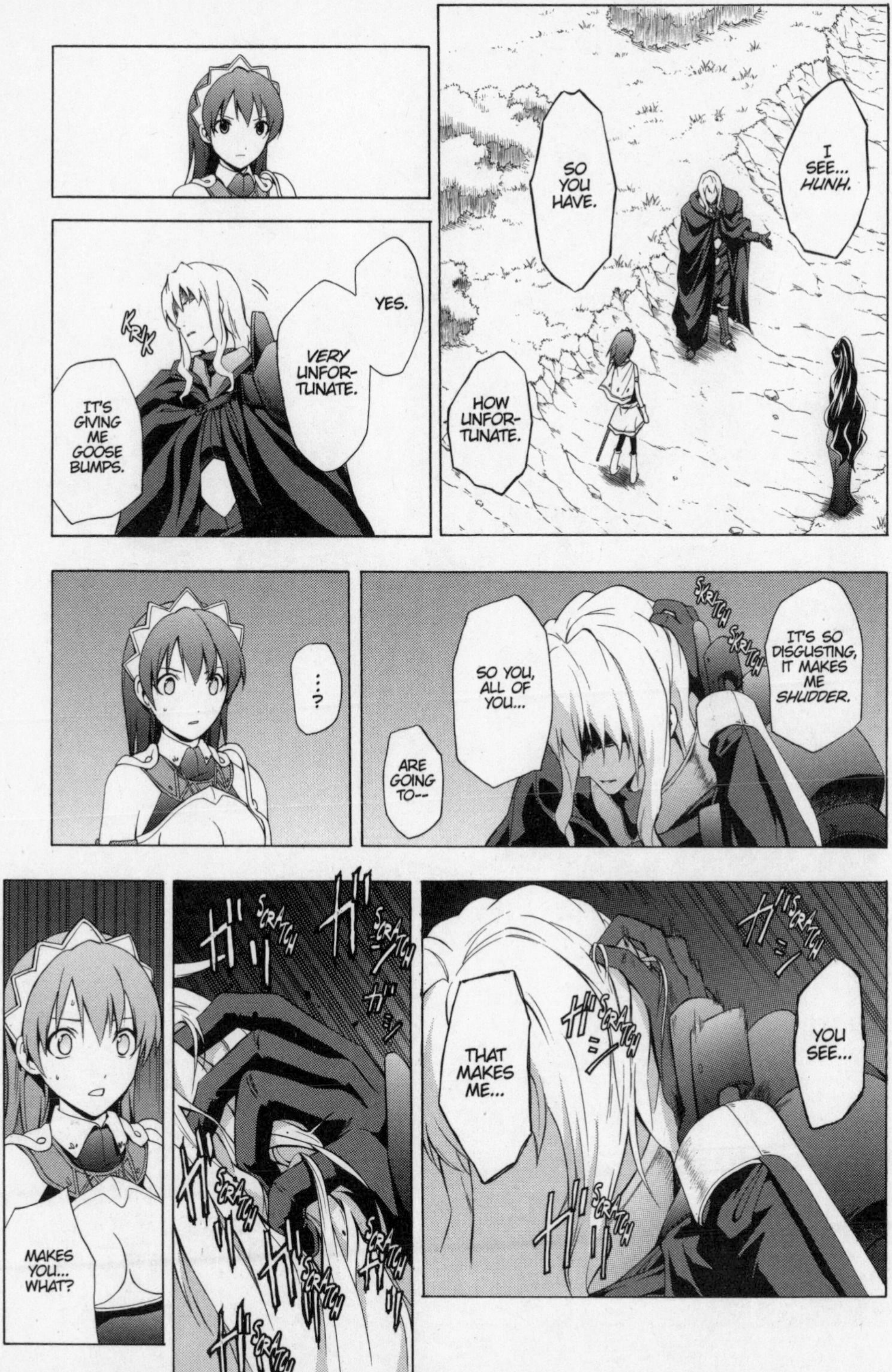
I SEE... HUNH.
SO YOU HAVE.
HOW UNFORTUNATE.
KRIK
YES.
VERY UNFORTUNATE.
IT'S GIVING ME GOOSE BUMPS.
SCRATCH
SCRATCH
IT'S SO DISGUSTING, IT MAKES ME SHUDDER.
SO YOU, ALL OF YOU...
ARE GOING TO--
...?
SCRATCH
YOU SEE...
SCRATCH
THAT MAKES ME...
SCRATCH
SCRATCH
SCRATCH
SCRATCH
SCRATCH
SCRATCH
SCRATCH
MAKES YOU... WHAT?

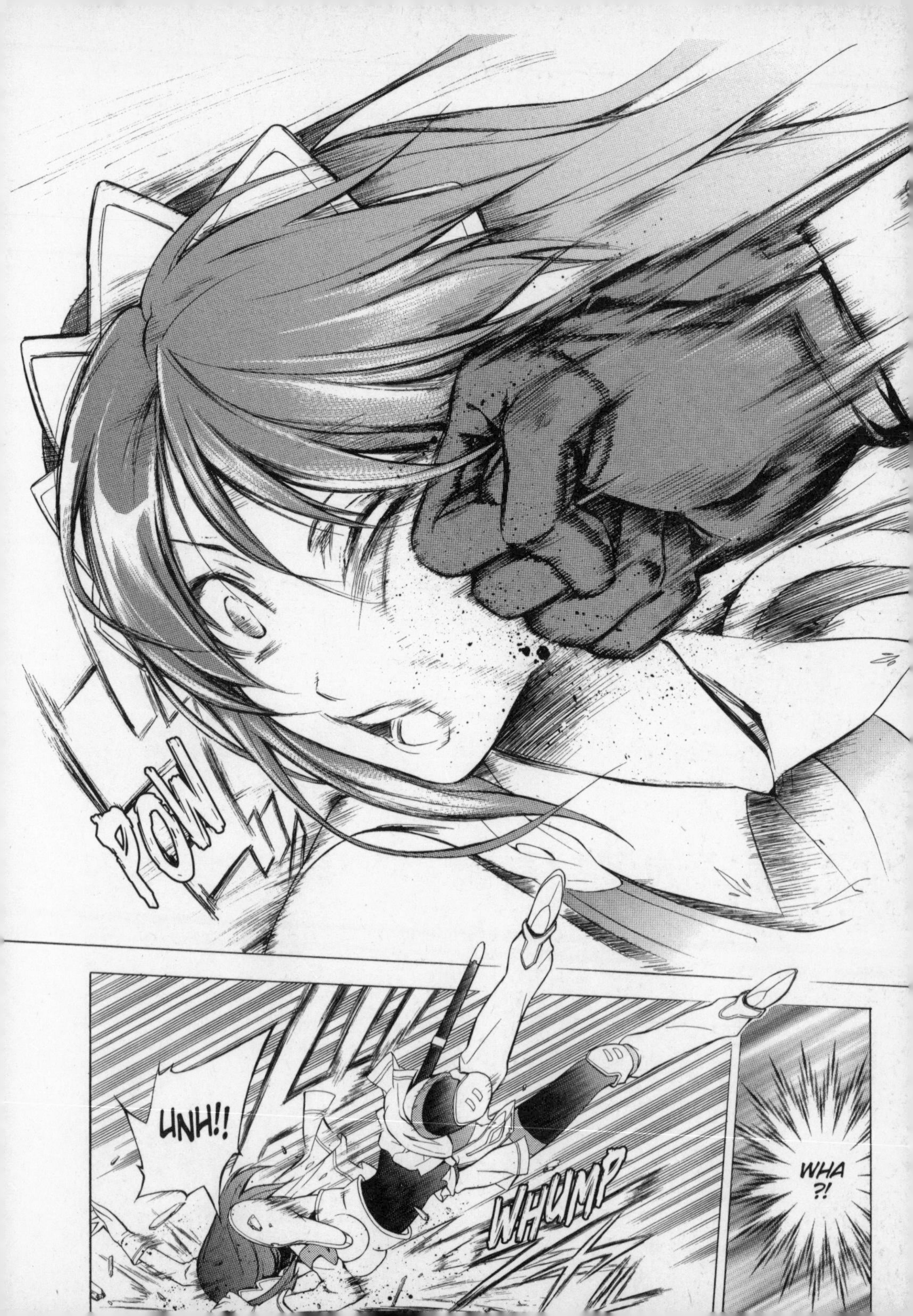
POW
WHA ?!
WHUMP
UNH!!

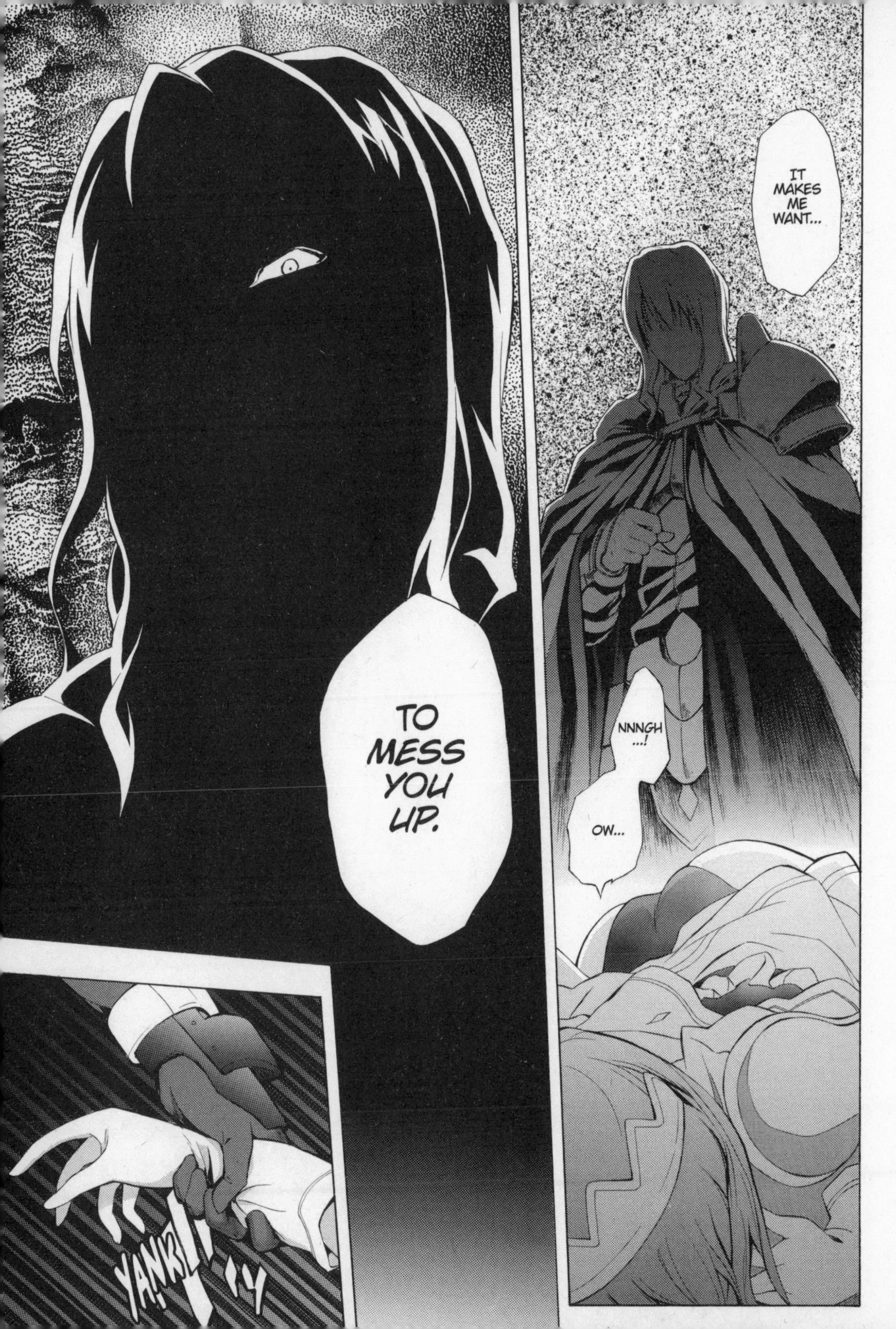
IT MAKES ME WANT...
NNNGH ...!
OW...
TO MESS YOU UP.
YANK!

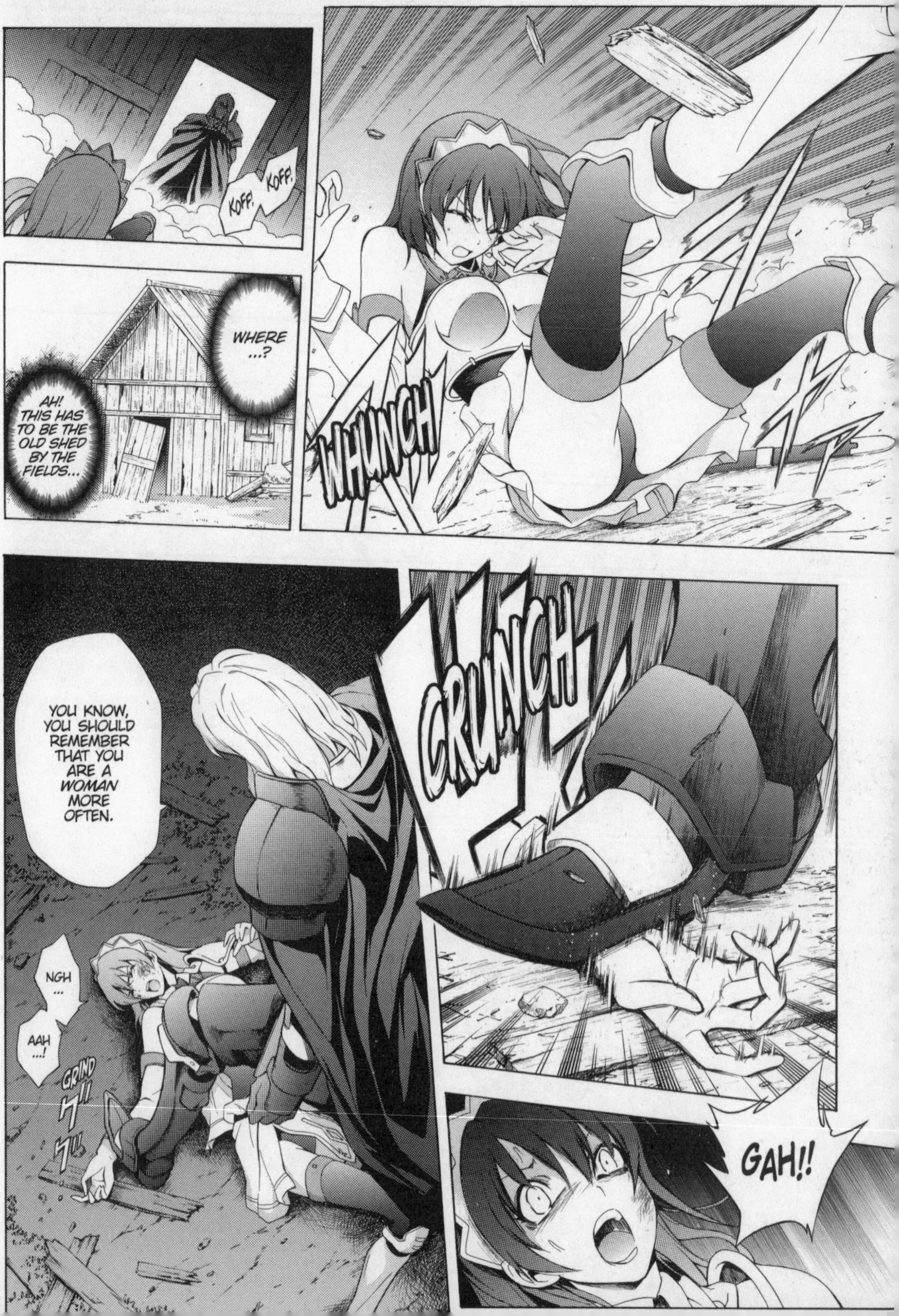
WHUNCH
KOFF! KOFF!
WHERE ...?
AH! THIS HAS TO BE THE OLD SHED BY THE FIELDS...
CRUNCH
GAH!!
YOU KNOW, YOU SHOULD REMEMBER THAT YOU ARE A *WOMAN* MORE OFTEN.
NGH ...
AAH ...!
GRIND

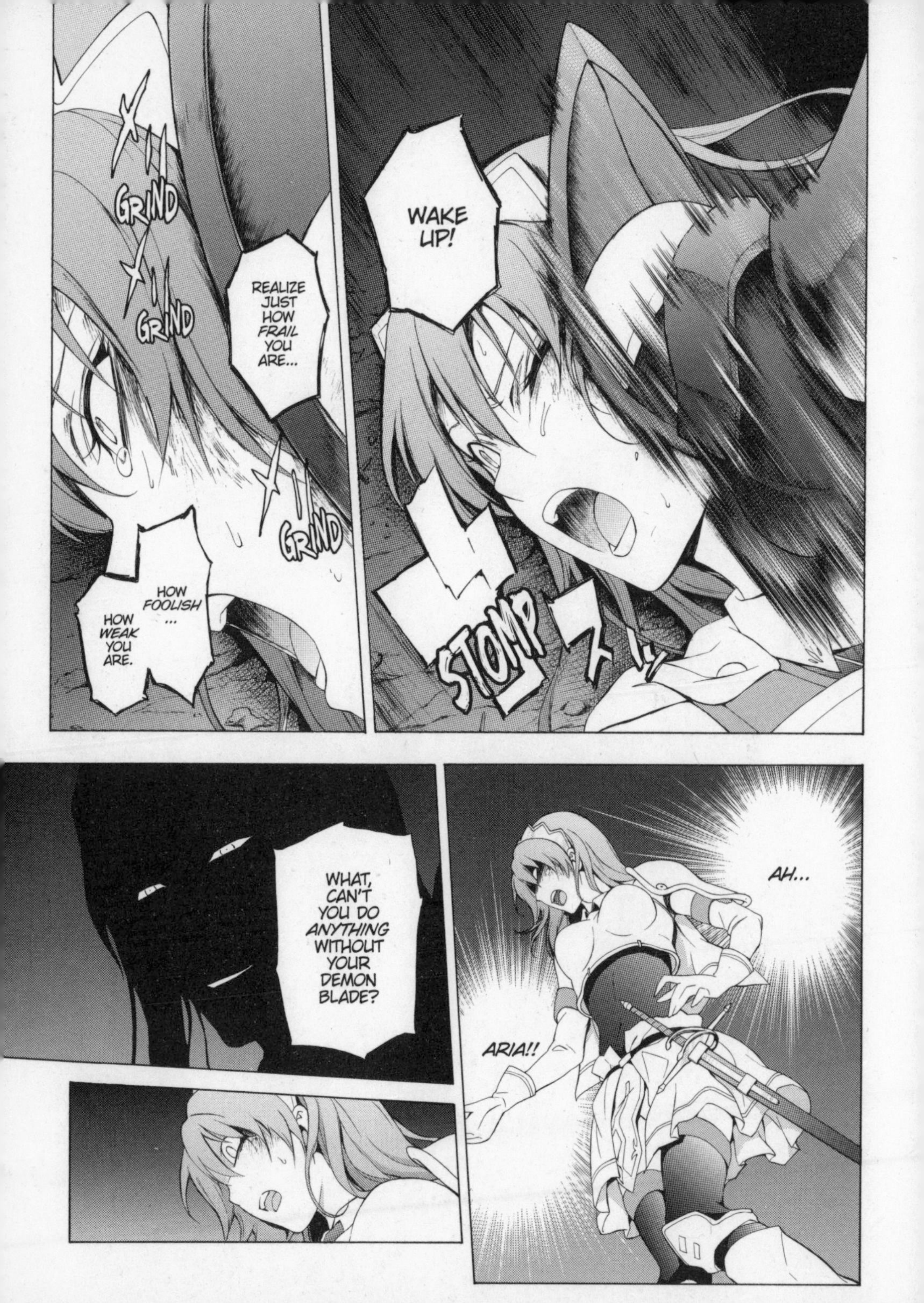
WAKE UP!
STOMP
REALIZE JUST HOW FRAIL YOU ARE...
GRIND
GRIND
GRIND
HOW FOOLISH...
HOW WEAK YOU ARE.
AH...
ARIA!!
WHAT, CAN'T YOU DO ANYTHING WITHOUT YOUR DEMON BLADE?

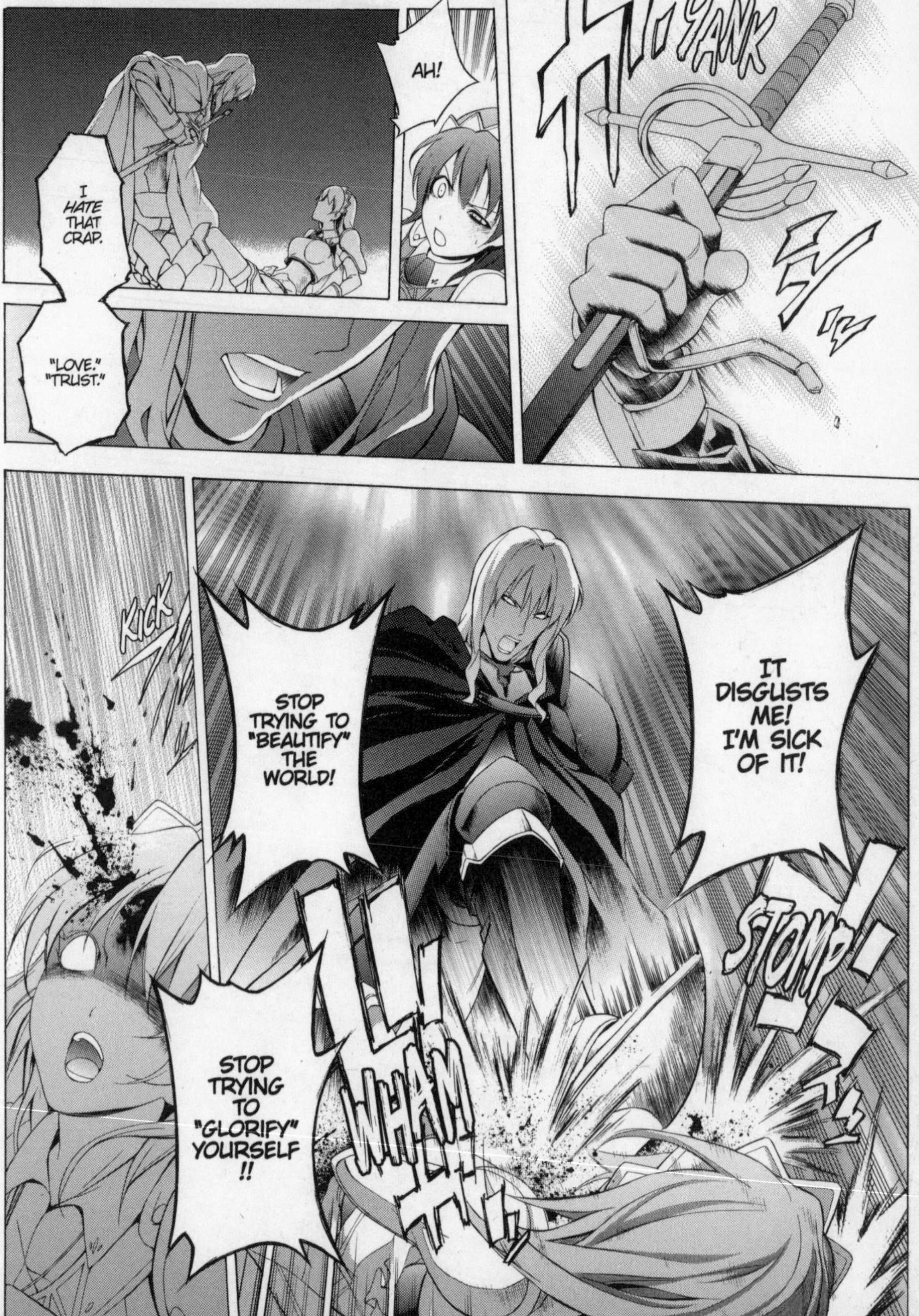
YANK
AH!
I HATE THAT CRAP.
"LOVE." "TRUST."
IT DISGUSTS ME! I'M SICK OF IT!
STOP TRYING TO "BEAUTIFY" THE WORLD!
STOMP!
WHAM
STOP TRYING TO "GLORIFY" YOURSELF !!
KICK

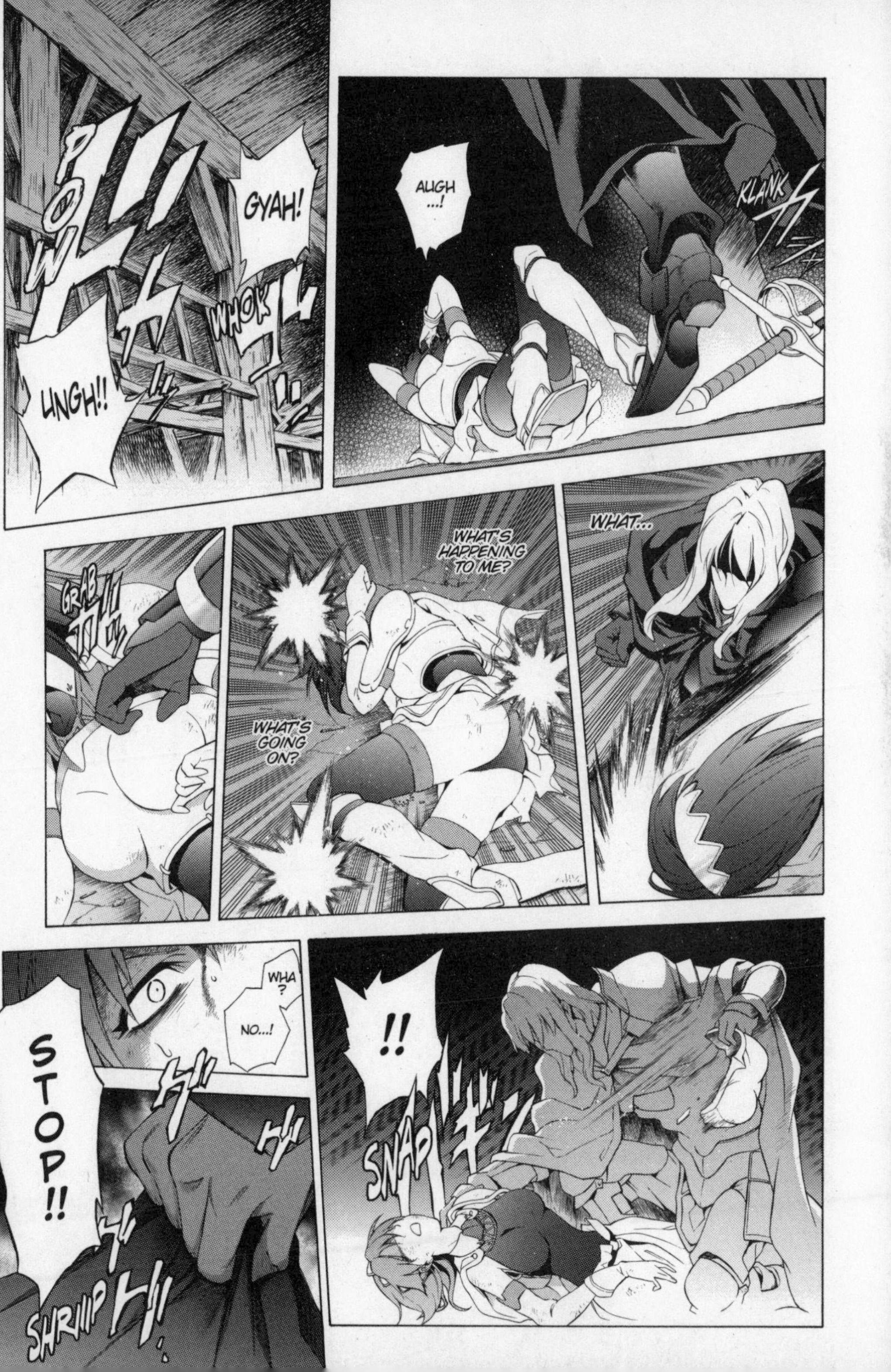
AUGH ...!
KLANK
GYAH!
POW
WHOK
UNGH!!
WHAT...
WHAT'S HAPPENING TO ME?
WHAT'S GOING ON?
GRAB
!!
SNAP
WHA?
NO...!
STOP!!
SHRIIP

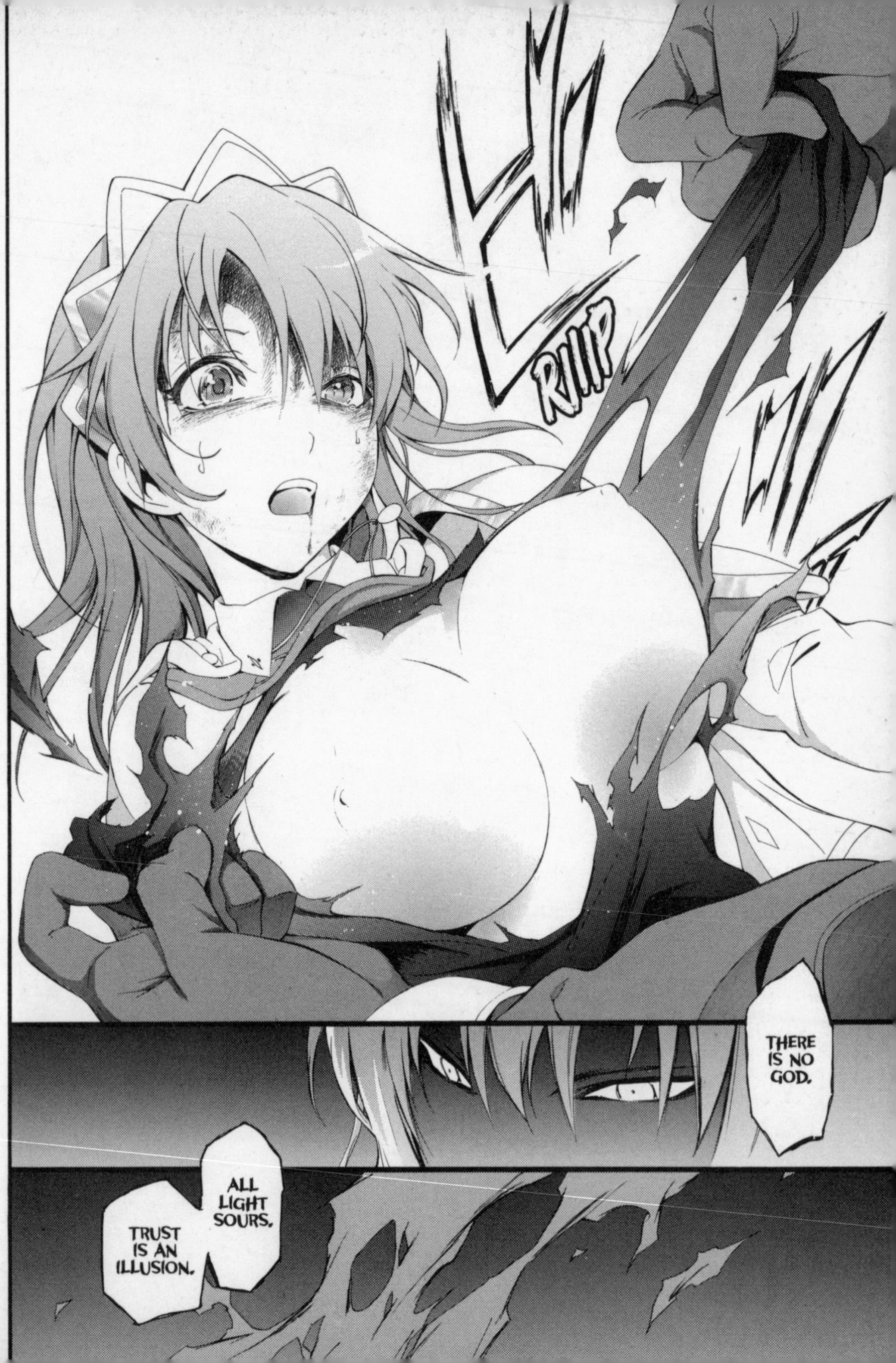
RIIIP
THERE IS NO GOD.
ALL LIGHT SOURS.
TRUST IS AN ILLUSION.

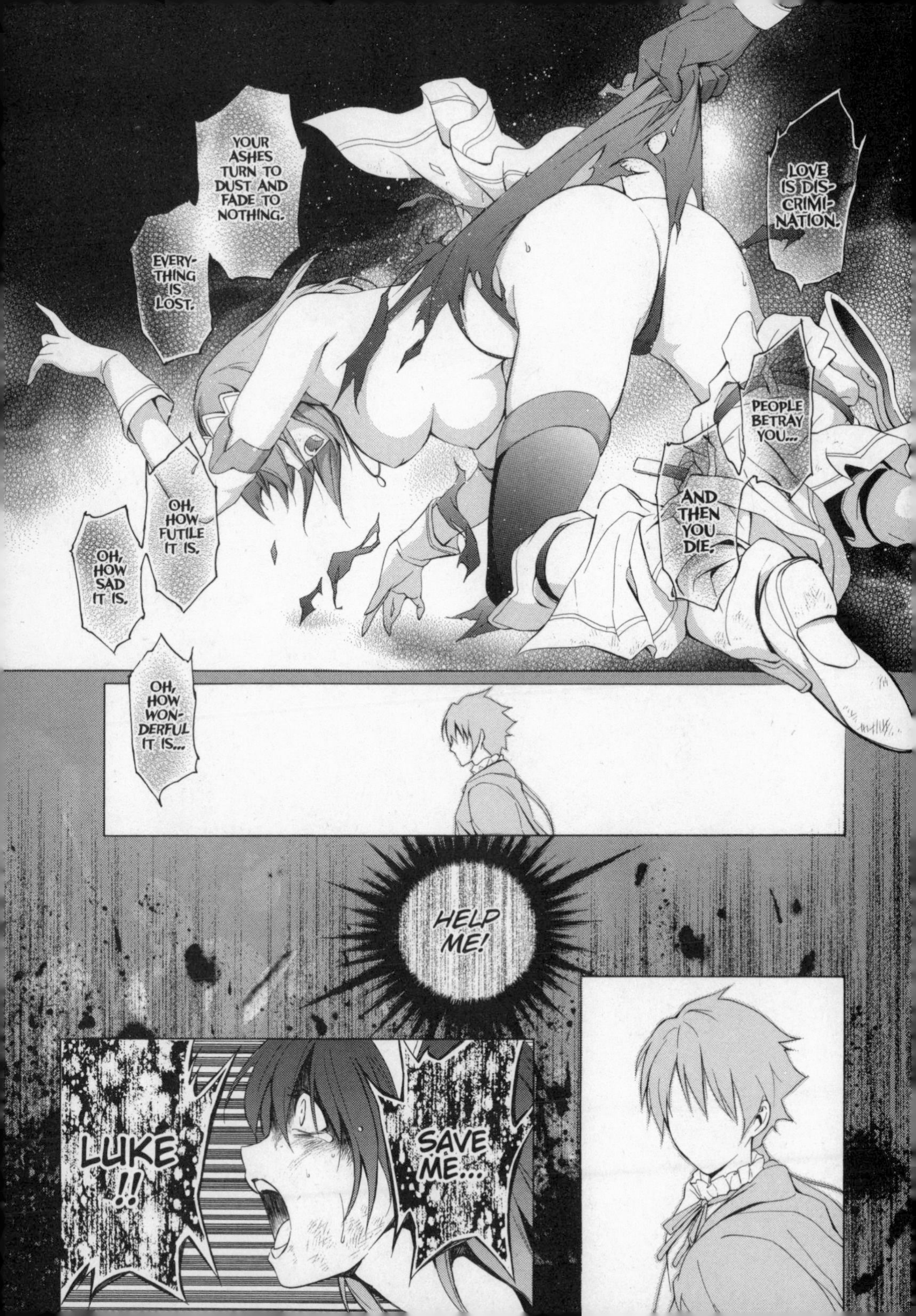
LOVE IS DISCRIMINATION.
PEOPLE BETRAY YOU...
AND THEN YOU DIE.
YOUR ASHES TURN TO DUST AND FADE TO NOTHING.
EVERYTHING IS LOST.
OH, HOW FUTILE IT IS.
OH, HOW SAD IT IS.
OH, HOW WONDERFUL IT IS...
HELP ME!
SAVE ME...
LUKE!!

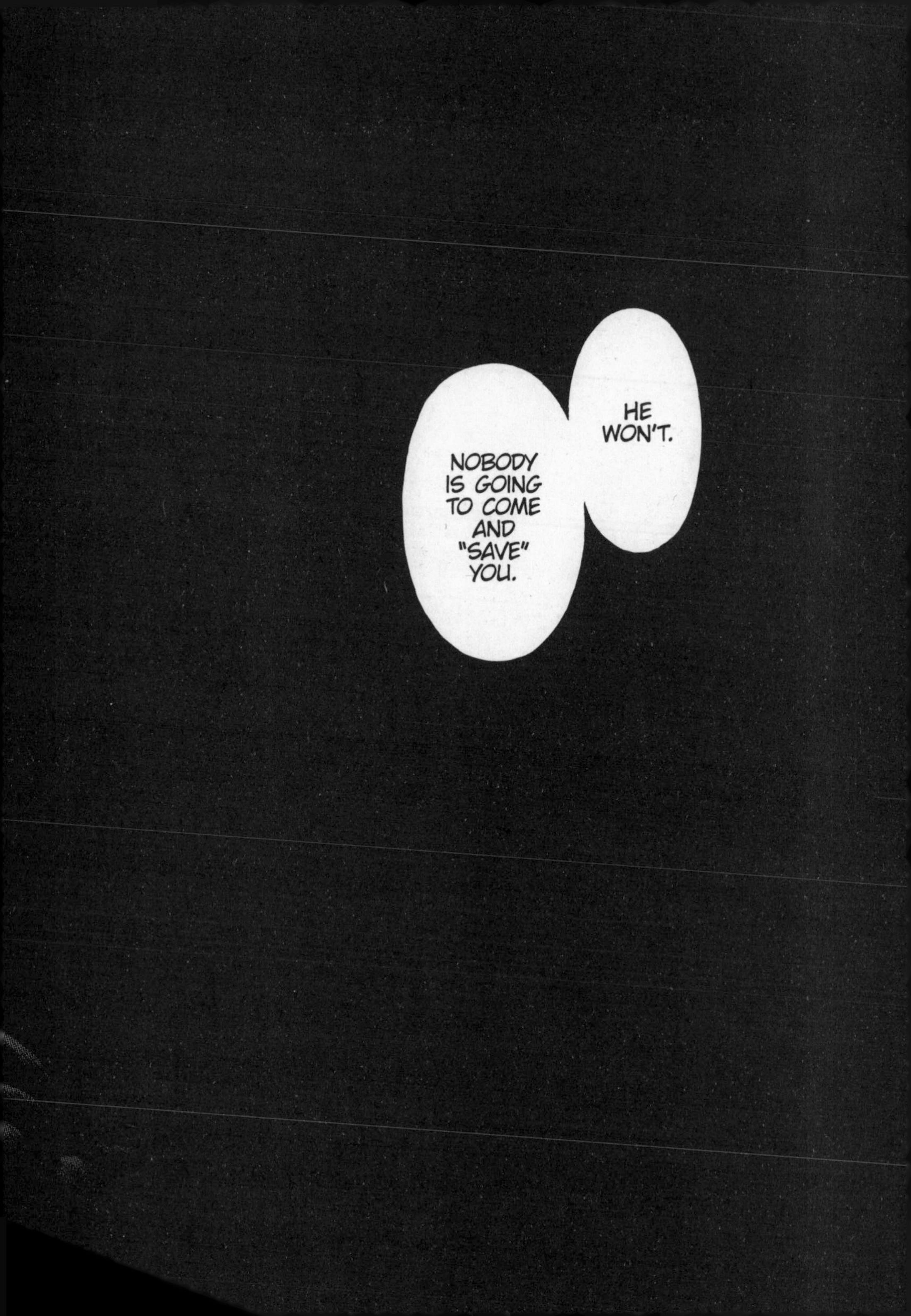
HE WON'T.
NOBODY IS GOING TO COME AND "SAVE" YOU.

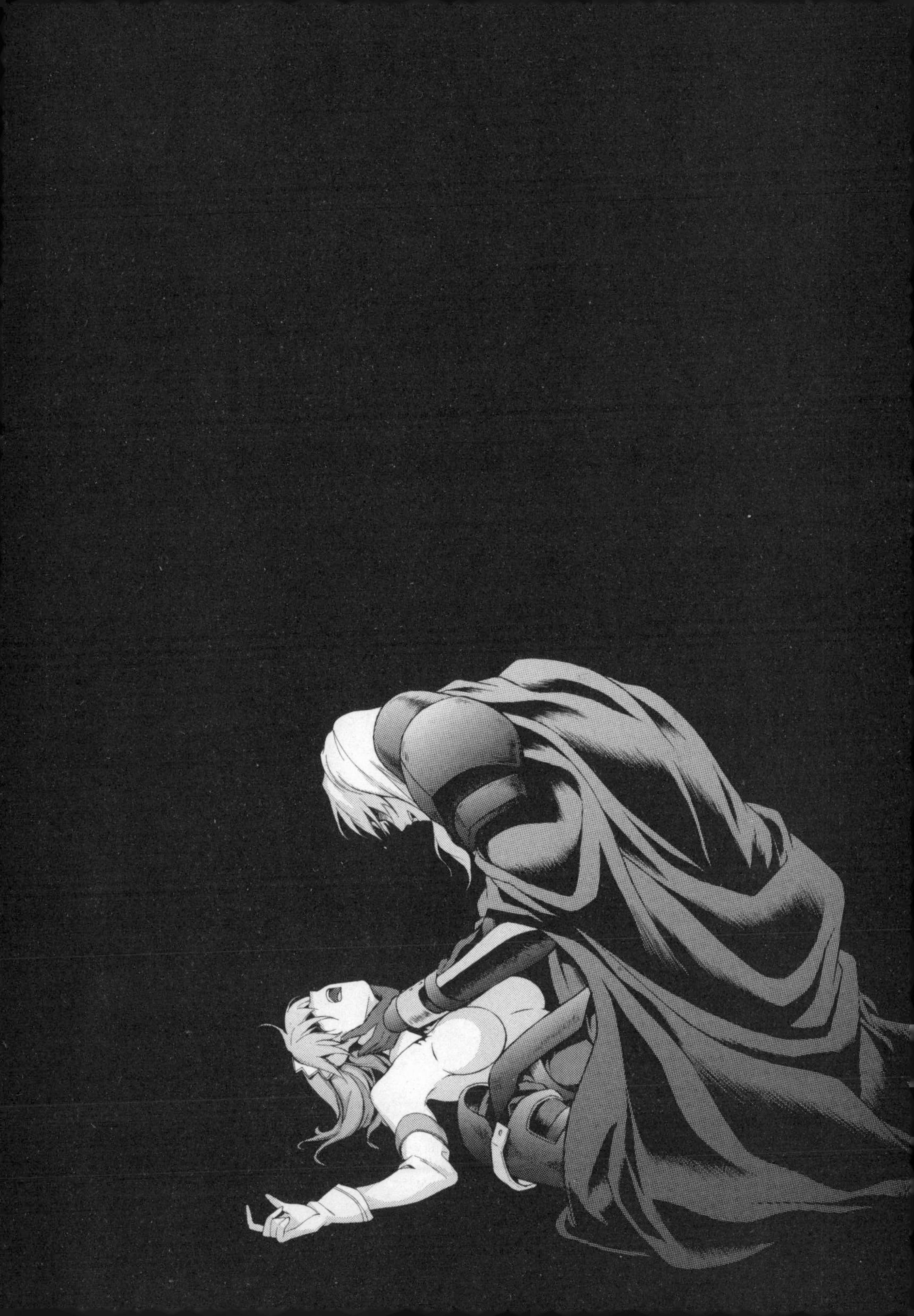

HE WON'T COME.

RIGHT NOW, HE IS TOO BUSY HOLDING HER IN HIS ARMS.

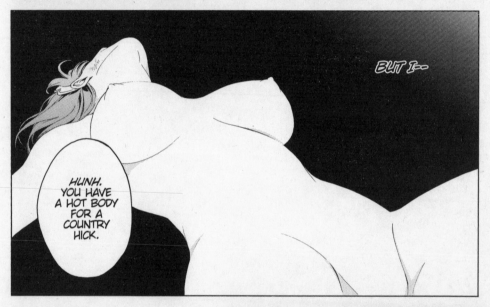

BUT I—

HUNH. YOU HAVE A HOT BODY FOR A COUNTRY HICK.

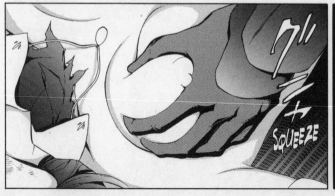

GU

SQUEEZE

HOW-EVER...

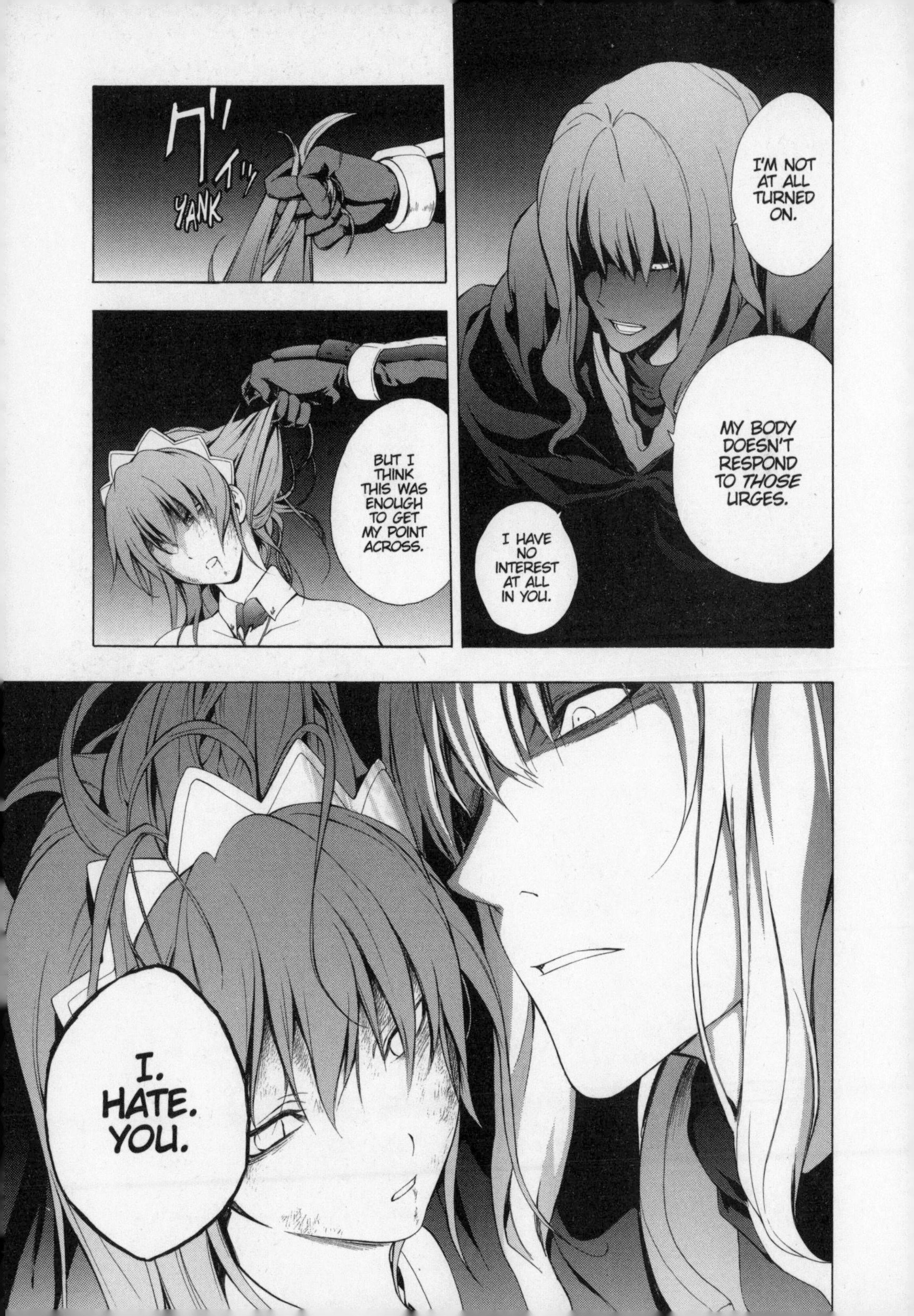
I'M NOT AT ALL TURNED ON.
MY BODY DOESN'T RESPOND TO *THOSE* URGES.
I HAVE NO INTEREST AT ALL IN YOU.
グイッ
YANK
BUT I THINK THIS WAS ENOUGH TO GET MY POINT ACROSS.
I. HATE. YOU.

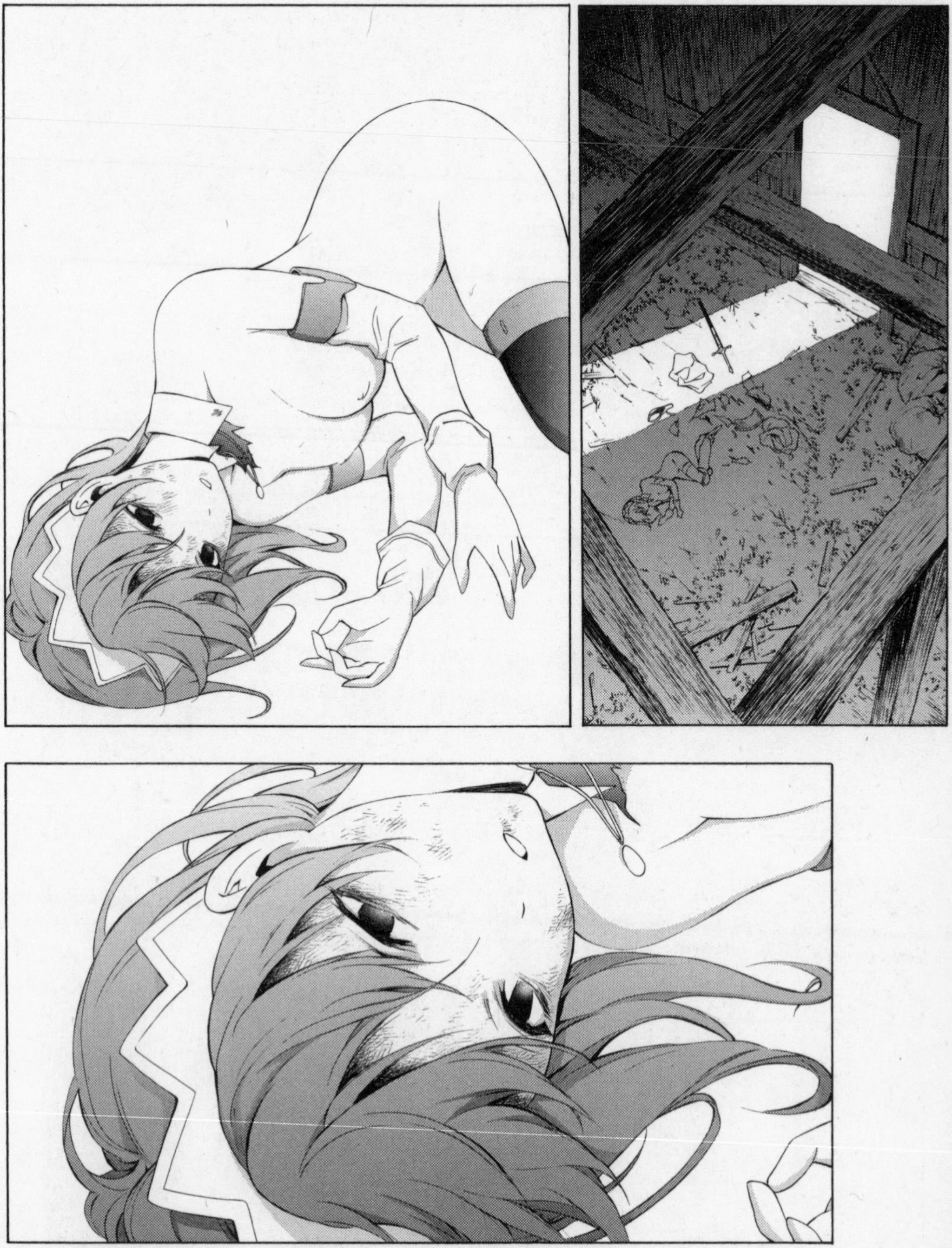

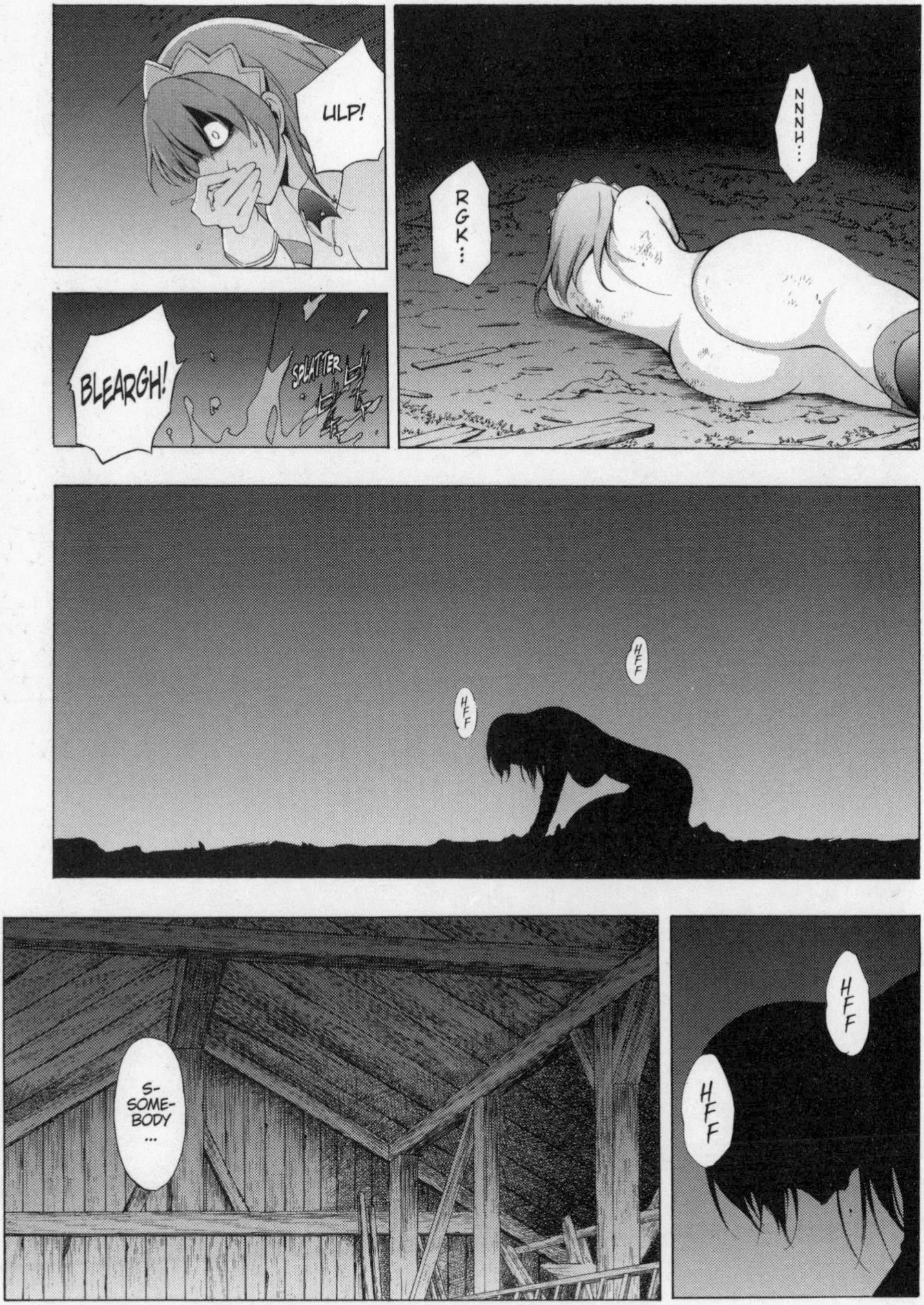
NNNH...
RGK...
ULP!
BLEARGH!
SPLATTER
HFF
HFF
HFF
HFF
S-SOMEBODY...

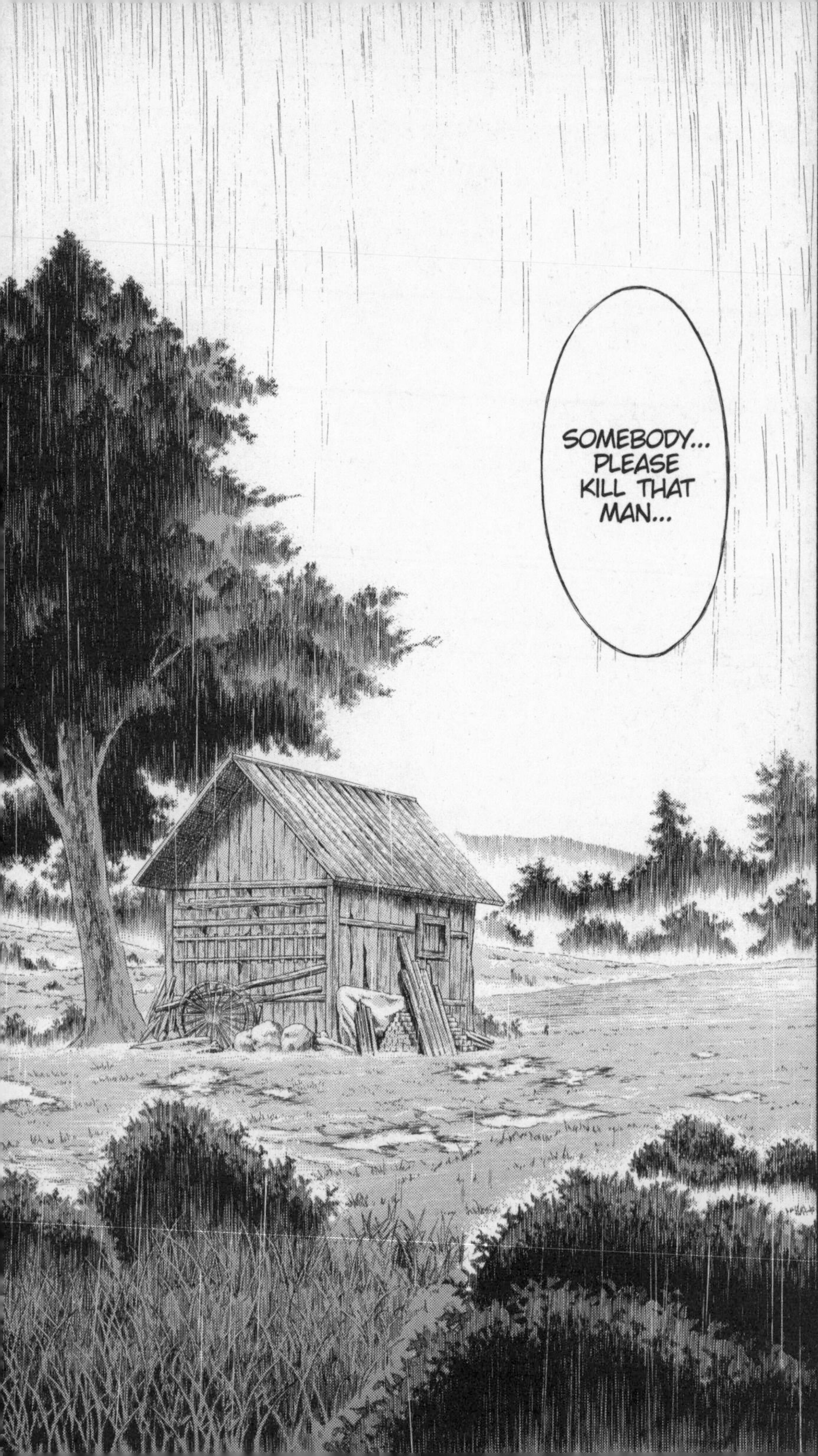
SOMEBODY... PLEASE KILL THAT MAN...

I DON'T WANT TO TELL ANYBODY...
ANYBODY... WHAT HAPPENED.

I DON'T WANT TO TALK ABOUT IT...
DON'T WANT PEOPLE TO KNOW.

ESPECIALLY *HIM*--

IF HE EVER FOUND OUT...
IT WOULD BE THE END OF EVERYTHING.

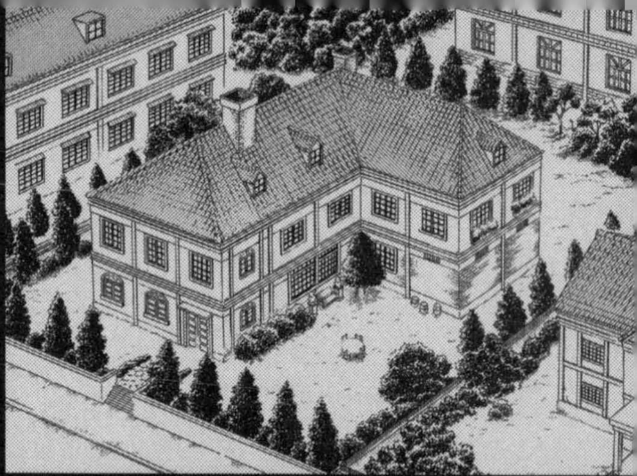

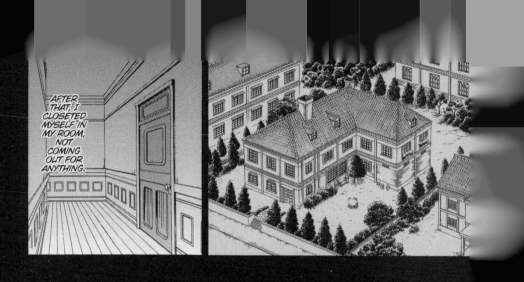

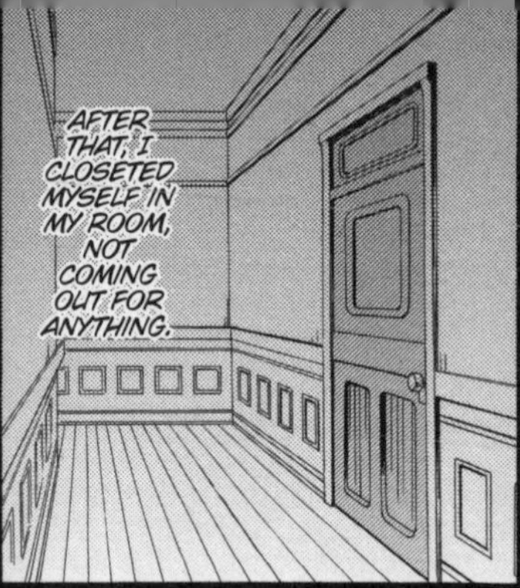
AFTER THAT, I CLOSETED MYSELF IN MY ROOM, NOT COMING OUT FOR ANYTHING.

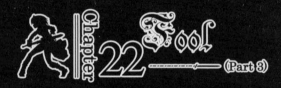

Chapter 22 Fool (Part 3)

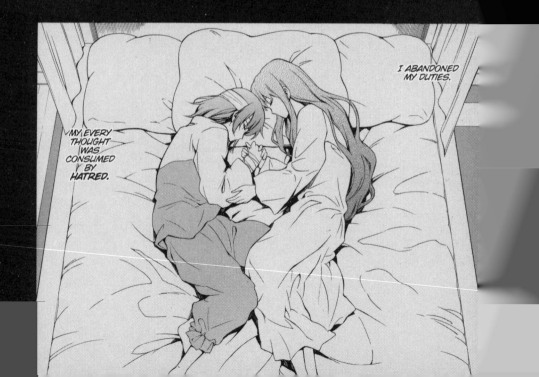

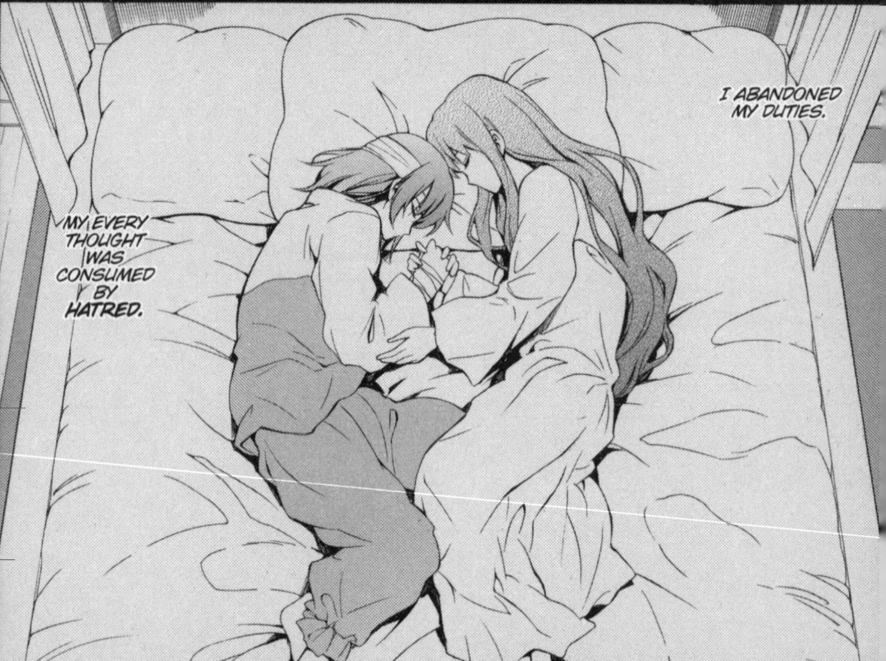
I ABANDONED MY DUTIES.
MY EVERY THOUGHT WAS CONSUMED BY HATRED.

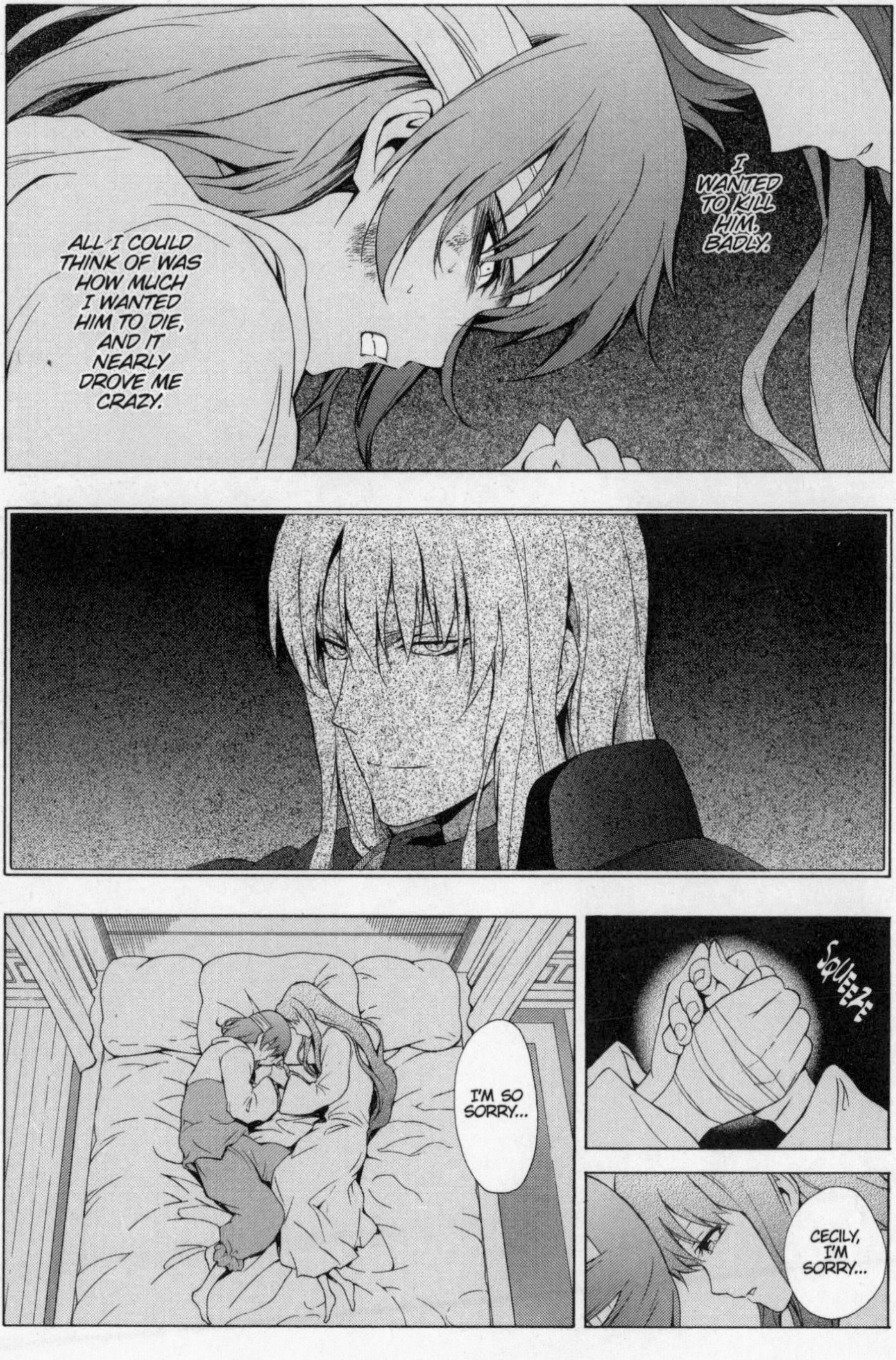
I WANTED TO KILL HIM. BADLY.
ALL I COULD THINK OF WAS HOW MUCH I WANTED HIM TO DIE, AND IT NEARLY DROVE ME CRAZY.
SQUEEZE
CECILY, I'M SORRY...
I'M SO SORRY...

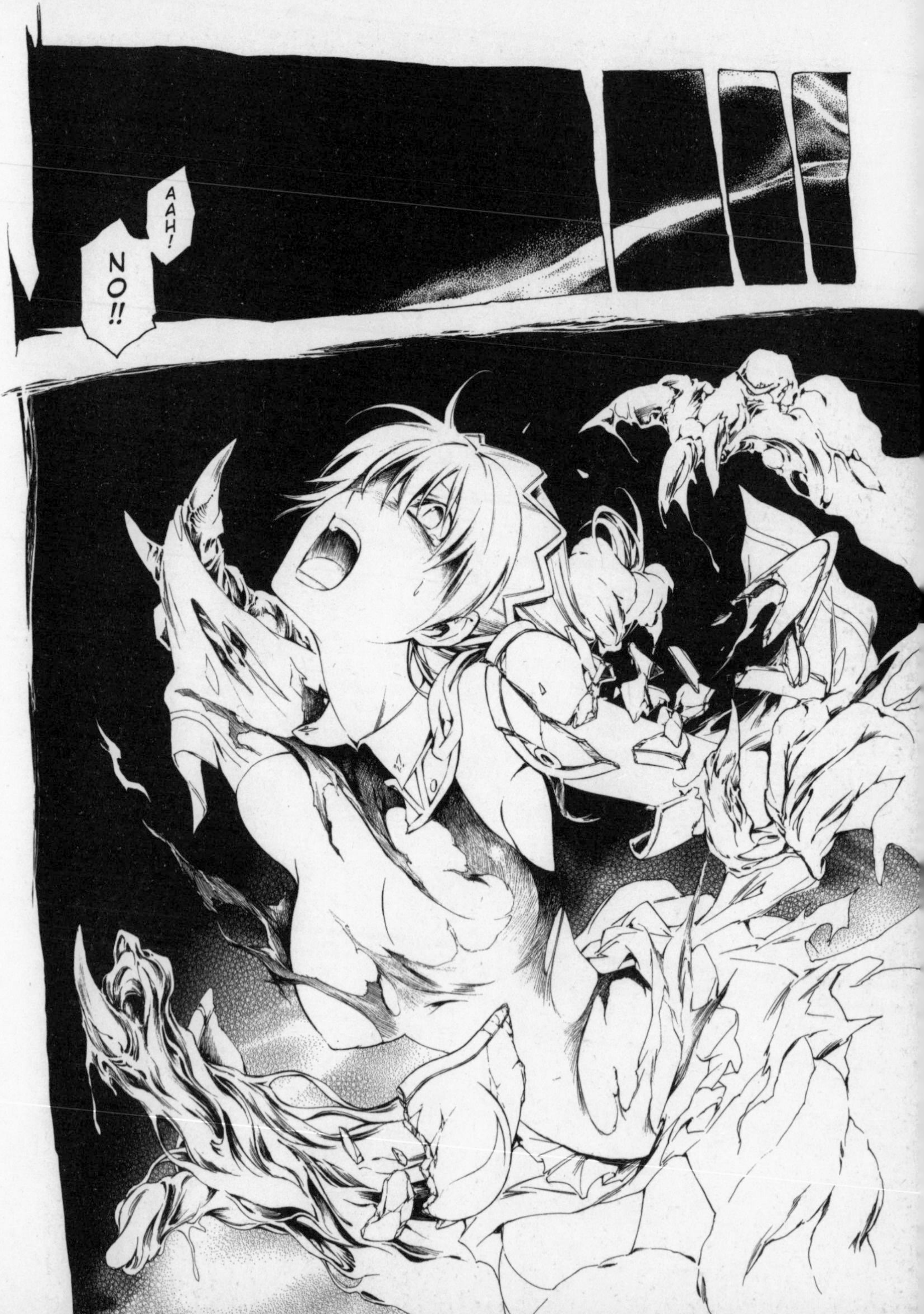
AAH!
NO!!

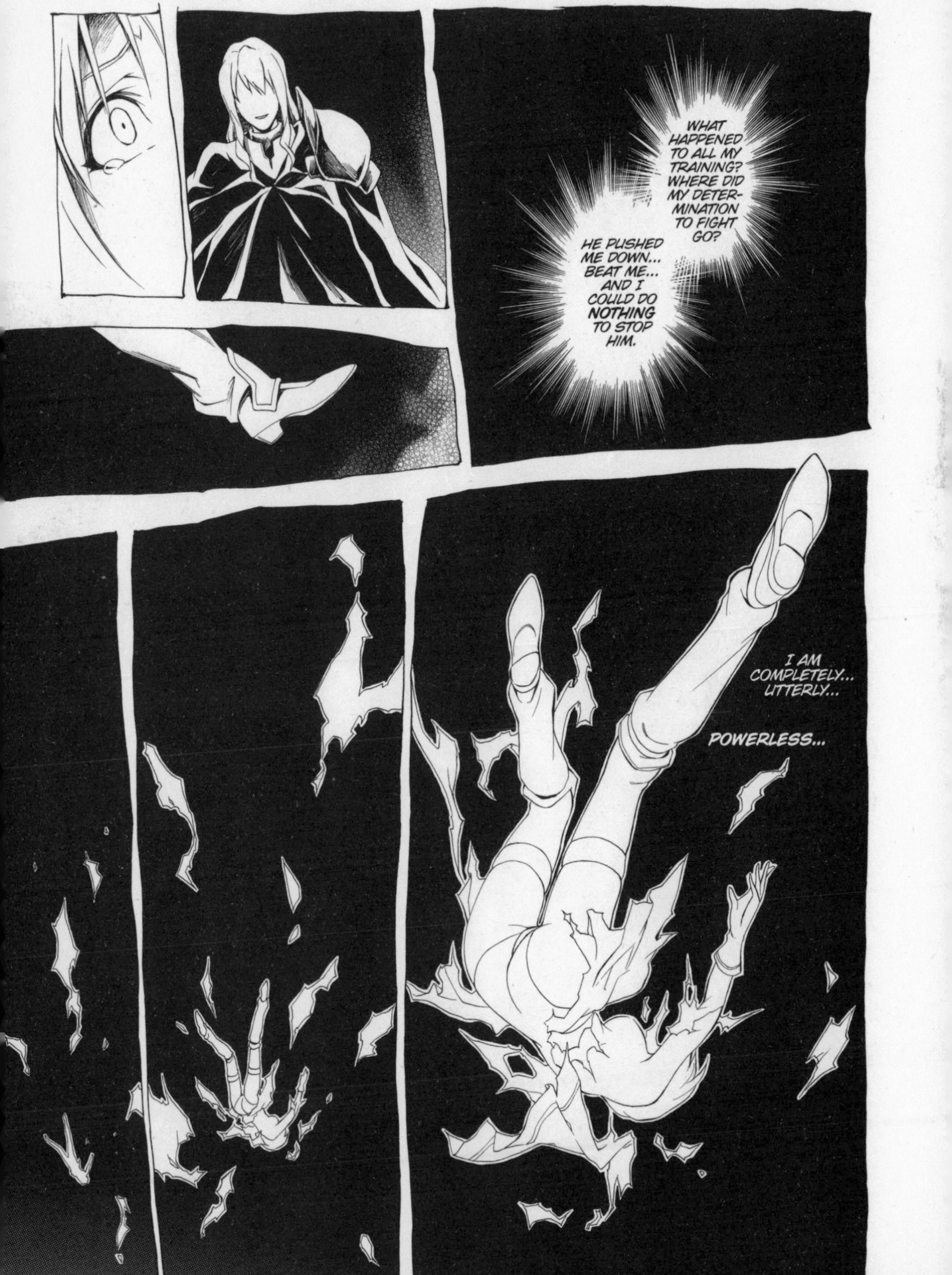
WHAT HAPPENED TO ALL MY TRAINING? WHERE DID MY DETERMINATION TO FIGHT GO?
HE PUSHED ME DOWN... BEAT ME... AND I COULD DO NOTHING TO STOP HIM.
I AM COMPLETELY... UTTERLY...
POWERLESS...

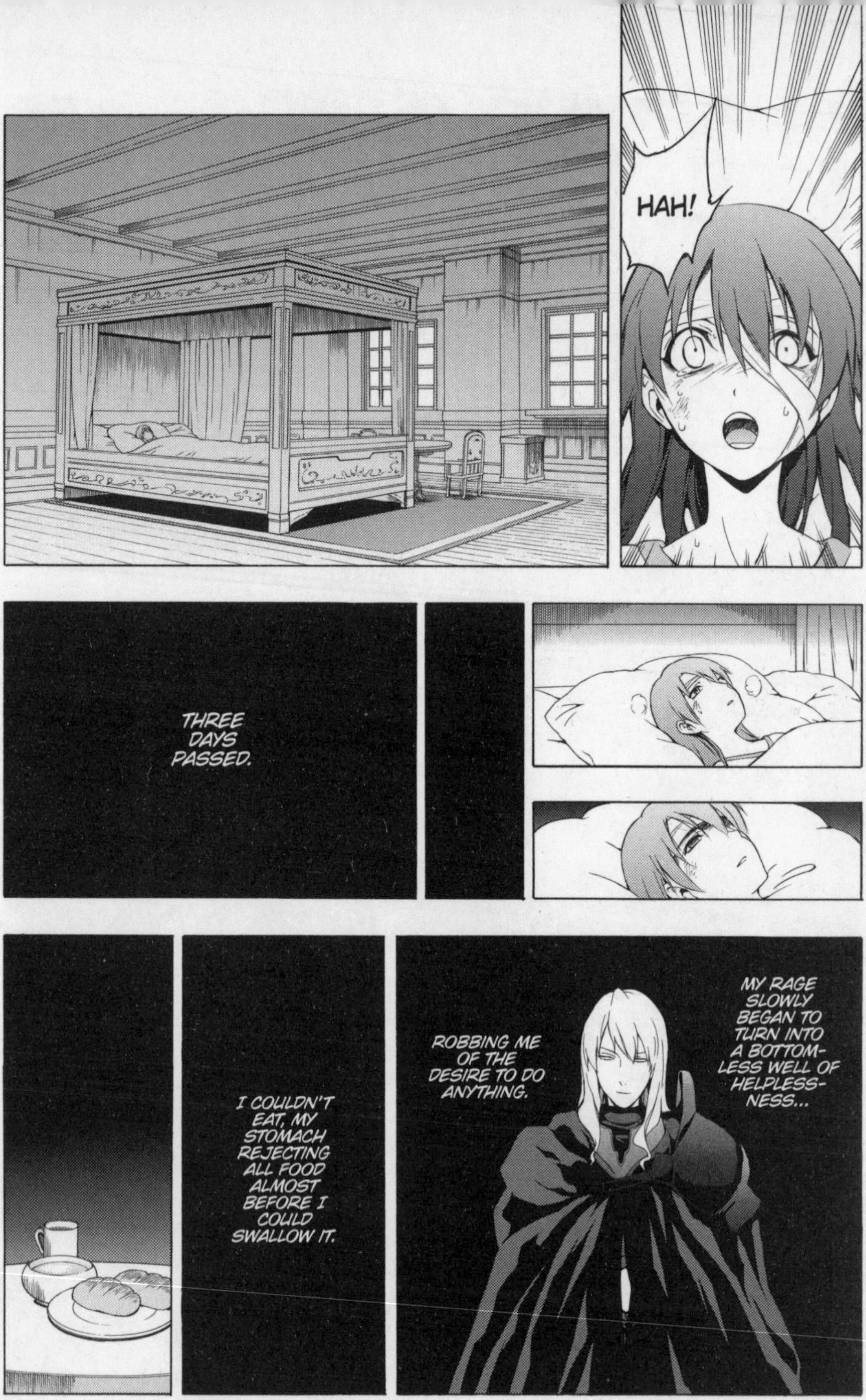
HAH!
THREE DAYS PASSED.
MY RAGE SLOWLY BEGAN TO TURN INTO A BOTTOM-LESS WELL OF HELPLESS-NESS...
ROBBING ME OF THE DESIRE TO DO ANYTHING.
I COULDN'T EAT, MY STOMACH REJECTING ALL FOOD ALMOST BEFORE I COULD SWALLOW IT.

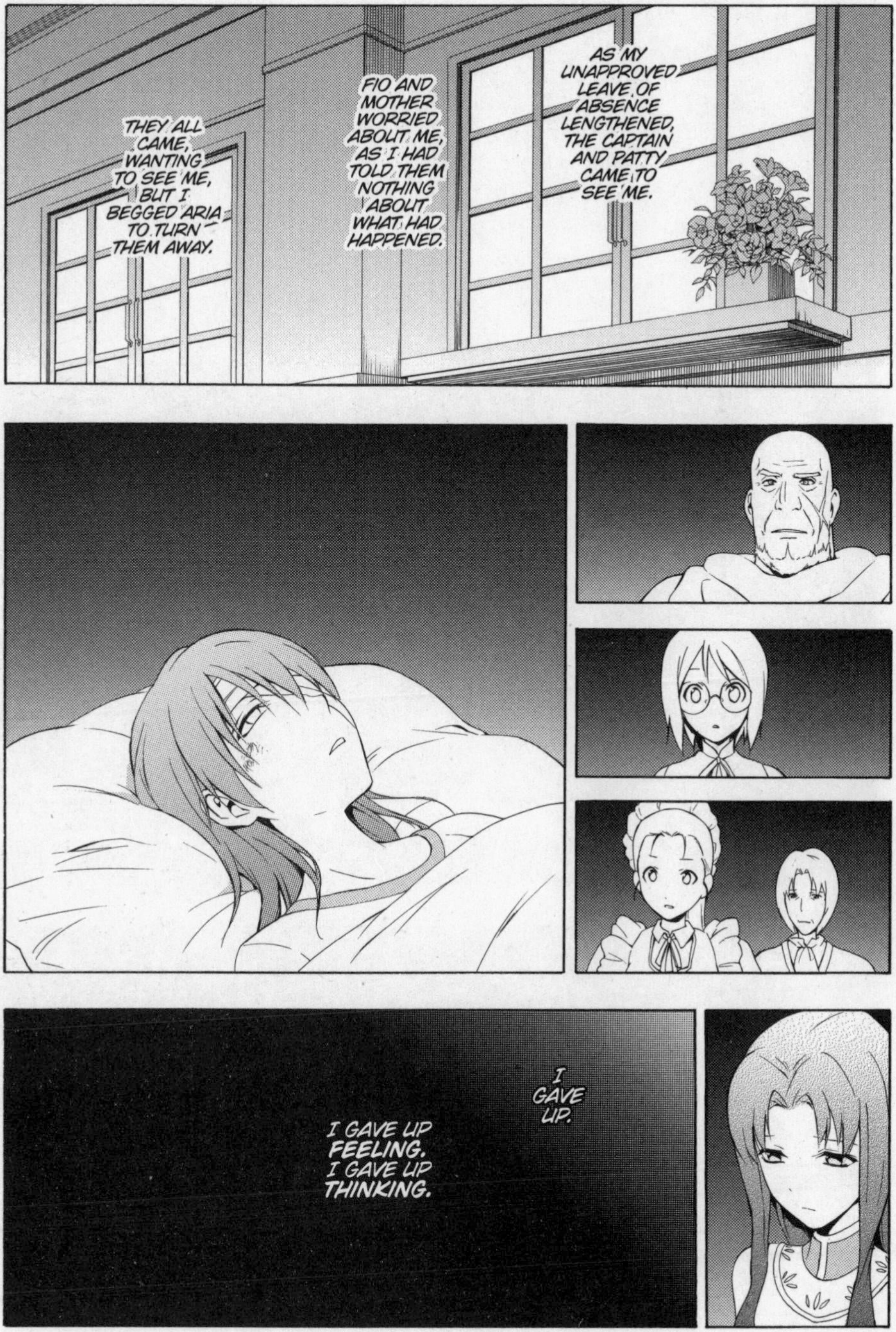
AS MY UNAPPROVED LEAVE OF ABSENCE LENGTHENED, THE CAPTAIN AND PATTY CAME TO SEE ME.
FIO AND MOTHER WORRIED ABOUT ME, AS I HAD TOLD THEM NOTHING ABOUT WHAT HAD HAPPENED.
THEY ALL CAME, WANTING TO SEE ME, BUT I BEGGED ARIA TO TURN THEM AWAY.
I GAVE UP.
I GAVE UP FEELING. I GAVE UP THINKING.

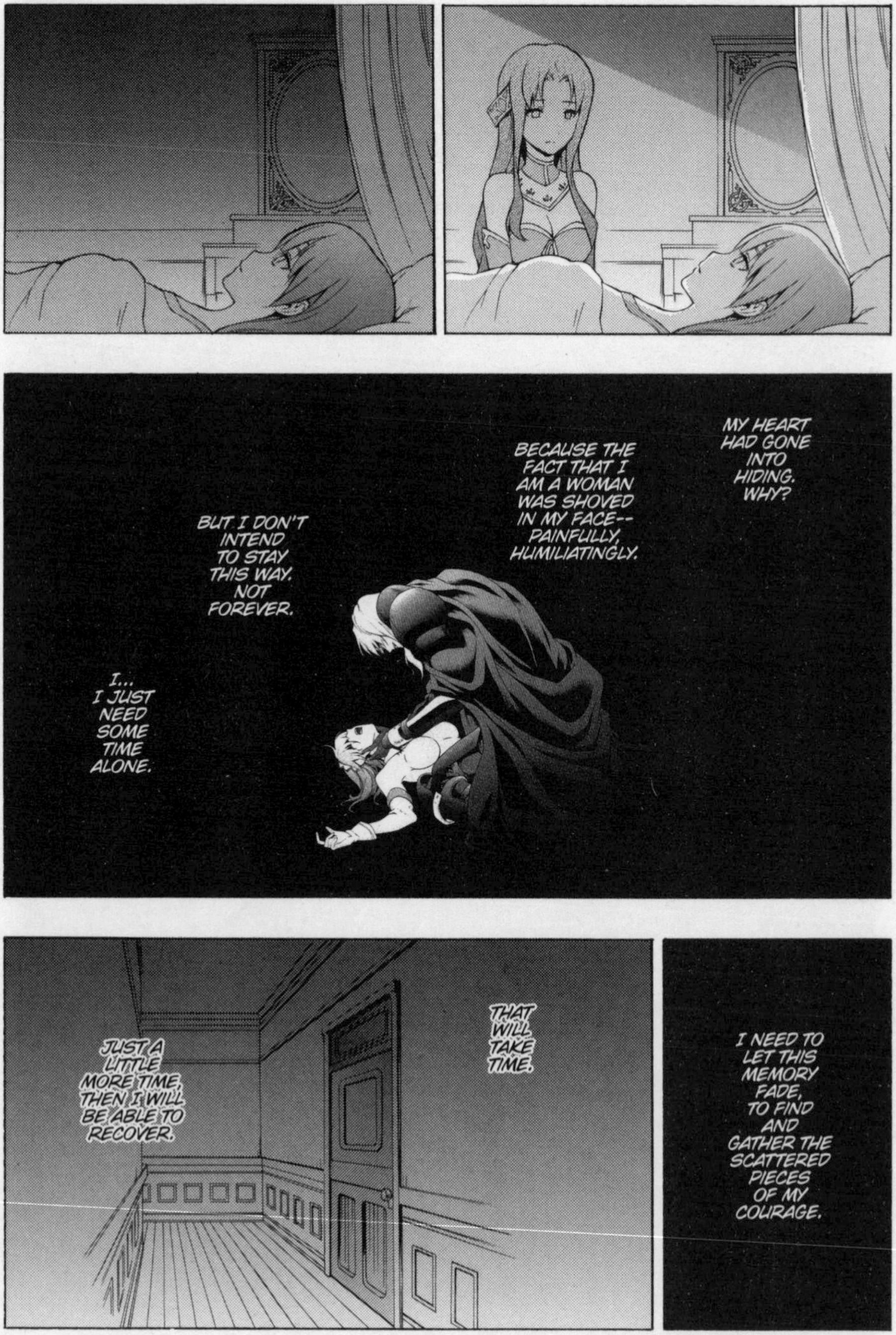
MY HEART HAD GONE INTO HIDING. WHY?
BECAUSE THE FACT THAT I AM A WOMAN WAS SHOVED IN MY FACE-- PAINFULLY, HUMILIATINGLY.
BUT I DON'T INTEND TO STAY THIS WAY. NOT FOREVER.
I... I JUST NEED SOME TIME ALONE.
I NEED TO LET THIS MEMORY FADE, TO FIND AND GATHER THE SCATTERED PIECES OF MY COURAGE.
THAT WILL TAKE TIME.
JUST A LITTLE MORE TIME, THEN I WILL BE ABLE TO RECOVER.

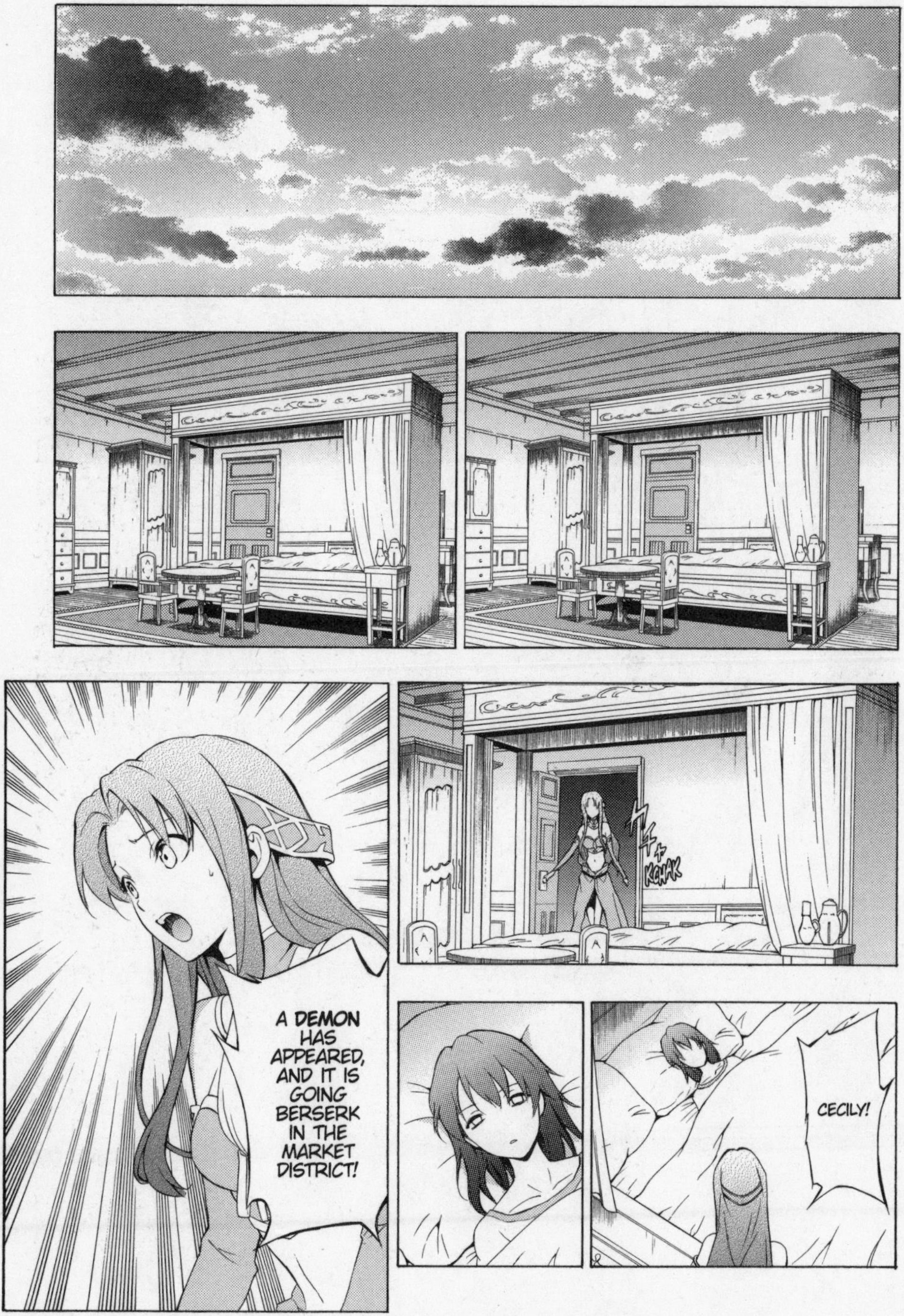
KCHAK
CECILY!
A DEMON HAS APPEARED, AND IT IS GOING BERSERK IN THE MARKET DISTRICT!

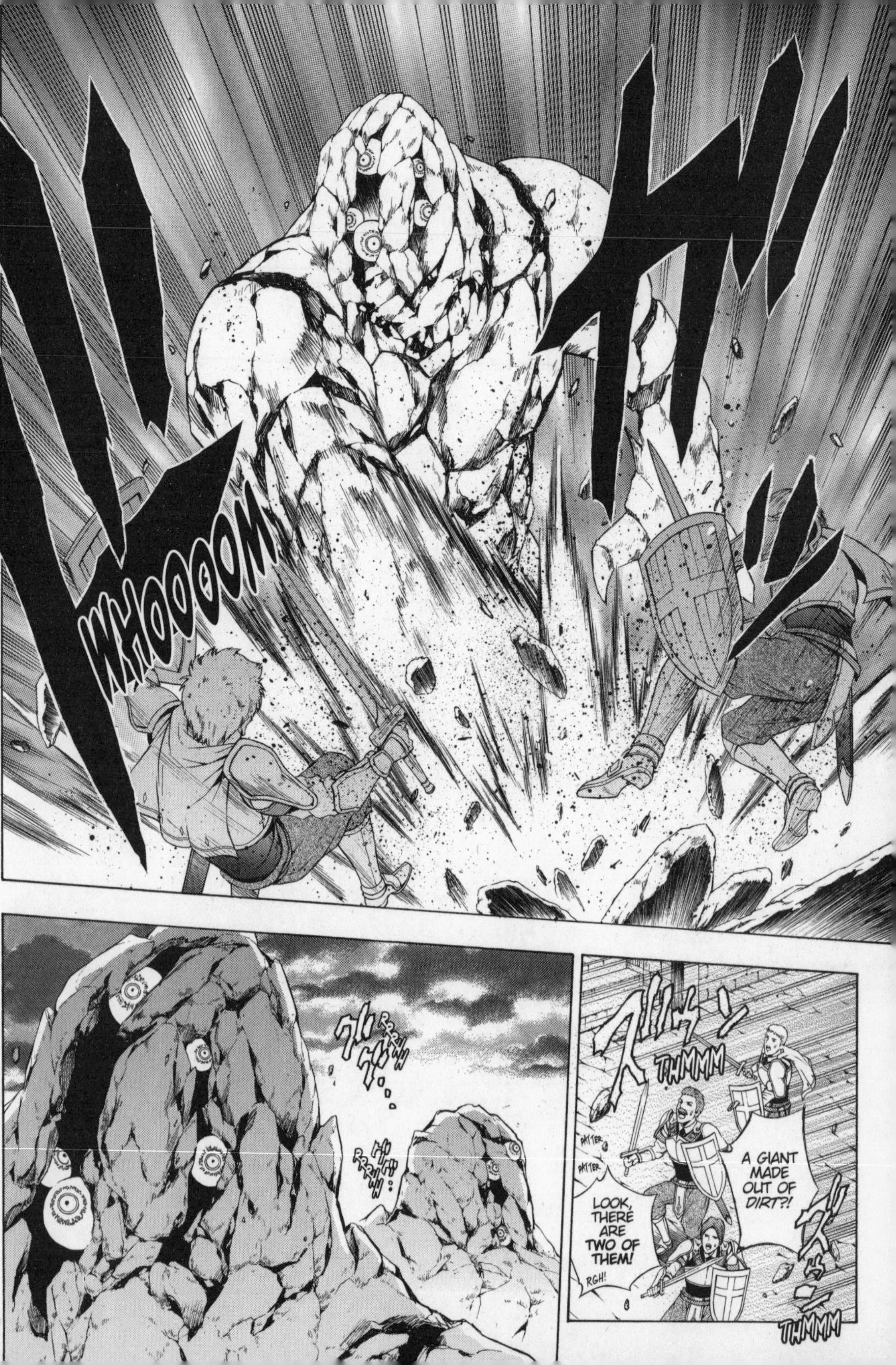
WHOOOOM
THMMM
A GIANT MADE OUT OF DIRT?!
PATTER
PATTER
LOOK, THERE ARE TWO OF THEM!
RGH!
THMMM
RRRUH
RRRUH

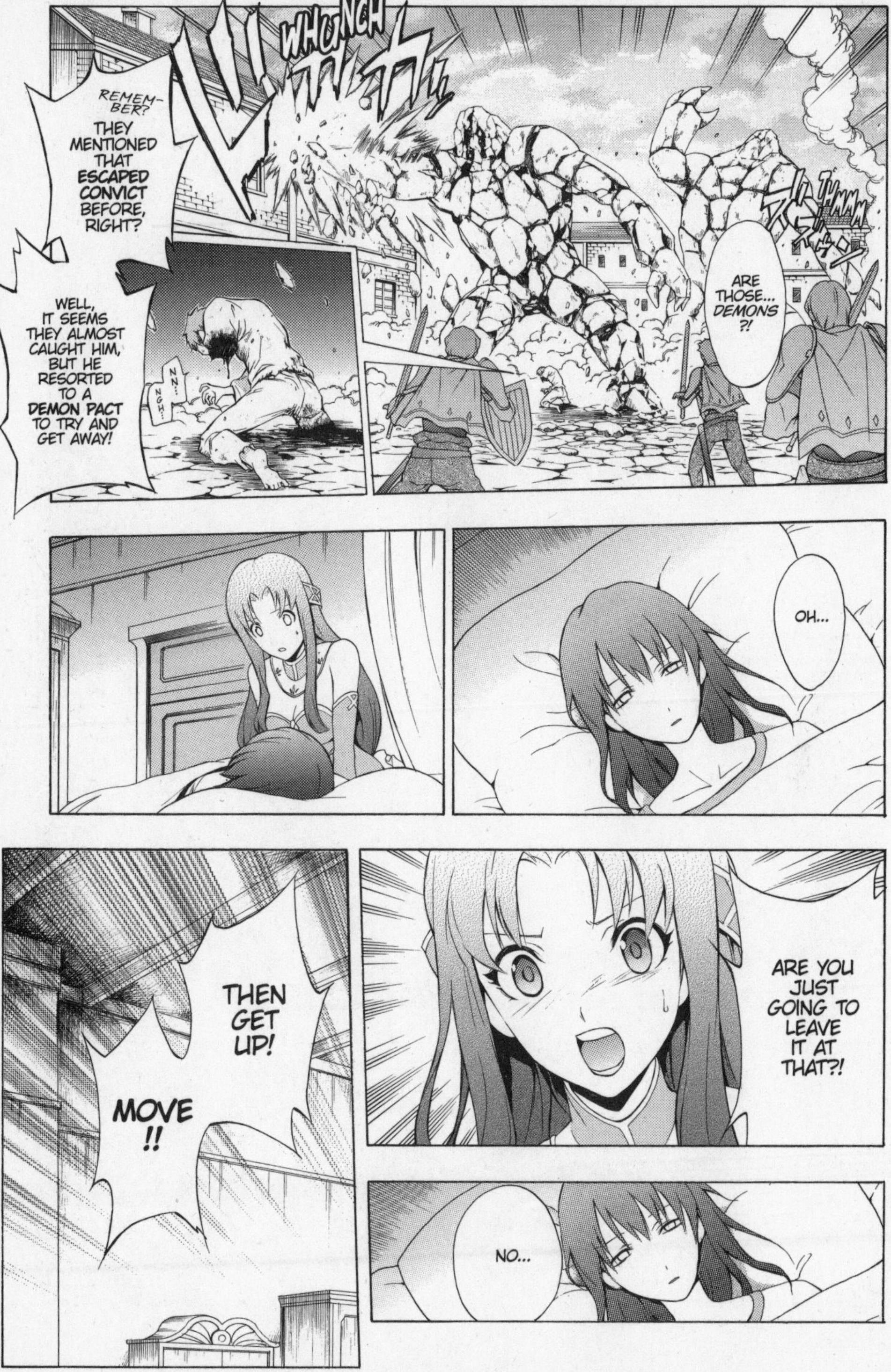
THWAM
ARE THOSE... DEMONS?!
WHUNCH
REMEMBER? THEY MENTIONED THAT ESCAPED CONVICT BEFORE, RIGHT?
WELL, IT SEEMS THEY ALMOST CAUGHT HIM, BUT HE RESORTED TO A DEMON PACT TO TRY AND GET AWAY!
NN... NGH!..
OH...
ARE YOU JUST GOING TO LEAVE IT AT THAT?!
NO...
THEN GET UP!
MOVE!!

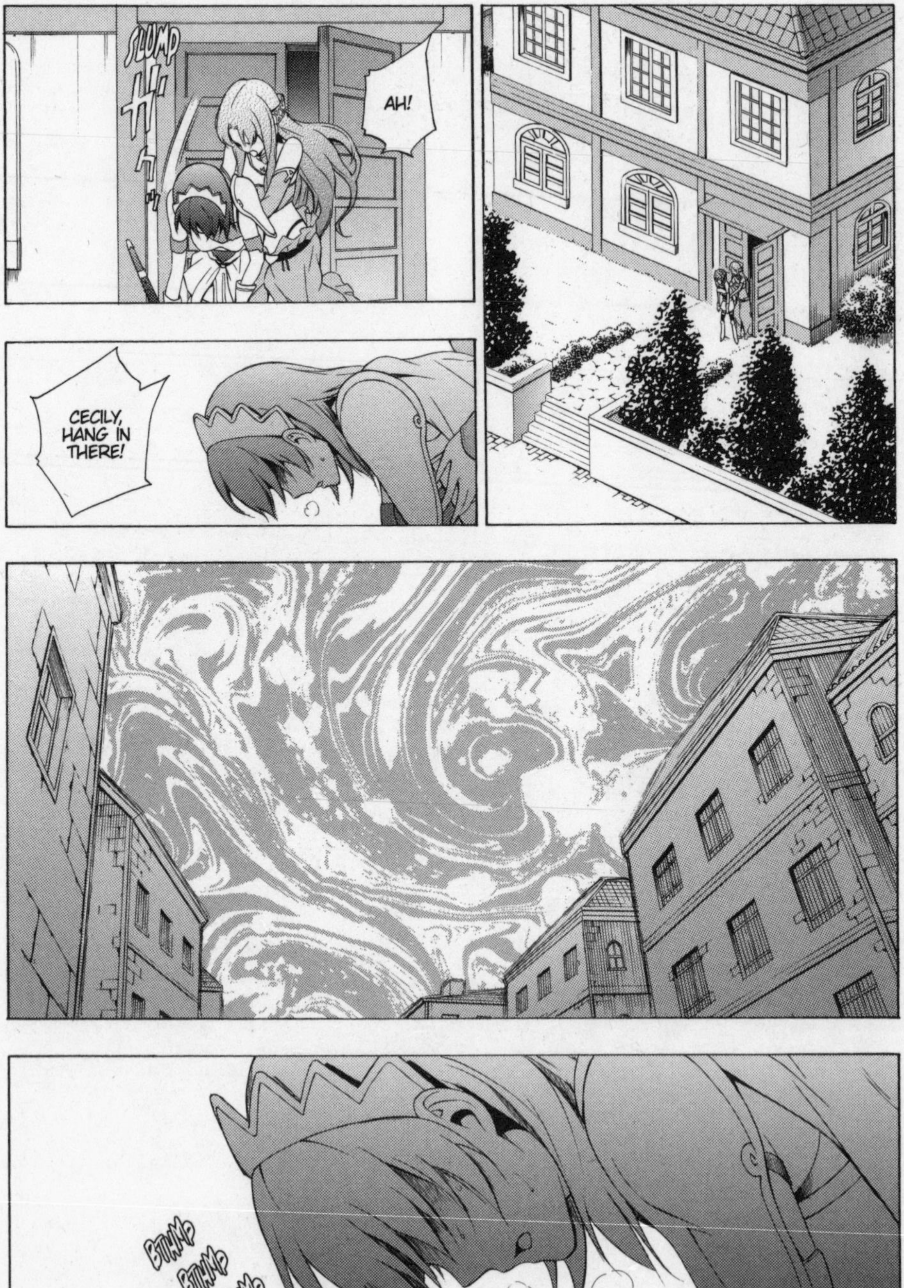
SLUMP
AH!
CECILY, HANG IN THERE!
BTHMP BTHMP BTHMP

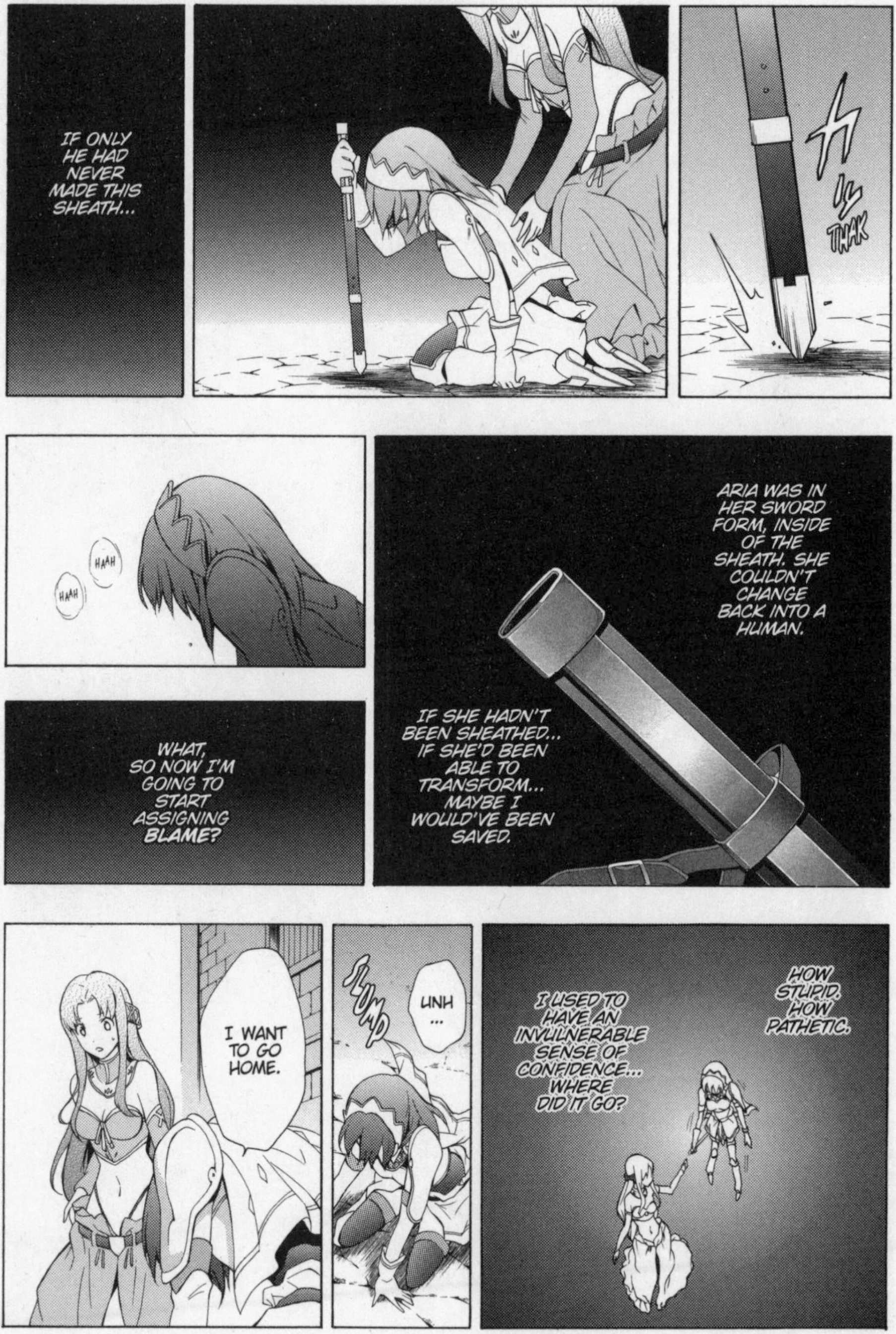
THAK
IF ONLY HE HAD NEVER MADE THIS SHEATH...
ARIA WAS IN HER SWORD FORM, INSIDE OF THE SHEATH. SHE COULDN'T CHANGE BACK INTO A HUMAN.
IF SHE HADN'T BEEN SHEATHED... IF SHE'D BEEN ABLE TO TRANSFORM... MAYBE I WOULD'VE BEEN SAVED.
HAAH
HAAH
WHAT, SO NOW I'M GOING TO START ASSIGNING **BLAME**?
HOW STUPID. HOW PATHETIC.
I USED TO HAVE AN INVULNERABLE SENSE OF CONFIDENCE... WHERE DID IT GO?
SLUMP
UNH ...
I WANT TO GO HOME.

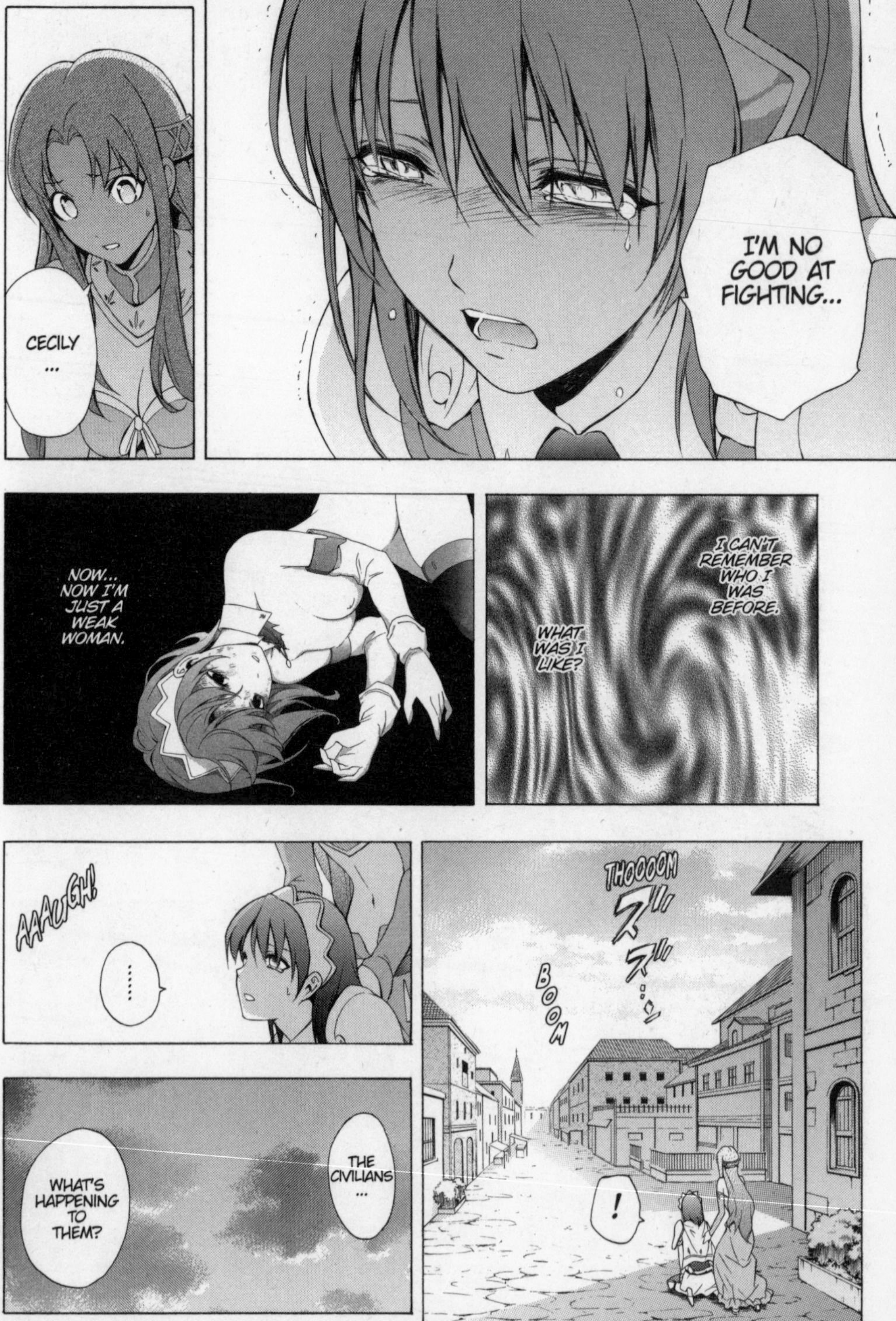
I'M NO GOOD AT FIGHTING...
CECILY ...
I CAN'T REMEMBER WHO I WAS BEFORE.
WHAT WAS I LIKE?
NOW... NOW I'M JUST A WEAK WOMAN.
THOOOOM
BOOM
!
AAAUGH!
......
THE CIVILIANS ...
WHAT'S HAPPENING TO THEM?

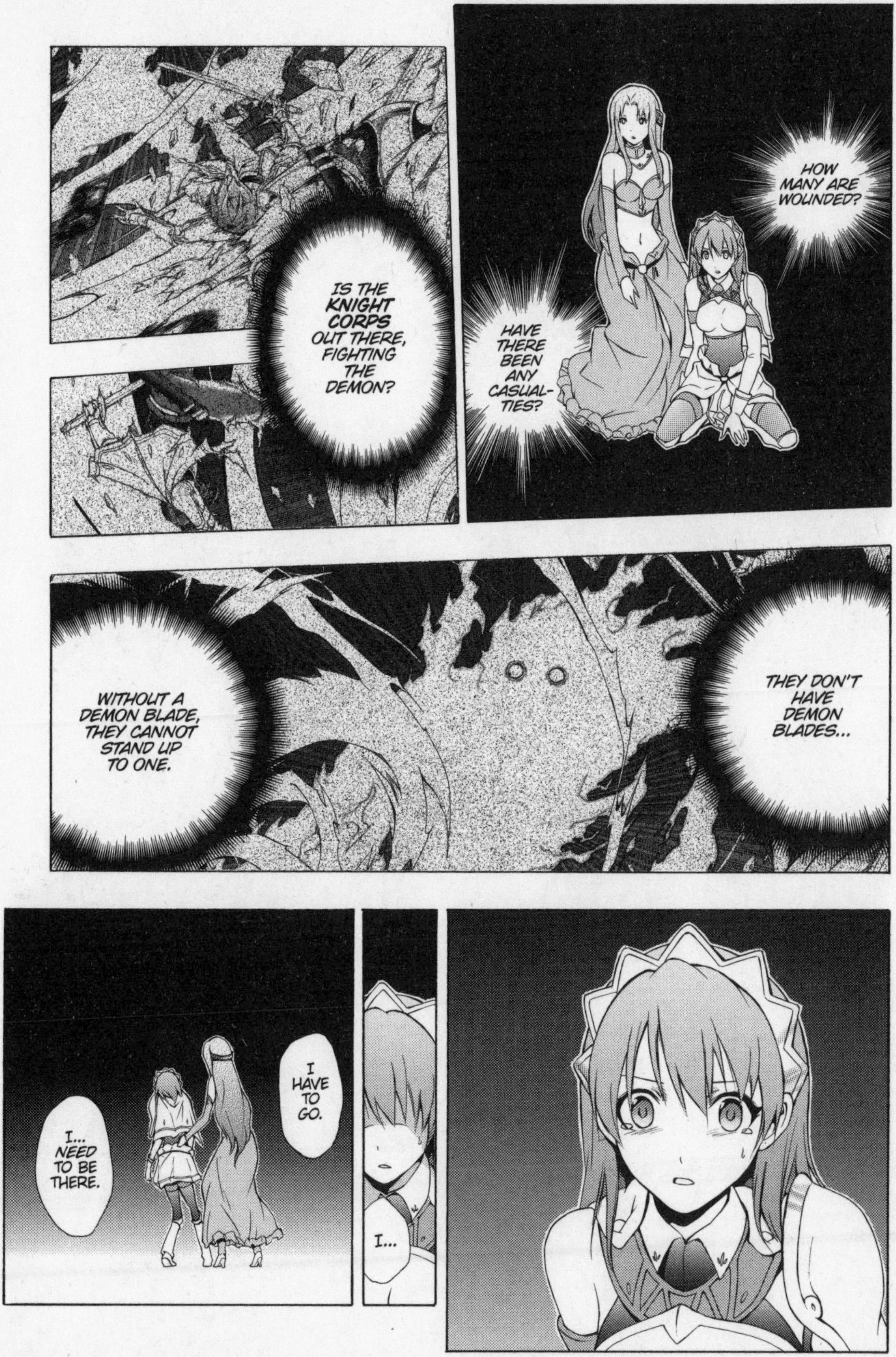

HOW MANY ARE WOUNDED?
HAVE THERE BEEN ANY CASUALTIES?
IS THE **KNIGHT CORPS** OUT THERE, FIGHTING THE DEMON?
THEY DON'T HAVE DEMON BLADES...
WITHOUT A DEMON BLADE, THEY CANNOT STAND UP TO ONE.
I...
I HAVE TO GO.
I... NEED TO BE THERE.

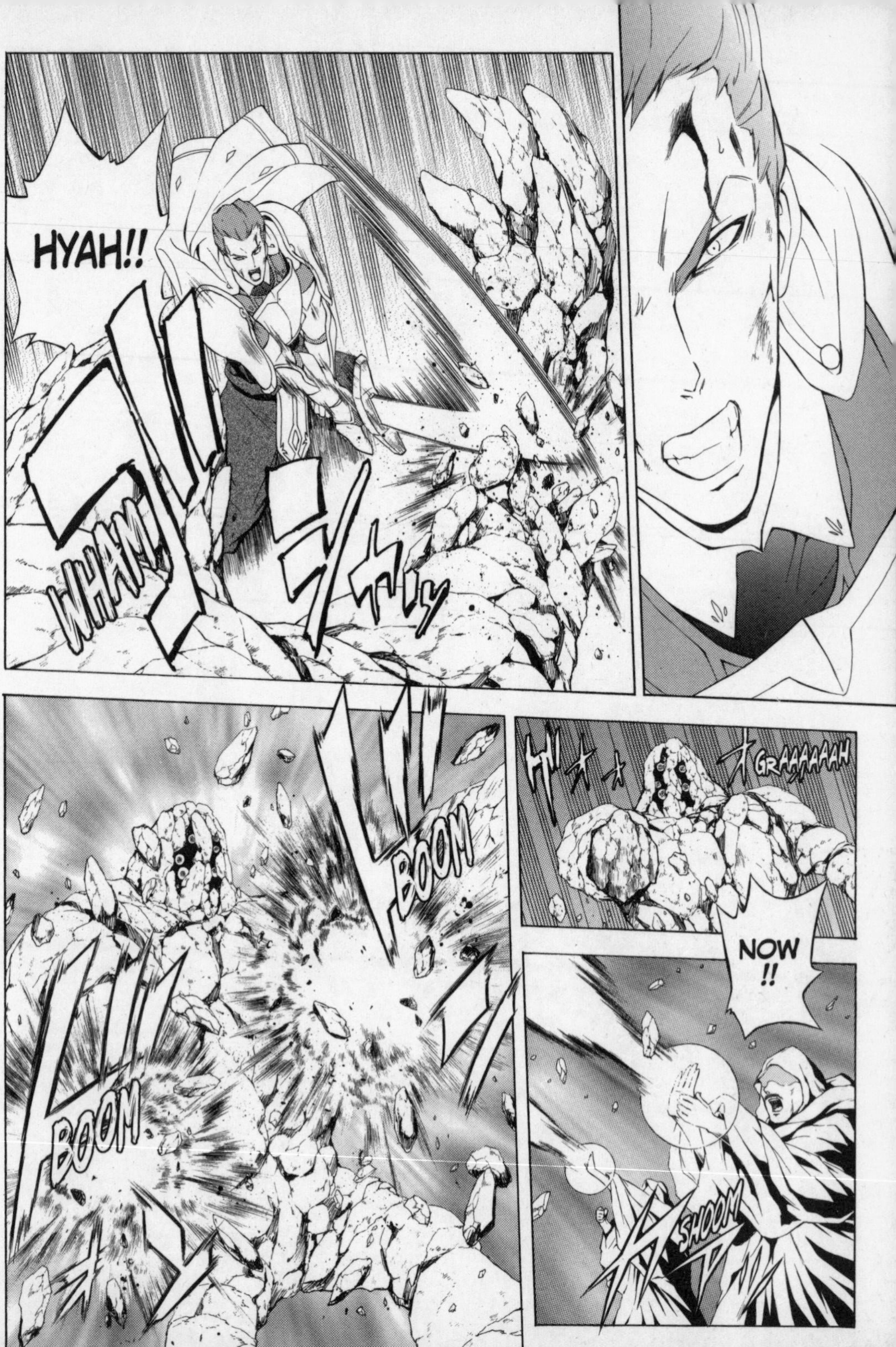
HYAH!!
WHAM
GRAAAAAAH
NOW!!
SHOOM
BOOM
BOOM

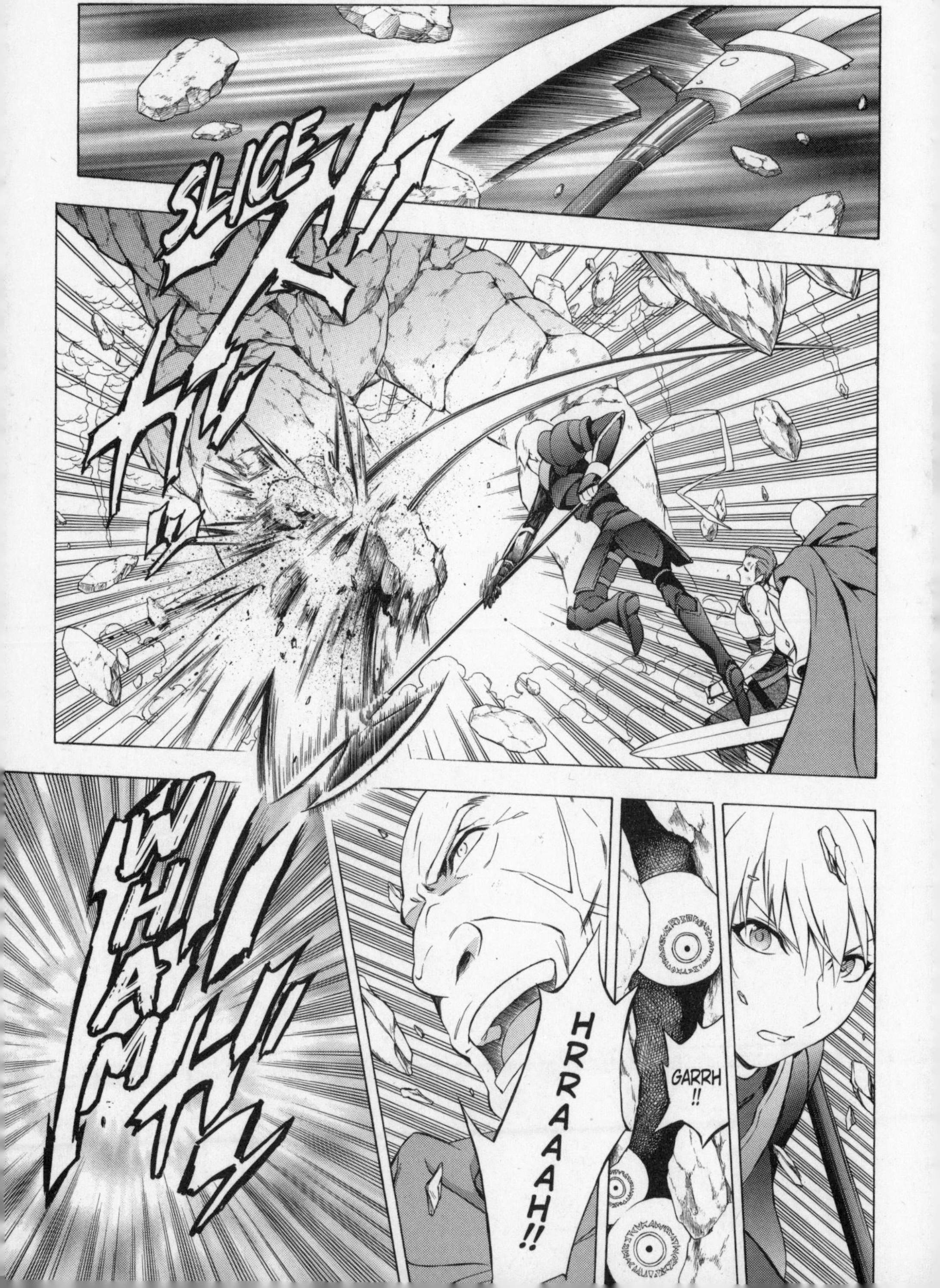
SLICE
GARRH!!
HRRAAAAH!!
WHAM

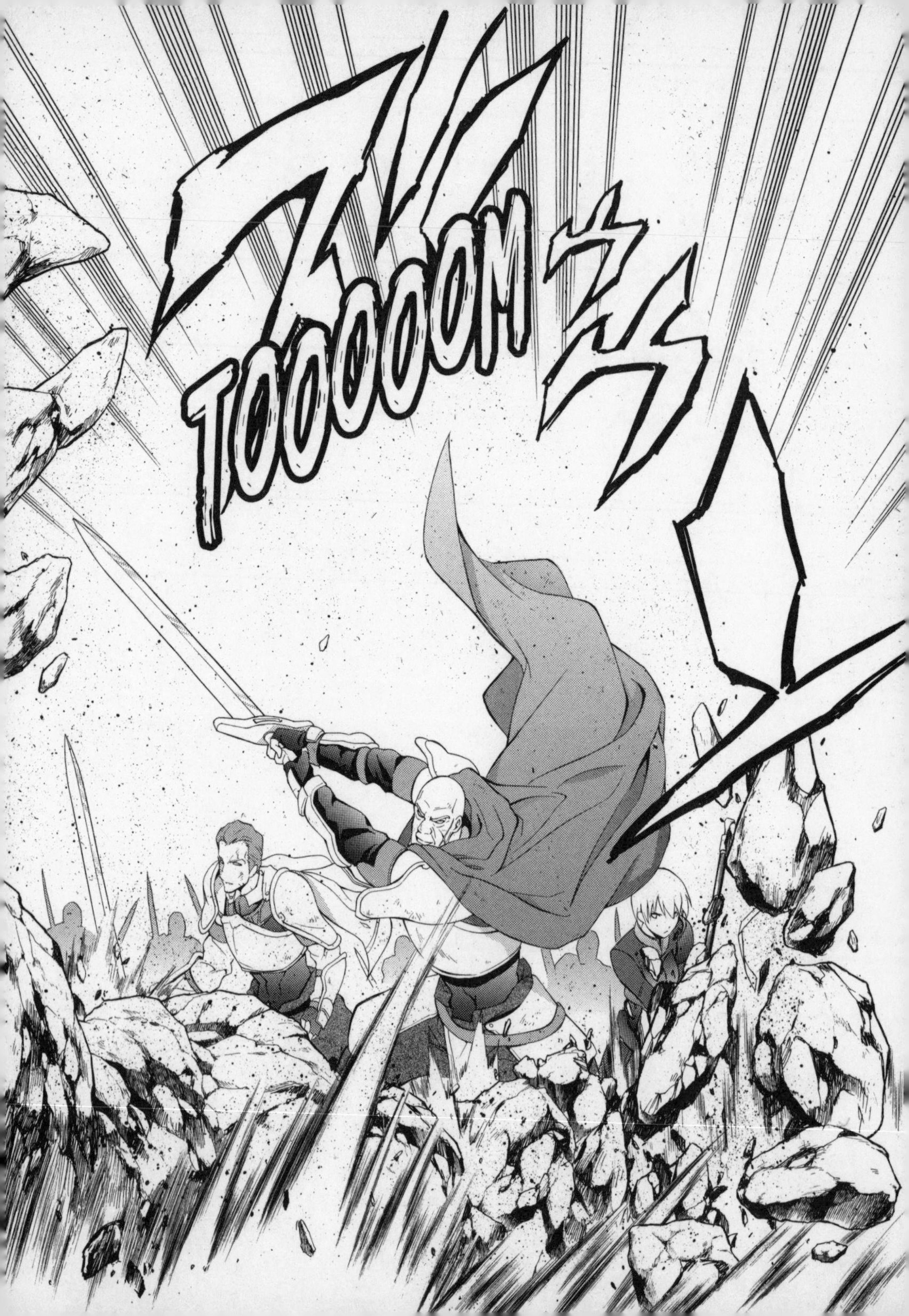
TOOOOOM

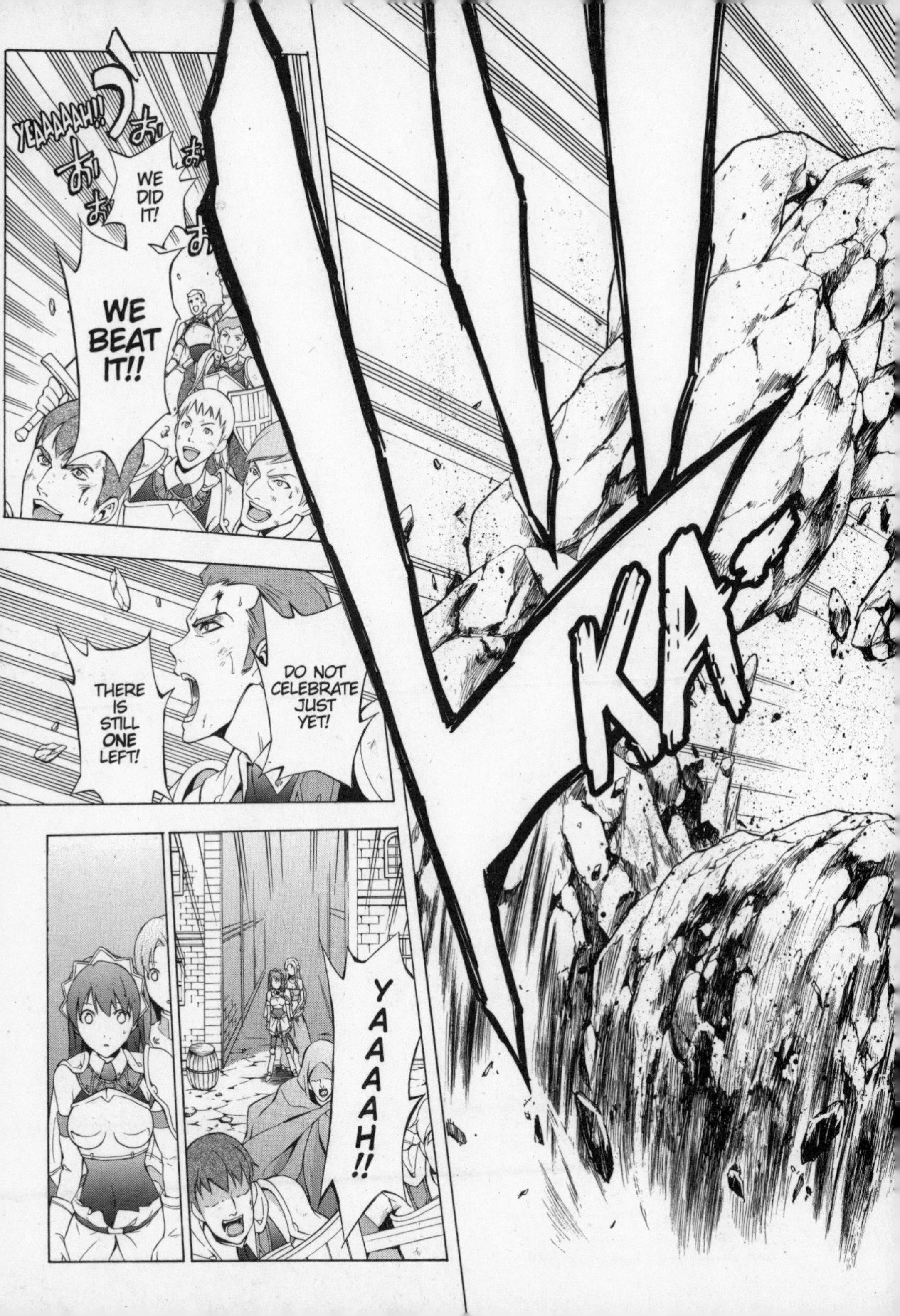
KA-
YEAAAAAH!!
WE DID IT!
WE BEAT IT!!
DO NOT CELEBRATE JUST YET!
THERE IS STILL ONE LEFT!
YAAAAAH!!

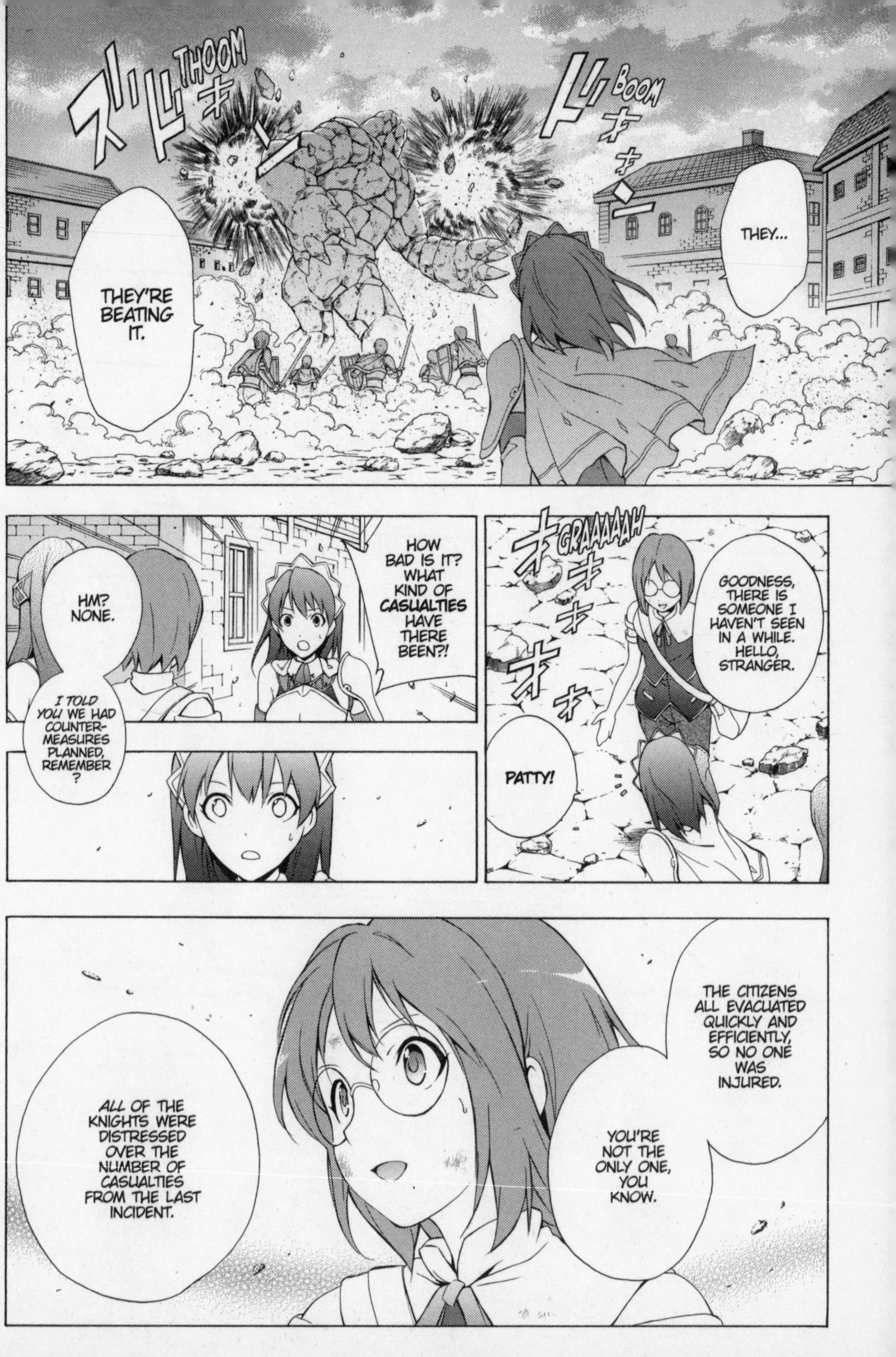
BOOM
THOOM
THEY...
THEY'RE BEATING IT.
GRAAAAAH
GOODNESS, THERE IS SOMEONE I HAVEN'T SEEN IN A WHILE. HELLO, STRANGER.
PATTY!
HOW BAD IS IT? WHAT KIND OF CASUALTIES HAVE THERE BEEN?!
HM? NONE.
I TOLD YOU WE HAD COUNTER-MEASURES PLANNED, REMEMBER?
THE CITIZENS ALL EVACUATED QUICKLY AND EFFICIENTLY, SO NO ONE WAS INJURED.
YOU'RE NOT THE ONLY ONE, YOU KNOW.
ALL OF THE KNIGHTS WERE DISTRESSED OVER THE NUMBER OF CASUALTIES FROM THE LAST INCIDENT.

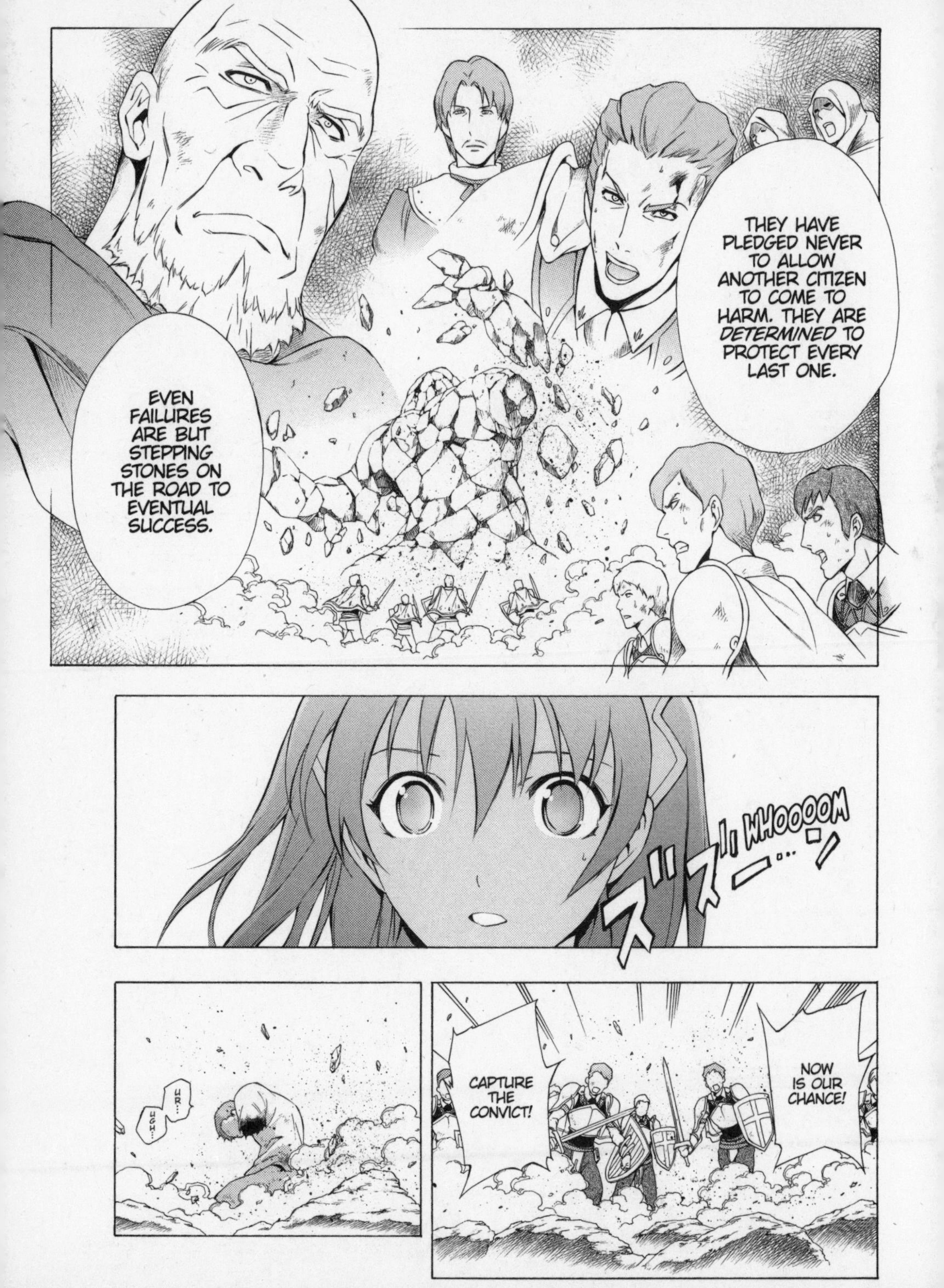
THEY HAVE PLEDGED NEVER TO ALLOW ANOTHER CITIZEN TO COME TO HARM. THEY ARE *DETERMINED* TO PROTECT EVERY LAST ONE.
EVEN FAILURES ARE BUT STEPPING STONES ON THE ROAD TO EVENTUAL SUCCESS.
WHOOOOM
NOW IS OUR CHANCE!
CAPTURE THE CONVICT!
UR...
UGH...

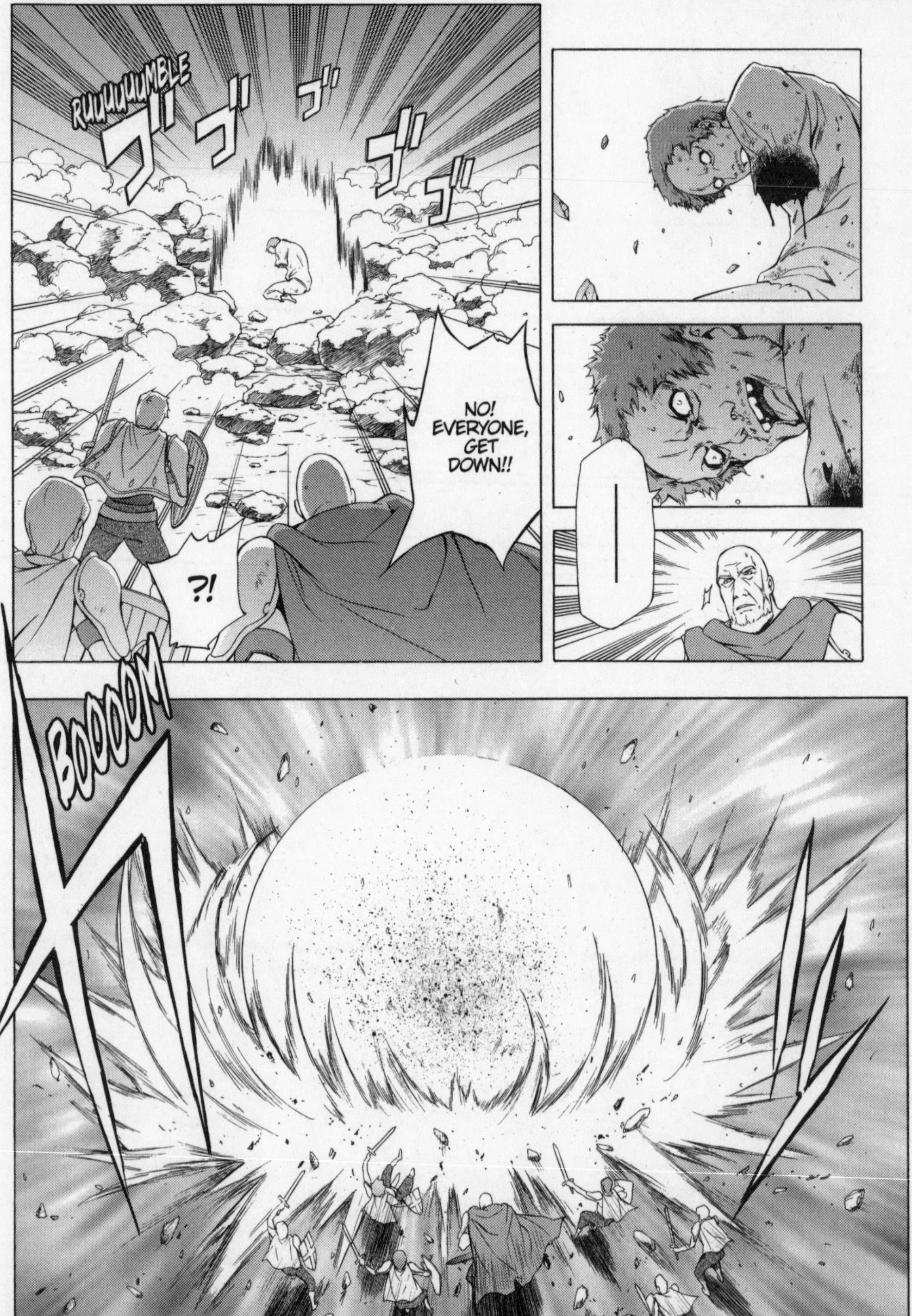
—
RUUUUUMBLE
ゴゴゴゴゴ
NO! EVERYONE, GET DOWN!!
?!
BOOOOM

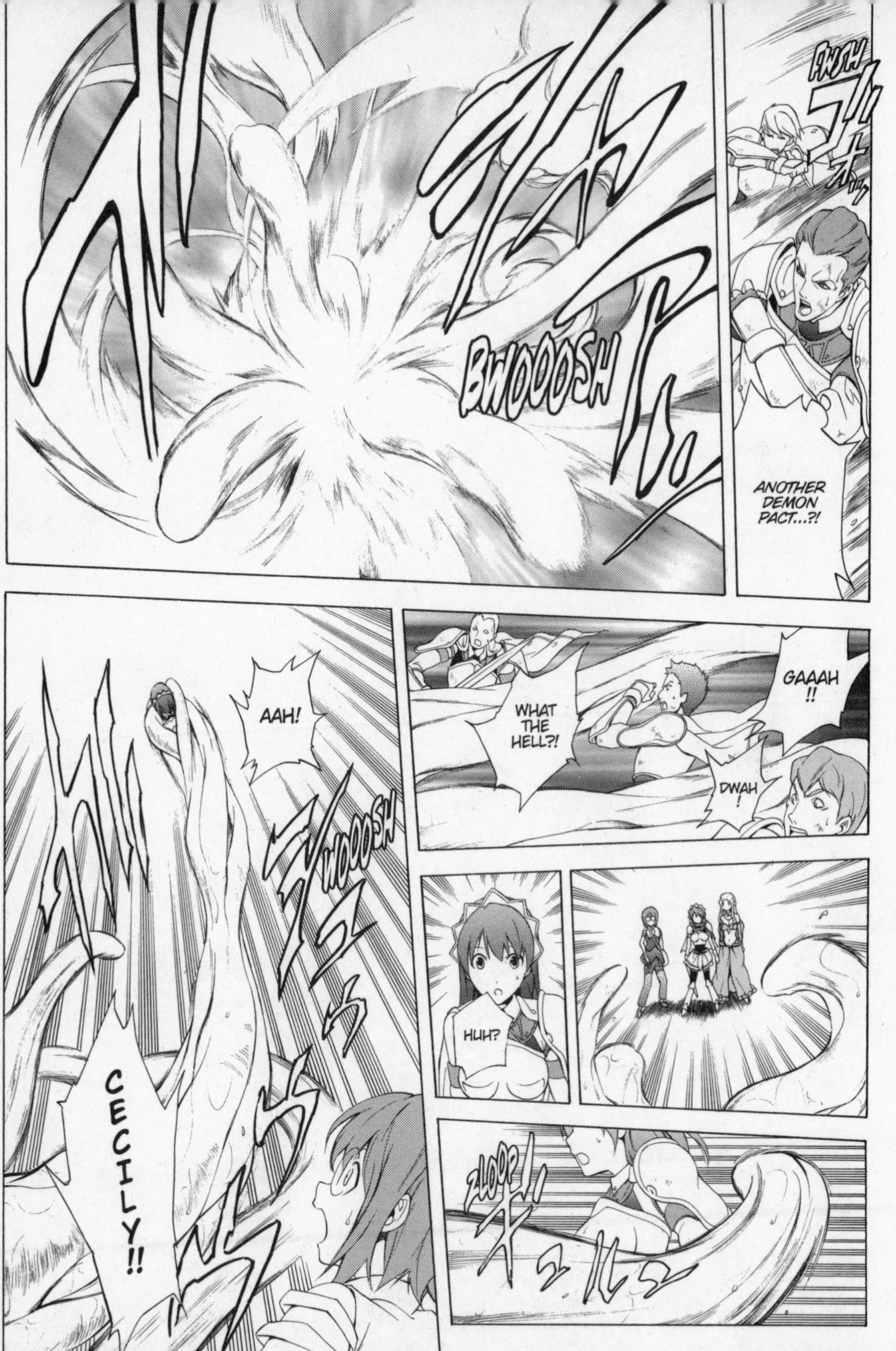
FWSH
ANOTHER DEMON PACT...?!
BWOOOSH
GAAAH!!
WHAT THE HELL?!
DWAH!
AAH!
WHOOOSH
CECILY!!
HUH?
ZLOOP

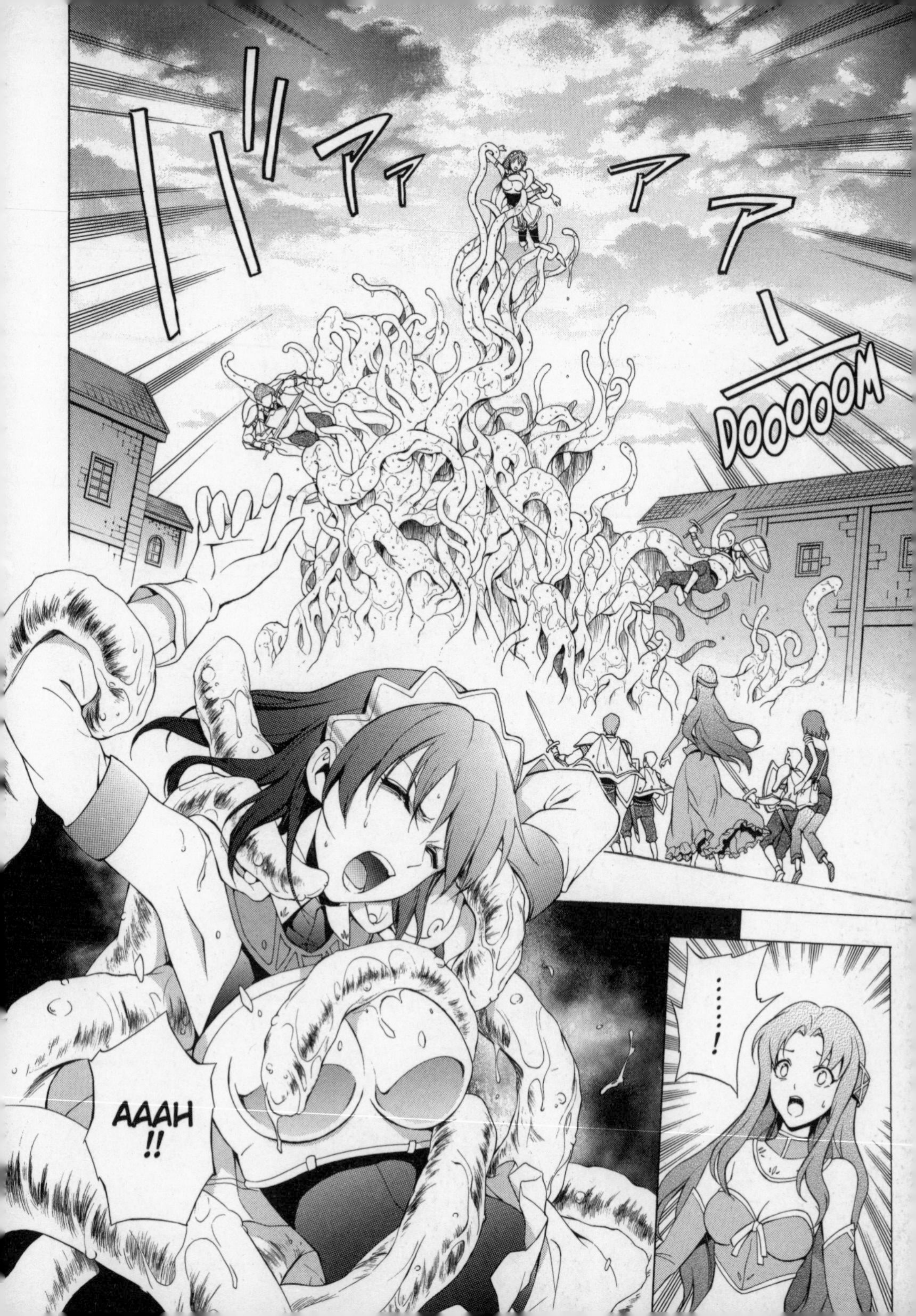
DOOOOOM
AAAH !!
......!

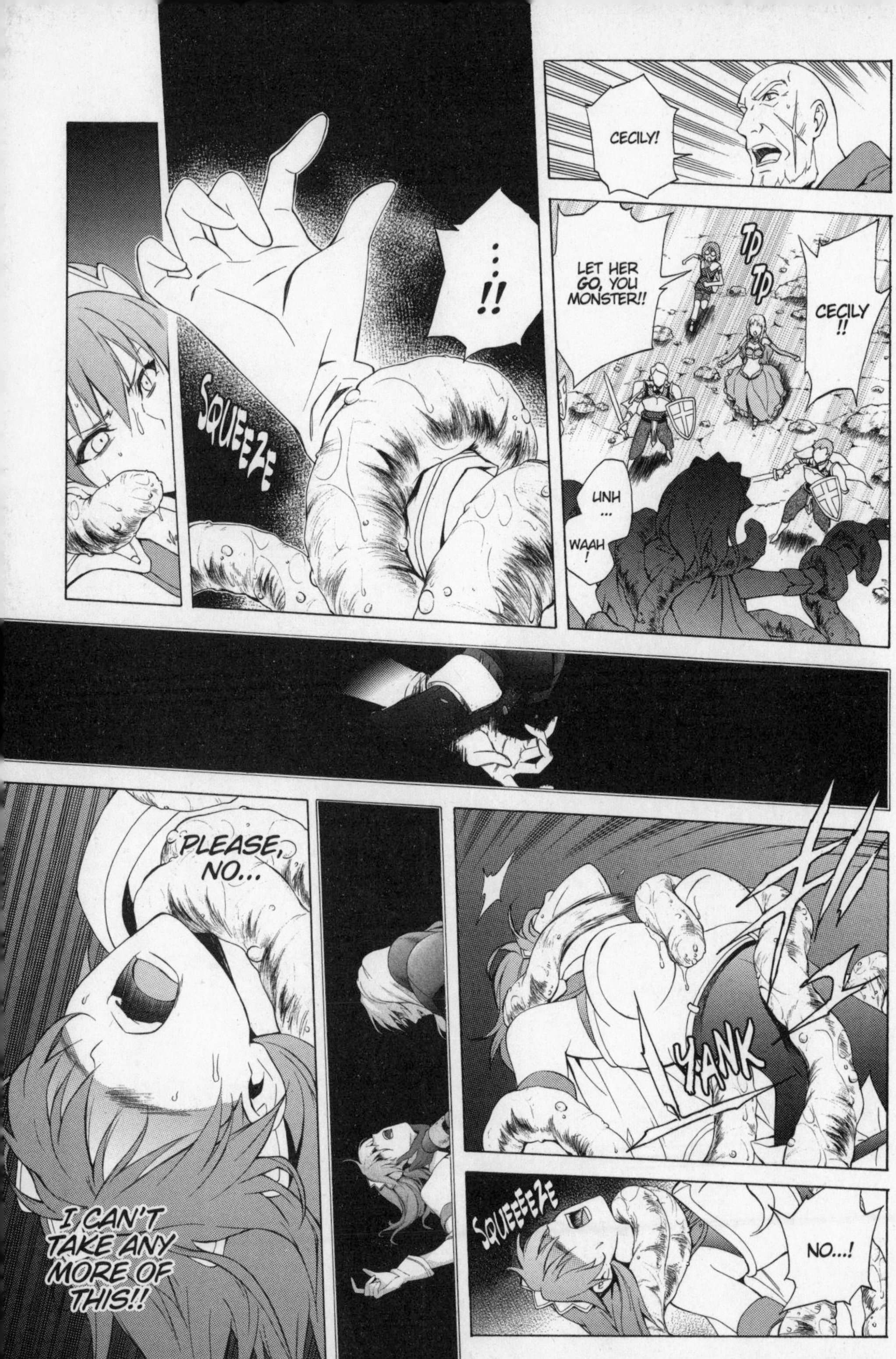
CECILY!
TP TP
CECILY !!
LET HER GO, YOU MONSTER!!
UNH ...
WAAH !
...!!
SQUEEEZE
YANK
NO...!
SQUEEEEZE
PLEASE, NO...
I CAN'T TAKE ANY MORE OF THIS!!

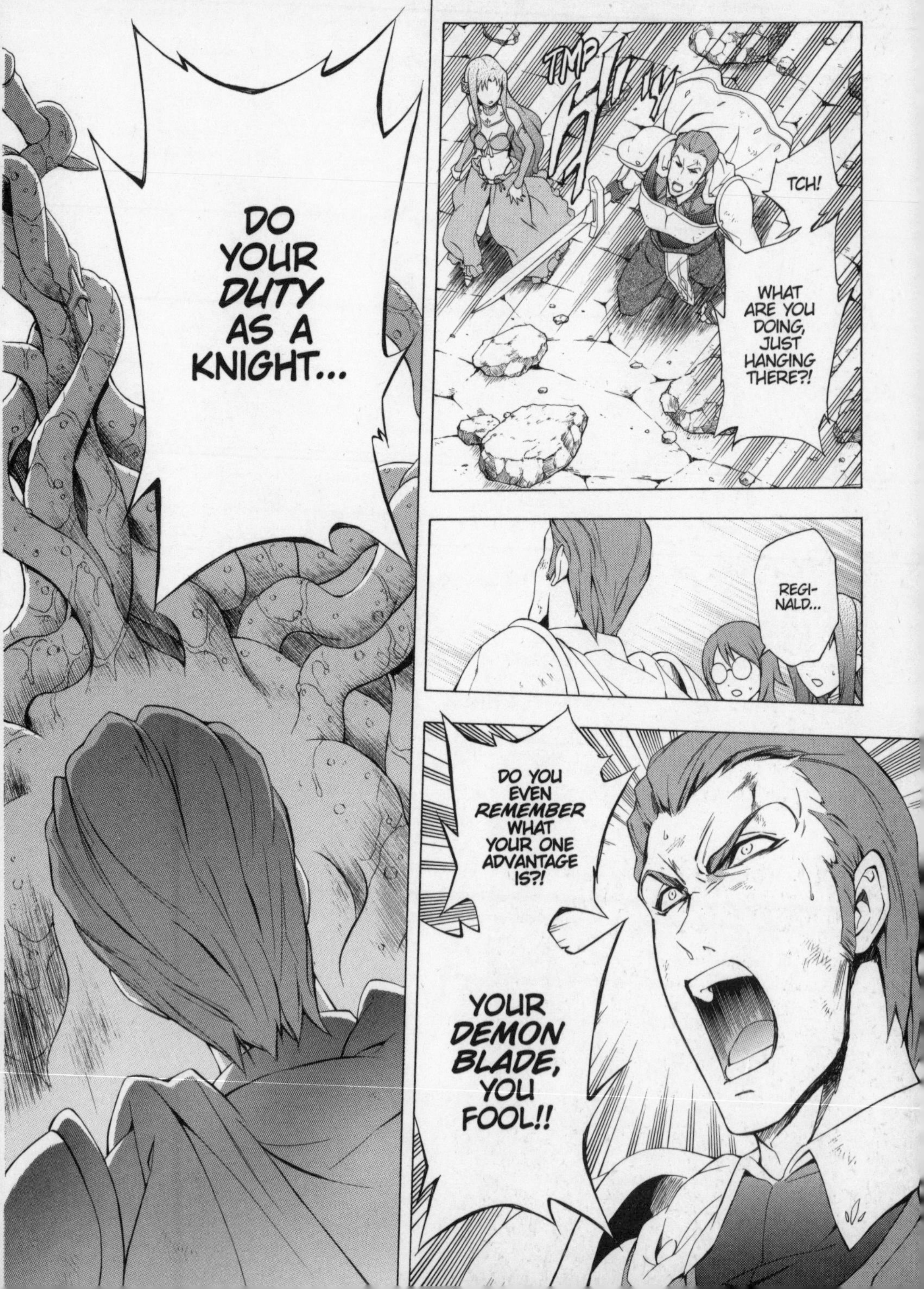
TMP
TCH!
WHAT ARE YOU DOING, JUST HANGING THERE?!
REGI-NALD...
DO YOU EVEN *REMEMBER* WHAT YOUR ONE ADVANTAGE IS?!
YOUR *DEMON BLADE*, YOU FOOL!!
DO YOUR *DUTY* AS A KNIGHT...

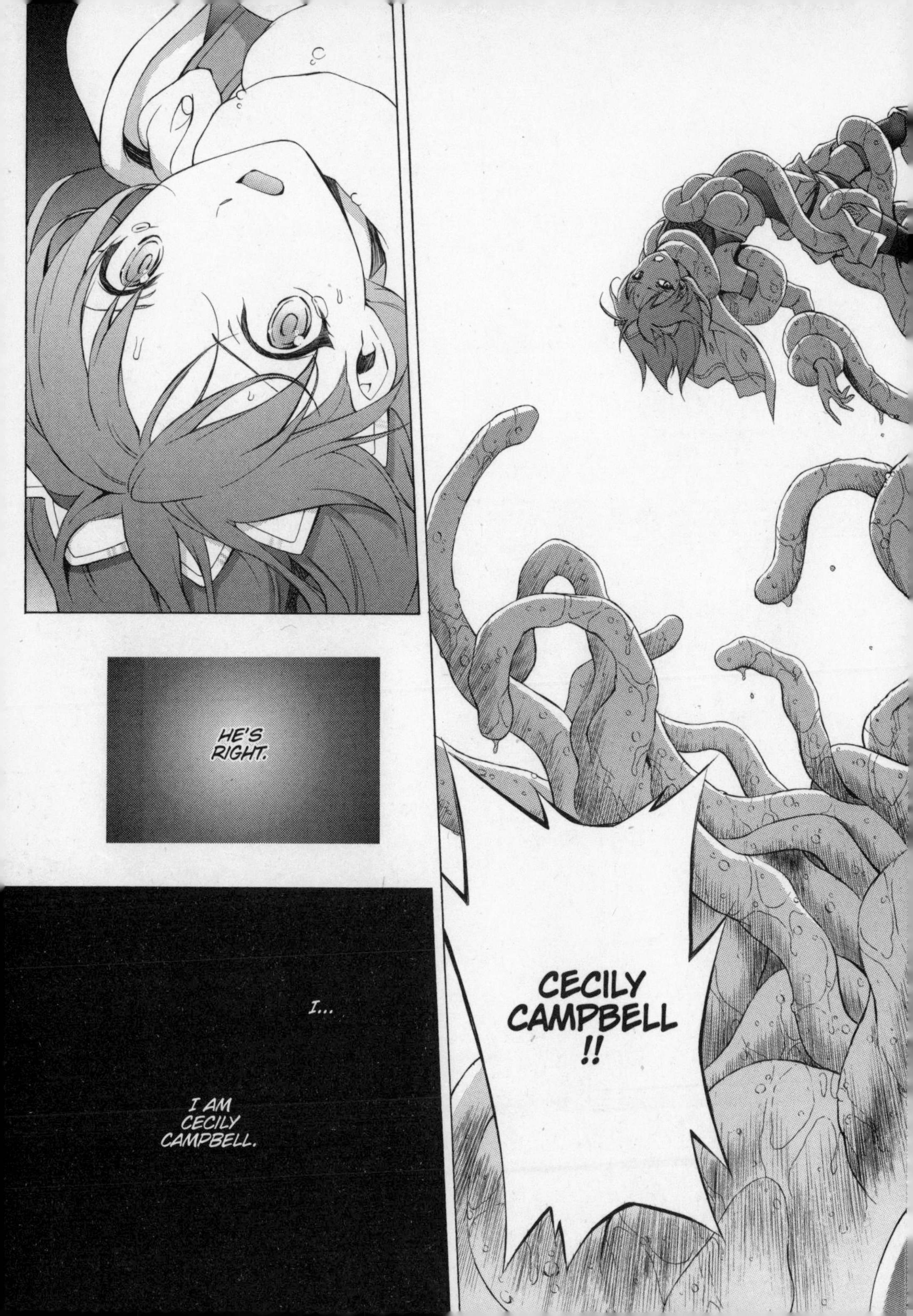
CECILY CAMPBELL !!
HE'S RIGHT.
I...
I AM CECILY CAMPBELL.

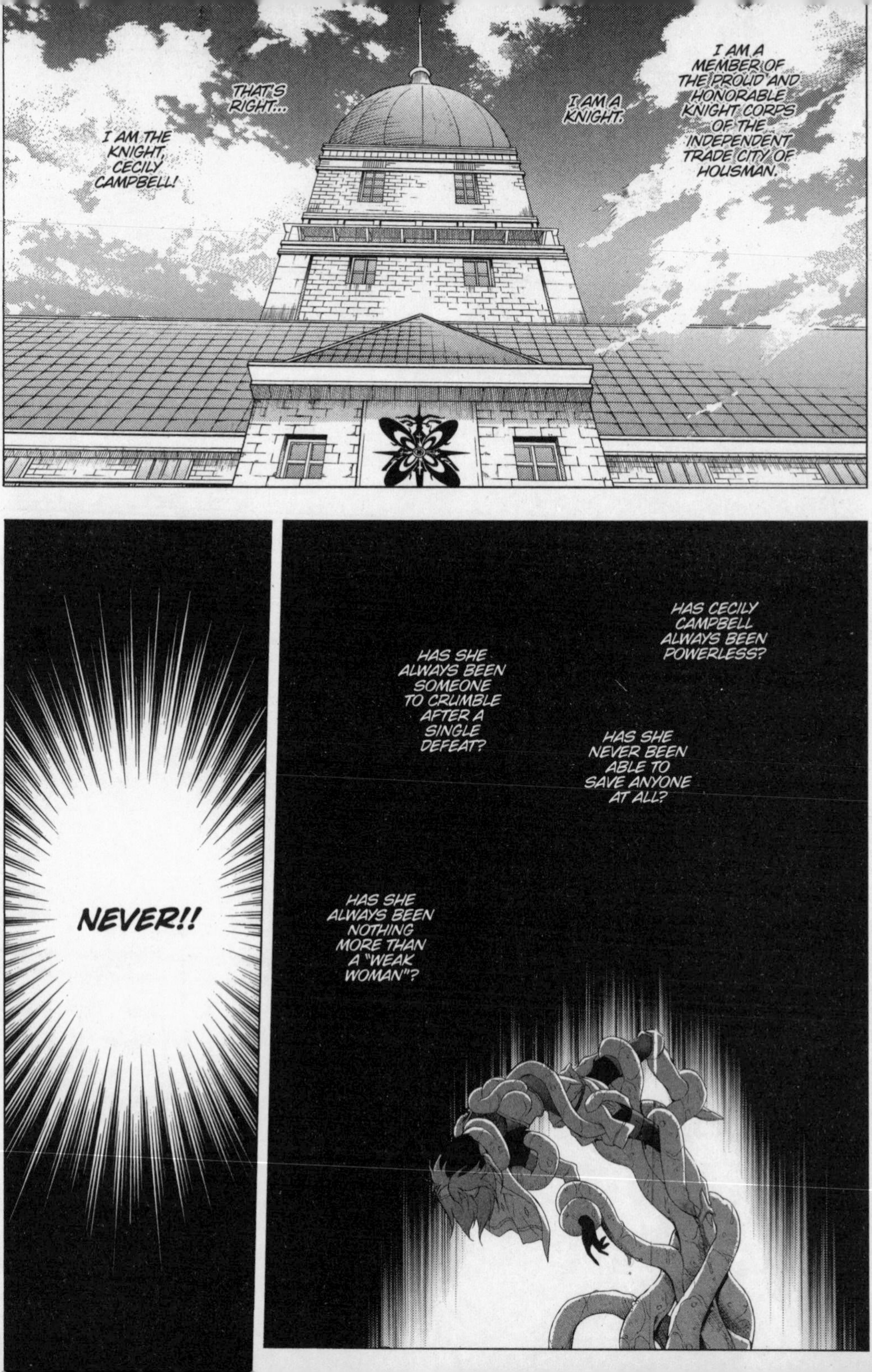
I AM A MEMBER OF THE PROUD AND HONORABLE KNIGHT CORPS OF THE INDEPENDENT TRADE CITY OF HOUSMAN.
I AM A KNIGHT.
THAT'S RIGHT...
I AM THE KNIGHT, CECILY CAMPBELL!
HAS CECILY CAMPBELL ALWAYS BEEN POWERLESS?
HAS SHE ALWAYS BEEN SOMEONE TO CRUMBLE AFTER A SINGLE DEFEAT?
HAS SHE NEVER BEEN ABLE TO SAVE ANYONE AT ALL?
HAS SHE ALWAYS BEEN NOTHING MORE THAN A "WEAK WOMAN"?
NEVER!!

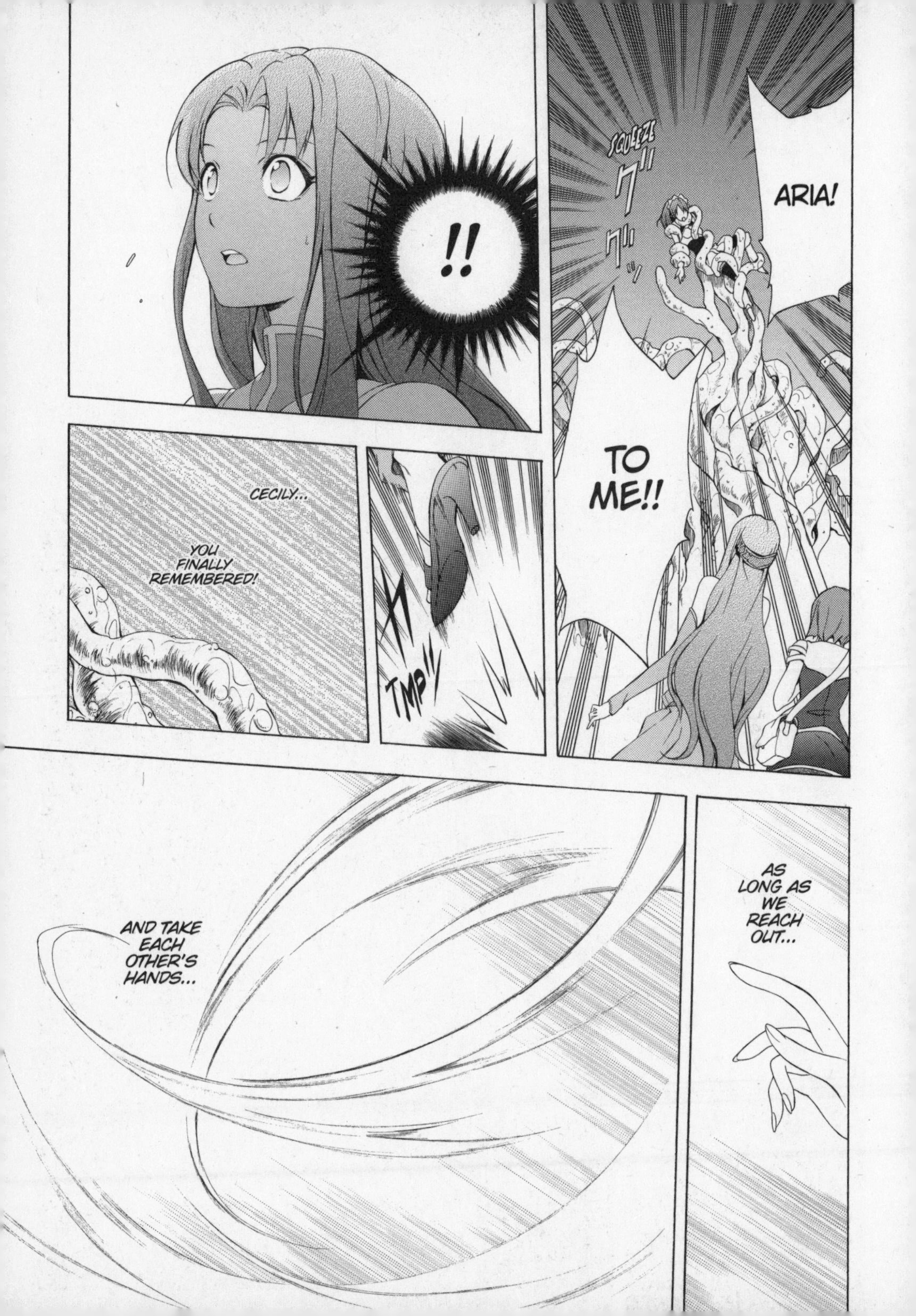
SQUEEZE
ARIA!
TO ME!!
!!
TMP!!
CECILY...
YOU FINALLY REMEMBERED!
AS LONG AS WE REACH OUT...
AND TAKE EACH OTHER'S HANDS...

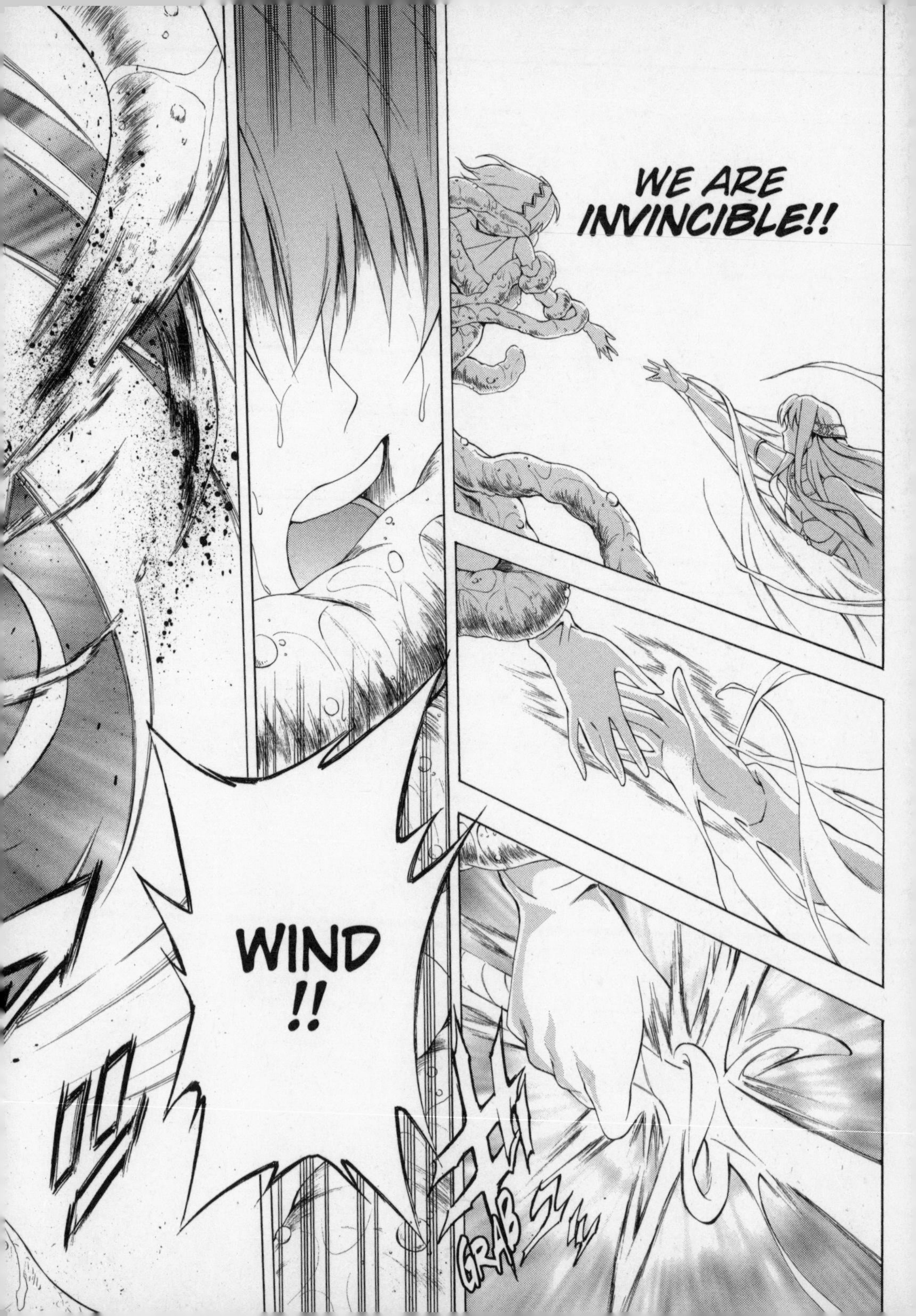
WE ARE INVINCIBLE!!
GRAB
WIND !!

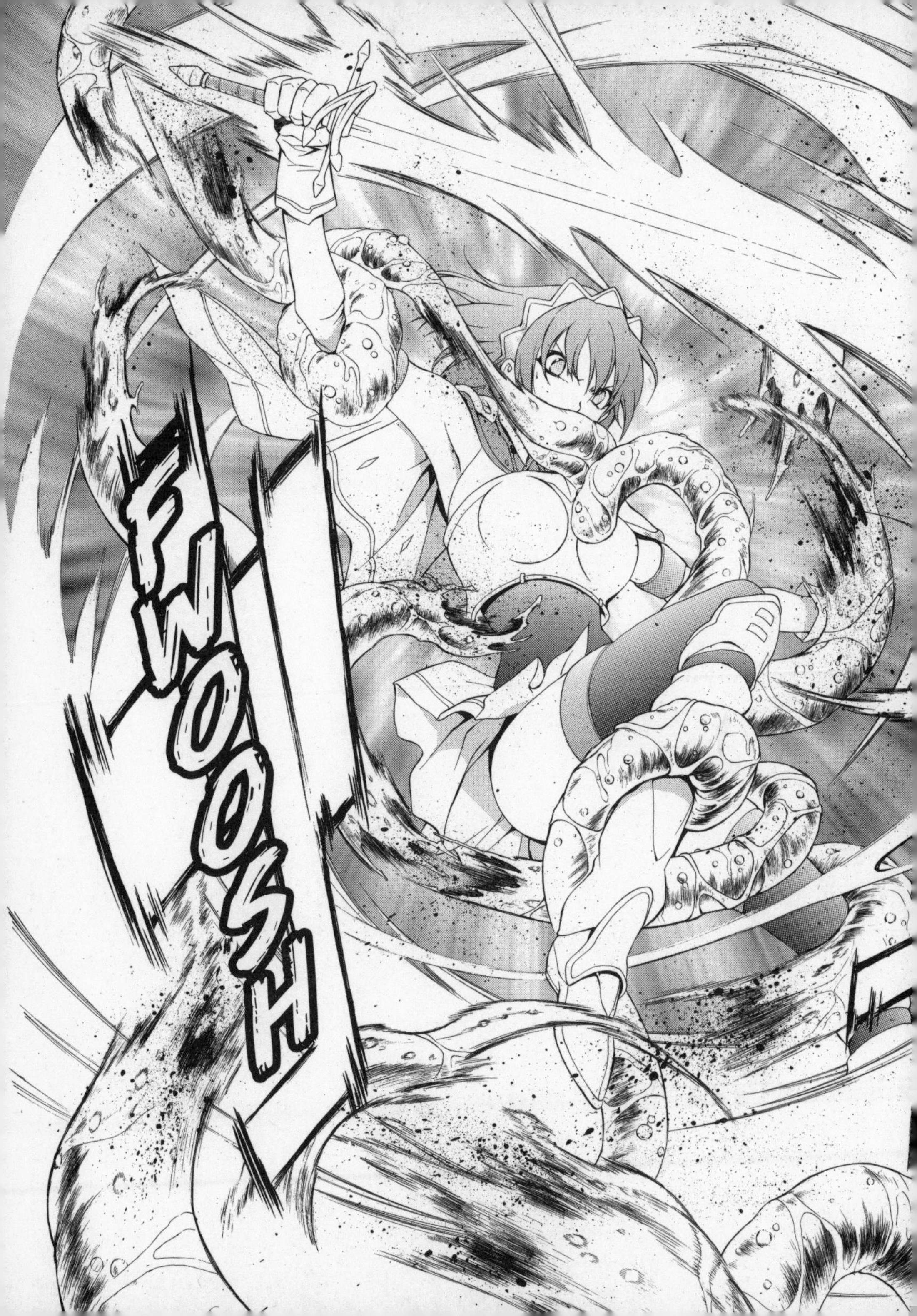
FWOOSH

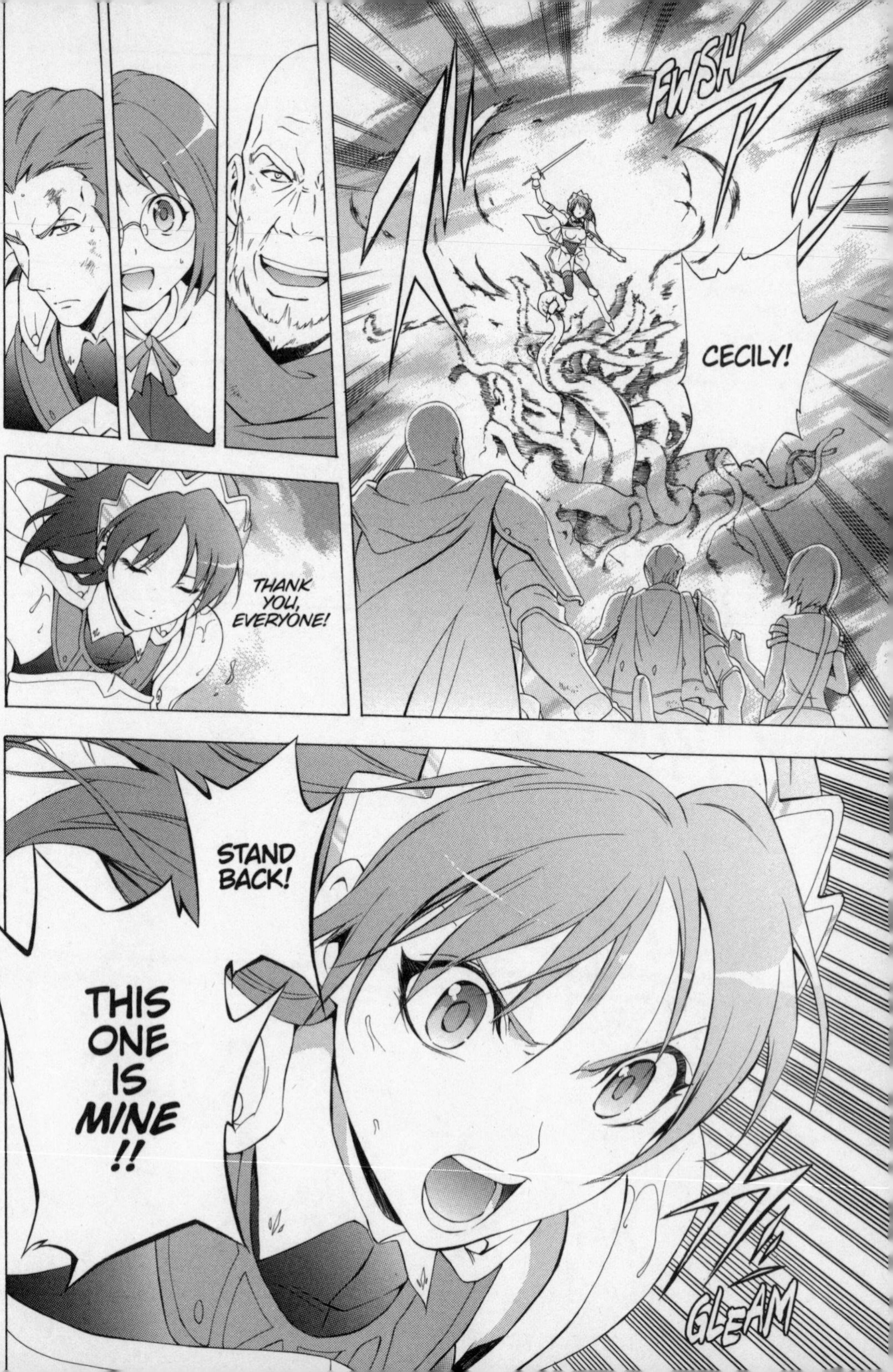
FWSH
CECILY!
THANK YOU, EVERYONE!
STAND BACK!
THIS ONE IS MINE!!
GLEAM

Chapter 23 Fool (Part 4)

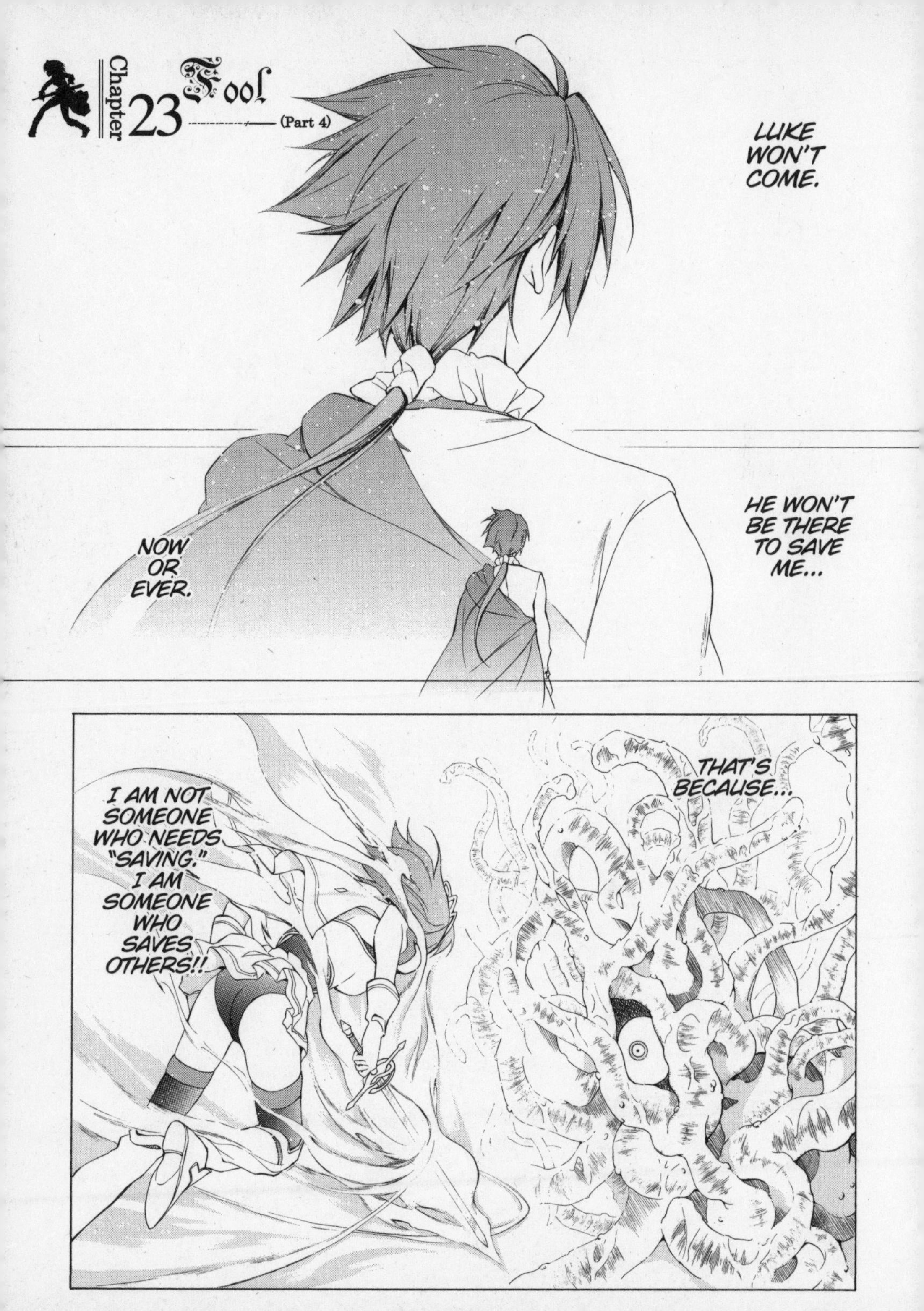
LUKE WON'T COME.
HE WON'T BE THERE TO SAVE ME...
NOW OR EVER.
THAT'S BECAUSE...
I AM NOT SOMEONE WHO NEEDS "SAVING." I AM SOMEONE WHO SAVES OTHERS!!

NO MATTER WHAT HAPPENS...

THE ONLY ONE WHO SHOULD EVER SAVE ME IS MYSELF.

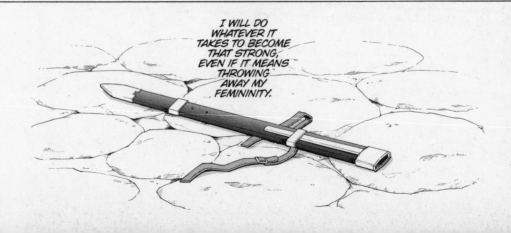

I WILL DO WHATEVER IT TAKES TO BECOME THAT STRONG, EVEN IF IT MEANS THROWING AWAY MY FEMININITY.

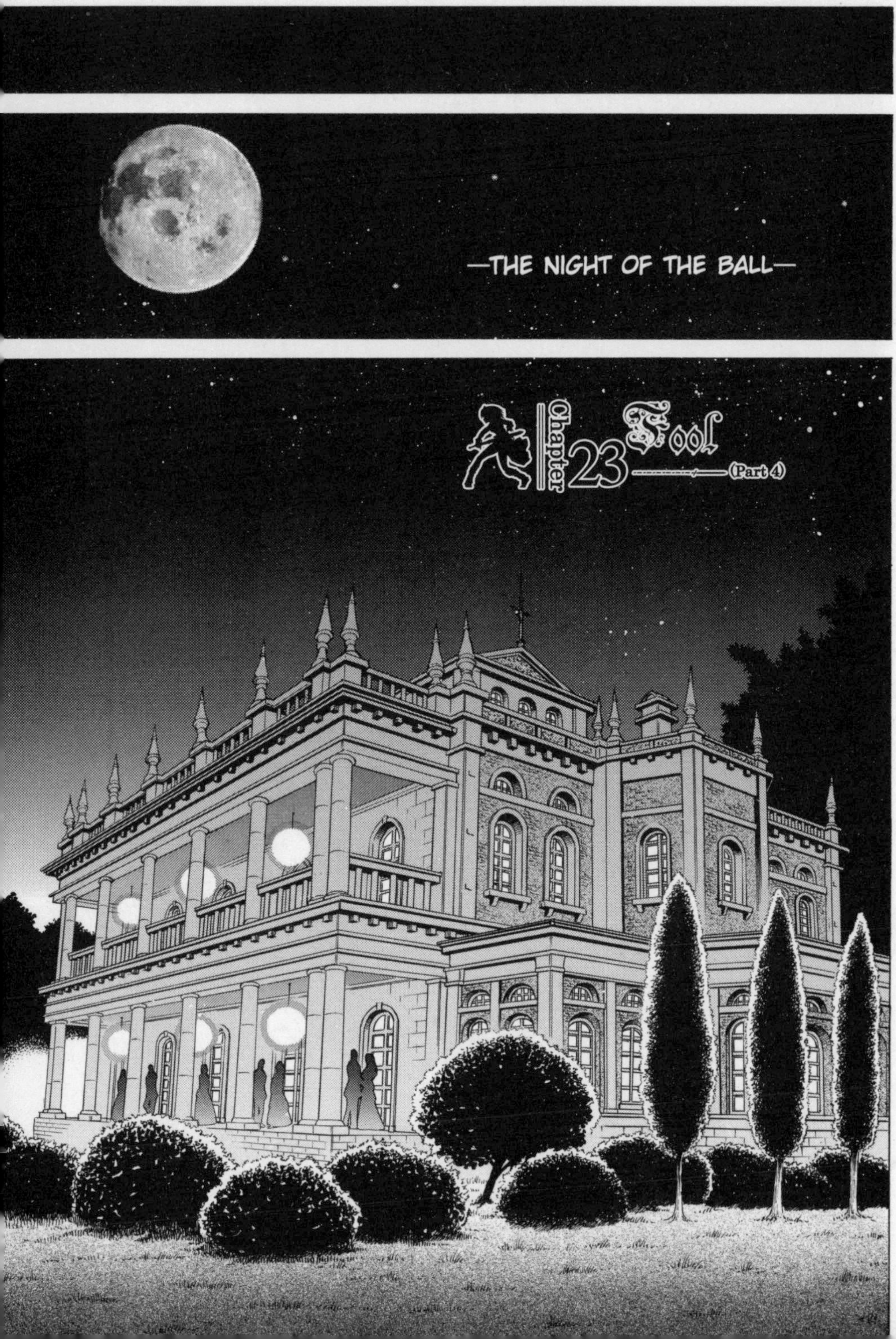
—THE NIGHT OF THE BALL—
Chapter 23 Fool
(Part 4)

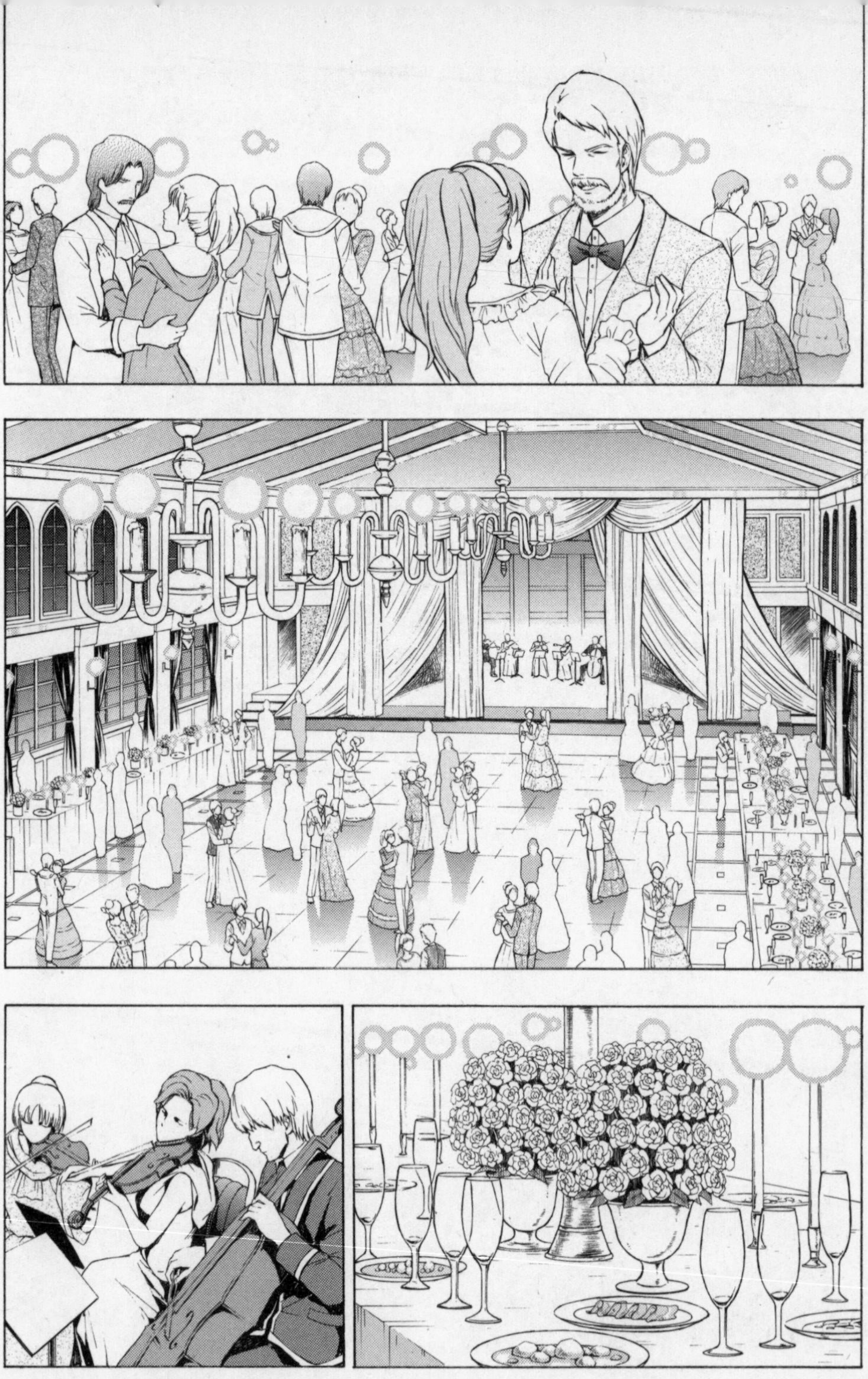

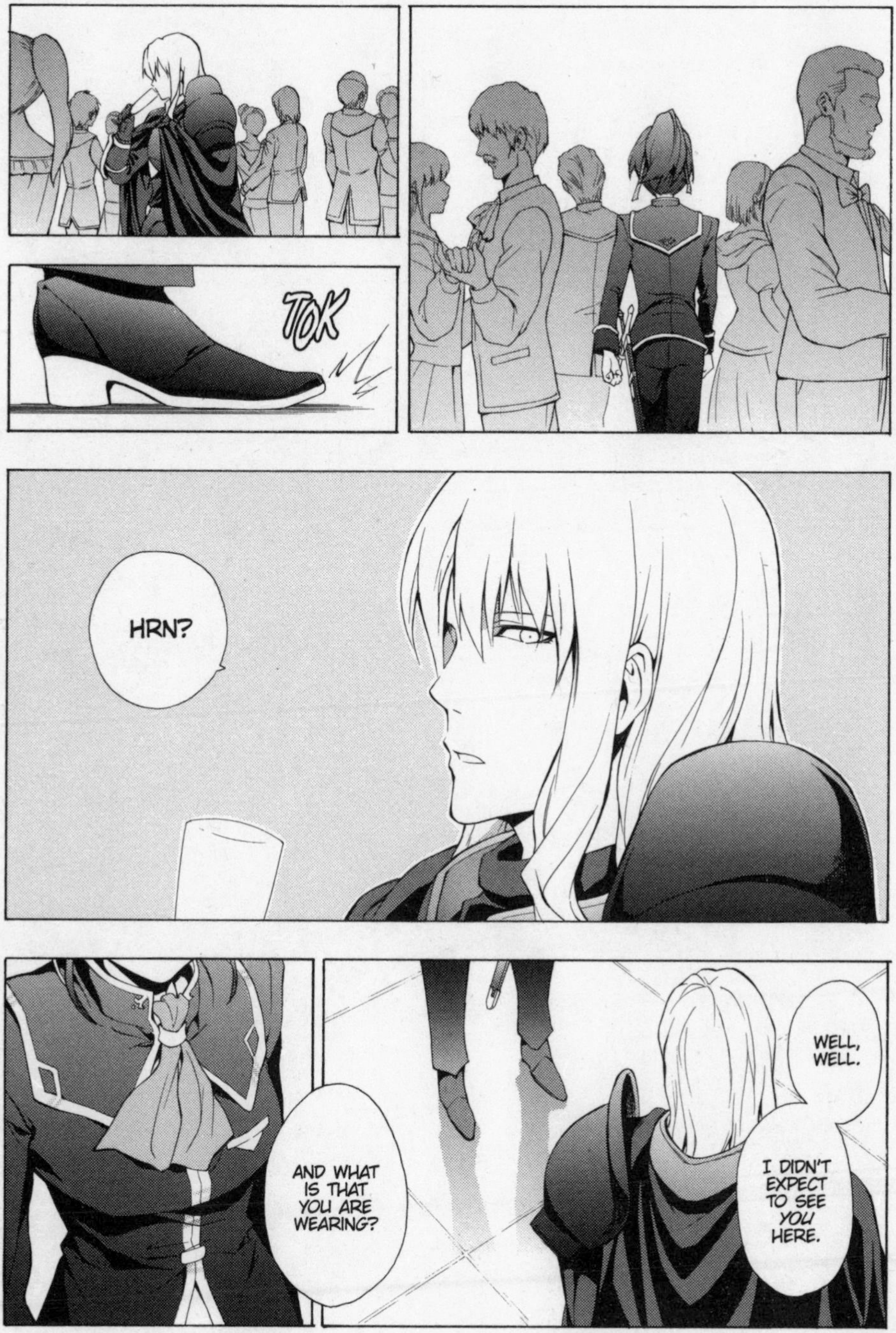
TOK
HRN?
WELL, WELL.
I DIDN'T EXPECT TO SEE *YOU* HERE.
AND WHAT IS THAT YOU ARE WEARING?

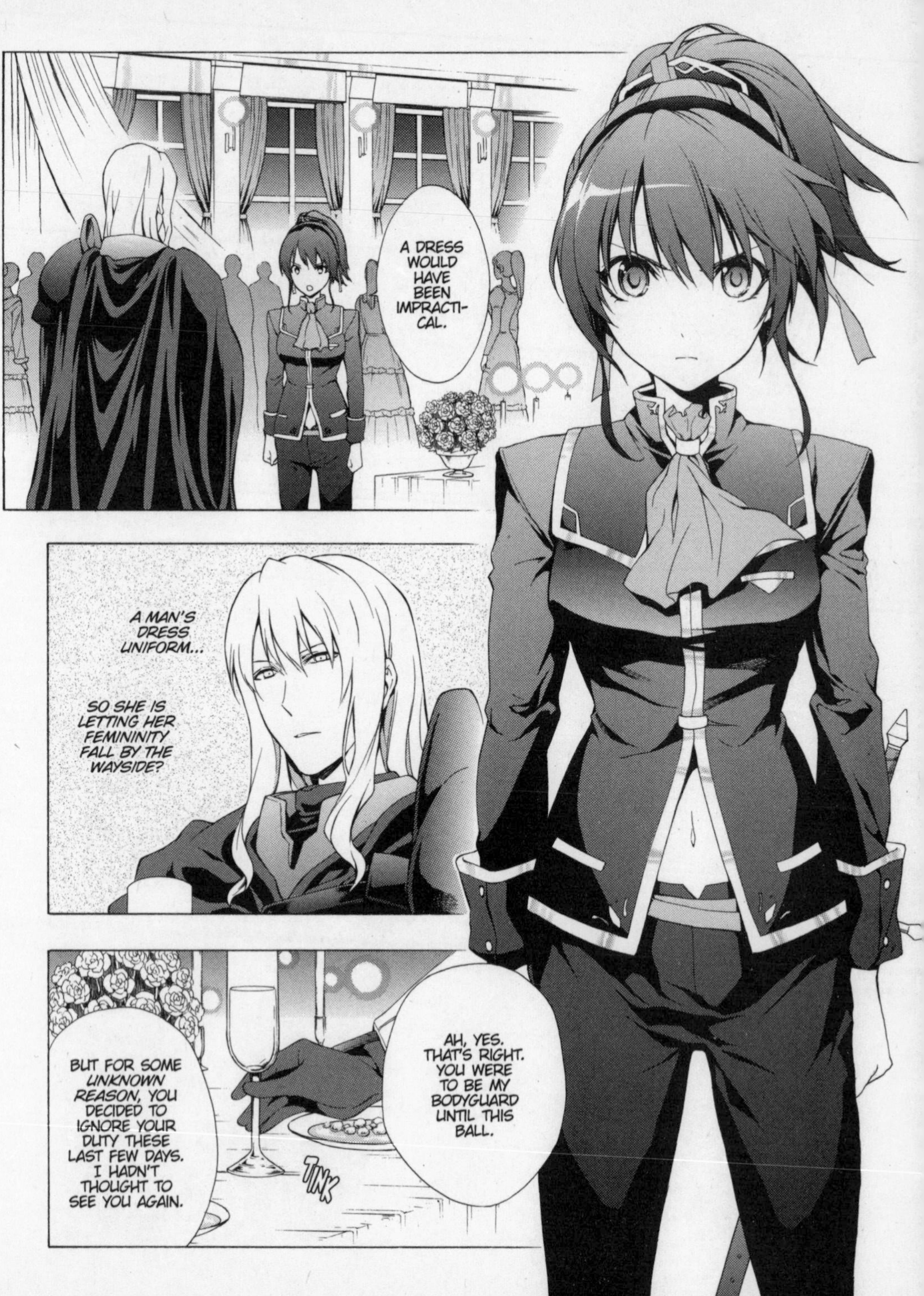
A DRESS WOULD HAVE BEEN IMPRACTICAL.
A MAN'S DRESS UNIFORM...
SO SHE IS LETTING HER FEMININITY FALL BY THE WAYSIDE?
AH, YES. THAT'S RIGHT. YOU WERE TO BE MY BODYGUARD UNTIL THIS BALL.
BUT FOR SOME UNKNOWN REASON, YOU DECIDED TO IGNORE YOUR DUTY THESE LAST FEW DAYS. I HADN'T THOUGHT TO SEE YOU AGAIN.
TINK

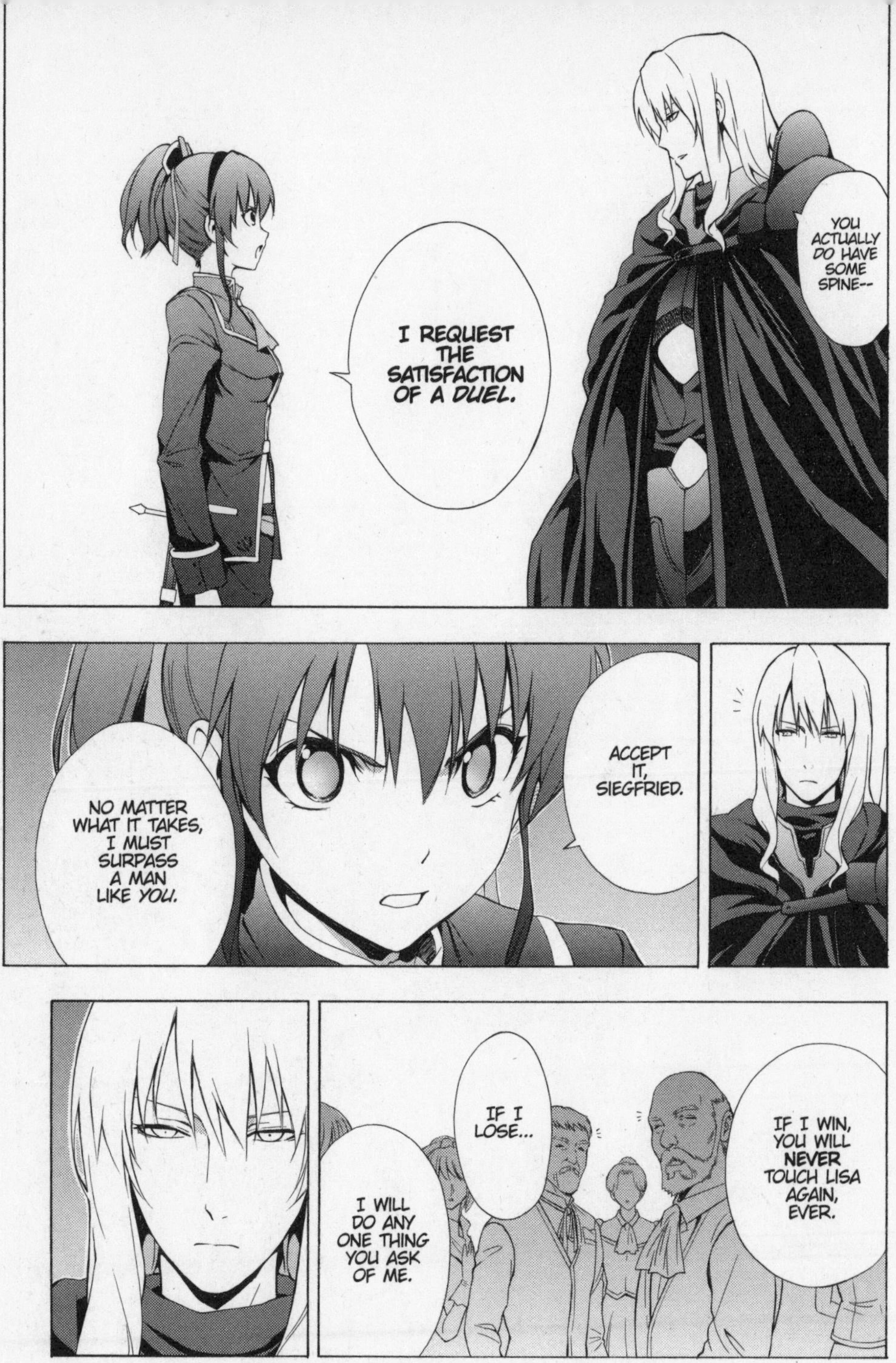
YOU ACTUALLY DO HAVE SOME SPINE--
I REQUEST THE SATISFACTION OF A DUEL.
ACCEPT IT, SIEGFRIED.
NO MATTER WHAT IT TAKES, I MUST SURPASS A MAN LIKE YOU.
IF I WIN, YOU WILL NEVER TOUCH LISA AGAIN, EVER.
IF I LOSE...
I WILL DO ANY ONE THING YOU ASK OF ME.

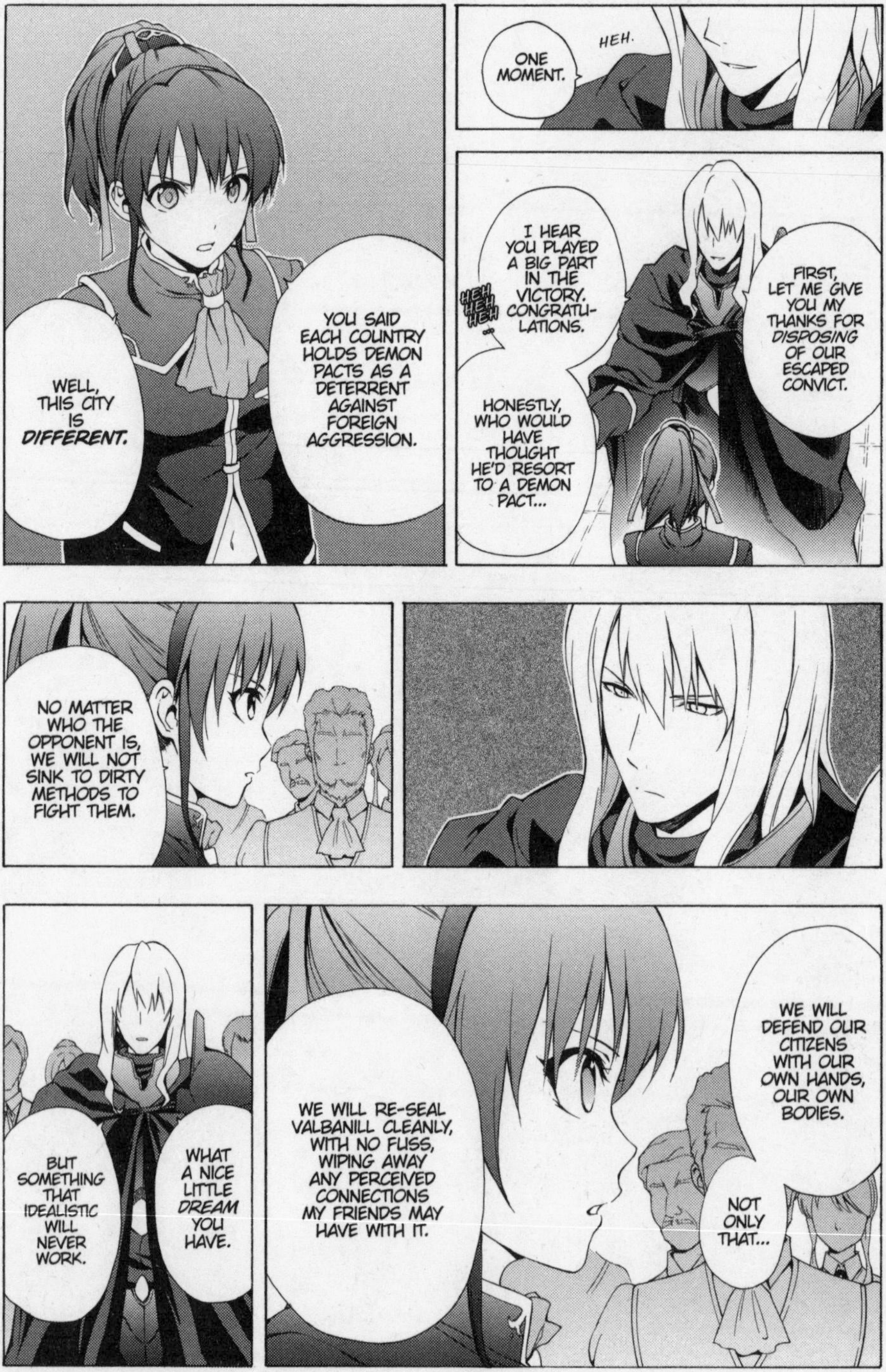
HEH.
ONE MOMENT.
FIRST, LET ME GIVE YOU MY THANKS FOR *DISPOSING* OF OUR ESCAPED CONVICT.
I HEAR YOU PLAYED A BIG PART IN THE VICTORY. CONGRATULATIONS.
HEH HEH HEH
HONESTLY, WHO WOULD HAVE THOUGHT HE'D RESORT TO A DEMON PACT...
YOU SAID EACH COUNTRY HOLDS DEMON PACTS AS A DETERRENT AGAINST FOREIGN AGGRESSION.
WELL, THIS CITY IS ***DIFFERENT.***
NO MATTER WHO THE OPPONENT IS, WE WILL NOT SINK TO DIRTY METHODS TO FIGHT THEM.
WE WILL DEFEND OUR CITIZENS WITH OUR OWN HANDS, OUR OWN BODIES.
NOT ONLY THAT...
WE WILL RE-SEAL VALBANILL CLEANLY, WITH NO FUSS, WIPING AWAY ANY PERCEIVED CONNECTIONS MY FRIENDS MAY HAVE WITH IT.
WHAT A NICE LITTLE *DREAM* YOU HAVE.
BUT SOMETHING THAT IDEALISTIC WILL NEVER WORK.

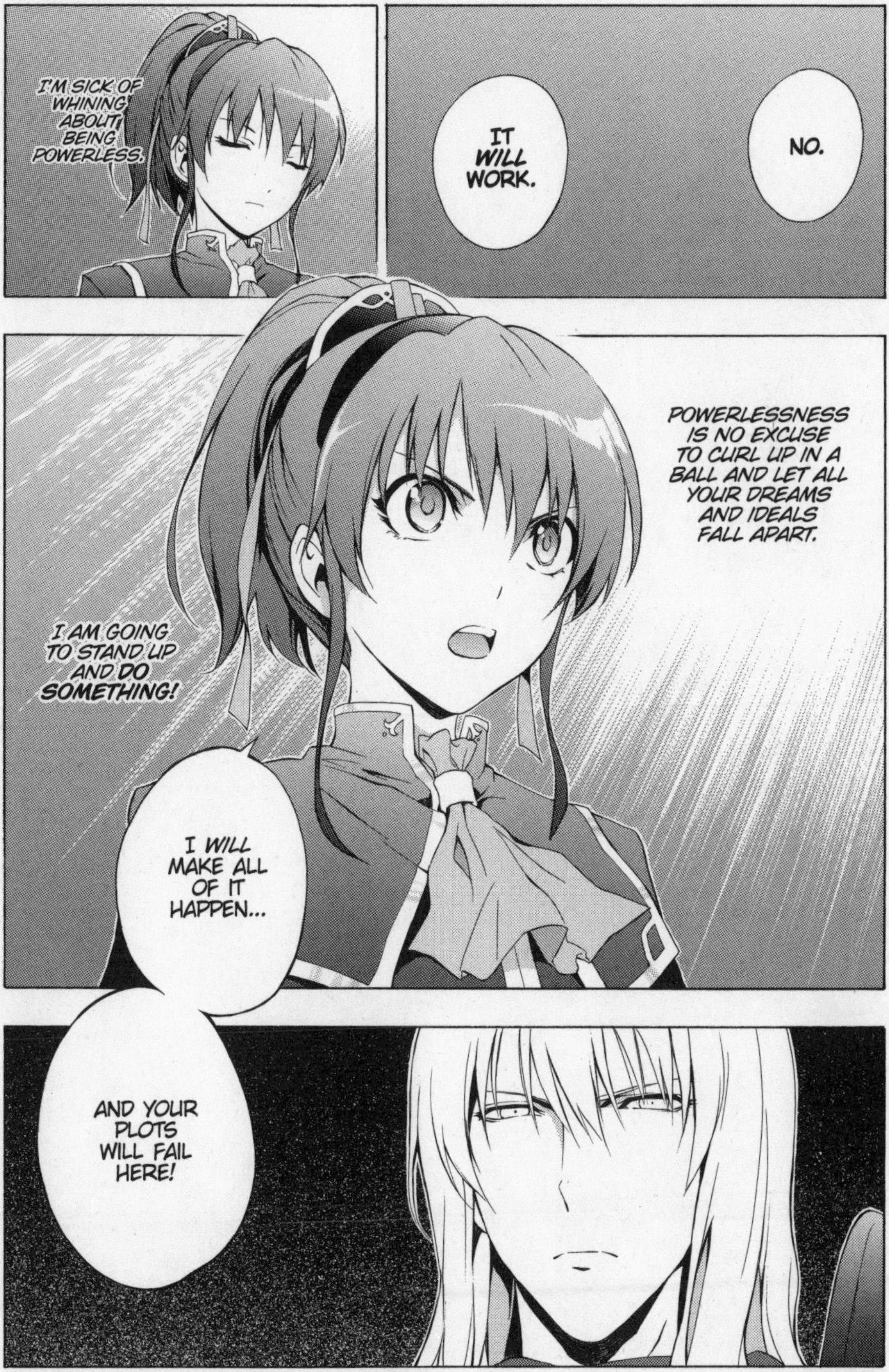
NO.
IT WILL WORK.
I'M SICK OF WHINING ABOUT BEING POWERLESS.
POWERLESSNESS IS NO EXCUSE TO CURL UP IN A BALL AND LET ALL YOUR DREAMS AND IDEALS FALL APART.
I AM GOING TO STAND UP AND DO SOMETHING!
I WILL MAKE ALL OF IT HAPPEN...
AND YOUR PLOTS WILL FAIL HERE!

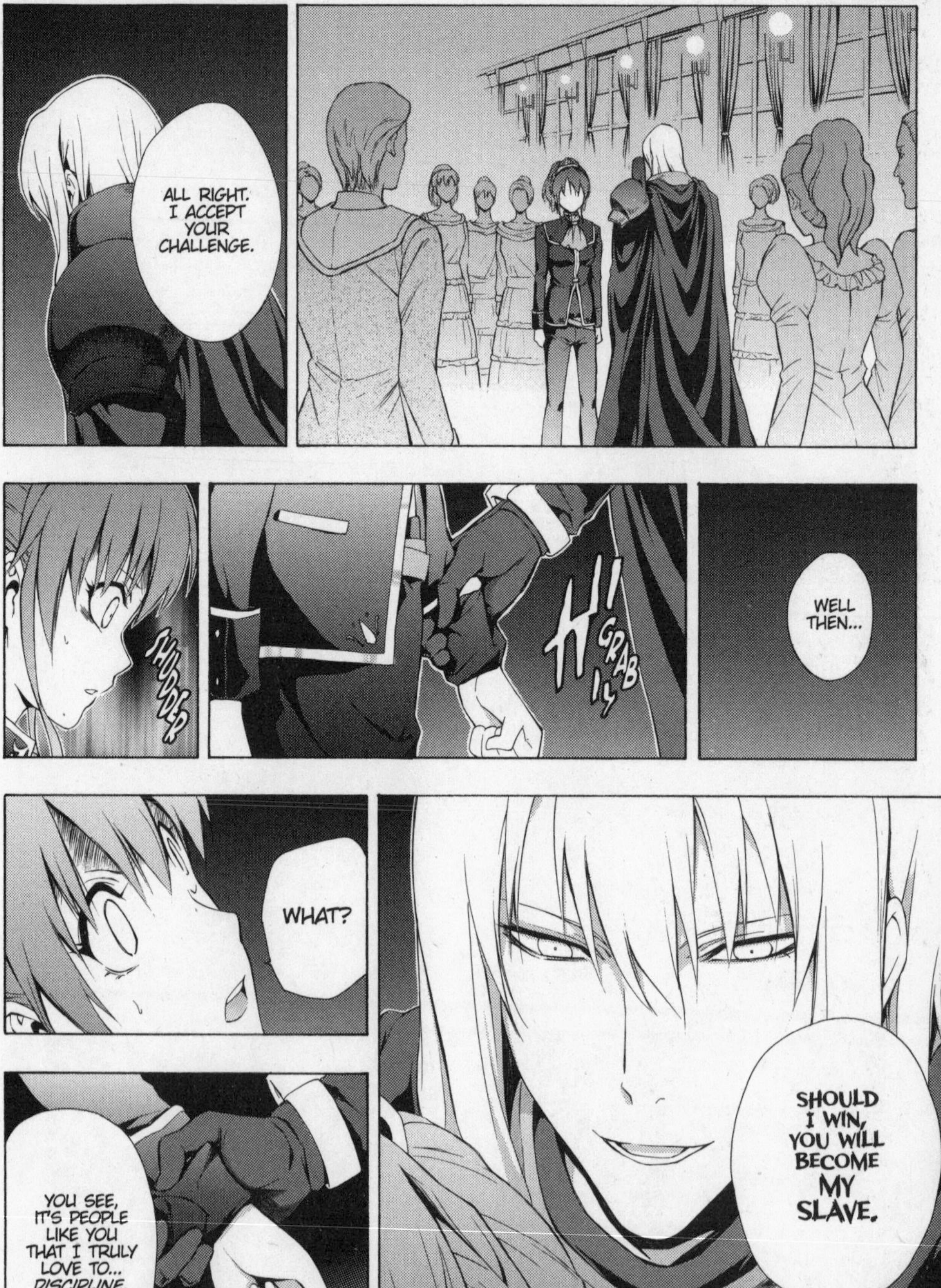
ALL RIGHT. I ACCEPT YOUR CHALLENGE.
WELL THEN...
GRAB
SHUDDER
SHOULD I WIN, YOU WILL BECOME MY SLAVE.
WHAT?
YOU SEE, IT'S PEOPLE LIKE YOU THAT I TRULY LOVE TO... DISCIPLINE.

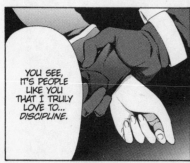

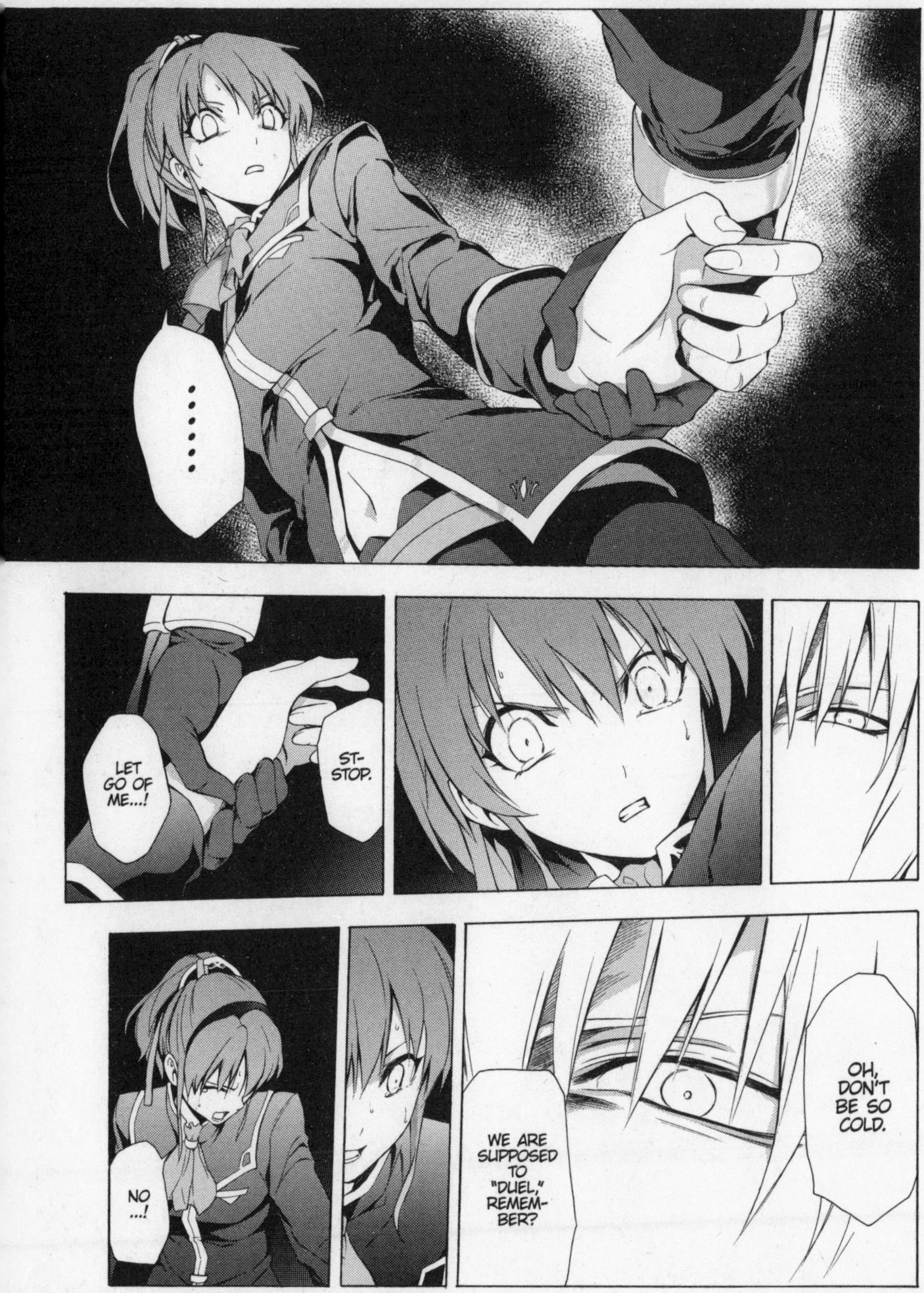
......
ST-STOP.
LET GO OF ME...!
OH, DON'T BE SO COLD.
WE ARE SUPPOSED TO "DUEL," REMEMBER?
NO ...!

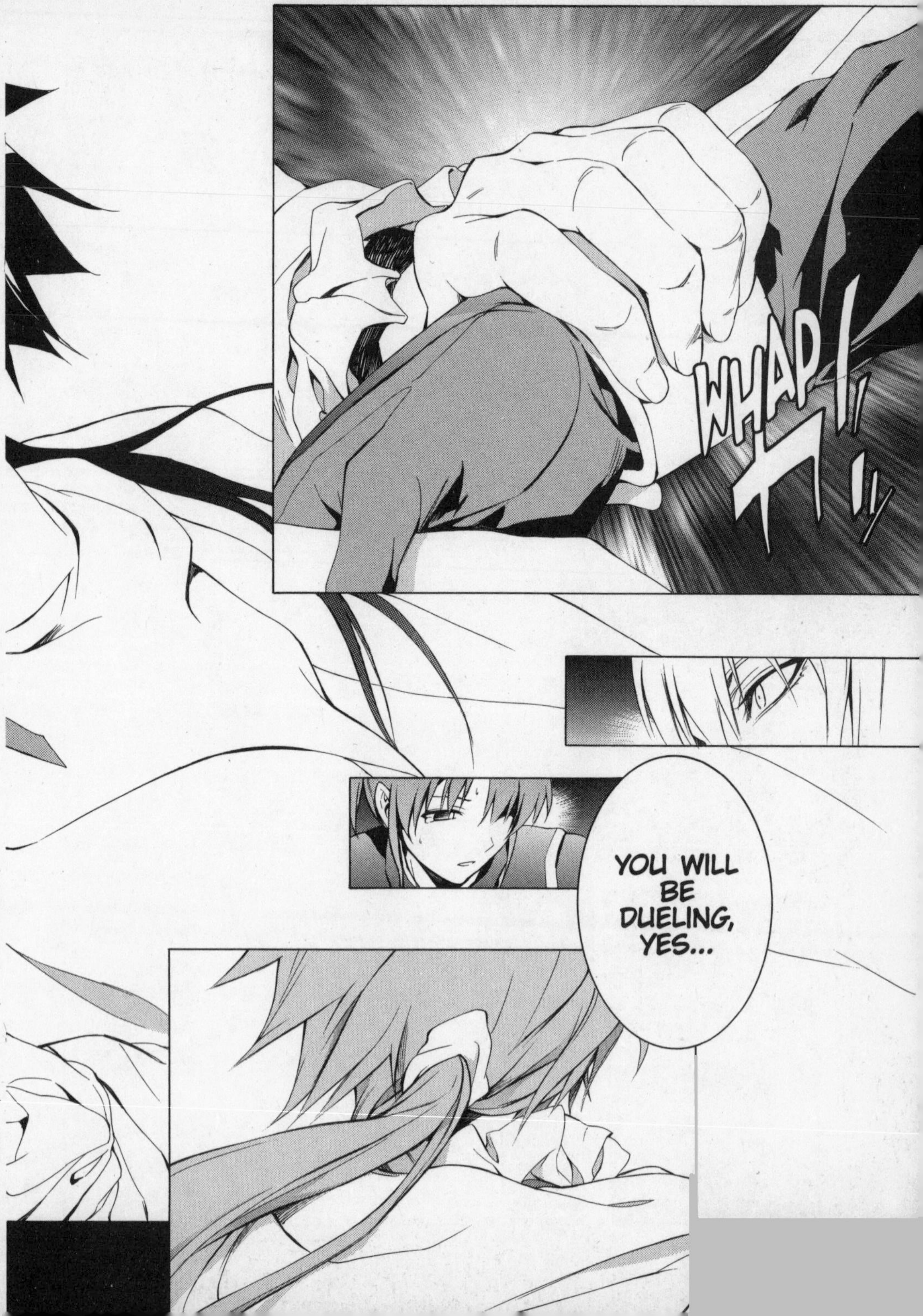
WHAP!!
YOU WILL BE DUELING, YES...

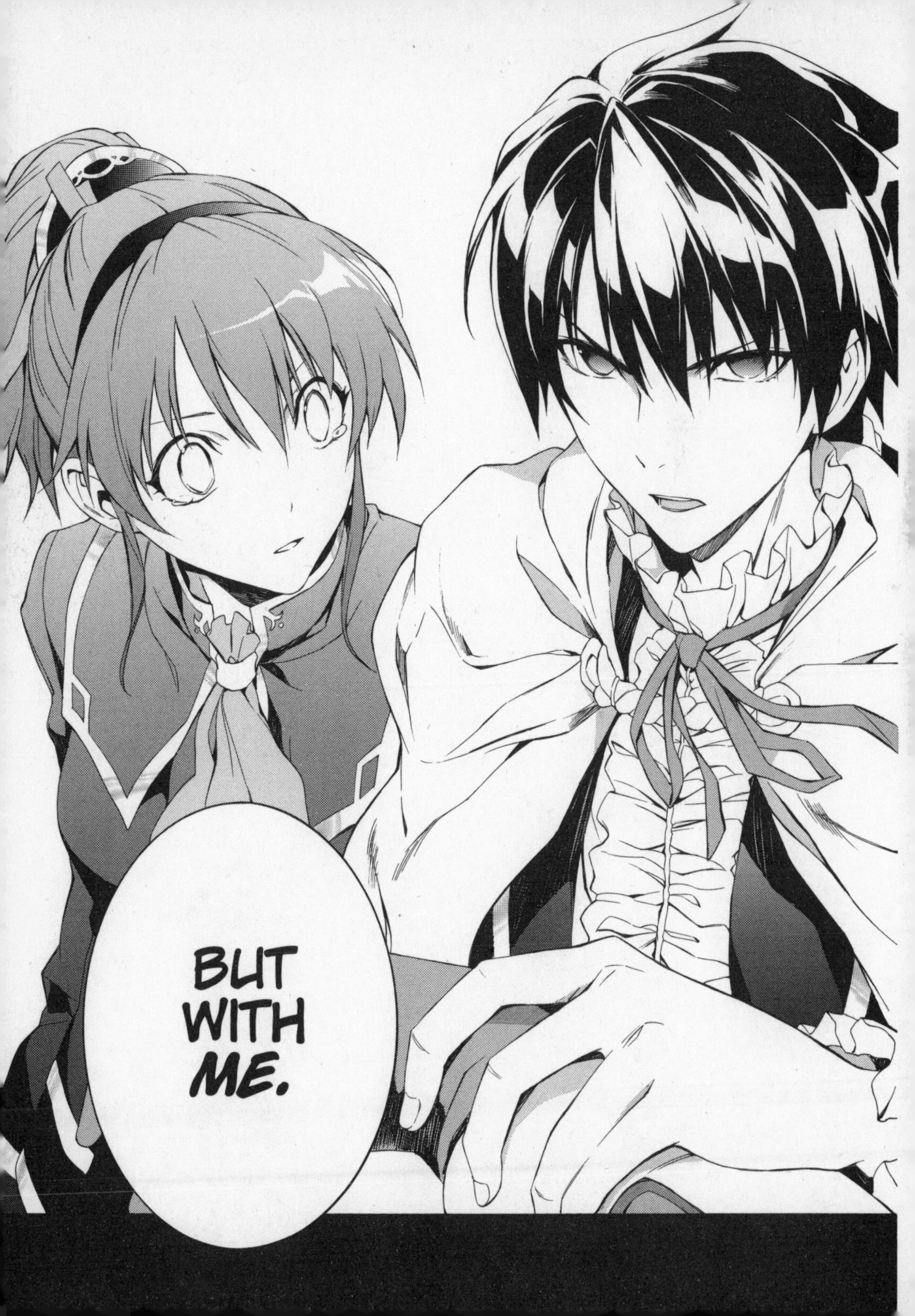
BUT WITH ME.

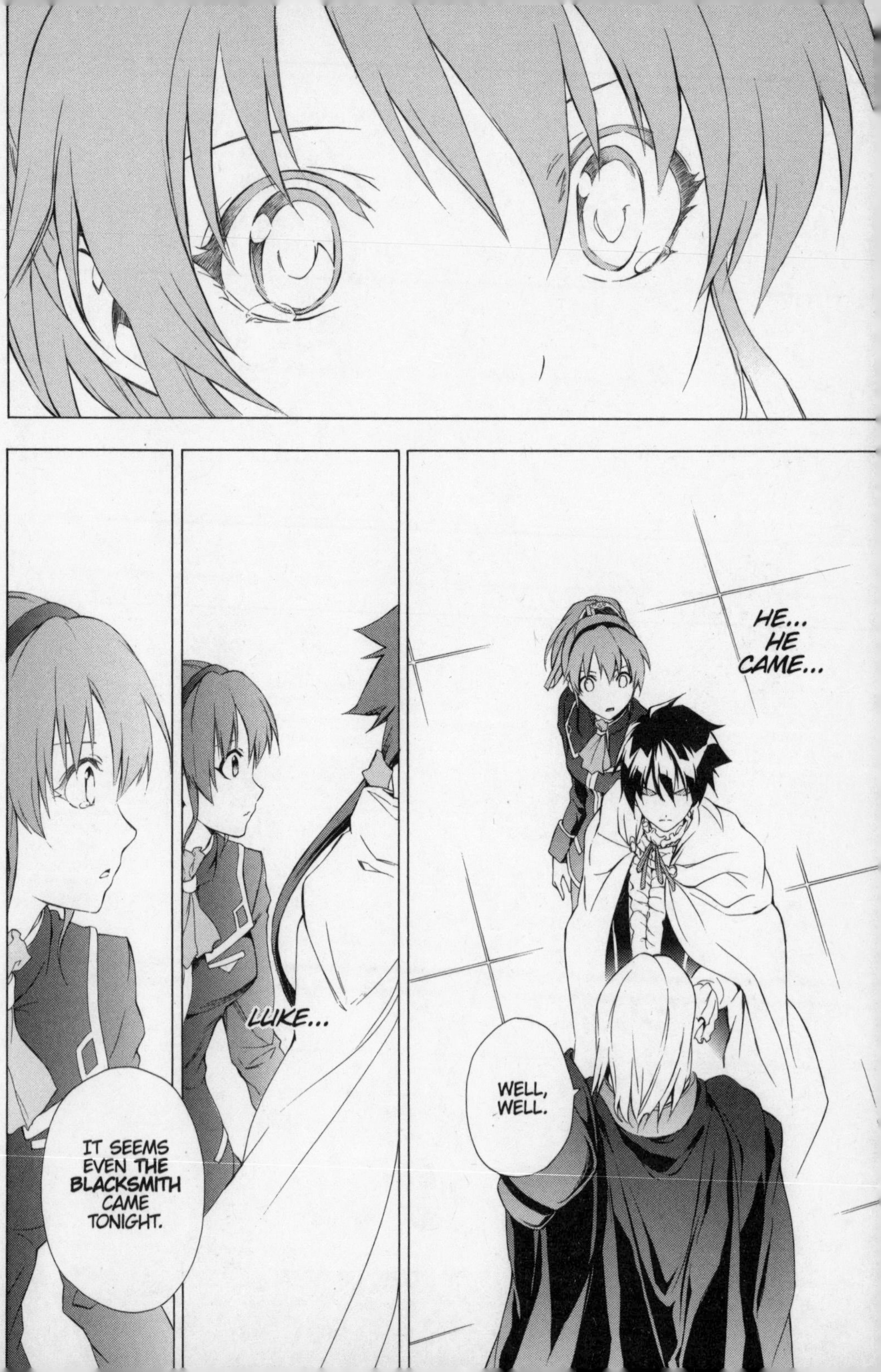
HE... HE CAME...
WELL, WELL.
LUKE...
IT SEEMS EVEN THE BLACKSMITH CAME TONIGHT.

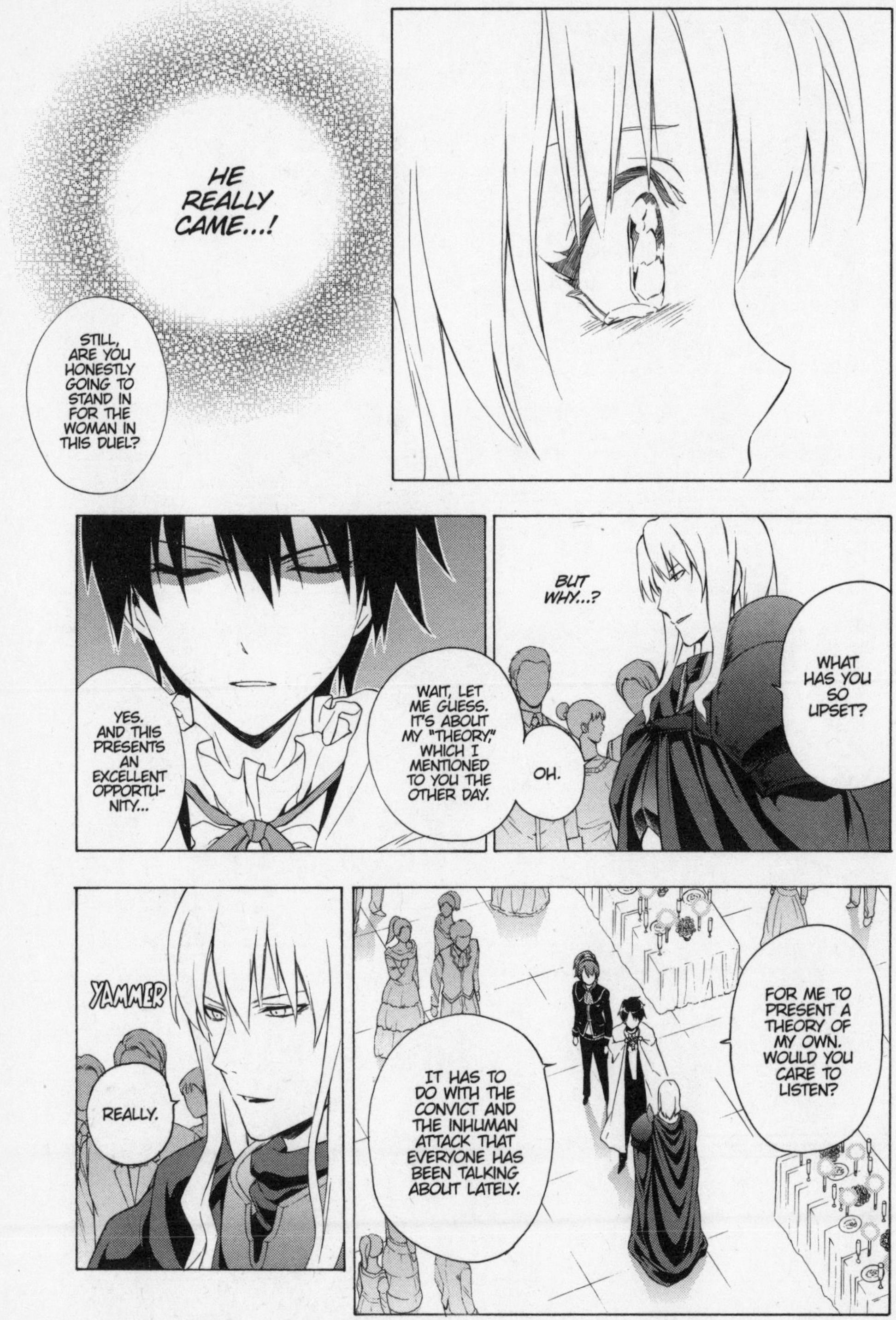
HE REALLY CAME...!
STILL, ARE YOU HONESTLY GOING TO STAND IN FOR THE WOMAN IN THIS DUEL?
BUT WHY...?
WHAT HAS YOU SO UPSET?
OH.
WAIT, LET ME GUESS. IT'S ABOUT MY "THEORY," WHICH I MENTIONED TO YOU THE OTHER DAY.
YES. AND THIS PRESENTS AN EXCELLENT OPPORTU-NITY...
FOR ME TO PRESENT A THEORY OF MY OWN. WOULD YOU CARE TO LISTEN?
IT HAS TO DO WITH THE CONVICT AND THE INHUMAN ATTACK THAT EVERYONE HAS BEEN TALKING ABOUT LATELY.
YAMMER
REALLY.

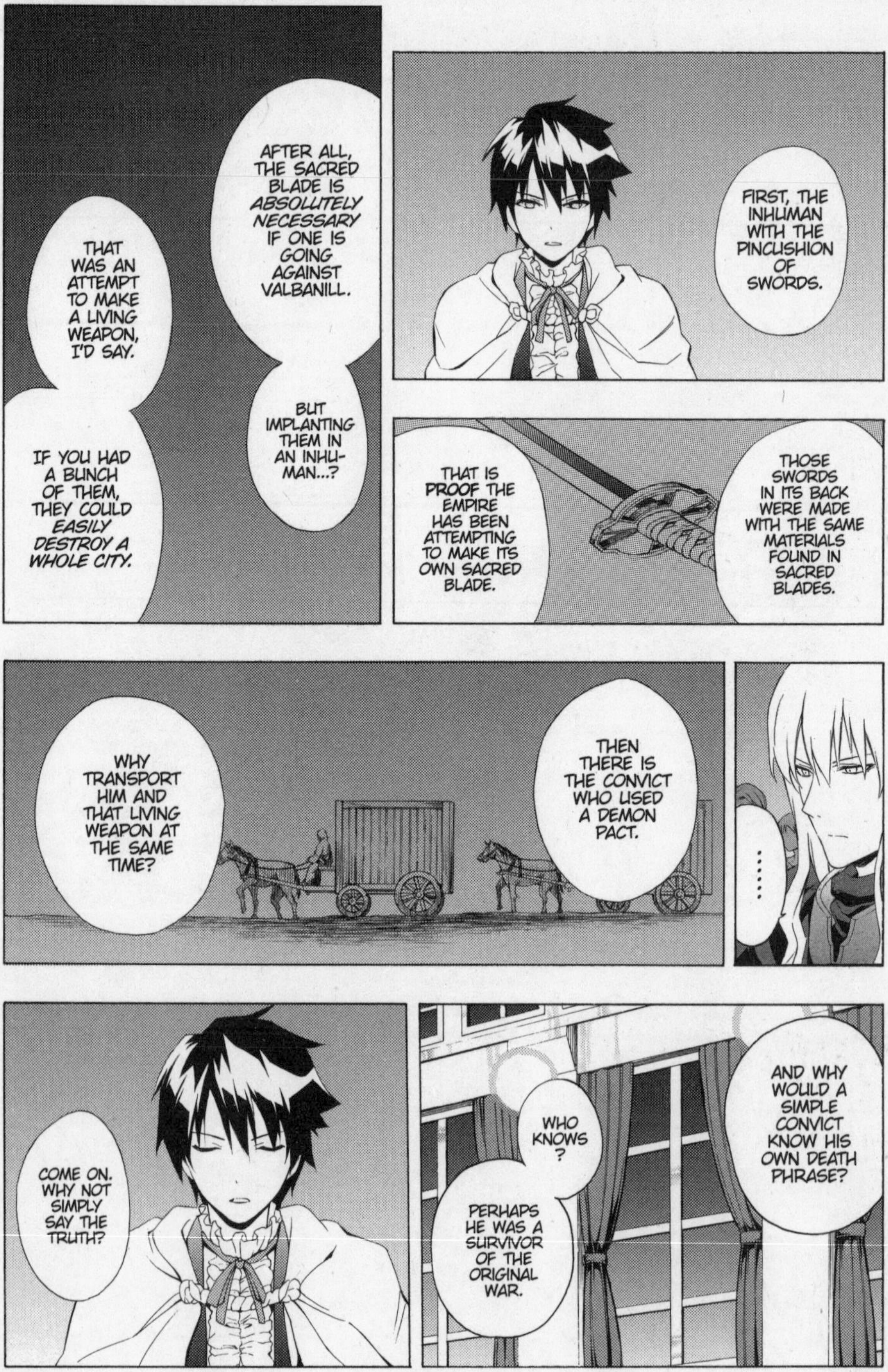

FIRST, THE INHUMAN WITH THE PINCUSHION OF SWORDS.
THOSE SWORDS IN ITS BACK WERE MADE WITH THE SAME MATERIALS FOUND IN SACRED BLADES.
THAT IS PROOF THE EMPIRE HAS BEEN ATTEMPTING TO MAKE ITS OWN SACRED BLADE.
AFTER ALL, THE SACRED BLADE IS ABSOLUTELY NECESSARY IF ONE IS GOING AGAINST VALBANILL.
THAT WAS AN ATTEMPT TO MAKE A LIVING WEAPON, I'D SAY.
BUT IMPLANTING THEM IN AN INHUMAN...?
IF YOU HAD A BUNCH OF THEM, THEY COULD EASILY DESTROY A WHOLE CITY.
......
THEN THERE IS THE CONVICT WHO USED A DEMON PACT.
WHY TRANSPORT HIM AND THAT LIVING WEAPON AT THE SAME TIME?
AND WHY WOULD A SIMPLE CONVICT KNOW HIS OWN DEATH PHRASE?
WHO KNOWS?
PERHAPS HE WAS A SURVIVOR OF THE ORIGINAL WAR.
COME ON. WHY NOT SIMPLY SAY THE TRUTH?

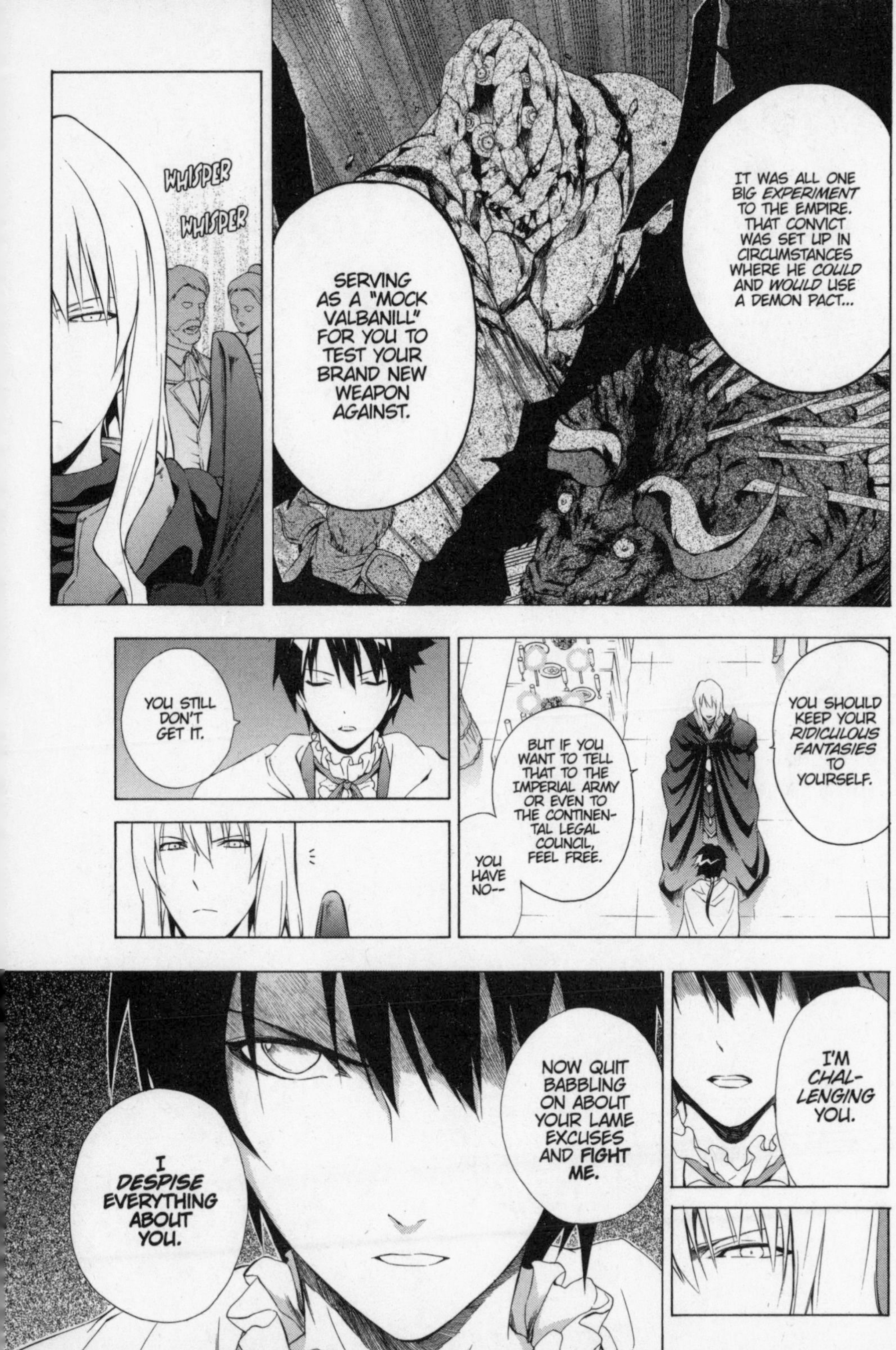

IT WAS ALL ONE BIG *EXPERIMENT* TO THE EMPIRE. THAT CONVICT WAS SET UP IN CIRCUMSTANCES WHERE HE *COULD* AND *WOULD* USE A DEMON PACT...
SERVING AS A "MOCK VALBANILL" FOR YOU TO TEST YOUR BRAND NEW WEAPON AGAINST.
WHISPER
WHISPER
YOU SHOULD KEEP YOUR *RIDICULOUS FANTASIES* TO YOURSELF.
BUT IF YOU WANT TO TELL THAT TO THE IMPERIAL ARMY OR EVEN TO THE CONTINENTAL LEGAL COUNCIL, FEEL FREE.
YOU HAVE NO--
YOU STILL DON'T GET IT.
I'M *CHAL-LENGING* YOU.
NOW QUIT BABBLING ON ABOUT YOUR LAME EXCUSES AND **FIGHT ME.**
I *DESPISE* EVERYTHING ABOUT YOU.

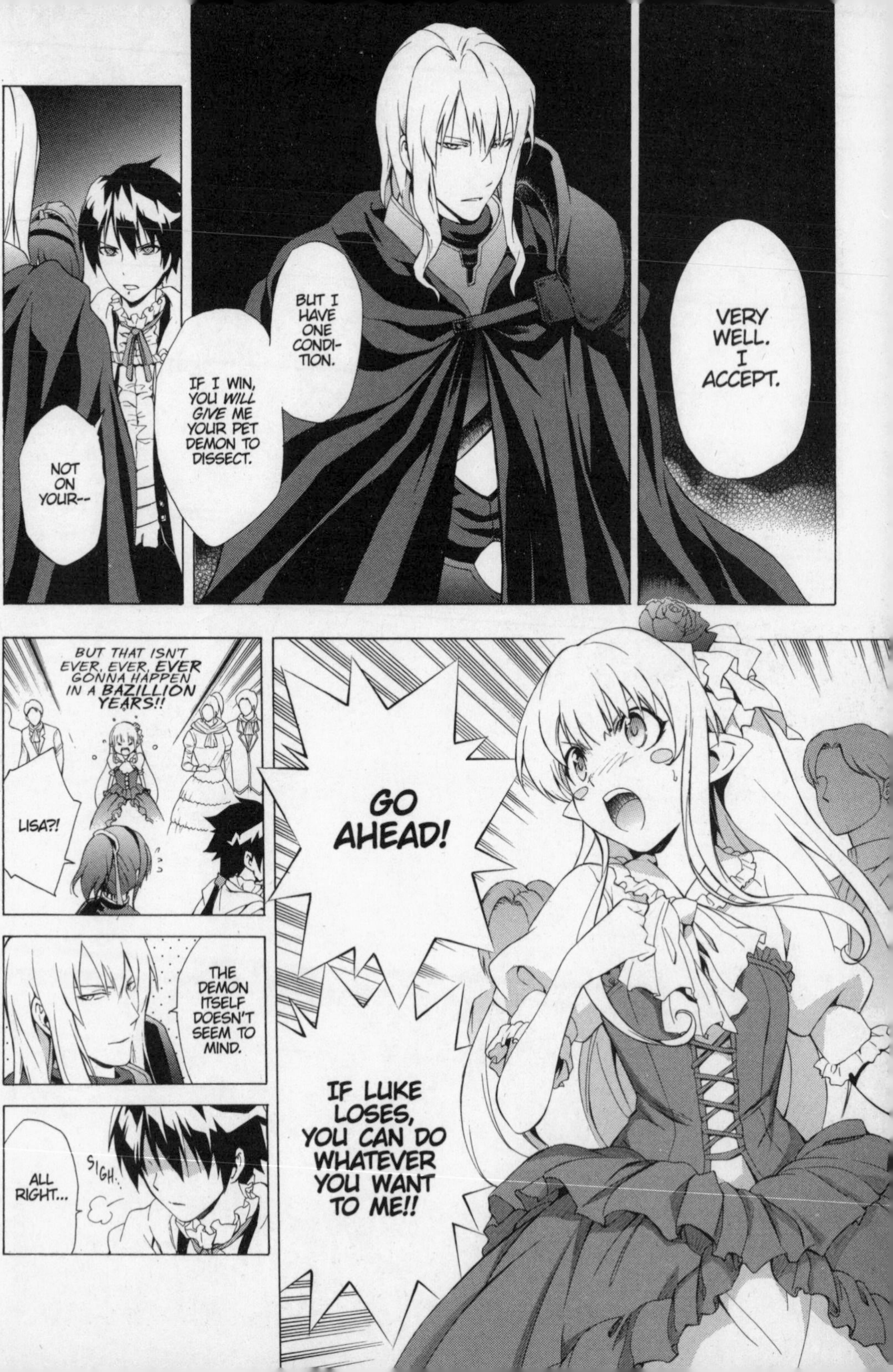
VERY WELL. I ACCEPT.
BUT I HAVE ONE CONDITION.
IF I WIN, YOU *WILL* GIVE ME YOUR PET DEMON TO DISSECT.
NOT ON YOUR--
GO AHEAD!
IF LUKE LOSES, YOU CAN DO WHATEVER YOU WANT TO ME!!
BUT THAT ISN'T EVER, EVER, EVER GONNA HAPPEN IN A BAZILLION YEARS!!
LISA?!
THE DEMON ITSELF DOESN'T SEEM TO MIND.
SIGH...
ALL RIGHT...

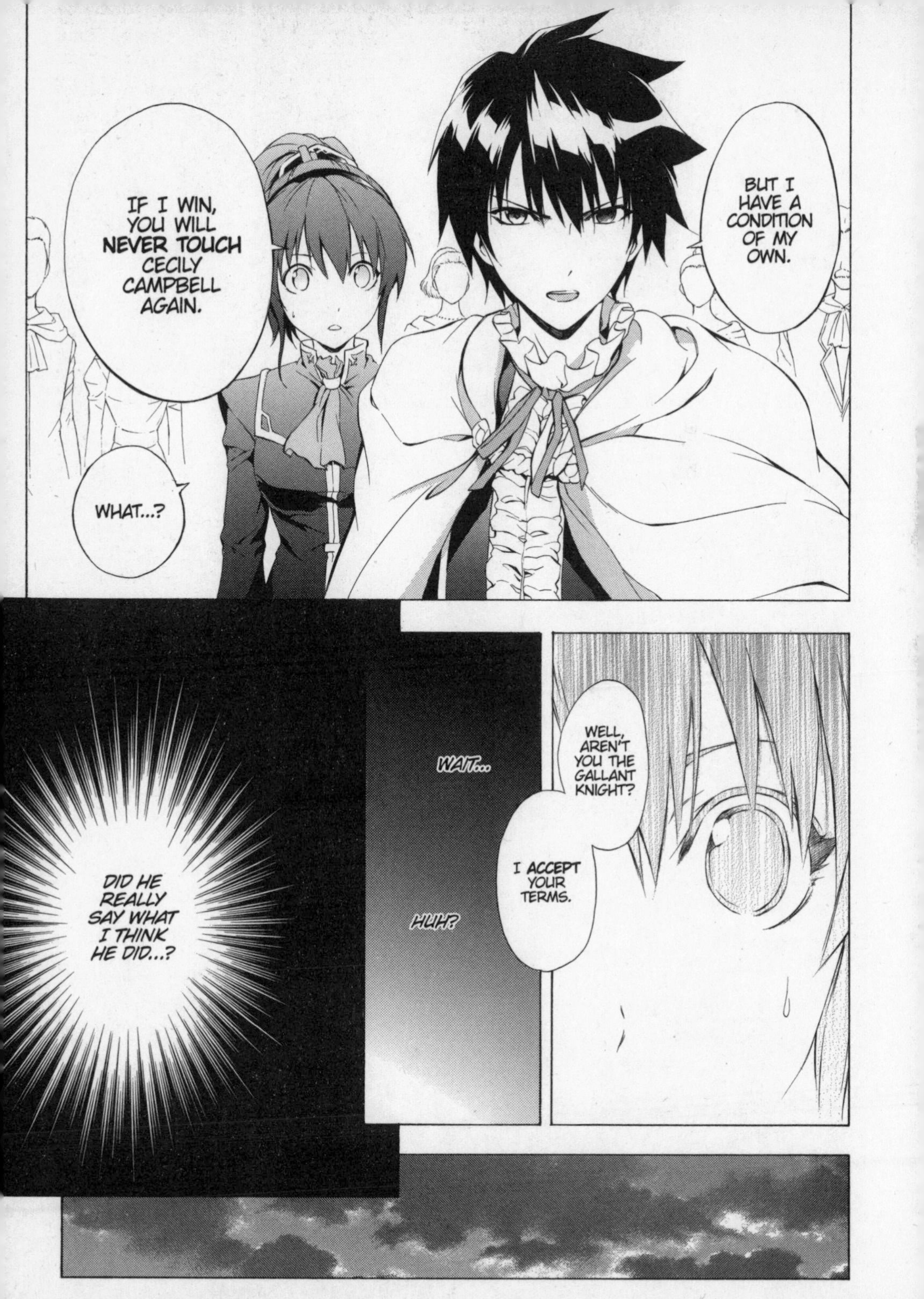
BUT I HAVE A CONDITION OF MY OWN.
IF I WIN, YOU WILL NEVER TOUCH CECILY CAMPBELL AGAIN.
WHAT...?
WELL, AREN'T YOU THE GALLANT KNIGHT?
I ACCEPT YOUR TERMS.
WAIT...
HUH?
DID HE REALLY SAY WHAT I THINK HE DID...?

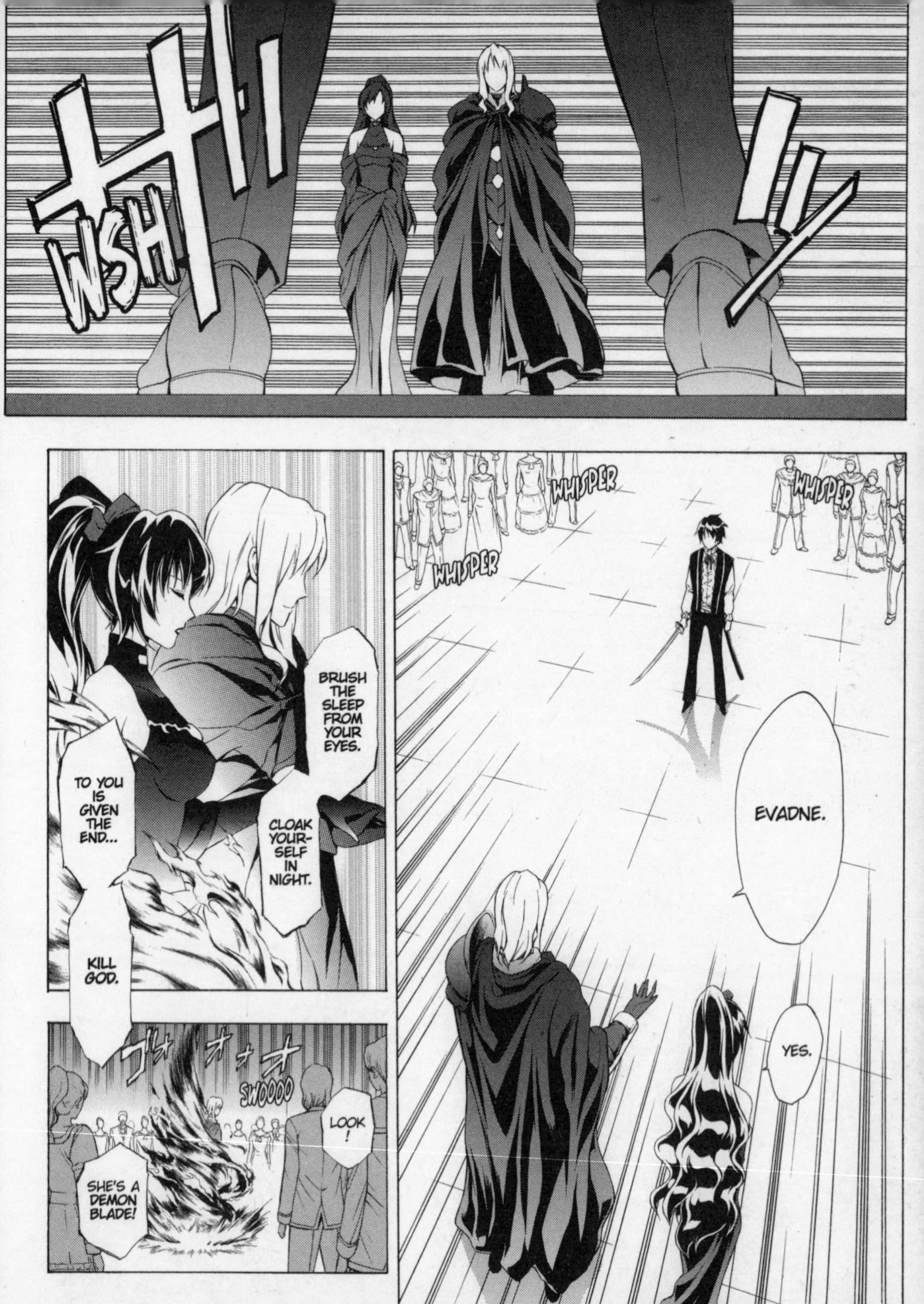
WSH
WHISPER
WHISPER
WHISPER
EVADNE.
YES.
BRUSH THE SLEEP FROM YOUR EYES.
CLOAK YOURSELF IN NIGHT.
TO YOU IS GIVEN THE END...
KILL GOD.
SWOOOO
LOOK!
SHE'S A DEMON BLADE!

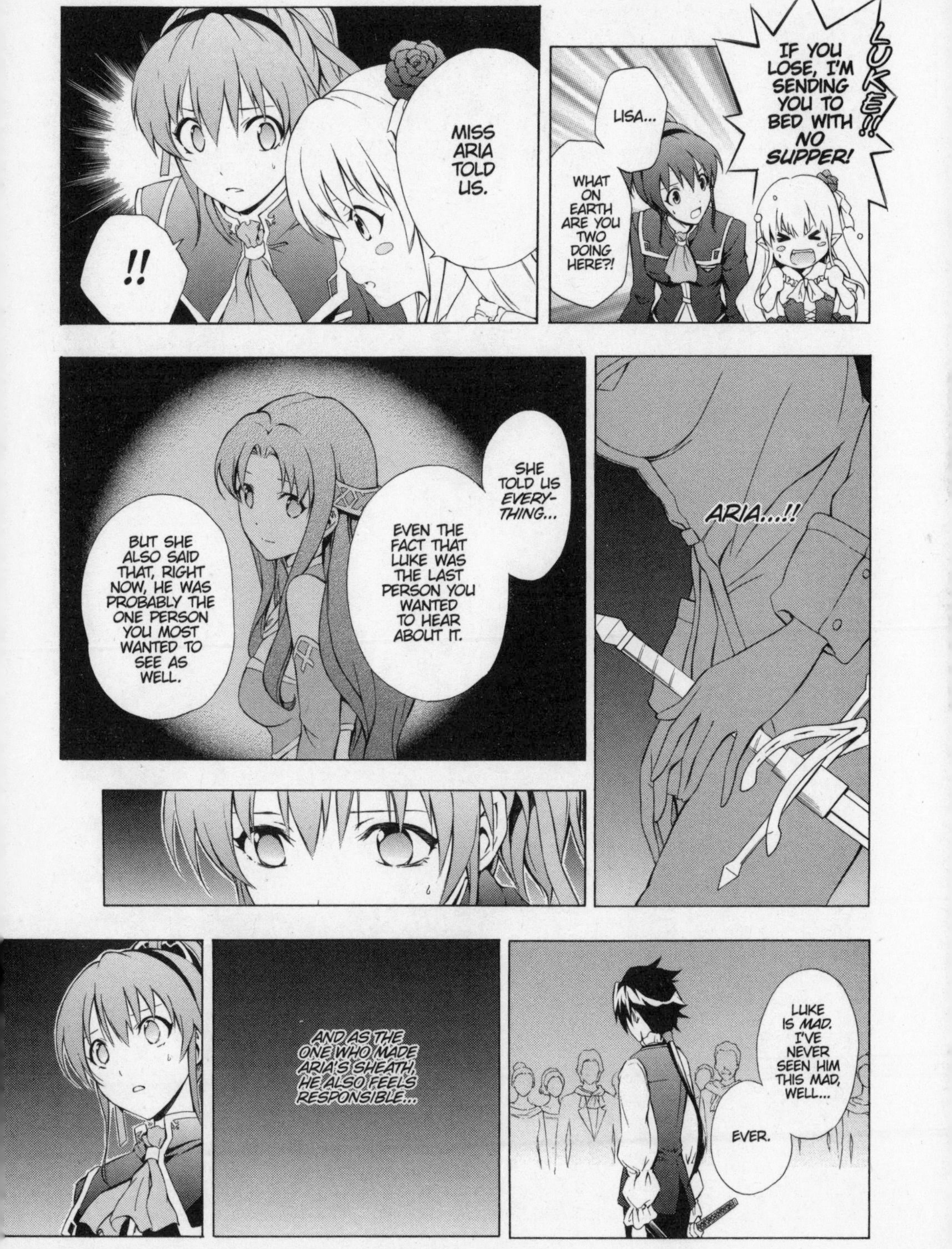
LUKE!!
IF YOU LOSE, I'M SENDING YOU TO BED WITH NO SUPPER!
LISA...
WHAT ON EARTH ARE YOU TWO DOING HERE?!
MISS ARIA TOLD US.
!!
ARIA...!!
SHE TOLD US EVERYTHING...
EVEN THE FACT THAT LUKE WAS THE LAST PERSON YOU WANTED TO HEAR ABOUT IT.
BUT SHE ALSO SAID THAT, RIGHT NOW, HE WAS PROBABLY THE ONE PERSON YOU MOST WANTED TO SEE AS WELL.
LUKE IS MAD. I'VE NEVER SEEN HIM THIS MAD, WELL...
EVER.
AND AS THE ONE WHO MADE ARIA'S SHEATH, HE ALSO FEELS RESPONSIBLE...

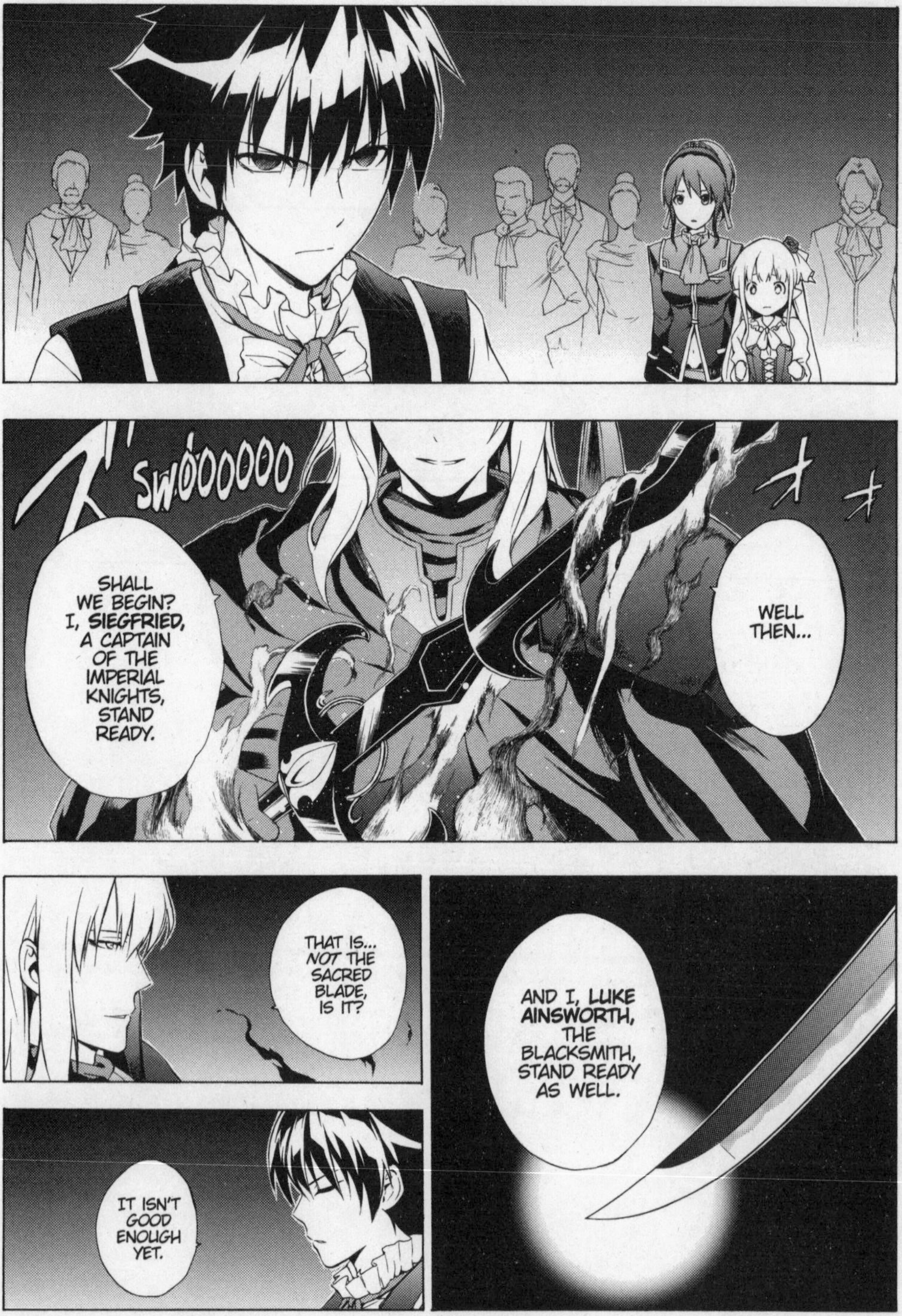
SWOOOOOO
WELL THEN...
SHALL WE BEGIN? I, SIEGFRIED, A CAPTAIN OF THE IMPERIAL KNIGHTS, STAND READY.
AND I, LUKE AINSWORTH, THE BLACKSMITH, STAND READY AS WELL.
THAT IS... NOT THE SACRED BLADE, IS IT?
IT ISN'T GOOD ENOUGH YET.

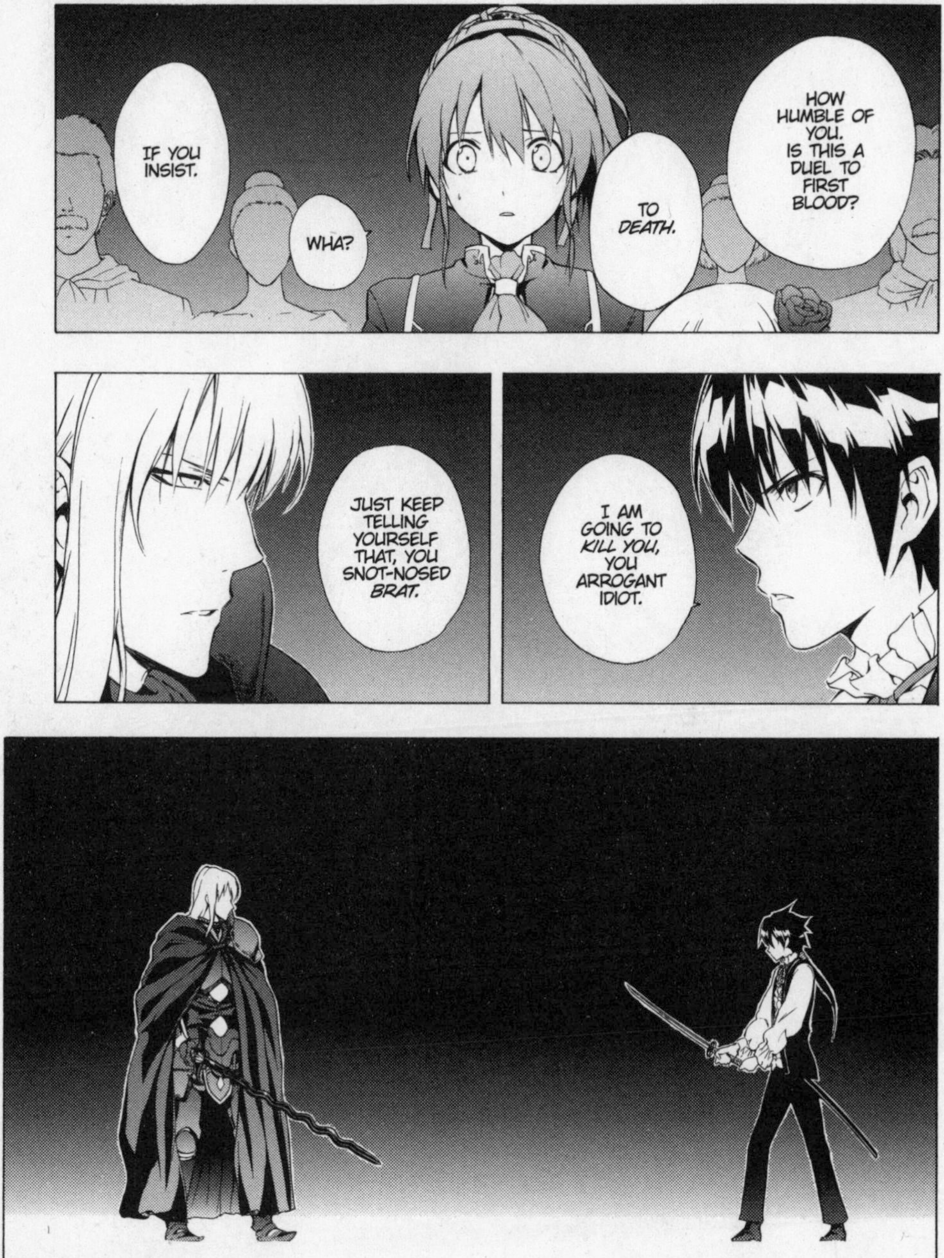
HOW HUMBLE OF YOU. IS THIS A DUEL TO FIRST BLOOD?
TO *DEATH.*
WHA?
IF YOU INSIST.
I AM GOING TO *KILL YOU,* YOU ARROGANT IDIOT.
JUST KEEP TELLING YOURSELF THAT, YOU SNOT-NOSED *BRAT.*

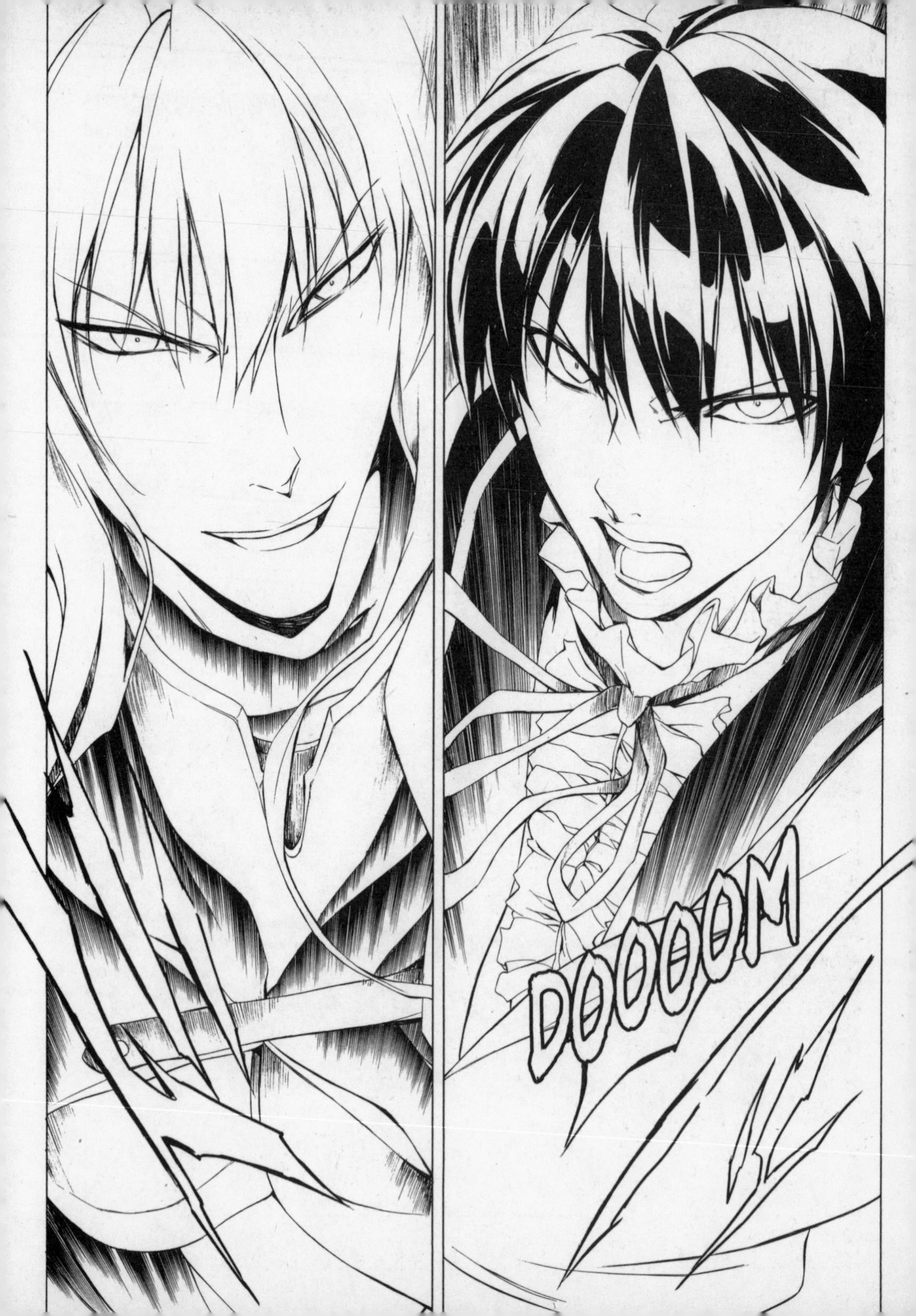
DOOOOM

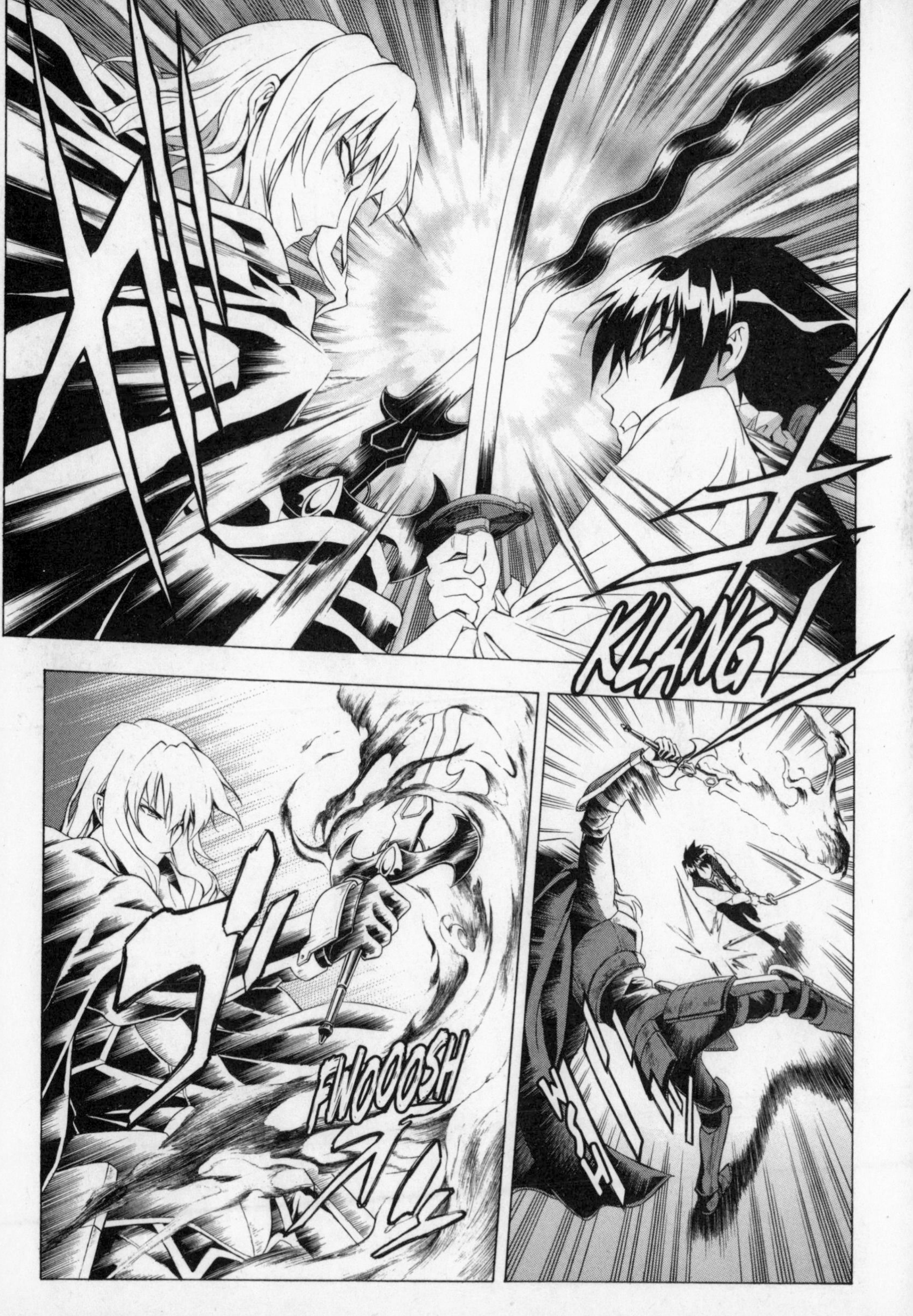
KLANG!
WSH
FWOOOSH

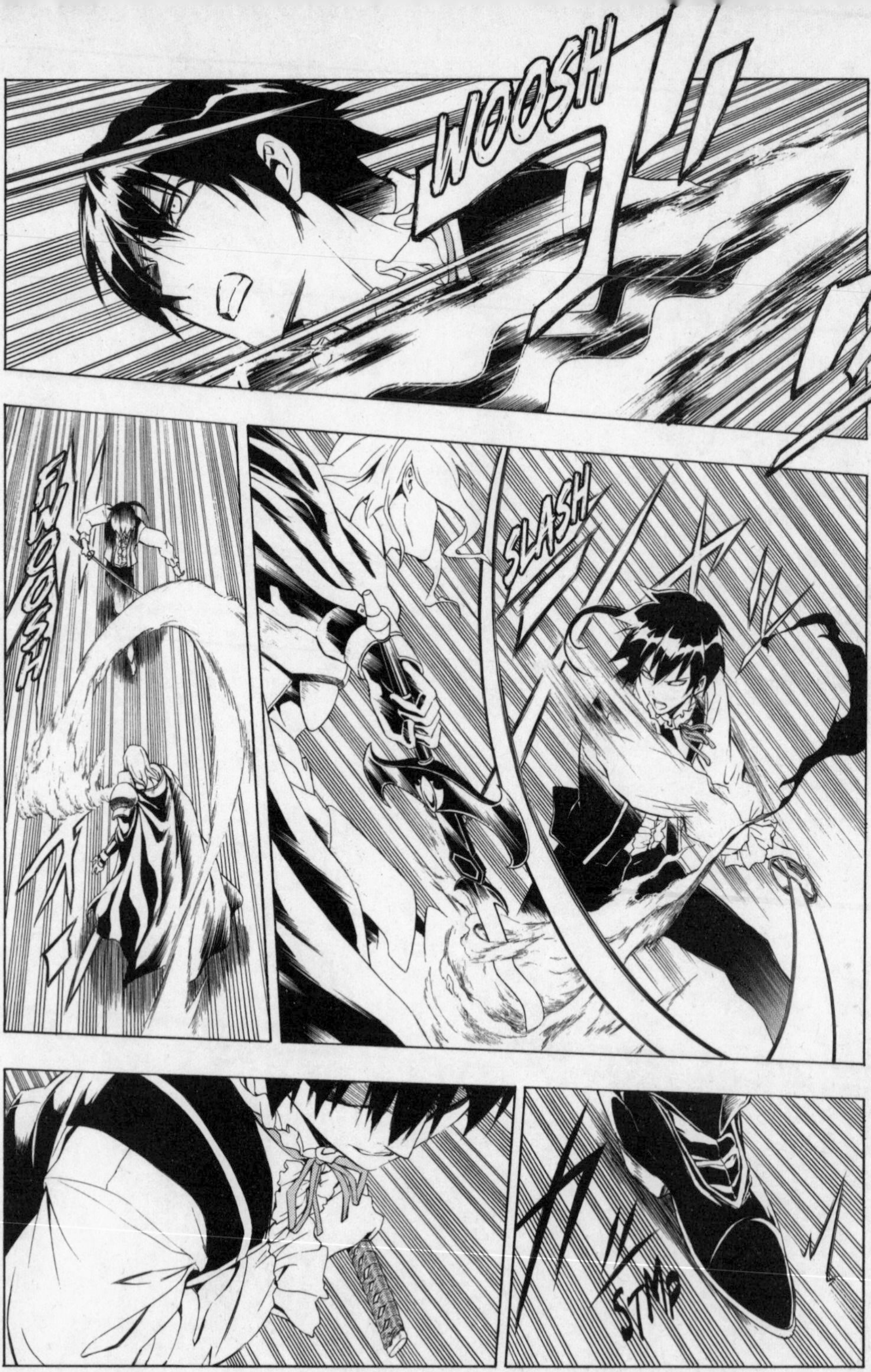
WOOSH
SLASH
FWOOSH
STMP

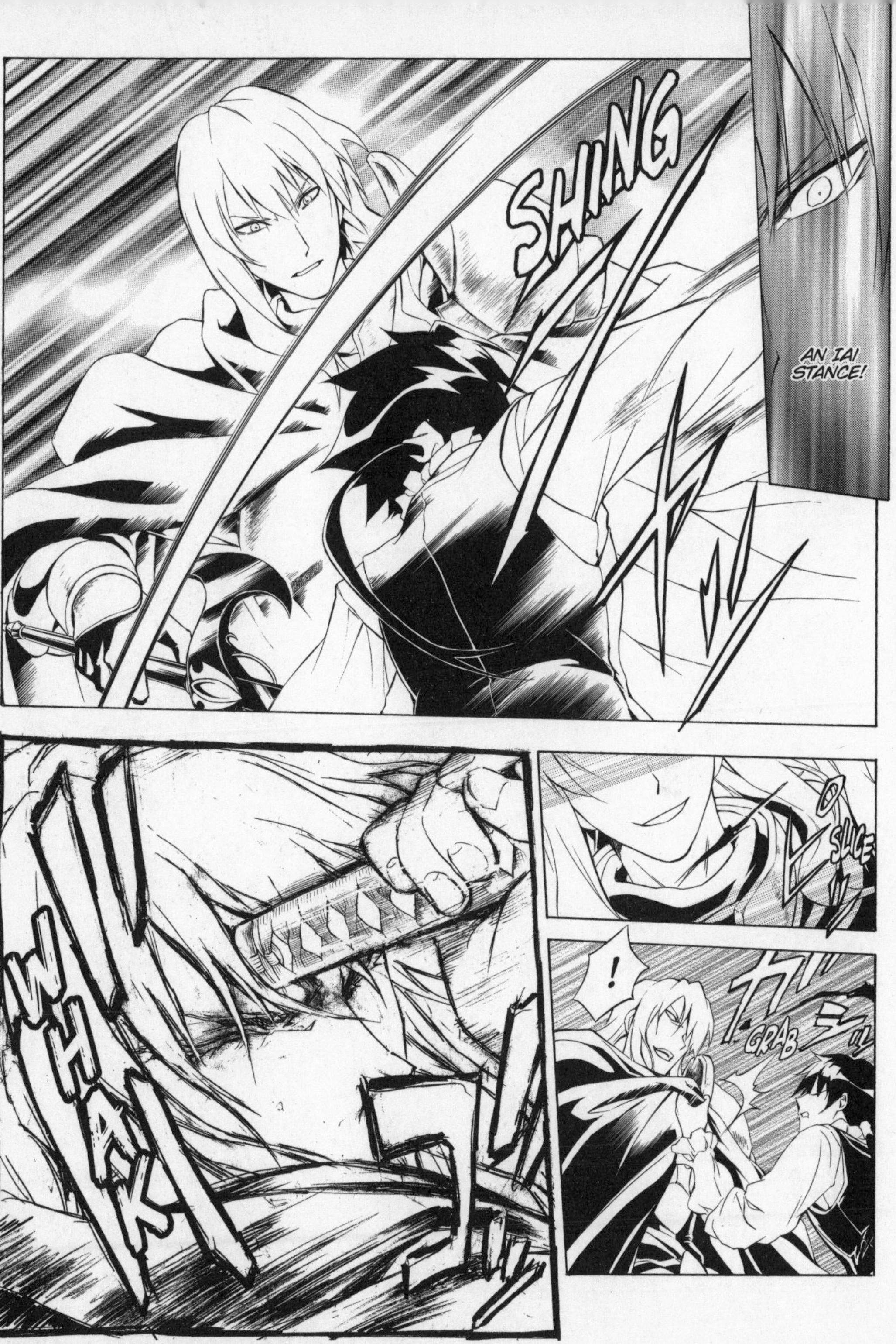
AN IAI STANCE!
SHING
SLICE
!
GRAB
WHAK

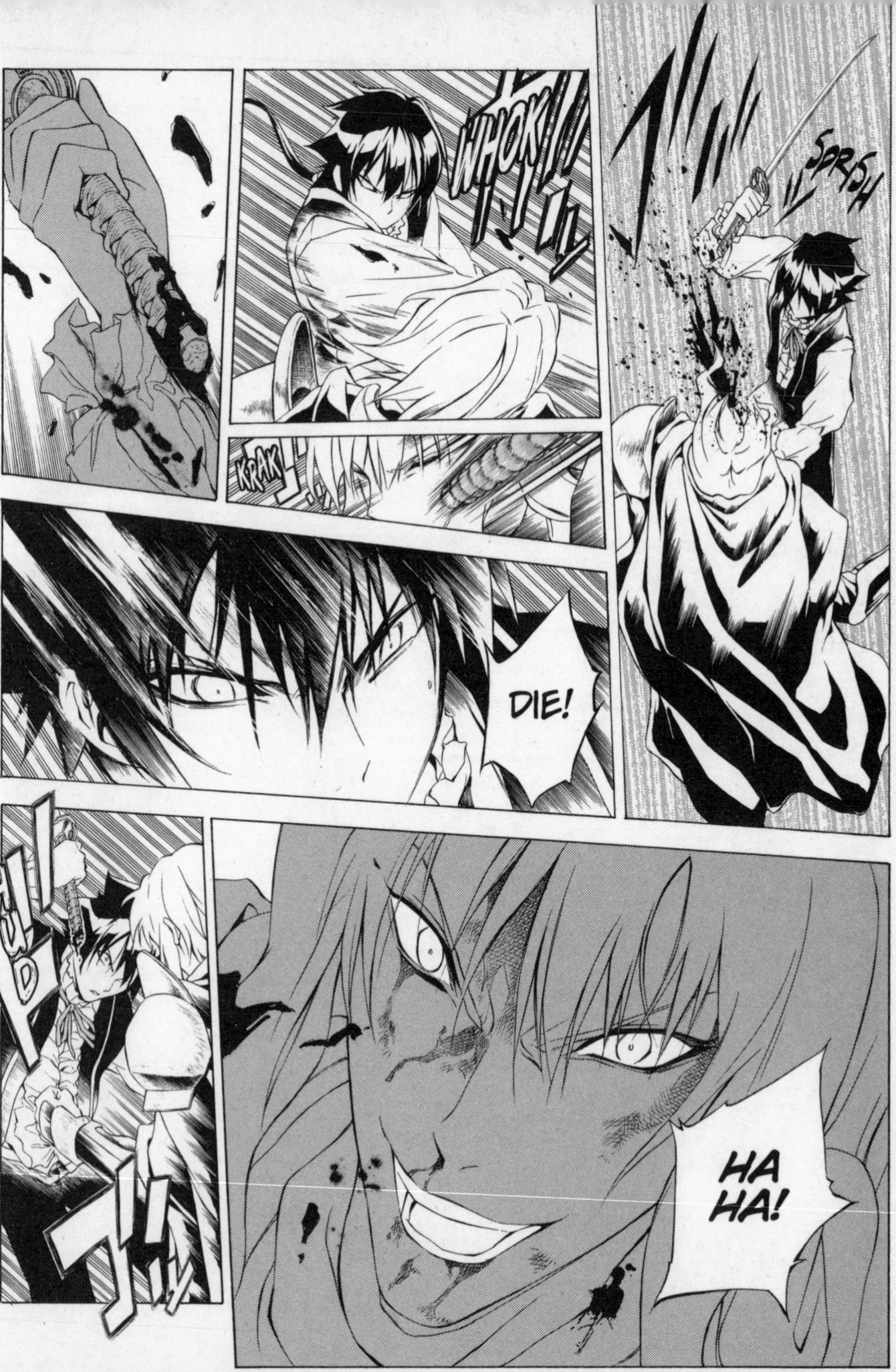
SPRISH
WHOK!!
KRAK
DIE!
HA HA!
WHUD!

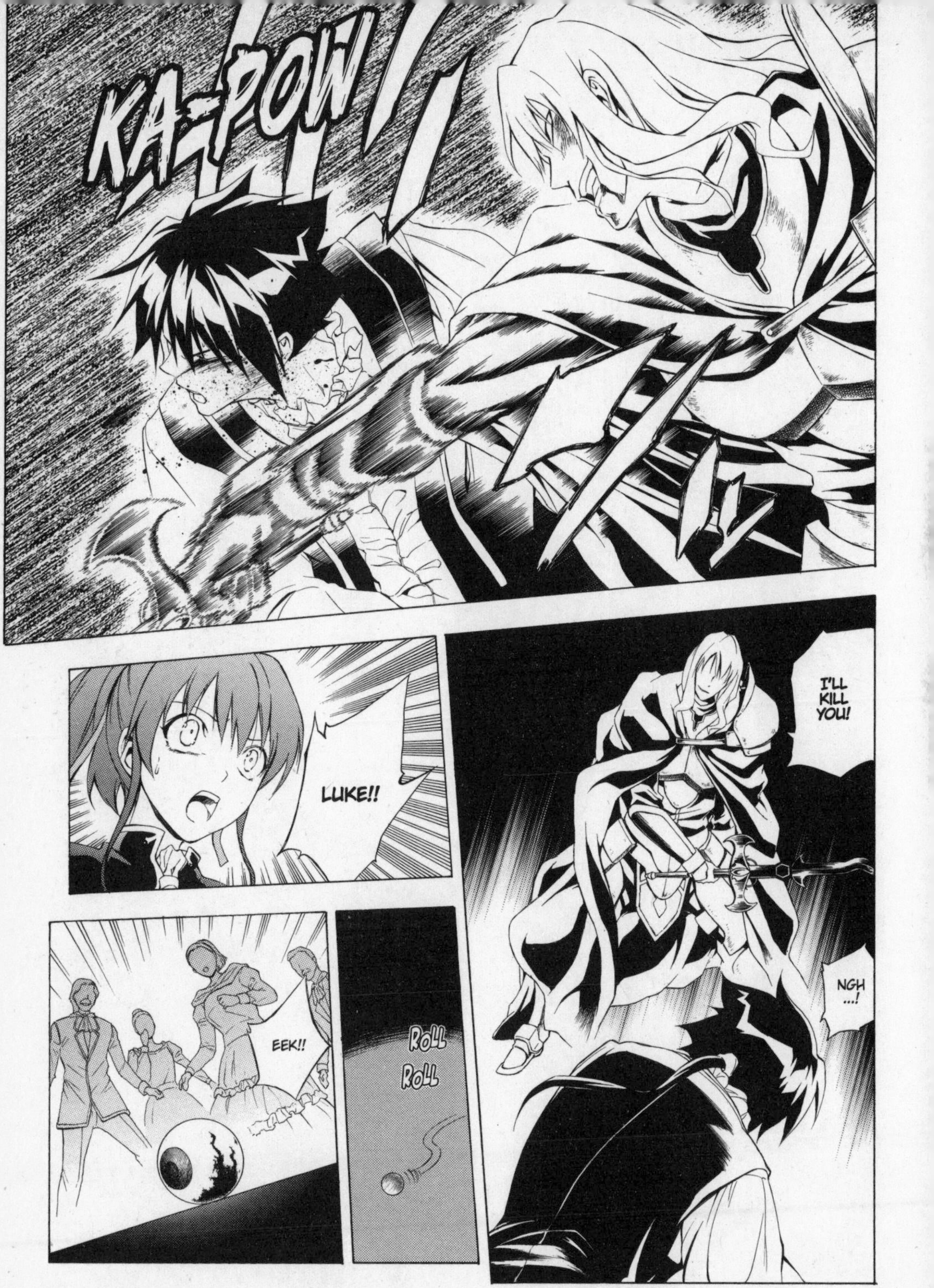
KA-POW
I'LL KILL YOU!
NGH ...!
LUKE!!
ROLL ROLL
EEK!!

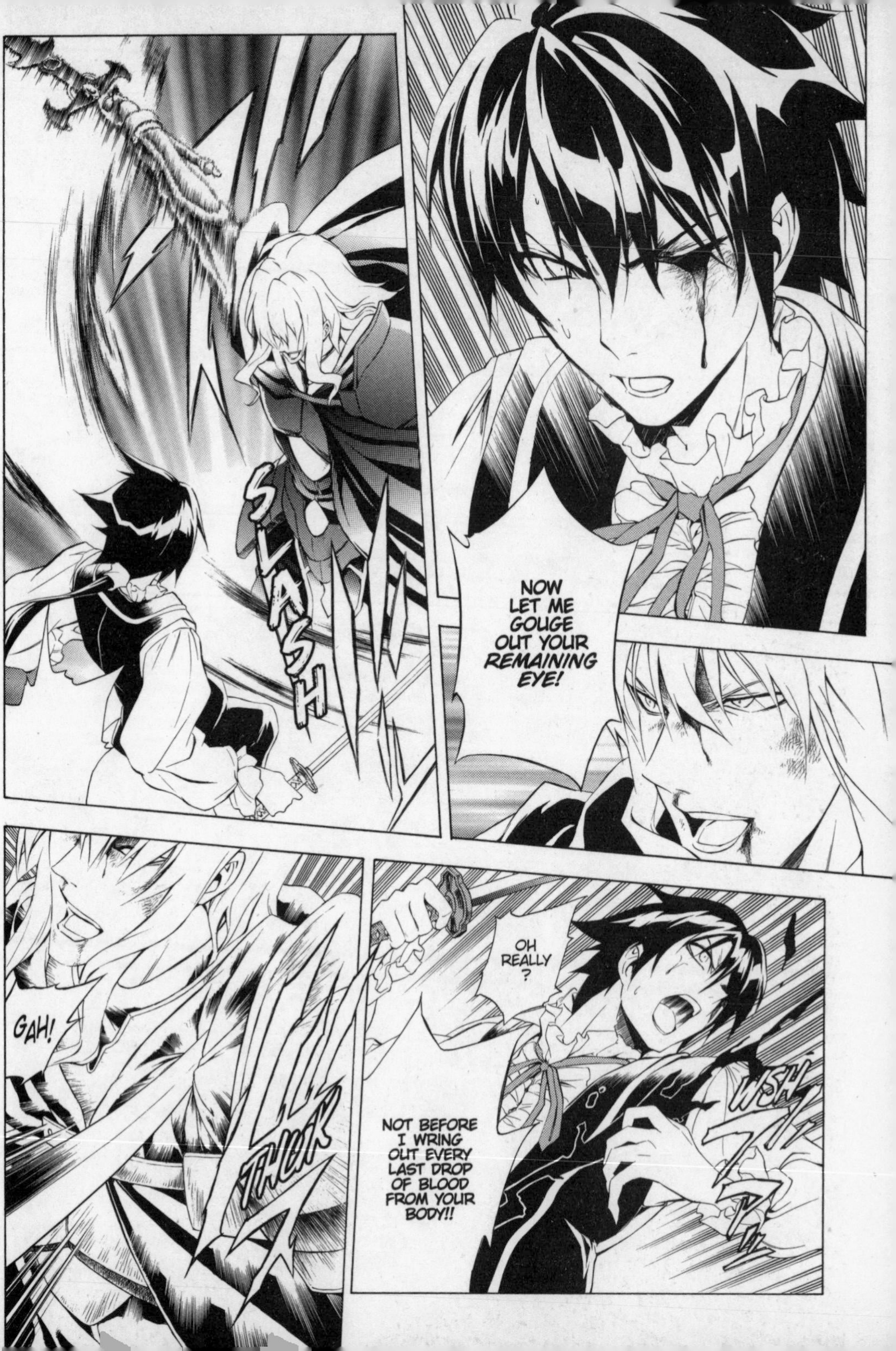
NOW LET ME GOUGE OUT YOUR REMAINING EYE!
SLASH
OH REALLY?
NOT BEFORE I WRING OUT EVERY LAST DROP OF BLOOD FROM YOUR BODY!!
WSH
GAH!
THUK

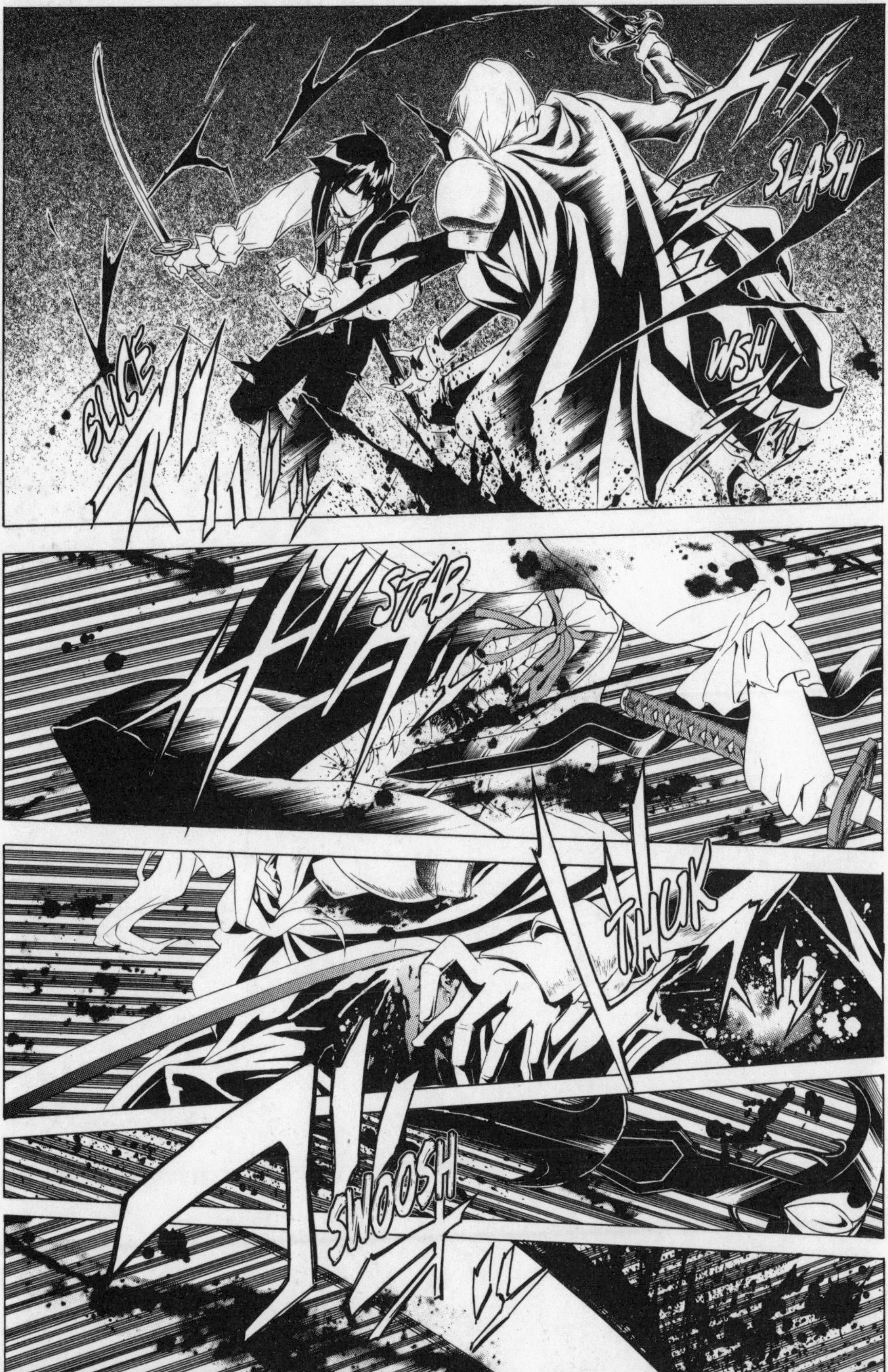
SLASH
WSH
SLICE
STAB
THUK
SWOOSH

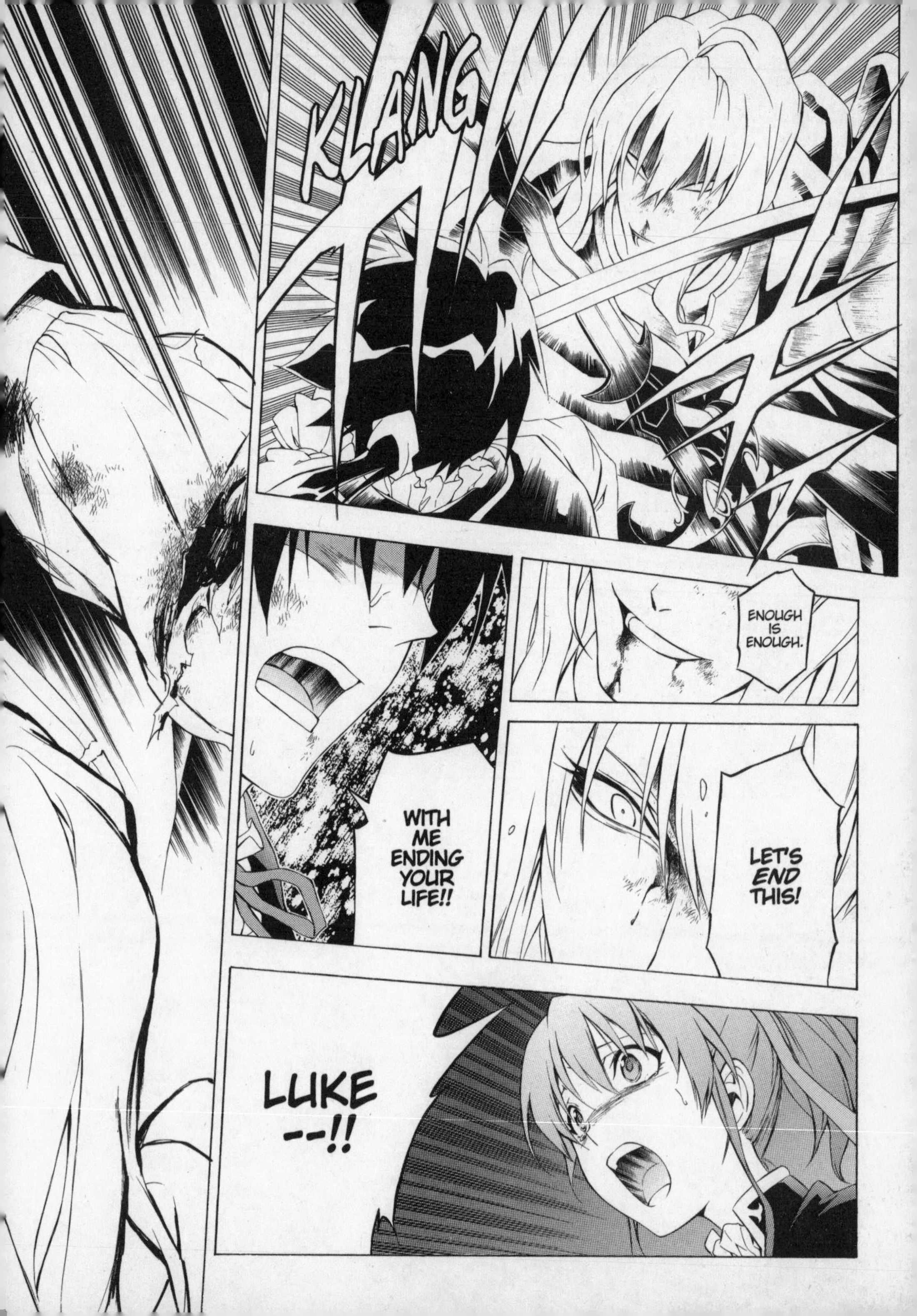
KLANG
ENOUGH IS ENOUGH.
LET'S END THIS!
WITH ME ENDING YOUR LIFE!!
LUKE --!!

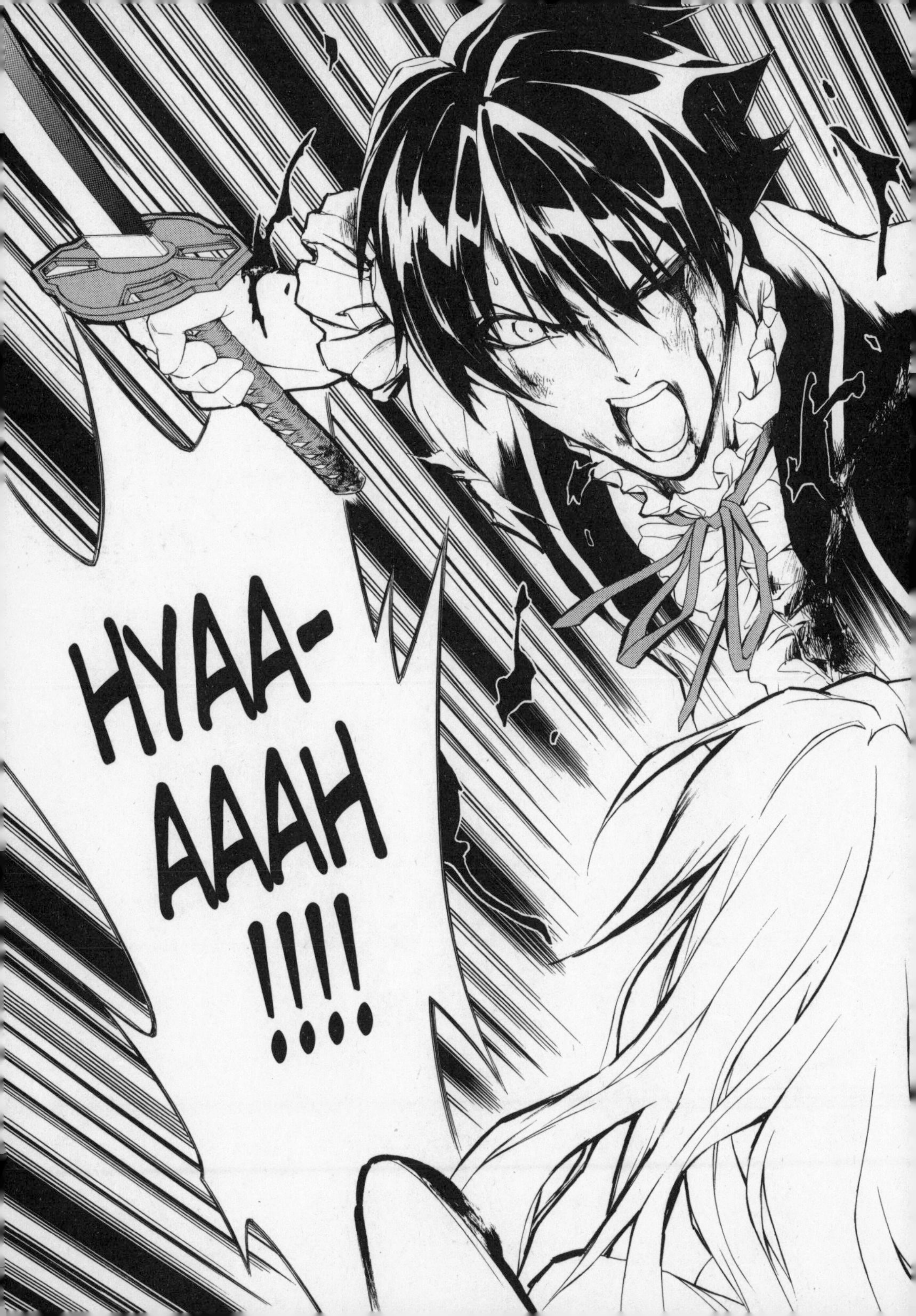
HYAA-
AAAH
!!!!!

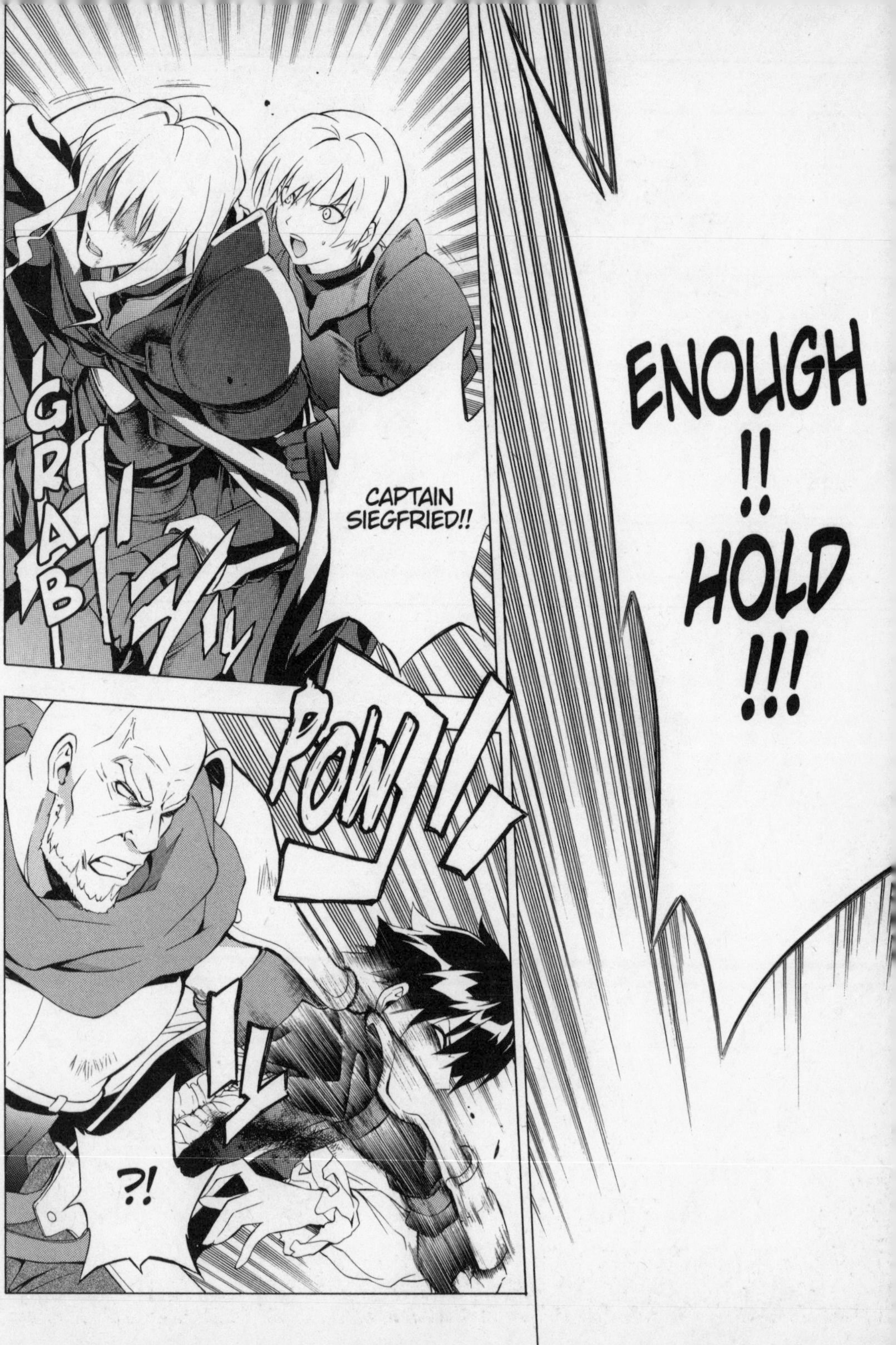
ENOUGH!! HOLD!!!
CAPTAIN SIEGFRIED!!
GRAB
POW!!
?!

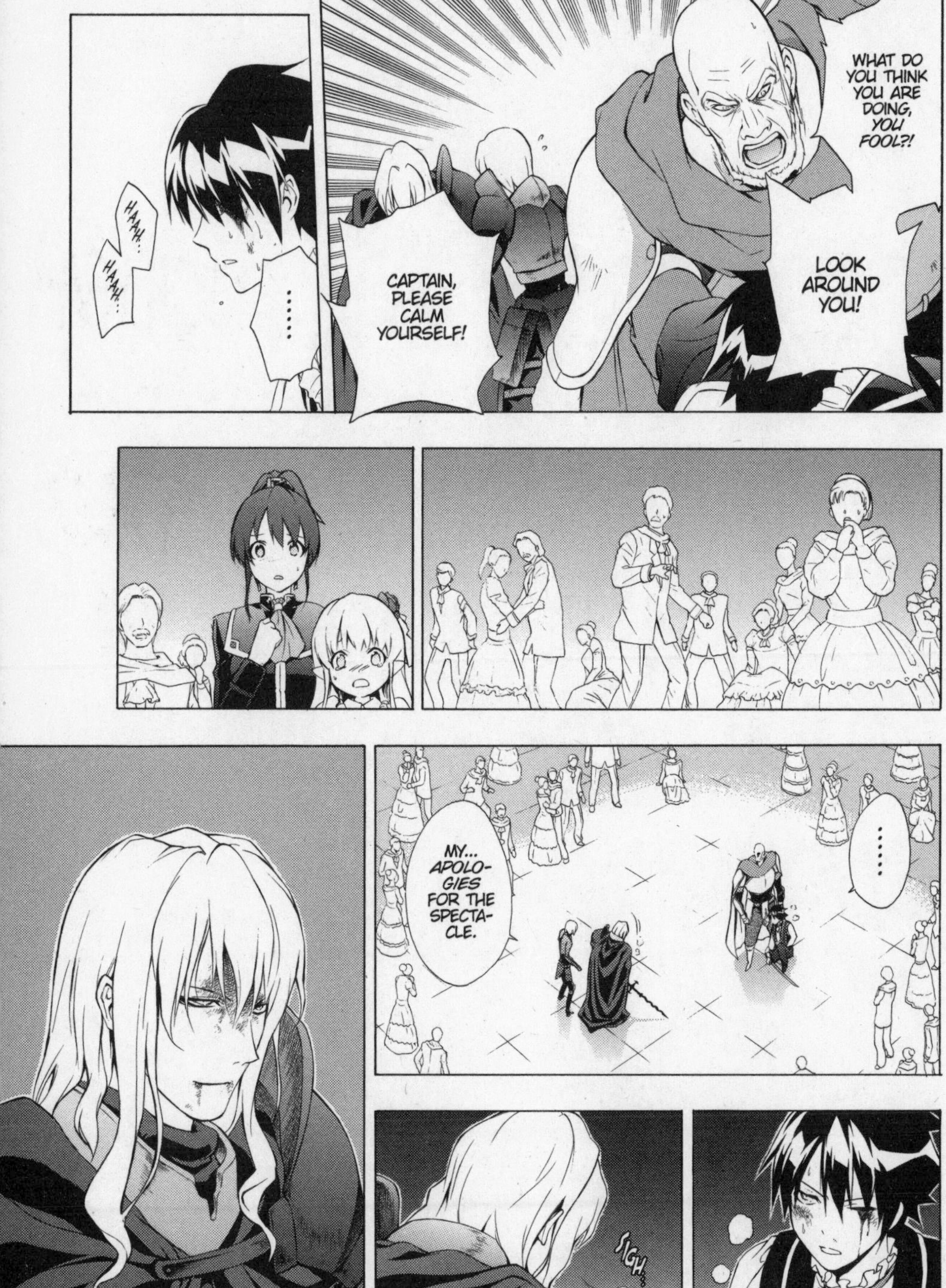
WHAT DO YOU THINK YOU ARE DOING, YOU FOOL?!
LOOK AROUND YOU!
CAPTAIN, PLEASE CALM YOURSELF!
HAAH...
HAAH...
......
......
MY... APOLOGIES FOR THE SPECTACLE.
SIGH...

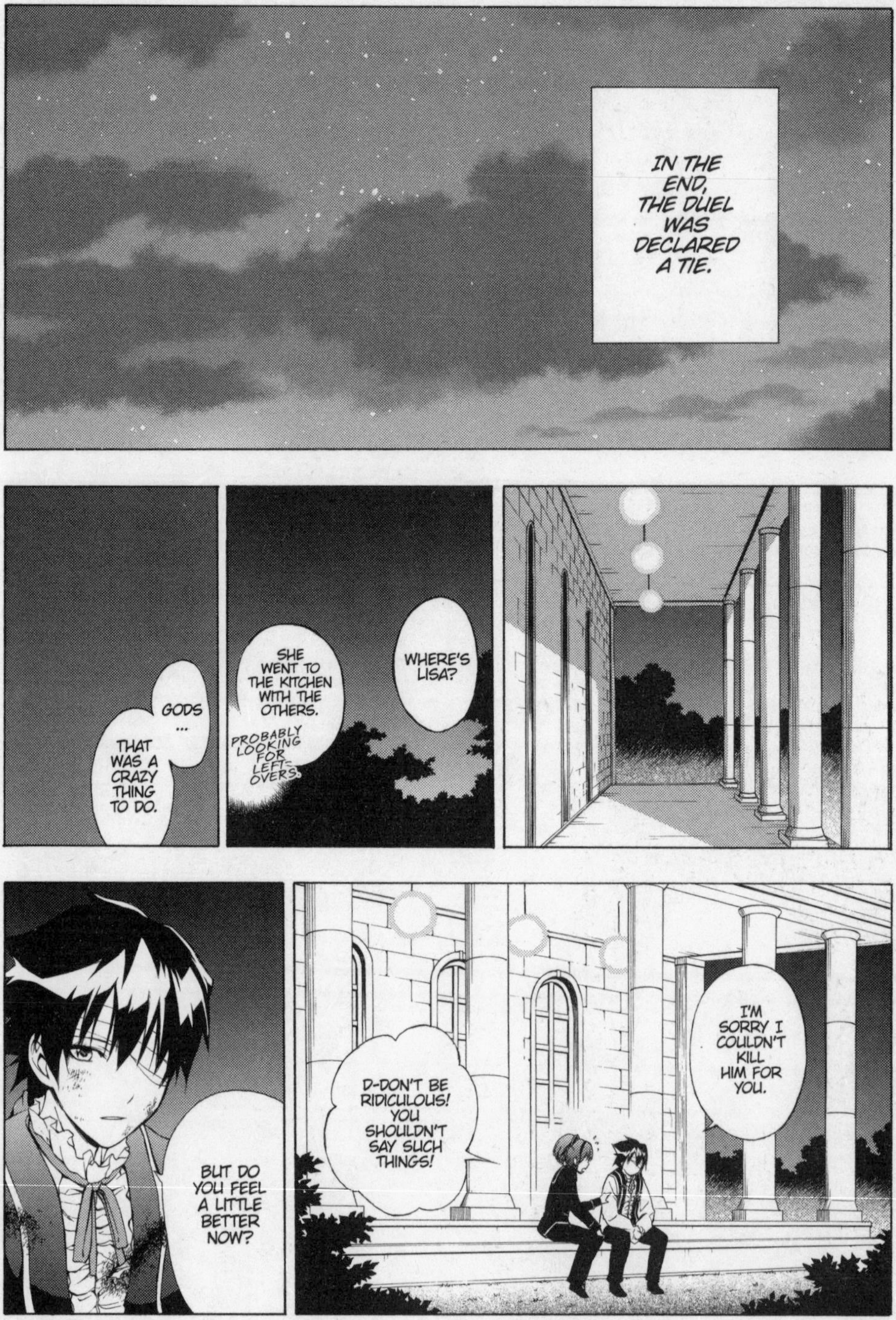
IN THE END, THE DUEL WAS DECLARED A TIE.
WHERE'S LISA?
SHE WENT TO THE KITCHEN WITH THE OTHERS.
PROBABLY LOOKING FOR LEFT-OVERS.
GODS...
THAT WAS A CRAZY THING TO DO.
I'M SORRY I COULDN'T KILL HIM FOR YOU.
D-DON'T BE RIDICULOUS! YOU SHOULDN'T SAY SUCH THINGS!
BUT DO YOU FEEL A LITTLE BETTER NOW?

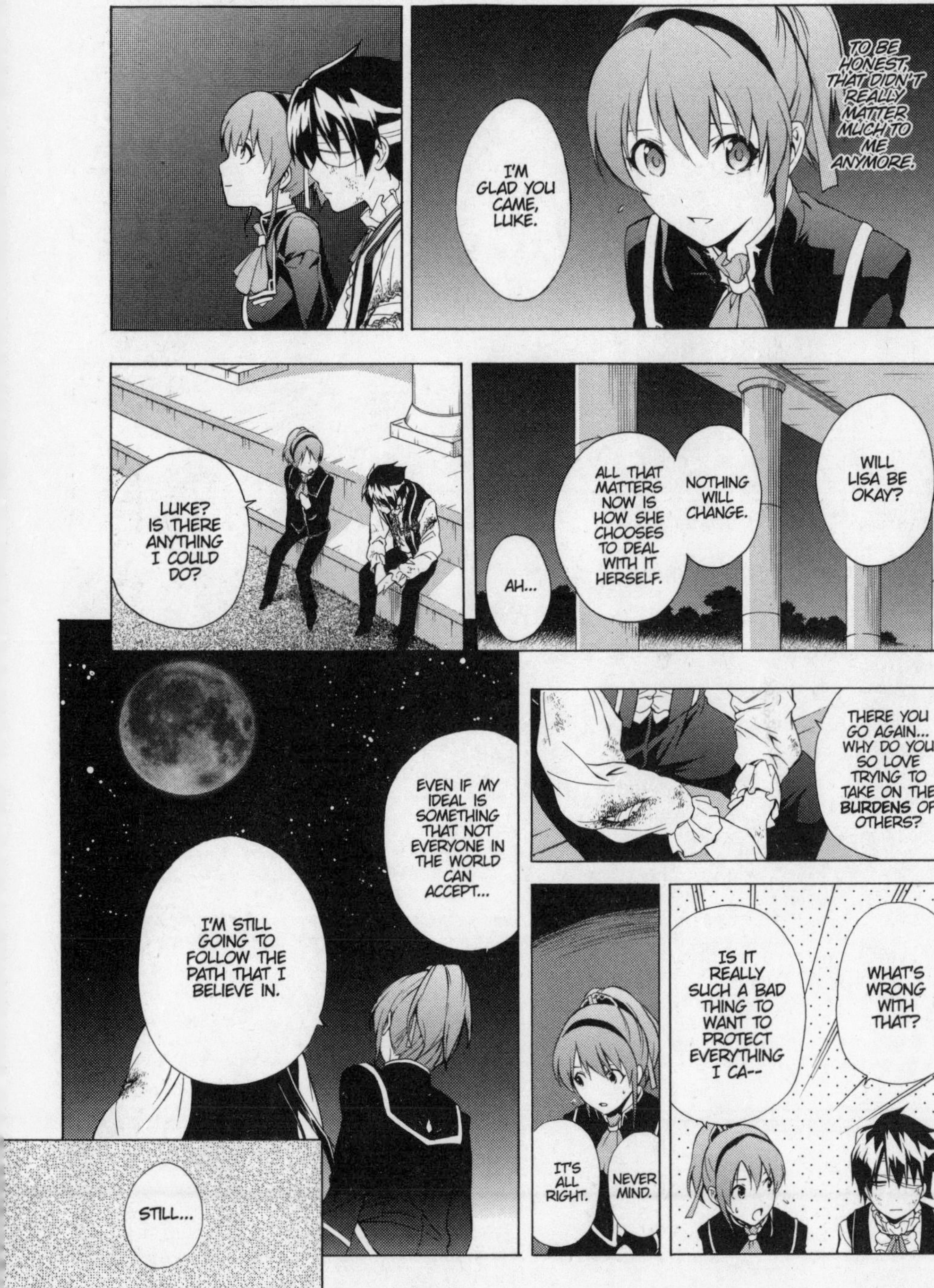
TO BE HONEST, THAT DIDN'T REALLY MATTER MUCH TO ME ANYMORE.
I'M GLAD YOU CAME, LUKE.
WILL LISA BE OKAY?
NOTHING WILL CHANGE.
ALL THAT MATTERS NOW IS HOW SHE CHOOSES TO DEAL WITH IT HERSELF.
AH...
LUKE? IS THERE ANYTHING I COULD DO?
THERE YOU GO AGAIN... WHY DO YOU SO LOVE TRYING TO TAKE ON THE BURDENS OF OTHERS?
WHAT'S WRONG WITH THAT?
IS IT REALLY SUCH A BAD THING TO WANT TO PROTECT EVERYTHING I CA--
NEVER MIND.
IT'S ALL RIGHT.
EVEN IF MY IDEAL IS SOMETHING THAT NOT EVERYONE IN THE WORLD CAN ACCEPT...
I'M STILL GOING TO FOLLOW THE PATH THAT I BELIEVE IN.
STILL...

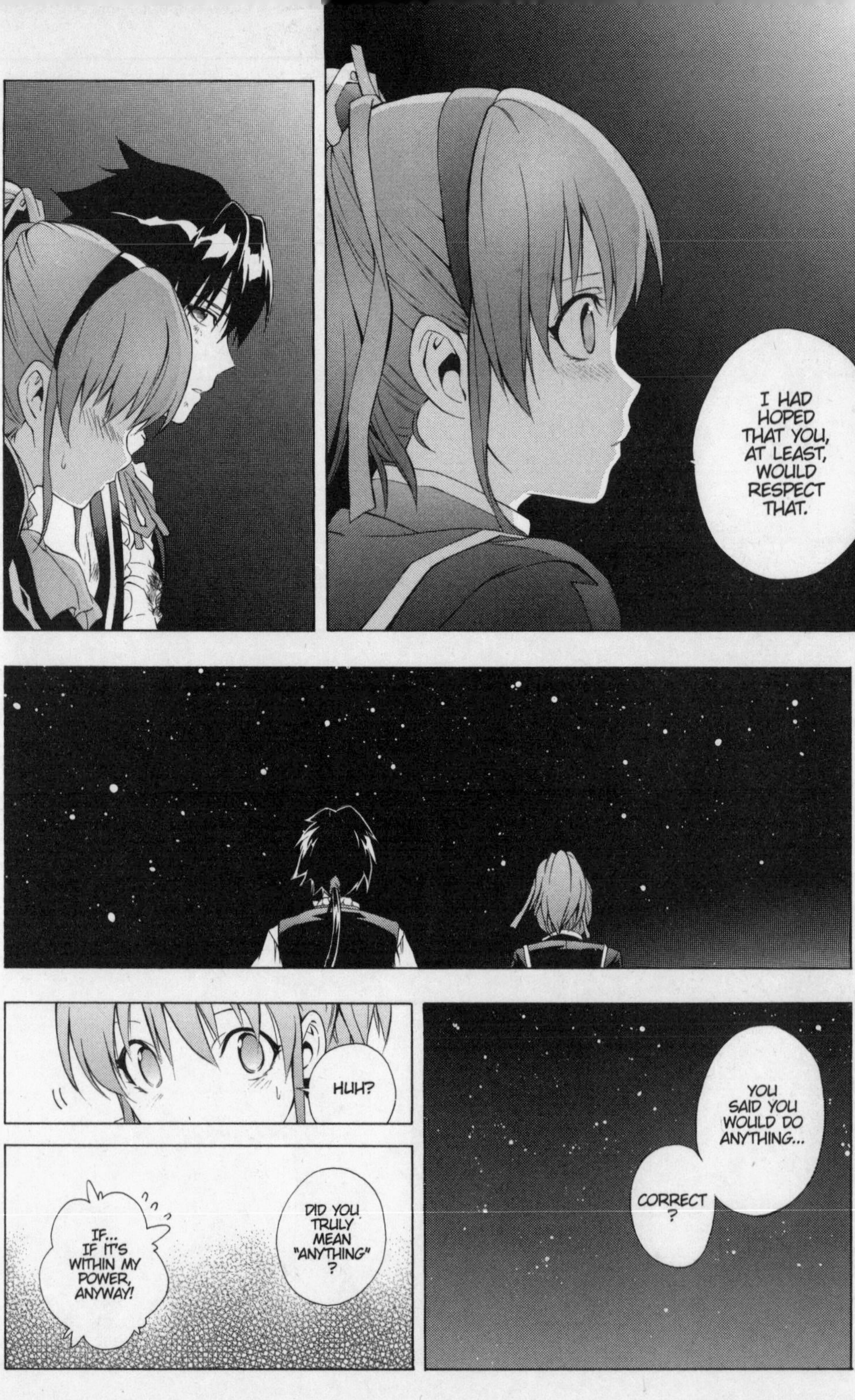
I HAD HOPED THAT YOU, AT LEAST, WOULD RESPECT THAT.
YOU SAID YOU WOULD DO ANYTHING...
CORRECT?
HUH?
DID YOU TRULY MEAN "ANYTHING"?
IF... IF IT'S WITHIN MY POWER, ANYWAY!

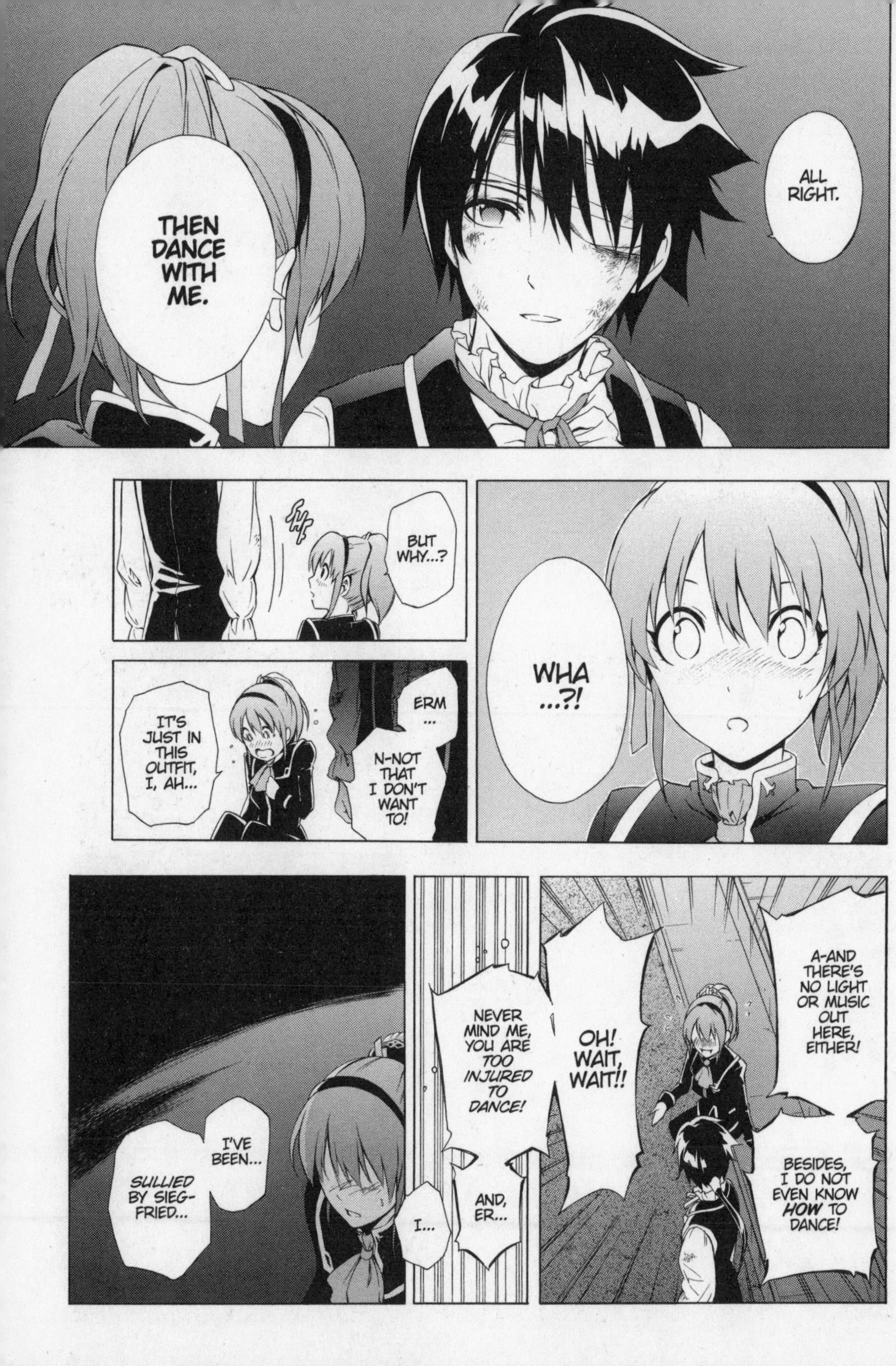
ALL RIGHT.
THEN DANCE WITH ME.
WHA ...?!
BUT WHY...?
ERM ...
N-NOT THAT I DON'T WANT TO!
IT'S JUST IN THIS OUTFIT, I, AH...
A-AND THERE'S NO LIGHT OR MUSIC OUT HERE, EITHER!
OH! WAIT, WAIT!!
BESIDES, I DO NOT EVEN KNOW *HOW* TO DANCE!
NEVER MIND ME, YOU ARE *TOO INJURED* TO DANCE!
AND, ER...
I...
I'VE BEEN...
SULLIED BY SIEG-FRIED...

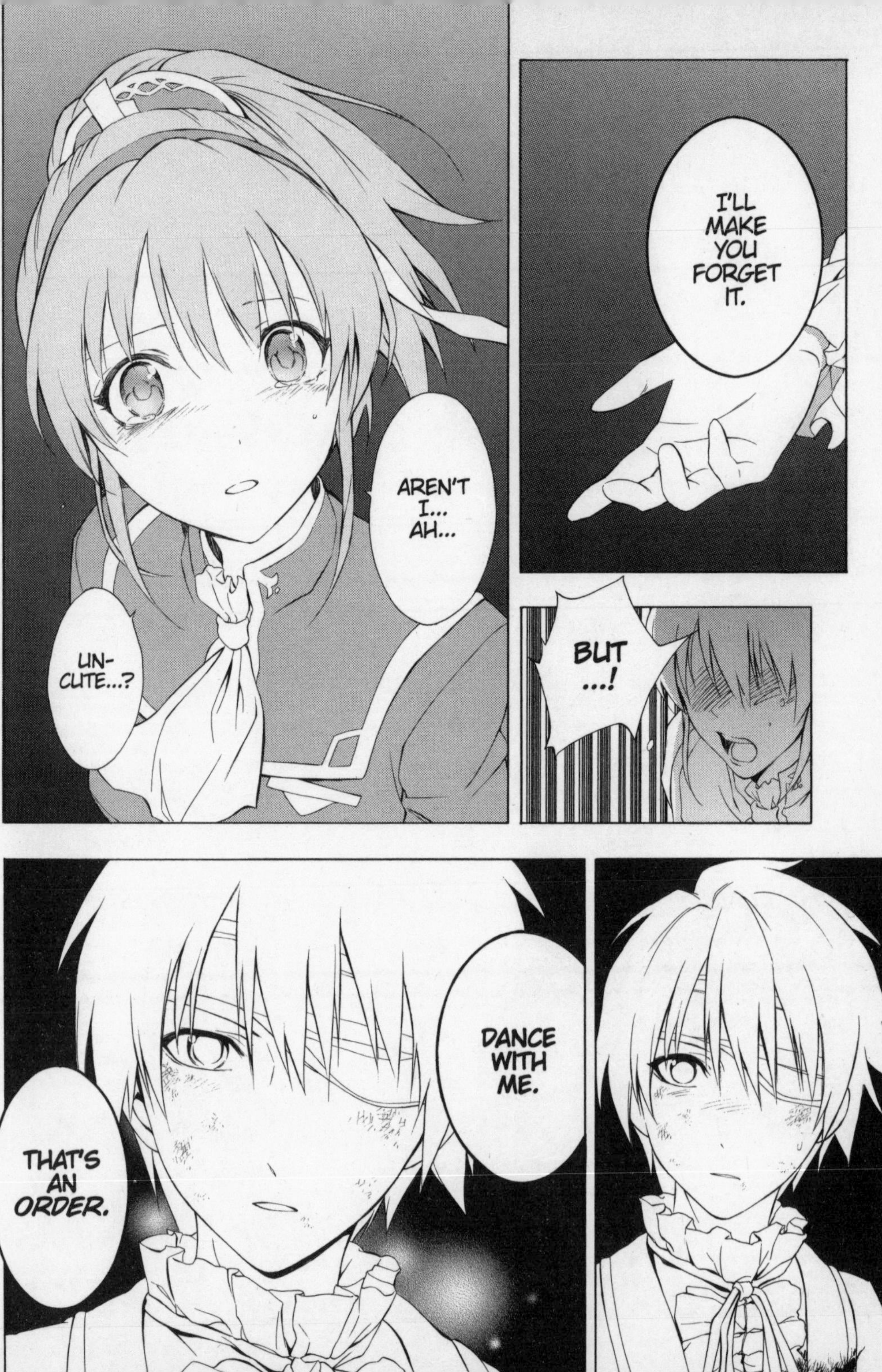
I'LL MAKE YOU FORGET IT.
BUT ...!
AREN'T I... AH...
UN-CUTE...?
DANCE WITH ME.
THAT'S AN ORDER.

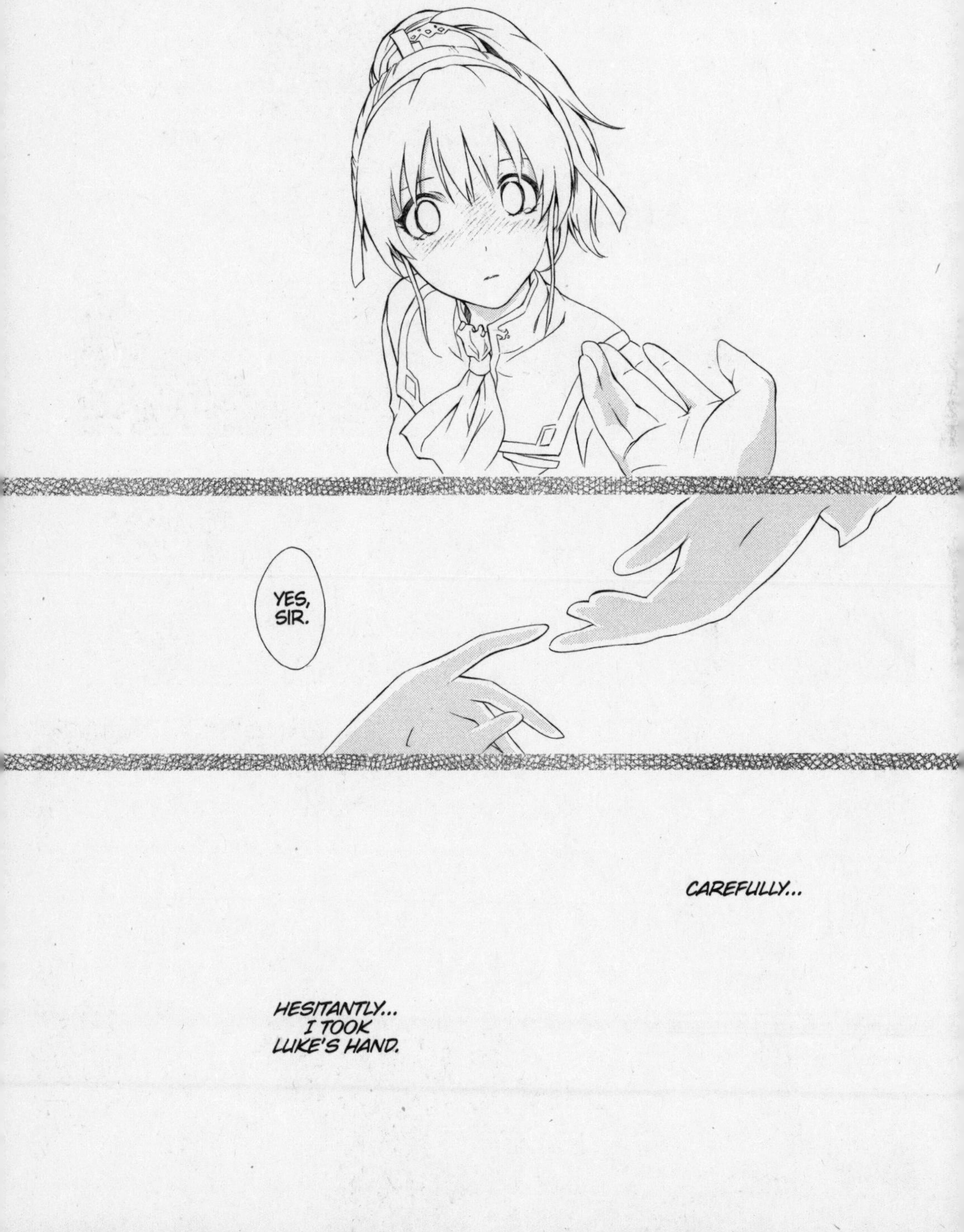
YES, SIR.
CAREFULLY...
HESITANTLY... I TOOK LUKE'S HAND.

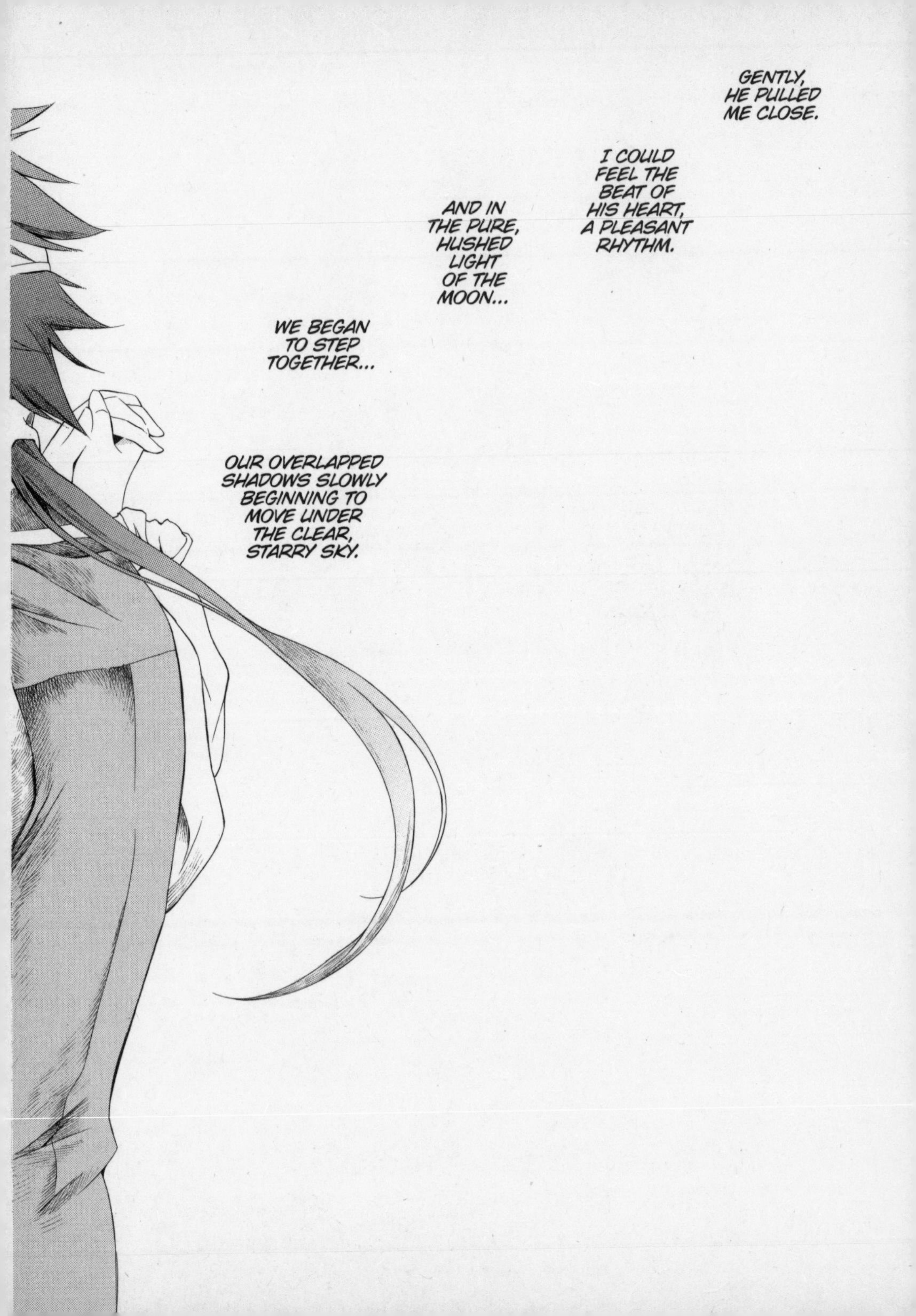
GENTLY, HE PULLED ME CLOSE.
I COULD FEEL THE BEAT OF HIS HEART, A PLEASANT RHYTHM.
AND IN THE PURE, HUSHED LIGHT OF THE MOON...
WE BEGAN TO STEP TOGETHER...
OUR OVERLAPPED SHADOWS SLOWLY BEGINNING TO MOVE UNDER THE CLEAR, STARRY SKY.

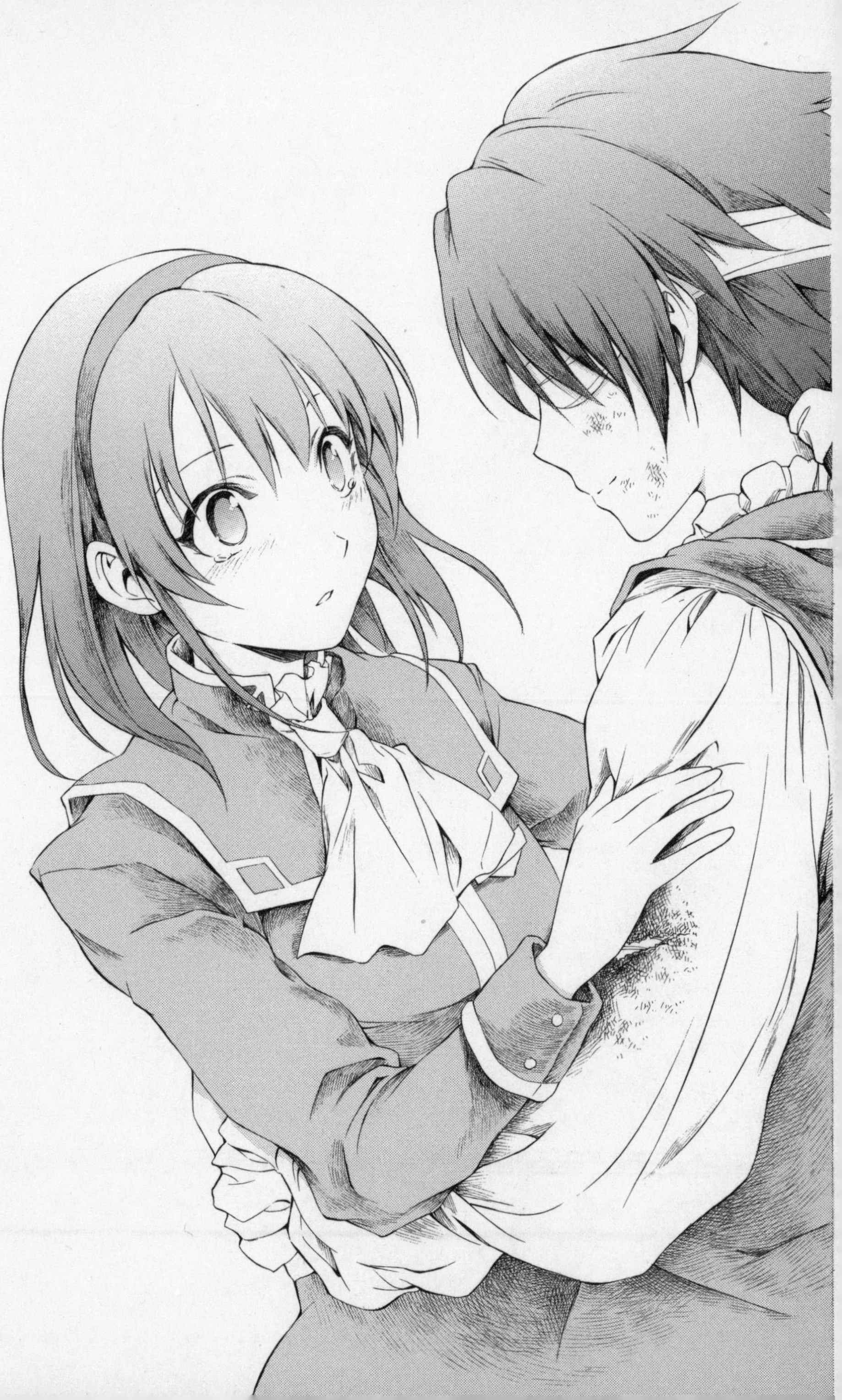

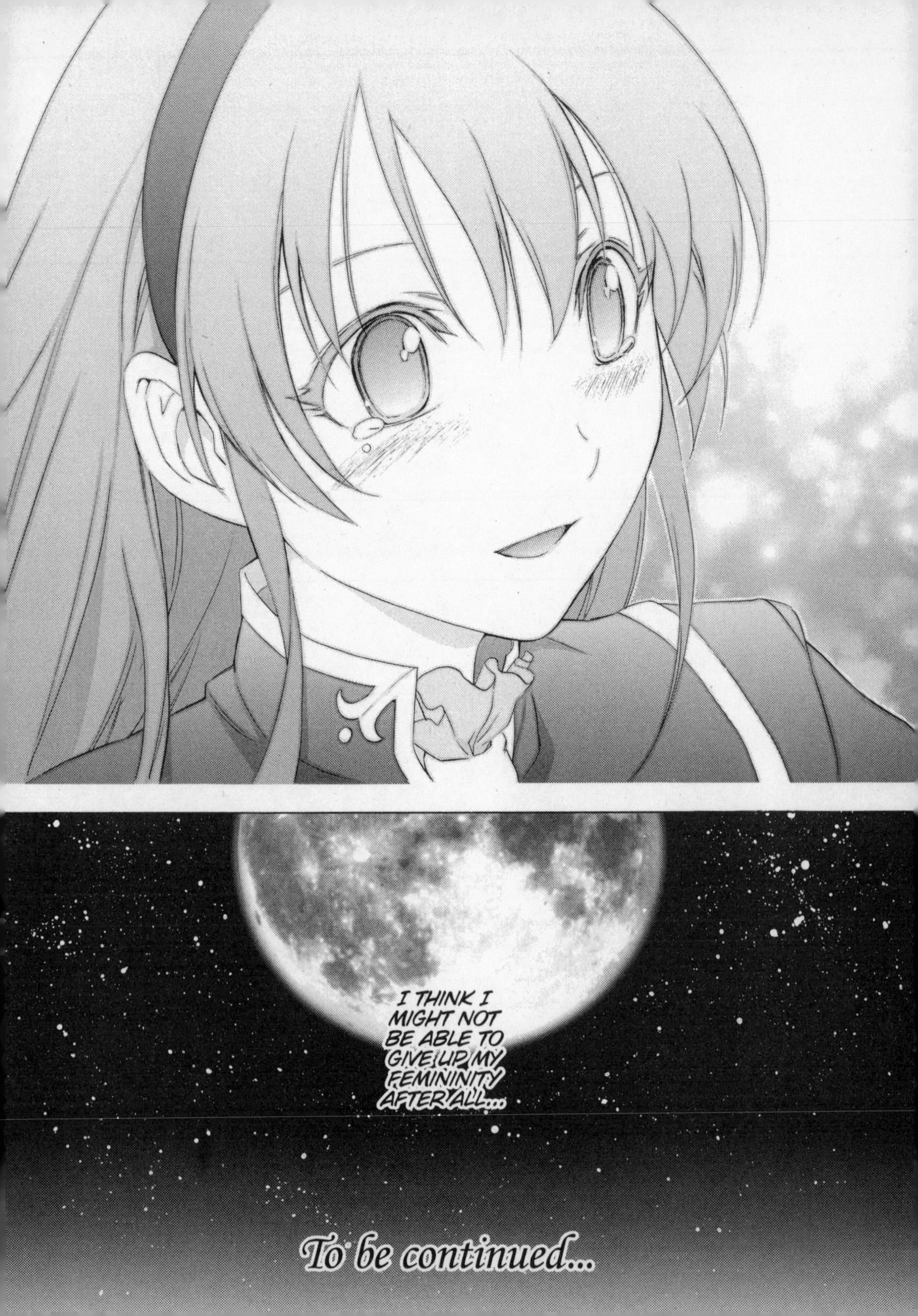
I THINK I MIGHT NOT BE ABLE TO GIVE UP MY FEMININITY AFTER ALL...
To be continued...

The Sacred Blacksmith

聖剣の刀鍛冶

SEVEN SEAS ENTERTAINMENT PRESENTS

THE SACRED BLACKSMITH

art by **KOTARO YAMADA** / story by **ISAO MIURA**

Original Character Designs by **LUNA**

VOLUME 5

TRANSLATION
Adrienne Beck

ADAPTATION
Janet Houck

LETTERING
Roland Amago

LAYOUT
Bambi Eloriaga-Amago

COVER DESIGN
Nicky Lim

PROOFREADER
Shanti Whitesides

MANAGING EDITOR
Adam Arnold

PUBLISHER
Jason DeAngelis

THE SACRED BLACKSMITH VOL. 5

Edited by MEDIA FACTORY.
First published in Japan in 2011 by KADOKAWA CORPORATION, Tokyo.

Seven Seas books may be purchased in bulk for educational, business, or promotional use. For information on bulk purchases, please contact Macmillan Corporate & Premium Sales Department at 1-800-221-7945 (ext 5442) or write specialmarkets@macmillan.com.

ISBN: 978-1-626920-40-8

Printed in Canada

First Printing: July 2014

10 9 8 7 6 5 4 3 2 1

FOLLOW US ONLINE: ***www.gomanga.com***

READING DIRECTIONS

This book reads from ***right to left***, Japanese style. If this is your first time reading manga, you start reading from the
take it from ther
numbered diagra
first, but you'll g

1
2
3
4
5
6
7
8
9

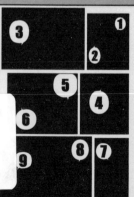